Studies in Cultural History

# BERLIN CABARET

D0775559

792.7
J390

# B E R L I N
# C A B A R E T

## Peter Jelavich

WITHDRAWN

LIBRARY ST. MARY'S COLLEGE

Harvard University Press
Cambridge, Massachusetts
London, England

Copyright © 1993 by the President and Fellows
of Harvard College
All rights reserved
Printed in the United States of America
Second printing, 1996

First Harvard University Press paperback edition, 1996

*Library of Congress Cataloging-in-Publication Data*

Jelavich, Peter.
Berlin cabaret / Peter Jelavich.
p.    cm.—(Studies in cultural history)
Includes bibliographical references (p.    ) and index.
ISBN 0-674-06761-4 (cloth)
ISBN 0-674-06762-2 (pbk.)
1. Music halls (Variety-theaters, cabarets, etc.)—Germany—Berlin—History.
2. Political satire, German—Germany—Berlin—History and criticism.
3. Theater—Political aspects—Germany—Berlin.
I. Title. II. Series.
PN1968.G3J45   1993
792.7'09431'55—dc20        93-16096
CIP

*Designed by Gwen Frankfeldt*

*For my parents,*
*Barbara and Charles Jelavich*

# Preface

Cabaret was an ephemeral art, and its material remains are widely scattered. I would like to express my deep gratitude to the librarians, archivists, and curators of the following institutions for their invaluable assistance: in (what was then) West Berlin, the Akademie der Künste, the Amerika-Gedenkbibliothek, the Berlin Document Center, the Berlin Museum, the Geheimes Staatsarchiv, the Landesarchiv, the Landesbildstelle, the Staatsbibliothek Preussischer Kulturbesitz, the Theaterhistorische Sammlung Walter Unruh, and the Ullstein Bilderdienst; in the former East Berlin, the documenta artistica collection of the Märkisches Museum; in Potsdam, the Brandenburgisches Landeshauptarchiv (formerly Staatsarchiv Potsdam) and the Bundesarchiv, Abteilungen Potsdam (formerly Zentrales Staatsarchiv Potsdam); in Koblenz, the Bundesarchiv; in Mainz, the Deutsches Kabarett Archiv/Reinhard Hippen; in Amsterdam, the Nederlands Theater Instituut and the Rijksinstituut voor Oorlogsdocumentatie; in Prague, the State Jewish Museum; in Terezín, the Památník Terezín; and in Jerusalem, Yad Vashem.

Research for this project was made possible by the generosity of the Wissenschaftskolleg zu Berlin, the American Council of Learned Societies, the University Research Institute of the University of Texas at Austin, and the Getty Center for the History of Art and the Humanities. I would especially like to thank the wonderful staffs, and the splendidly helpful librarians of the Wissenschaftskolleg, where I began this project, and of the Getty Center, where I (almost) completed it.

Throughout the years, as I have given talks and published essays on Berlin cabaret, I have benefited from conversations with numerous scholars, colleagues, and "nameless members of the audience." In the initial stages of this project, as well as thereafter, I received very valuable orientation from Ingrid Heinrich-Jost and Walter Rösler. I gained insights into the complexities of cabaret production, and the continuing relevance of these materials, from the performances of "Cabaret Verboten" organized by Jeremy Lawrence, and performed under the auspices of the Mark Taper Forum in Los Angeles and the CSC Repertory Theater in New York. For close and critical readings of the entire book manuscript, I would like to thank especially Sally Clarke, Barbara Jelavich, Michael Kater, and Ellen Handler Spitz. And, once again, I greatly appreciate the meticulous and thoughtful editing of Ann Louise McLaughlin.

To the extent that this project was a pleasurable undertaking, much of that delight derived from my extended stays in Berlin, where I enjoyed the hospitality of many wonderful people. For their friendship and generosity, I would like to thank in particular Cella and Georg Girardet; Christiane Lemke, Björn Dämpfling, and Christian Meyer; and Annerose and Walter Rösler.

Finally, in the briefest of words: This book is dedicated to my parents, Barbara and Charles Jelavich, who have given me encouragement and support in every possible way. They also introduced me to the study of history.

Cabaret, however, I had to discover on my own.

*P. J.*

# Contents

Introduction    1

**1** Cabaret as Metropolitan Montage    10

Berlin: Cosmopolitan Life, Consumerism, and Montage   *10*
Variety Shows and Nietzschean Vitalism   *20*
Berlin Wit: Laughter and Censorship   *30*

**2** Between Elitism and Entertainment: Wolzogen's Motley Theater    36

The Premiere of the Motley Theater   *36*
Critics and Competitors   *45*
New Theater, Rapid Demise   *53*

**3** From Artistic Parody to Theatrical Renewal: Reinhardt's Sound and Smoke    62

Theatrical Parody for Connoisseurs   *62*
A Temporary Turn to Political Satire: Serenissimus   *72*
The Path to a New Theatricality   *80*

**4** Cosmopolitan Diversions, Metropolitan Identities    85

Policing the Pub-Cabarets   *85*
Two Sides of Metropolitan Cabaret: Rudolf Nelson and Claire Waldoff   *95*
Fashioning Berlin: The Metropol Revues   *104*

**5** Political Satire in the Early Weimar Republic    118

Nationalism in Wartime and Postwar Entertainment   *118*
Limitations of Republican Satire: Kurt Tucholsky   *128*
Dada and Metropolitan Tempo: Walter Mehring   *141*

**6** The Weimar Revue    154

Nude Dancing on the Early Weimar Stage   *154*
The Americanization of Entertainment: Jazz and Black Performers   *165*
"Girls and Crisis"   *175*

**7** Political Cabaret at the End of the Republic                    187
   The Politics of Revues and Cabaret-Revues   *187*
   Cabaret and the Crises of the Late Republic   *197*
   Red Revues and Agitprop   *209*

**8** Cabaret under National Socialism                                228
   The Suppression of Critical Cabaret   *228*
   From "Positive Cabaret" to Total Depoliticization   *241*
   Only the "Girls" Remain   *250*

   Epilogue: Cabaret in Concentration Camps                          258

   *Notes*                                                           285

   *Index*                                                           317

# Illustrations

1. Leipziger Strasse. From *Album von Berlin* (Berlin: Globus Verlag, ca. 1904). *15*
2. Wertheim department store. From *Album von Berlin*. *16*
3. Wintergarten variety theater. From *50 Jahre Wintergarten: Festschrift 1888–1938* (Berlin: 1938). *22*
4. Ernst von Wolzogen. Postcard. *37*
5. "The Merry Husband." Courtesy of documenta artistica, Märkisches Museum. *42*
6. August Endell's Motley Theater. From *Berliner Architekturwelt* 4 (1902): 378. From the Resource Collections of the Getty Center for the History of Art and the Humanities. *55*
7. Martin Zickel, Friedrich Kayssler, and Max Reinhardt at Sound and Smoke. From Max Ehrlich, *Von Adalbert bis Zilzer: Gesammelte Theater-Anekdoten* (Berlin: Eden-Verlag, 1928), 249. *66*
8. Interior of Sound and Smoke (designed by Peter Behrens). From Benno Jacobson, *Das Theater* (Berlin: N. Israel Album, 1906). *70*
9. Kindermann and Serenissimus. Courtesy of documenta artistica, Märkisches Museum. *74*
10. Hungry Pegasus cabaret. Courtesy of documenta artistica, Märkisches Museum. *87*
11. Performers of the Roland von Berlin. From Benno Jacobson, *Das Theater*. *97*
12. Cover of Rudolf Nelson/Willy Hagen, "Jacques Manasse," sheet music (Berlin: Bote & Bock, 1912). *98*
13. Claire Waldoff. Postcard. *101*
14. "Kodak Song." From Julius Freund, *Neuestes!! Allerneuestes!!!* (Berlin: Harmonie, 1904). *107*
15. The dissolved Reichstag at the Metropol. From *Bühne und Welt*, October 1907, 47. *111*
16. Touting undergarments at the Metropol. Postcard. *115*
17. "Miss Fashion" promotes paper clothing. Postcard. *122*
18. Paul Graetz. Courtesy of documenta artistica, Märkisches Museum. *132*
19. "Woodrow Apollon." From Walter Mehring, *Einfach klassisch! Eine Orestie mit glücklichem Ausgang* (Berlin: Adolph Fürstner, 1919), following p. 28. *142*

20. Trude Hesterberg. Courtesy of documenta artistica, Märkisches Museum. *151*

21. Members of the Ballet Celly de Rheidt. Postcard. *155*

22. Chocolate Kiddies. From *Die Woche,* April 30, 1927, 509. *172*

23. Josephine Baker. From *Das Theater,* December 1928, 528. *173*

24. Charell revue: "What Sailors Dream Of." From *Querschnitt,* 5 (1925), following p. 904. From the Resource Collections of the Getty Center for the History of Art and the Humanities. *177*

25. The Tiller Girls. From Hans W. Fischer, *Körperschönheit und Körperkultur* (Berlin: Deutsche Buch-Gemeinschaft, 1928), plate 128. *178*

26. Paul Simmel: Ford produces Tiller Girls. From *Berliner Illustrirte Zeitung,* March 28, 1926, 411. From the Resource Collections of the Getty Center for the History of Art and the Humanities. Reproduced by permission of Ullstein Bilderdienst. *182*

27. Tiller Girls shoulder arms. From *Wintergarten Magazin,* January 1930, 13. *183*

28. Grit and Ina van Elben as "Tingel-Tangel-Girls." From *Querschnitt,* 11 (1931), opposite 271. From the Resource Collections of the Getty Center for the History of Art and the Humanities. Reproduced by permission of Ullstein Bilderdienst. *184*

29. Valeska Gert: "Charleston." From Fred Hildenbrandt, *Die Tänzerin Valeska Gert* (Stuttgart: Walter Hädecke Verlag, 1928), opposite 17. *185*

30. Scene from Friedrich Hollaender's *That's You!* Courtesy of documenta artistica, Märkisches Museum. *191*

31. Margo Lion and Marlene Dietrich. From *Das Theater,* June 1928, 286. *193*

32. Interior of the Kadeko (designed by Erich Mendelsohn). From *Das Theater,* October 1928, 446. *199*

33. Scene from Erwin Piscator's *Red Revel Revue.* Courtesy of documenta artistica, Märkisches Museum. *212*

34. Red Wedding agitprop troupe. From *Arbeiterbühne und Film,* September 1930, 9. *215*

35. Werner Finck parodies the Wandervogel movement. From *Querschnitt,* 10 (1930), following 122. From the Resource Collections of the Getty Center for the History of Art and the Humanities. Reproduced by permission of Ullstein Bilderdienst. *237*

36. The Hiller Girls at the Scala. Cover of Scala program booklet, April 1940. *255*

37. Max Ehrlich performs at Westerbork. From photo album of *Humor und Melodie* (1943). Courtesy of Yad Vashem. *264*

38. Schoolgirl scene from *Humor and Melody.* Courtesy of Yad Vashem. *265*

39. Camilla Spira in *Humor and Melody.* Courtesy of Yad Vashem. *270*

40. Fritta (Fritz Taussig): caricature of Kurt Gerron. From H. G. Adler, *Die verheimlichte Wahrheit: Theresienstädter Dokumente* (Tübingen: J. C. B. Mohr, 1958). Reproduced by permission of J. C. B. Mohr. *276*

# BERLIN CABARET

# Introduction

Every metropolis tends to generate an urban mythology, and Berlin is no exception. One of the more enduring fables associated with that city is that it was a hotbed for cabaret. This book seeks to assay that tale, by examining cabaret in Berlin from 1901 to 1944.

Berlin cabaret was not what most people today think it was. In the United States the prevalent image of 1920s cabaret seems to have been formed by a combination of Marlene Dietrich's Lola Lola in *The Blue Angel*, the Sally Bowles character in Christopher Isherwood's Berlin stories (most memorably portrayed by Liza Minnelli in the filmed musical *Cabaret*), as well as the socially critical songs of Bertolt Brecht and Kurt Weill. None of these figures, however, corresponded to cabaret as it was understood at that time. *The Blue Angel* was set in the dive of a Hanseatic harbor town, while Sally Bowles appeared in sleazy nightclubs. Brecht appeared only once on a Berlin cabaret stage, to sing two numbers that he had composed. His collaborations with Weill were rarely performed in such venues, but rather were embedded in full-length works of musical theater performed in opera houses or on dramatic stages.

Although these figures cannot be equated with cabaret, it would not be wrong to link them to cabaret's environment. Lola Lola performed in what was usually called a "Tingeltangel," a third-rate variety show that was a direct precursor of cabaret. Moreover, even though the sets of *The Blue Angel* deny a cabaret setting, the music was written by Friedrich Hollaender and performed in part by Weintraub's Syncopators. These were major figures in Weimar cabaret, as were Kurt Gerron and Rosa Valetti, the film's major supporting players. As for the Isherwood stories, in the 1920s bars with sleazy entertainment often dubbed themselves cabarets, to the horror of the cabaret purists. Indeed, in order to avoid this linguistic confusion, the German language now differentiates *Cabaret* and *Kabarett*. The words were used interchangeably through the Weimar era, but since the 1950s, *Cabaret* has referred to a strip show, while *Kabarett* is reserved for social criticism or political satire. Finally, it can be said that although Brecht and Weill did not write for cabaret, they were part of a wider culture of satirical, mildly critical, often cynical songwriting which found its best expression on cabaret stages. Lola Lola, Sally Bowles, and Brecht and Weill were, in short, on the boundaries of cabaret. And those boundaries were very fluid.

For the purposes of this book, I would like to propose the following definition (or at least image) of an "ideal type" cabaret. It consisted of a small stage in a relatively small hall, where the audience sat around tables. The intimacy of the setting allowed direct, eye-to-eye contact between performers and spectators. The show consisted of short (five- or ten-minute) numbers from several different genres, usually songs, comic monologues, dialogues and skits, less frequently dances, pantomimes, puppet shows, or even short films. They dealt in a satirical or parodistic manner with topical issues: sex (most of all), commercial fashions, cultural fads, politics (least of all). These numbers were usually presented by professional singers and actors, but often writers, composers, or dancers would perform their own works. The presentations were linked together by a conferencier, a type of emcee who interacted with the audience, made witty remarks about events of the day, and introduced the performers.

Even Max Weber admitted that ideal types are hard to find in reality. Likewise, this pure type of cabaret was rare, and when it miraculously appeared, it was short-lived. All aspects of cabaret were subject to change. With increasing popularity, a troupe might move to larger quarters: the stage would expand and, more important, the auditorium would be enlarged to be filled no longer with tables, but rather with rows of chairs facing the performers. The intimacy of ideal-type cabaret, an intimacy between actors and audience (and among the spectators themselves), would thereby be lost. The content of performances likewise might be transformed. It could become more literary and dramatic. When mainly professional actors were involved, when there was a dearth of good cabaret material, or when the audience preferred more conventional dramatic forms, one-act skits would come to dominate the program, and eventually a total conversion to drama would be made. The cabaret would, in short, become a regular theater. In contrast, a cabaret might become less literary, or decidedly nonliterary. If censorship hindered parody or satire, or if an audience wanted more show and less tell, then the stage would be left with variety acts, and the cabaret would end up as just another vaudeville hall. If a troupe felt commercially compelled to appeal to the absolutely lowest common demominator of public taste, it could mutate into a purveyor of what Germans in the twenties called "nude dancing." That is precisely what most stages calling themselves "cabarets" are today.

Cabaret was thus not only bounded by dramatic theater, variety shows, and nude dancing; those other types of performance could even be part of the trajectories of individual cabaret troupes. Two further genres must be considered as well: revue and agitprop. Revues were performed on large stages with an abundance of often gaudy production numbers, and held together by something vaguely resembling a plotline. The revue was related to cabaret inasmuch as it comprised a smattering of songs and dialogues of a satirical or parodistic nature. While revue was the most commercial (because most costly) of these entertainments, agitprop was the most political. As we shall see, politics was never the central theme of Wilhelmine or Weimar cabaret; to the extent that those stages were politicized at all, they lacked a clear standpoint and tended to make fun of all parties. The agitprop movement, which flourished in the last years of the Weimar Republic, tried to alleviate that situation by developing cabaret-style performances that centered on political issues and espoused a firm standpoint, however flawed—that of the Communist Party.

In sum, the history of cabaret cannot be written without considering developments in theater, vaudeville, nude dancing, revue, and agitprop—as well as operetta, popular music, dance crazes, film, and many other facets of public and commercial entertainment. How is one to pull this together? At first I planned to write a slim book, on the principle that one should not produce a large volume about *Kleinkunst*. Yet as I pursued a number of disparate themes, the project expanded inexorably, and I had to establish some limiting parameters. Consequently, various important aspects of cabaret had to be neglected. Performers were, in a sense, the lifeblood of cabaret; both the "stars" and the lesser entertainers, each with a distinct style and personality, gave shows their special character. Yet with a few notable exceptions, I have not sought to paint a full portrait gallery of Berlin's cabaret scene. This is due partially to limitations of space, but also to the difficulty of capturing in words the spirit of performances that were aural, gestural, and visual. Unfortunately, no cabaret performances of the Weimar era were recorded on sound film. The best one can do to reexperience particular entertainers like Kurt Gerron, Paul Graetz, Trude Hesterberg, Paul Morgan, or Rosa Valetti is to contemplate still photos, listen to gramophone recordings, or see their performances in film (where they did not play cabaret roles). Obviously, a book is not a proper medium to reproduce these effects.

Language has intruded at another level as well: since I am writing in English, I have had to forgo reproducing much of the untranslatable verbal wordplay, the witty or awful puns that were rampant in cabaret. Still, I have tried to examine some of the more important cabaret lyrics, and I apologize in advance for the quality of my rhymed-verse translations (where I have sought to retain the meter and rhyme sequence of the original, sometimes at the expense of the literal wording). Finally, I have concentrated on a middle-ground of commercial cabaret, and have left out some institutions at both ends of the cultural scale. At the "low" end, restaurants with live entertainment sometimes called themselves cabarets during the Imperial era; so did most night spots featuring nude dancing shows under the Republic. I allude to this fact whenever it impinges on "genuine" cabarets, but I do not examine those faux stages in any detail. At the "high" end, there were evenings of poetry readings or musical recitals that also dubbed themselves cabarets. The most significant were probably the occasional performances of "Gnu" and the "Neopathetisches Cabaret," which were extremely important forums for the presentation of Expressionist lyrics. Yet they too fall outside the boundaries of commercial entertainment that is the focus of my work.

So what is left? Generally I have been guided by thematic concerns. Here too one has to be selective, since a study of cabaret can raise a host of significant issues. The ones I found most important—or at least most interesting—are politics, sex, fashion, and race.

In the cabaret of the Wilhelmine and Weimar eras (unlike *Kabarett* today), political themes played a secondary role. Nevertheless, to the extent that they were addressed, they raised some important questions: Is satire a useful political tool? How focused can satire be? To what extent does humor detract from political messages? These questions plagued politically committed entertainers, even in the agitprop movement, where Communist ideologues increasingly worried that workers were being amused but not mobilized by the shows. While Communists found satire a difficult propagandistic tool, their firm political beliefs saved them from cynicism, a pitfall of "bourgeois" cabaret. In the Weimar era, many entertainers made jokes about all political parties—hardly a difficult task in any age. Over time, however, this could lead to an oppressive sense of disillusionment. The resulting cynicism logically implied the end of satire, which works only when one can confront ideals and reality. Satire pits stated purpose against actual practice, essence against surface appearance, ingredients against packaging. At the very least, it is a useful vehicle for unmasking hypocrisy. But what if one discovers that hypocrisy is all-pervading? In the Weimar era that problem was compounded by the fact that satirists themselves were caught up in the very compromises they mocked. Even the best of them routinely toned down political statements to curry favor with the public or avoid conflicts with the state. Faced with these dilemmas, the more introspective performers and writers, like Kurt Tucholsky, fought an increasingly desperate battle to avoid cynicism, to cling to shreds of ideals.

Whereas such issues were internal to the cabaret movement, politics also intervened from the outside. The years 1901 to 1944 saw three very distinct regimes in power, which handled cabaret in substantially different ways.

In Imperial Germany, theater was subject to preliminary censorship. Although Berlin's censors were (in my opinion) quite open-minded, nothing could be said on stage that had not been approved by the police. The Weimar Republic, in contrast, abolished censorship. Although strictures by the state crept back in attenuated forms, cabaret performers quickly realized that their main "censor" was now the audience. Since many spectators took great offense at having their political ideas mocked, the box office dictated that satirists exercise restraint. Predictably, the Nazi era saw the most radical changes in the cabaret landscape. Entertainers who were Jewish or left-of-center fled the cabarets, and the country as well, leaving insipid variety-show programs in their wake. Thereafter, performers who tried the make even benignly jocular references to life in the Third Reich invariably fell afoul of the Nazis' numerous cultural watchdogs.

Compared to political issues, sexuality and gender were much more prominent themes on cabaret stages. Of course, this was true not just of cabaret. Love, romance, courtship, marriage; sexual hunting, conquest, and intercourse—the sentimental and the unsentimental modes of sexuality have dominated popular music and theater for a long time. But those themes underwent dramatic changes between 1900 and 1930, as individuals transformed their actual sexual practice. The Great War was a watershed, and the 1920s saw an ongoing "sexual revolution" for men and women. Simultaneously, the lifting of censorship permitted the popular arts to address sexual themes more freely. To be sure, this opened the door to greater prurience, since women could be seen naked on stage. But the loosening of strictures also allowed a more explicit, and perhaps more honest, portrayal of intergender relations, as popular music transcended the saccarine sentimentality of Wilhelmine lovesongs.

Within this context, cabaret had a field day. Its numbers mocked the kitschy romanticism of much popular entertainment; they satirized conservative moralists who denounced the loosening of sexual mores; and they made fun, in turn, of those liberalized sexual manners. Moreover, cabaret dealt with themes that were not addressed in most types of popular music or theater: prostitution, homosexuality, lesbianism. But this image of cabaret standing at an ironic distance to the sexual practices, the sentimental entertainment, or (after 1918) the flesh-baring of the time is not quite accurate, since cabaret also counted sentimentality and skin as part of its own appeal. A typical evening at a cabaret would have both cynical and nostalgic lovesongs; and even a number that made fun of nude dancers or the kicklines of "Girls" might be performed by a woman wearing skimpy clothing. In this sense, cabaret was something of a tease: it simultaneously satirized and sustained the erotic energy of the day.

To the extent that it was contemporary, topical, and *aktuell,* cabaret dealt primarily with fashion, with current styles and trends. Politics and sex were realms of fashion in this sense. Cabaret zeroed in on fadishness in other areas as well: high culture, popular entertainment, habits of speaking, styles of clothing, new commercial goods and the advertisements that touted them. This aspect of cabaret made it an art form that was continually up-to-date. But just as there were ambiguities in its political stances and elements of bad faith in its sexual parodies, cabaret's send-up of fashion was ambivalent. Cabaret became a parasite that lived off its age: it could ridicule, it could criticize, but it put nothing in place of the objects it attacked. Moreover, cabaret itself was a fashion from the very beginning: the initial success of Wolzogen's Motley Theater inspired a host of imitators, and led to an "Überbrettl" fad in 1901 and 1902. Other cabaret fashions appeared in the ensuing decades. The more self-conscious troupes were aware of this and made light of their own trendiness. But that fact underscored the problem that lay at the heart of cabaret, whether political or not: What was its purpose? If everything is just a fad, if anything can be mocked, then what has happened to the Good and the True and the Beautiful? If they are irreplaceably lost, then we are left, once again, with cynicism.

Or are we? There is, after all, a bright side to "relativism." If there are no eternal verities, then you are free to fashion your own values; if there is no timeless art, then you can create art for your time. If you can mock anything, then nothing has the moral authority to claim your allegiance, to weigh you down. Cabaret represented freedom and creativity and play. Many of the writers and performers, and probably much of the audience, valued it for precisely this reason. It was no wonder that the ideas of Friedrich Nietzsche were invoked by cabaret's first practitioners.

The issue of race, however, underscores the fact that while cabaretists might have been playing, other historical actors were deadly serious. Of the four major themes that I discuss, racial or ethnic identity was raised least frequently. There was quite a bit of joking about the various German "tribes," especially Prussians, Bavarians, Saxons, and Austrians. I do not discuss that benign form of humor, although I do suggest ways in which popular stages helped define the character of "the Berliner." Much more serious, I believe, were the ways that Jews and blacks were depicted in cabarets and revues. Many of the entertainers were Jewish, and they told jokes about Jews to audiences that were primarily Gentile. That rarely led to protests by Jewish citizens in the Imperial era, but by the 1920s, the rise of virulent political anti-Semitism made the subject much less funny, and Jewish jokes became rarer. Simultaneously, some stages made light of Adolf Hitler. While they ridiculed the logical absurdity of his ideas, they failed to fathom the immensity of the Nazi danger. As for blacks, German stages had hosted African American song-and-dance numbers since the turn of the century. They received considerably more attention during the Weimar era, as jazz—or what passed for it—became a prominent style of popular music. Seemingly liberal critics praised black entertainment, but in a manner that perpetuated racial stereotypes: African Americans were equated with a healthy, "primitive" vitality, a sensibility derived from the African "jungle." That questionable rhetoric was intended to be complimentary. In contrast, German conservatives, horrified by jazz and the black entertainers, engaged in vicious and unambiguous racist attacks against "Negro culture."

Like politics, racism was not only a theme of cabaret numbers but also a potent force that could intervene from the outside. That became most apparent in 1933. "Negro culture" was proscribed, although jazz managed to survive in various forms. A much more drastic fate awaited Jewish entertainers. They were banished from Germany's stages, and the most prominent figures fled abroad. The lucky ones found a haven in England or the United States. The less fortunate emigrated to countries like Austria, France, Czechoslovakia, or the Netherlands, where several years later they were captured by the agents of the expanding Reich. In the concentration camps at Westerbork and Theresienstadt/Terezín some of Berlin's most famous entertainers put on shows for their fellow Jewish prisoners. Cabaret had always lacked a firm purpose, and in these "transit" camps that were way stations to Auschwitz, the performers and the audience asked the most agonizing questions about the value of that art.

This book seeks to weave together the themes of politics, sexuality, fashion, and race as treated in cabarets and related types of popular entertainment. There is no straightforward manner of doing this. Aesthetic theorists have long debated whether form should or should not reflect content. If this volume's structure were to mirror its cabaretic subject matter, then it would consist of an array of disconnected numbers. Since that goes against my narrative grain, I suggest that the book be read as something closer to a revue: it has several themes, but they are woven very loosely, they sometimes break off abruptly, and they are not tied together in the end. I admit that this approach has pitfalls. In 1930 Friedrich Hollaender and Marcellus Schiffer scripted a show, with music by Rudolf Nelson, entitled *Der rote Faden*—a reference to the proverbial "red thread," the tenuous plotline that was supposed to run through a revue. The title was ironic, however, since a "red thread" was precisely what the script lacked; the characters spent the whole show looking for it in vain. I hope that this book is not like that revue. But just in case, I now provide a synoptic program guide.

The first chapter delineates the environment in which cabaret arose, by focusing on Berlin as a modern metropolis with a tradition of critical wit. It also describes the variety show, a form of urban entertainment that was the immediate precursor of cabaret. The second chapter takes an in-depth look at Berlin's first cabaret, Wolzogen's Motley Theater, which already displayed the commercial and political compromises that were to characterize cabaret in the Imperial era and beyond. Chapter 3 examines a different type of parodistic stage, Max Reinhardt's Sound and Smoke. Unlike the Motley Theater, which soon gave up any highbrow artistic pretentions, Sound and Smoke represented a new theatrical sensibility which Reinhardt was to incorporate into his world-famous productions of classical and modernist drama. The ensuing chapter presents an overview and analysis of other forms of cabaret-type entertainment in the decade before the Great War. Berlin's metropolitan modernity found expression in various guises: bohemian pub-cabarets on the Parisian model, the urbane suavity of Rudolf Nelson's upscale cabarets, Claire Waldoff's immensely popular representation of the lower-class Berliner, and the spectacular revues of the Metropol-Theater.

Chapter 5 examines the political tone of cabaret in World War I and the early years of the Weimar Republic. As in all belligerent nations, popular entertainment during the war was virulently nationalistic. That mood persisted on most popular stages throughout the republican era. Left-liberal cabaret authors had a hard time finding an appreciative audience for their critical works. Kurt Tucholsky soon honed down the satirical edges of his lyrics and introduced sentimental notes. Walter Mehring gained acclaim not for his political messages, but rather for his formal experimentations based on Dadaist aesthetics. The next chapter deals with the most popular form of live entertainment on Berlin's stages during the mid-twenties: the revue. One element of the revue derived from nude dancing, which proliferated after the abolition of stage censorship in 1919. Other notes were contributed by "American" forms of entertainment, such as jazz, which was implicated in a debate about black culture. But the most sensational number of any revue was the kickline of "Girls," which generated a major discourse concerning gender, machine aesthetics, and militarism. Chapter 7 returns to more explicitly political themes, as it surveys the final years of the Republic. While some cabarets and the new genre of "cabaret-revue" had some mildly critical numbers, they tended to lack political focus. That was not a fault of the agitprop movement, which sought to employ cabaret-style entertainment to spread the Communist message. Both "bourgeois" cabarets and leftist agitprop made fun of Hitler, but neither of them correctly assessed the Nazi threat or predicted the horrors to come.

Chapter 8 describes the fate of cabaret in the Third Reich. Almost all prominent Jewish entertainers fled the country in the spring of 1933. Of the "Aryan" cabaretists that remained, few dared to make jokes about the realities of National Socialism. Those who did were brought into line: in 1935, members of the Catacombs and the Tingel-Tangel spent several weeks in a concentration camp. The Nazis attempted to replace the "negative" satire of the Weimar era with a "positive cabaret" that would support the regime's goals, but the effort failed on account of its total humorlessness. By the time the war broke out, German cabaret had been fully depoliticized. The epilogue describes the final vestiges of genuine "Berlin cabaret" after 1940. Many prominent Jewish entertainers who had fled in 1933 were caught by Germany's advancing armies. Interned in Westerbork and Theresienstadt, they staged shows for the Jewish captives, until performers and audience were transported to Auschwitz, Sobibor, and Treblinka.

# CHAPTER ONE

# Cabaret as Metropolitan Montage

Friedrich Hollaender, one of the outstanding songwriters of the Weimar era, noted that cabaret was "engendered in dissolute passion by theater, the variety show, and the political tribunal."[1] If the child had several fathers, then the incubating and nurturing mother clearly was the metropolis. Berlin cabaret was a product of changes in urban life and artistic taste at the beginning of the twentieth century. As Berlin became a cosmopolis, social theorists and cultural critics recorded the development of a new mentality, strongly affected by the city's dynamism and consumerism. The disruptions of big-city life encouraged the creation of forms of art and entertainment that were likewise heterogeneous and fragmented. The variety show was the most popular of these new diversions. Proponents of cabaret copied the variety show's format, as well as its sensuality, but they also sought to give it a "higher" literary and artistic content. Moreover, they tried to infuse it with some of the aggressive humor that had characterized Berliners for generations. Hollaender's formula—the serious aspirations of elite "theater," the framework of the "variety show," and the "political tribunal" of local antiauthoritarian sarcasm—was the recipe for Berlin cabaret.

## Berlin: Cosmopolitan Life, Consumerism, and Montage

By the eve of World War I, Berlin, the capital of the second greatest industrial nation (after the United States), had become the world's third largest city (after London and New York). That was a startling distinction for a community that had numbered only 200,000 citizens at the close of the Napoleonic Wars. For the first half of the nineteenth century Berlin remained, above all, the administrative capital of the Kingdom of Prussia, a city in which the state was the largest employer. At that time the government also left its visual imprint on the city, as it sponsored the public buildings designed by the outstanding neoclassical architect, Karl Friedrich Schinkel. His mature and elegant works, which complemented the city's eighteenth-century structures, contributed to the designation of Berlin as the "Athens on the Spree" *(Spreeathen)*. This appellation, which referred to the city's location on the river Spree, not only alluded to its architecture but also evoked its importance as a center of learning. During the Enlightenment, Berlin could claim the presence of Gotthold Ephraim Lessing and Moses Mendelssohn, while Frederick the Great hosted Voltaire and La Mettrie for several years in nearby Potsdam. The city's intellectual preeminence was established after 1810, when the university was founded by Wilhelm von Humboldt. Already in its first two decades it could boast a faculty that included the philosophers Johann Gottlob Fichte, Friedrich Schleiermacher, and Georg Wilhelm Friedrich Hegel.[2]

By the end of the century that age would be portrayed as a lost idyll. In 1899 Walter Rathenau wrote: "The Athens on the Spree is dead, and the Chicago on the Spree grows apace."[3] In true Hegelian fashion, the seeds of *Spreechicago* had been planted under the neoclassical veneer. The abrogation of Prussia's internal tariffs in 1818, followed by the progressive expansion of the German customs union since 1834, opened new markets and allowed Berlin to develop into a center of industry. Textiles and garmentworking had been important manufactures for well over a century, since the Prussian armies needed uniforms; but now these enterprises could shift toward production for a civilian mass market. Machine and locomotive construction and metalworking industries rapidly acquired prominence as well. In the wake of economic expansion, Berlin saw the rapid growth of what came to be called the proletariat, which played a major role in the revolution of 1848. Working-class desperation caused by an economic depression, combined with middle-class discontent at royal authoritarianism, resulted in barricade fighting on March 18, 1848. The king was forced to order his troops out of Berlin, abolish censorship, and convene a Prussian parliamentary assembly. Over the ensuing months, however, rifts divided the classes that had made the revolution, as workers demanded social and economic rights that the middle classes found unacceptable. With his opposition disunited, the king ordered his troops back into Berlin on November 10 and imposed martial law. The ensuing decade was generally a period of authoritarian governmental policies matched by public depoliticization. Nevertheless, the events of 1848 fashioned Berlin's political framework for the next seventy years: a conservative monarchy, liberal bourgeoisie, and radical working class were to contend with each other until 1918.

Berlin again became a center of liberal agitation in the 1860s. When the new monarch, Wilhelm I (ruled 1861–1888), was unable to persuade the Prussian assembly to approve reforms that would have greatly strengthened the standing army, he named Otto von Bismarck as prime minister. The tough Junker politician decreed the reforms without parliamentary approval, an act that provoked a constitutional crisis. Despite calls for a tax boycott and other measures of civil disobedience, the parliament was unable to assert its prerogatives. In the ensuing years Prussian victories in three successive wars—with Denmark (1864), Austria (1866), and France (1870)—seduced many liberals into placing nationalism above political rights. When Bismarck finally forged a united Germany in January 1871, he could count on the support of these so-called National Liberals, even though the new Empire's parliament, the Reichstag, had greatly restricted power. Berlin, however, continued to remain a bastion of left liberals, who persisted in demanding democratic reforms. In the elections of 1871 all of the city's six Reichstag seats went to members of the Progressive Party, and ten years later Bismarck was still complaining that the city was dominated by a "progressive clique."

The proclamation of the Reich in 1871 marked a new phase in Berlin's development. Although it remained the capital of Prussia, it now was also the *Reichshauptstadt,* the capital of a united German Empire. Moreover, by then economic and demographic developments had turned it into a true *Weltstadt,* an industrial, commercial, and banking metropolis of global significance. As Berlin increasingly became Europe's capital of modernity, challenging London and Paris, members of the Prussian court looked upon it with growing distaste: to them it was a city of industrial parvenus, left-liberal bourgeois, and socialist workers. Much of Berlin's modernity was determined by its economy. Occupations that had been generated by the "first industrial revolution" of iron, coal, and steam—metalworking, textile mills, and machine construction—remained important. By the end of the century Berlin could attribute most of its global economic clout to the fact that it had helped pioneer important sectors of the "second industrial revolution," based on chemicals and electricity.

Since industry needed workers, a primary fact of life in Imperial Berlin was a persistent demographic explosion, based largely on immigration into the city. Its population doubled between 1849 and 1871, when it reached 826,000; it topped one million in 1877, two million in 1905—and that did not include outlying suburbs. In 1861 the city's first detailed census revealed an acute housing crisis. Over 40 percent of Berlin's population lived in one-room units, which housed 4.3 people on average, yet tens of thousands of individuals lived in rooms that each harbored 7 or more occupants. Despite the public outcry, little was done to alleviate the situation throughout the Wilhelmine period. Disease remained rampant, owing to the lack of ventilation, light, and adequate sanitary facilities. In 1905 infant mortality in Wedding, a working-class district, was a staggering 42 percent. Heinrich Zille, a popular graphic artist who portrayed the life of the poor, noted: "You can kill a person with a tenement as easily as with an axe." Conditions at home and at work hastened the radicalization of Berlin's proletariat. A united German working-class party, heavily influenced by Marxist thought, was formed in 1875. In the Reichstag elections of 1878 the socialists received 52 percent of the vote in Berlin's six electoral districts. In that same year the Reichstag passed Bismarck's package of antisocialist legislation, which initiated twelve years of repression. After the repeal of those laws in 1890, the workers' party, now named the Social Democratic Party of Germany (SPD), expanded its electoral base in Berlin even more. In 1912, when the socialists received 35 percent of the national vote, they won 75 percent of the ballots cast in the capital.

Despite Berlin's growing reputation as a "red" city, in the 1880s it also was the center of an anti-Semitic movement. Many citizens suffered in the wake of the financial crash of 1873, which inaugurated a prolonged period of economic depression. In particular, members of the lower middle class were scared: independent craftsmen suffered increasingly from the competition of large industry, and small shopkeepers could not stand up to the marketing capabilities of the new department stores. The percentage of self-employed people in Berlin's working population fell from 32 in 1882 to just under 20 in 1907. The socialists argued that this was the inevitable result of free trade and capitalism. But many small producers, who abhorred socialism as a threat to private property, chose to listen instead to a new, politically updated brand of anti-Semitism (which opponents dubbed the "socialism of fools"). Its spokesmen argued that Jews were to blame for the "little man's" miseries. According to this theory, Jewish industries, backed by Jewish bankers, produced goods for Jewish department stores that undersold Christian craftsmen and shopkeepers, while Jewish newspapers hushed up the whole conspiracy. Berlin's anti-Semites liked to point their fingers at prominent local Jewish businessmen. Relatively few industrialists were Jewish; Emil Rathenau, founder of the electrical giant AEG (and Walter Rathenau's father), was an exception. Yet many of Berlin's banks, department stores (Wertheim, Tietz, Jandorf), and publishing houses (Mosse, Ullstein) had been launched by members of Jewish families. Berlin's anti-Semites were mobilized by Adolf Stöcker, a pastor with ties to the Imperial court. A coalition of right-wing and anti-Semitic groups gained up to 30 percent of the Berlin vote in the Reichstag elections of the 1880s. The movement subsided in the 1890s as economic conditions improved; it seemingly lay dormant for a generation. Anti-Semitism continued to appear, however, in individual cases. As we shall see, even Ernst von Wolzogen, the founder of Berlin's first cabaret, blamed the financial ruin of his project on "the Jews."

Although the socialists on the Left and the anti-Semites on the Right deplored the conditions generated by commercial and industrial capitalism, many middle-class citizens found Imperial Berlin exhilarating. The city was characterized above all by continuous, all-pervasive change. During the Wilhelmine era Berlin became, in the oft-quoted words of the critic Karl Scheffler, a city that "was damned to perpetual becoming, never to being." In 1912 Arthur Eloesser, who penned numerous vignettes of city life, noted that "Berlin used to have a physiognomy when it still was poor, when it consisted of philistines, officers, civil servants, and academics." But now "everything is provisional, and whoever was born in Berlin finds himself less at home there than a newly arrived inhabitant, who does not have to cast off any inhibiting memories or troublesome sentiments in order to jump into the flowing present and swim toward a shoreless future."[4]

Much of the change was physical and geographic; as the population exploded, new neighborhoods were created and social classes were increasingly segregated. While industries and their attendant proletariat moved to the periphery, the heart of Berlin became functionally differentiated. Unter den Linden, which stretched from the Brandenburg Gate to the Royal Palace and was flanked by the opera, the university, and other representational structures, remained the capital's most prestigious boulevard. Other centrally located streets became foci of administration (Wilhelmstrasse), banking (Behrenstrasse), shopping (Leipziger Strasse), and entertainment (Friedrichstrasse). Moreover, by the turn of the century a "push to the west" was well underway. The Tauentzienstrasse and the Kurfürstendamm became new centers of shopping and after-hours diversions, while further west, rich villas were arising in the Grunewald neighborhood. To connect the various segments of the burgeoning metropolis, newer and faster methods of transport were needed. Horse-drawn streetcars, introduced in 1865, were replaced by electric ones at the turn of the century. A municipal railroad system was begun in 1882, and the first subway was inaugurated twenty years later. The proliferation of transportation and traffic became one of the visual signs of the hectic tempo of the new Berlin (fig. 1).

For the well-to-do middle classes, Imperial Berlin was characterized above all by consumerism. Commercial arcades could be found in the city's center in the 1870s, but by the turn of the century, the true palace of commodities was the *Warenhaus,* the department store. The essayist Leo Colze noted in 1908: "There are four rulers in Berlin, uncrowned Kaisers"—the stores of Wertheim, Tietz, Jandorf, and the Kaufhaus des Westens. Functionally efficient, internally spacious, filled with light, they presented the consumer with the wonders of modern mass production (fig. 2). For the worker toiling in the factory or the small shopkeeper losing his clientele, the department store might symbolize voracious commercial capitalism; but for the bourgeois with money to spend, it was a paradise of

1. Leipziger Strasse, the major shopping avenue of Imperial Berlin, at the corner of Friedrichstrasse, the axis of the entertainment district.

consumerism, catering under one roof to the most refined and most banal of needs. The essayist Franz Hessel, a self-proclaimed flaneur and perceptive observer of modern Berlin, noted: "In luminous atria and winter gardens we sit on granite benches, our packages in our laps. Art exhibitions, which merge into refreshment rooms, interrupt the stack of toys and bathroom furnishings. Between decorative baldachins of silk and satin we wander to the soaps and toothbrushes." The children of the bourgeoisie were especially taken by this consumerist ambience. Eloesser noted "not without disapproval, that children above all respect the large department

2. The glass-roofed atrium of Wertheim on Leipziger Platz (completed 1904), Berlin's most renowned department store at the beginning of the century.

stores as the most imposing monuments that they recognize. They stroll with greedy fascination around the modern temple, in which the golden and silken idols dwell." In recollections of his childhood in fin-de-siècle Berlin, Walter Benjamin wrote: "In those early years I came to know the 'city' only as the theater of 'shopping'. . . A chain of impenetrable mountains, nay, caverns of commodities—that was 'the city.'"[5] Such impressions of commercial diversity and plenitude, to which young and old succumbed, helped fashion the metropolitan spirit from which cabaret was born.

Scheffler contended that "what is decisive for the conception of the modern metropolis [*Grossstadt*] is not the number of inhabitants, but rather the metropolitan spirit [*Grossstadtgeist*]." The man who analyzed that spirit most thoroughly was Georg Simmel, whose discussions of social interaction, commerce, and culture in the modern world were inspired by lifelong observations in Imperial Berlin. He noted repeatedly that "the development of Berlin from a big city to a world city [*von der Grossstadt zur Weltstadt*] in the years around and after the turn of the century coincides with the period of my own strongest and most general development," and "the special achievements that I made during these decades are undoubtedly tied to the Berlin milieu." Simmel was an extremely popular lecturer among both students and a broader educated public, and his essays constitute some of the most trenchant analyses of the society and culture of modernity. In his famous lecture on "The Metropolis and Mental Life" (1903), Simmel contended that "the psychological foundation" of individuals in the metropolis was "the intensification of nervous life, which proceeds from the rapid and uninterrupted fluctuation of external and internal impressions." In contrast to "the slower, more customary, more uniformly flowing rhythm" of small-town life, the modern metropolis confronted its inhabitants with a dizzying variety of sensations. "With every walk across the street, with the tempo and multiplicity of economic, professional, and social life," human consciousness came to be shaped in a uniquely modern and metropolitan manner, one characterized by what Simmel called the blasé outlook. In the modern city, which for Simmel meant Berlin, "the rapidity and the contradictory quality" of changing sense impressions "compel the nerves to make such violent responses and tug them back and forth so brutally that they surrender their last reserves of strength." The nervous exhaustion resulting from this daily civil war of sense impressions led to an attitude of indifference. Ultimately, and ironically, the nerves reacted to metropolitan experiences "by refusing to react to them."[6]

In numerous essays as well as the concluding sections of his monumental *Philosophy of Money* (1900), Simmel explored the cultural implications of this mentality. The display of commodities in shop windows, department stores, and exhibitions became a paradigm for modern experience. Observing the plethora of commodities presented at the Berlin Trade Exhibition of 1896, Simmel noted that "precisely this wealth and variety of fleeting impressions is appropriate to the desire for the stimulation of irritated and exhausted nerves." In part, such displays made amends for the monotony of labor: "it seems as if modern man desires to compensate for the one-sidedness and uniformity of the division of labor by seeking, in the realm of consumption and amusement, a growing concatenation of heterogeneous impressions, an increasingly hasty and motley fluctuation of stimulations." The monotony of the division of labor created a desire for variety outside of working hours. Fortunately, what was collectively produced—the wealth of commodities that the division of labor itself made possible—provided the diversity of impressions for which citizens hungered, when it was displayed in the shop windows and the exhibitions of the metropolis. But because this same diversity, carried to extremes, resulted in nervous exhaustion and a blasé outlook, ever stronger enticements were needed to attract the attention of potential consumers. Modern advertising developed as goods needed to have not only use-value, but also an "enticing exterior." They had to be fashioned, packaged, and displayed in an aesthetic manner to increase their "external appeal," since "internally" there often was little differentiation among competing products. The "shop-window-quality" of commodities came to supersede their practical utility for the consumer. Simultaneously, "ordinary advertisement has advanced to the art of the poster," as ever more extreme means were required to attract the attention of the blasé shopper. As commodities and their advertisements acquired aesthetic traits, shopping and "window-shopping" became forms of entertainment.[7]

The arts more generally came to reflect this condition. Artistic fashions, like commercial ones, came and went with increasing frequency, since the hollowness at the core of the blasé person caused him or her to seek ever new, albeit necessarily fleeting, stimulations: "The lack of something definite at the center of the soul impels us to search for momentary satisfaction in ever-new stimulations, sensations, and external activities. Thus it is that we become entangled in the instability and helplessness that manifests itself as the tumult of the metropolis, as the mania for travelling, as the wild pursuit of competition and as the typically modern disloyalty with regard to taste, style, opinions and personal relationships." In time, the forms of art favored by the urbanite came to reflect the diversity and fragmentation of the world of commodities: he or she responded to the "charm of the fragment, the mere allusion, the aphorism, the symbol, the undeveloped artistic style."[8]

Simmel's observations referred to a fundamental revolution that was taking place in various artistic media. Throughout the nineteenth century writers and artists had attempted to capture the spirit of the big city. One form that initially had seemed promising was the novel; its ability to evoke numerous lives and events appeared especially appropriate for encompassing the sprawling life of the metropolis. Yet despite the abilities of novelistic giants like Balzac, Dickens, Dostoevsky, and Zola, the expansiveness and narrative cohesion of that medium seemed to contradict the actual experience of fragmentation and disassociation evoked by the big city. That aspect of metropolitan experience required the generation of new artistic forms, whose brevity stood in direct opposition to the novel's breadth. In *Paris Spleen* (1869), Charles Baudelaire presented short vignettes of city life, based upon the innovative form of "poetic prose, musical without rhythm and without rhyme, supple and abrupt enough to adapt itself to the lyrical movements of the soul." This new style was born, he said, from "the frequentation of enormous cities [*des villes énormes*], from the cross-ings of their innumerable connections."[9] Baudelaire's vignettes appeared in the feuilleton columns of Parisian newspapers, and eventually Berlin's daily papers also printed reflections on city life, by such noted observers as Arthur Eloesser, Bernhard von Brentano, Franz Hessel, and Walter Benjamin.

In the visual arts many Impressionist and Postimpressionist painters likewise sought to freeze moments of urban experience. Although the German Impressionists never approached the quality of their French coun-terparts, talented painters like Lesser Ury used that style to capture the hectic spirit of Berlin traffic and street life. As for the stage, experimental playwrights came to reject multiact works with conventional dramatic unity and closure in favor of more open-ended forms. The one-act play, an increasingly prevalent genre, presented a "slice of life" torn from a larger context, while the new "station-dramas" depicted an individual's progression from incident to incident, without any overarching meaning. In 1907 the German art critic Richard Hamann surveyed these develop-ments in the various arts and claimed that they expressed an "impression-istic" aesthetic infusing all aspects of modern culture. By this he meant a profusion of artistic styles based upon the evocation of momentary im-pressions, and a decline of grander forms based upon dramatic or narrative continuities. Not surprisingly, Hamann regarded the metropolis as the incubator of these developments.[10]

By the eve of World War I, another especially promising technique was developed to fashion art from the fragments of urban life: collage. Origi-nally used by Picasso and Braque in 1912, it was appropriated by artists in several countries, most notably by the Berlin Dadaists at the end of the war. By adding clipped or torn newspaper articles, advertisements, sheet music, and "found objects" to the painted canvas, they made explicit an aesthetic based on the collation of diverse impressions. Such works con-cretized the principles that had been evolving in the other media. Art no longer strove for a consistent form and a unified content; rather it aimed at expressing heterogeneity and discontinuity. Clear spatial ordering was replaced by disruptive juxtapositions that evoked the simultaneity of di-vergent experiences. As collage spread among practitioners of the two-dimensional arts, and the related practice of assemblage inspired three-dimensional works, montage came to characterize the new medium of film. Still photography, a product of the nineteenth century, had not only docu-mented the growth of cities but also contributed to the "impressionistic" aesthetic through the "snapshot," the visual capturing of isolated mo-ments. In the mid-1890s a temporal dimension was added with the intro-duction of "moving pictures," which further documented the confusion of the modern city. As early as 1896 a short film entitled "Life and Activity on Unter den Linden" recorded the goings-on of Berlin's central boulevard. More significantly, the new cinematic medium, based on the splicing together of short takes, opened up novel possibilities for juxtaposing visual materials.[11]

Needless to say, many novels, plays, paintings, and films continued to strive for the depiction of "linear," self-contained stories. Yet the innovators in those arts, most of whom were based in urban milieus, increasingly abandoned the visual, dramatic, or narrative conventions of the past. Instead, they devised a new paratactic grammar, which juxtaposed divergent elements without claiming to see any logical unities to their relationships. Montage came to be seen as the appropriate principle for replicating big-city life, and parataxis was its new syntax. Cabaret employed both. Unlike other art forms, however, cabaret drew directly upon a type of urban entertainment that had embodied those principles long before they were formulated by writers, artists, critics, and social theorists: the variety show. "Completely on instinct and without any theory," as the writer Ludwig Rubiner noted, Variété had inaugurated a formal revolution that gave birth to German cabaret.[12]

### Variety Shows and Nietzschean Vitalism

Georg Simmel regarded the metropolis as a locus where human subjectivity was constantly challenged: a dynamic was established between city and psyche, such that both were continually destructured and refashioned. Popular entertainment could not help but be entangled in this exchange. Unlike many of the later social thinkers whom he influenced—Siegfried Kracauer, Ernst Bloch, Walter Benjamin—Simmel never discussed cabaret or revues directly, but many of his observations complemented other ongoing debates about the nature of modern life and popular culture. At the center of those discussions stood the variety show.

In Berlin the creation of cabarets was above all a reaction to the growing popularity of vaudeville and variety shows—Variétés or Specialitäten-Theater—in the years following the unification of the Reich. As their name suggests, they provided a "variety" of unconnected and "specialized" entertainments, primarily songs, acrobatic stunts, and animal acts, but also skits, magic tricks, tableaux, and even popular opera arias. The variety show was an urban institution that had originated in England, where it was called music hall, in the first half of the nineteenth century. The concept of the variety show soon spread to the continent, as well as to America, where it was known as vaudeville. It became the dominant form of urban entertainment until the advent of film. German vaudeville halls appeared in different guises. Those at the lower end of the spectrum were little more than raised stages at the side of a cheap restaurant or pub, where aspiring (or down-and-out) entertainers would perform. Some, with male waiters, were considered decent establishments to which one could take the whole family. Far less reputable were establishments where waitresses served beverages to a male clientele, while soubrettes performed risqué songs. Often several women would appear on stage at once, and each would sing a suggestive song. Afterward they might wander among the audience and sell "naughty" postcards, encourage the men to order more drinks, or even make assignations for later. The tavern scenes of the film *The Blue Angel* illustrated that type of venture. Such joints were commonly, and disparagingly, dubbed "Tingeltangel." Although the origins of the name are disputed, it probably derived from the verb *tingeln*, which described the clinking of coins onto a plate passed around during the show. The repetition of this root word with a single vowel shift gave Tingeltangel a further plebeian quality, much like the American honky-tonk. The official attitude toward such venues can be gleaned from the definition of Tingeltangel established by a German court in 1904: "commercial presentations at a fixed place of operation, consisting of musical performances, especially vocal music, declamations, dances, shorter musicals and similar works, devoid of any higher artistic or scholarly interest, and which are capable, through either their content or their manner of presentation, of arousing the lower instincts, in particular the sexual lust of the audience."[13]

At the upper end of the vaudeville spectrum were large commercial establishments, seating well over a thousand spectators, that could afford to engage the most famous entertainers. As variety shows spread throughout Europe and the United States, an international star system of especially talented (or at least well-advertised) performers developed, and their high-priced acts would be purchased for two-week stints by the premier vaudeville halls. The most distinguished variety theater in Berlin was the Wintergarten. When the Central-Hotel opened in Berlin in 1880, it boasted an enormous, glass-decked winter garden. Its owners soon put it to more profitable use, first as a ballroom, and by 1887 as a vaudeville hall (fig. 3). They proceeded to book the most famous stars of the variety-show circuit, and over the years its entertainers included Yvette Guilbert, Loie Fuller, La belle Otéro, Cleo de Mérode, Saharet, The Five Sisters Barrison, and Lillian Russell. The world's first public film projection took place at the Wintergarten on November 1, 1895, when the Skladanowsky brothers presented their "Bioskop" as part of the evening's entertainments. Somewhat superfluously, the short film clips depicted other variety-show numbers: a juggler, an athlete on horizontal bars, acrobats, wrestlers, Russian

3. Auditorium and stage of the Wintergarten variety theater.

dancers, Italian children's dances, and a certain Mister Delaware with his boxing kangaroo.[14]

Many vaudeville halls were neither cheap Tingeltangel nor extravagant establishments, but simply regular theaters that hosted variety shows. Indeed, this was precisely what worried German observers by the turn of the century: vaudeville was becoming so popular that it was driving conventional dramatic theaters out of business. The trend was especially pronounced in Berlin at an early date. The Tonhallen-Theater (founded 1869), the Bellevue-Theater (1872), the Neues American Reichs-Theater (1877), and the Reichshallen-Theater (1881), among others, switched from concerts or spoken theater to variety shows within a few months after opening. By the 1880s it had become apparent that broad sectors of the middle class, which had initially looked down upon vaudeville, were being won over to its popular theatricality. The Wintergarten played a key role in this transition, inasmuch as attendance there became fashionable for Berliners as well as tourists. A cabaret journal of 1902 noted in retrospect that "Julius Baron, the former director of the Wintergarten, was probably the first person to build a large and wide bridge between vaudeville artistry and bourgeois society." The success of the Wintergarten and other prestigious variety theaters was so great that Conrad Alberti, a noted naturalist writer, could write in 1901: "The fact that vaudeville halls have increasingly supplanted and diminished interest in theater has caused a stir for quite some time in all circles which still take an interest in the fate and the future of art in Germany. Perhaps this has never been so apparent as this winter in Berlin, where attendance at the performances of theaters dwindles day by day and has become limited almost exclusively to inferior farces, while the vaudeville halls can boast of sold-out houses nearly every evening."[15]

Numerous attempts were made to explain this abandonment of theater in favor of variety shows. Some authors made the obvious point that the demands of work during the day left people exhausted in the evening. In *Das Variété* (1902) Artur Moeller van den Bruck, an increasingly conservative essayist and cultural critic, noted that the pleasure-urge was "the flip side of productivity," and that vaudeville allowed the masses to experience some of the instinctive sensuality that they were forced to repress in the workplace. Another observer contended: "Whoever has to strain hand and head from early in the morning to late in the evening has neither the composure nor the receptivity for intellectual products that demand strict concentration. The tortured spirit seeks relaxation and the lightest form of diversion; thus it is really no wonder that the most superficial farces are the greatest draws at theaters, and the broad masses prefer vaudeville halls." Other authors argued that vaudeville was not only a source of release from the pressures of labor, but simultaneously, and paradoxically, a reflection of values that had been instilled in the workplace. Conrad Alberti noted that "the passionate partiality for gymnastics, for bodily agility and exercise, accords well with an age in which technology rules everything, in which dexterity and practical ability outweigh philosophical thought and aesthetic perception." In such an age, people actively participate in sports—"sport is technology without a practical goal"—or passively admire the "technically" perfect gymnastic feats of vaudeville performers.[16] Such leisure-time activities might allow one to relax from the pressures of a hard week's work, but they also reinforced the attitudes inculcated on the shop floor or in the office. This aspect of entertainment was to persist into the twenties, when the kicklines of "Girls" updated the industrial aesthetic for audiences of the Weimar era.

Some writers contended that vaudeville not only alleviated the rigors and reproduced the values of the workplace but also reflected modern experience more generally. They asserted that vaudeville was in fact a quintessentially modern art form, a logical and inevitable outcome of urban life. The hustle and bustle of the modern city, with its crowds and traffic, its constant variation of sights and sounds, fragmented consciousness and shattered all sense of stability and continuity. Ernst von Wolzogen, who founded Berlin's first cabaret, noted that vaudeville's popularity was "a sign of our nervous, precipitate age, which finds no repose for long and prolix entertainments. We are all, each and every one of us, attuned to aphoristic, terse, and catchy tones." In the introduction to *Deutsche Chansons* (1900), an influential collection of lyrics that helped usher in the cabaret movement, Otto Julius Bierbaum wrote: "The contemporary city-dweller has vaudeville nerves; he seldom has the capacity of following great dramatic continuities, of tuning his senses to the same tone for three hours. He desires diversity—Variété."[17] The fragmentation and intensification of sense experience in everyday metropolitan life transformed the perceptual apparatus of modern urbanites to such an extent that they were no longer capable of the continuous reflection demanded by conventional drama. Stage presentations thus had to become as multiform and disjunct as the presentation of everyday life in the streets, shops, and offices of the modern metropolis.

These arguments paralleled Simmel's analysis of the metropolitan psyche and its effects on the marketing of commodities. Modern life fashioned citizens who felt at home in surroundings that changed constantly; too much stability placed excessive demands on the concentration of the modern observer. Moreover, increasingly extreme means were needed to attract the attention of modern urbanites, bewildered and exhausted by the plethora of external stimuli. As Wolzogen said, everyone was "attuned to aphoristic, terse, and catchy tones": the melodies of modern life needed to be not only succinct, but "catchy"; they had to reach out and ensnare the consumer. This became a vicious circle. As the number and intensity of stimulations increased, the observer became more confused and exhausted, which necessitated ever greater exertions to attract his or her attention. Shop-window displays became more extravagant, advertisements became more colorful, and entertainments as well became more lavish and sensually enticing in order to feed the hunger for overt stimulation. Just as window displays and trade exhibitions presented a growing diversity of goods attractively packaged and presented, vaudeville provided a variety of different entertainments that increasingly claimed to be "the world's best," "the most beautiful," "the most daring," "the sensation of Europe."

Such arguments implied that any artist who desired to address a modern public would have to adopt sooner or later the "terse and catchy" forms of vaudeville. By the 1890s conventional theater was beginning to adapt itself to the style of vaudeville, as gymnastic stunts, songs, and other variety-show elements were inserted into some dramas, comedies, and farces. This trend was given theoretical justification by Oskar Panizza, a highly controversial Bavarian playwright who published an influential essay on "Classicism and the Infiltration of Vaudeville" (1896). He defined vaudeville very broadly in order to argue that modern culture was becoming increasingly infused with a variety-show spirit, so that the classical foundations of nineteenth-century culture were about to collapse. For Panizza vaudeville was the "absolute contradiction" of classicism, insofar as it respected no moral or aesthetic categories and had no social consciousness: it expressed joy in existence pure and simple. It represented "the total lack of character in the arts . . . It is absolute naiveté in the use of artistic media; it is the crudest (because unselfconscious) use of makeup and powder, of lipstick and eyelash black, of tutus and tights—I speak figuratively—in art, it is sparkling joy, childish enthusiasm, and purest delight in the result, whatever its origin. That is Variété." According to Panizza, this spirit, this "poetry of the people" that had originated in "the lowest music-halls," irrevocably changed the aesthetic taste of those who had experienced it. "It is not without import if we decide to spend an evening seeing the Huline-Brothers, some musical clowns, or the Barrison Sisters instead of Goethe's *Iphigenia*. Whoever sees a serpentine-dance with its ravishing mysticism in the evening cannot quietly sit down the next morning and continue to write a fifth act in a classical mode." Just as Bierbaum contended that modern audiences could no longer sit through multiact plays, Panizza argued that modern writers could not compose them anymore: once vaudeville destroyed the aura of classicism, it never could be restored. He pointed to the paintings of Franz Stuck, Frank Wedekind's play *Spring Awakening,* and Otto Erich Hartleben's version of the lyric cycle, *Pierrot lunaire,* as examples of the intrusion of the vaudeville spirit into all spheres of the arts. Panizza's own blasphemous drama, *The Council of Love* (1894), for which he was sentenced to a year in jail, likewise included gymnastics, wrestling bouts, boisterous sexuality, and other vaudevillian elements.[18]

Many writers concurred with Moeller van den Bruck's assertion that "if our age has a style at all, then it must be a vaudeville-style [*Variétéstil*]." They sought to use this fact as a basis for reforming both high and low culture, by infusing them with a new vitality. They contended that many aspects of popular vaudeville were tasteless, and they sought to improve or "ennoble" *(veredeln)* its artistic forms. At the same time, they believed that high culture as well was in serious need of reform. While much of elite art had degenerated into a lifelessly epigonal neoclassicism, the so-called avant-garde trends were too distant from the concerns or the comprehension of the broader educated public. Some critics argued that much serious art, already marked by modernist tendencies, made too many demands on the average audience. Noting that the public was abandoning opera in favor of vaudeville, one music critic laid the blame on the disappearance of simple melodic lines in post-Wagnerian operas and symphonies: "The music-loving public does not in the long run want to be served contrapuntal curiosities and pointy-headed [*geistreichelnde*] note combinations in place of melodies and healthy music appreciation. If opera houses and concert halls continue to deny the public what it desires and demands, then it turns to vaudeville or to operettas." And a critic in the conservative journal *Der Kunstwart* pointed disapprovingly to the "convoluted polyphony" and motifs of modern music-dramas, "or a play by Ibsen, with its hesitant unfolding of antecedent events, with its dialogue, where one has to read the true meaning between the lines, and where the words themselves provide only slight intimations and halfway-hinted thoughts." No wonder the audience sought "a desirable counterbalance to the exhausting nature of great art."[19]

By the turn of the century many observers of German culture concluded that a new performing art was needed. It should appeal to the modern audience's predilection for the fragmented form of vaudeville, and it should occupy a middle ground between the mindlessness of popular variety shows and the incomprehensible esoterism of the avant-garde. The solution to this equation was cabaret. That French word originally had a twofold meaning: it designated a lower-class wine-house or pub, and it referred to a type of tray that held a variety of different foods or drinks. Both definitions came together in the "cabaret artistique," where a variety of different numbers would be performed in a pub setting. The first such venture was the "Chat noir" (Black Cat) of Rodolphe Salis, an *artiste manqué* turned tavern keeper. Initially a circle of Parisian writers and artists entertained each other with their own poems and songs at his Montmartre pub. When he noticed that the lively goings-on began to attract a wider, bourgeois public, he formalized the performances. From 1881 on, every evening would feature writers and artists presenting their own works to the tavern's clientele. Although the performers received little or no pay, it was a means of advertising themselves to a wider audience. Salis reaped the profits from the venture, as word-of-mouth soon turned his establishment into a fashionable venue. He moved to larger quarters in 1885, where he expanded the repertory to include elaborately staged shadow plays.

Salis's original venue was taken over by Aristide Bruant, an imposing figure who composed and sang argot songs with a strong populist bent. Renamed "Le Mirliton," a word that can mean either a reed flute or doggerel verse, it became a place where the audience could pretend to engage in social and cultural slumming. Whereas Salis treated his guests with excessive (and hence ironic) courtesy, Bruant heaped vulgar verbal abuse on his patrons and subjected them to accusatory songs that deplored the fate of workers, criminals, and the poor. Unfortunately, the Chat noir and the Mirliton were the only two artistically respectable Parisian cabarets, and they lasted little more than a decade. Bruant sold his venture in 1895, and Salis died two years later. Their successors and numerous imitators created what were little better than tourist traps, each with a different gimmick to inspire levity. There was a cabaret that pretended to replicate heaven, next door to one that represented hell; one was decked out like a catacomb, and several claimed to be modeled on the haunts of criminals. None of them displayed any of the literary or artistic quality that characterized the ventures of the 1880s.[20]

The German proponents of cabaret were forewarned. The Parisian prototypes demonstrated that such ventures could be centers of artistic innovation, experimentation, and conviviality, but could just as easily degenerate into commercial kitsch. The first sustained call for the creation of German cabarets took note of this problem. Otto Julius Bierbaum's novel *Stilpe* (1897) recounted the misadventures of its eponymous antihero, a bright but unstable writer who dabbled in the various cultural trends of the fin de siècle. The cabaret founded by Stilpe turned into a commercial and artistic debacle, and he ended up hanging himself on stage during a performance. Despite the novel's warnings about the many ways in which a cabaret could become derailed, its arguments in favor of founding such ventures were taken seriously by many readers. They concurred with Stilpe's observations: "Just look at the theaters! They're empty! Go into the Wintergarten! It's full! Death in one spot, revival in the other!" However, both were "ripe for destruction": "Theater, because its structure is too clumsy, heavy, and immovable to satisfy the hunger for tidbits in the modern artistic urge; and today's vaudeville, because it does not know how to give truly artistic substance to its otherwise auspicious form, which conforms to all of the demands of a nervous age." Stilpe placed great hopes in Tingeltangel, which he believed might bring about "a renaissance of all arts and of life in its entirety."[21]

Heretofore art had played a secondary role in people's lives, but Stilpe believed that a new movement could infuse everyday existence with aesthetic vitality. That idea was a central precept of art nouveau, the Jugendstil movement of the turn of the century. Taking cues from developments in England and Belgium, German artists in the 1890s had begun to focus on applied arts as a means of infusing the everyday surroundings of the middle classes with new aesthetic forms. Whereas nineteenth-century design had consisted of historicist imitations of previous styles (classic, gothic, renaissance, baroque), a new generation of applied artists sought to create an ahistorical, supposedly modern style based upon organic, crystalline, and geometric forms. This style was employed to shape objects of daily life, from house facades to interior design, from wallpaper to furniture and silverware. The center of the German Jugendstil movement was Munich, where Bierbaum resided for most of the 1890s. He explained and applauded its endeavors in numerous essays, and his theory of cabaret drew directly upon its precepts. Just as Jugendstil sought to bring visual art out of the museum and into the living room, Bierbaum believed that literature should be aimed more directly at the modern public. He contended that cabaret could perform this function by presenting "applied lyrics" *(ange-wandte Lyrik)* to complement the "applied arts" *(angewandte Kunst)*. In the introduction to *Deutsche Chansons* he wrote: "We too have serious objectives, insofar as we place our art in the service of Tingeltangel. We have the idée fixe that all of life should be saturated with art. Today painters build chairs, and their ambition is to make chairs which one not only can admire in museums, but to which one can also apply one's posterior without suffering injury. Similarly, we want to write poems that not only can be read in the quiet of one's room, but also be sung before an audience desiring amusement. Applied lyrics—that is our slogan."[22] Bierbaum hoped that the poems and songs heard at cabarets would address everyday concerns, and would be lyrical or melodic enough to be spoken or sung at home as well.

Cabaret's "application" of literature and music to a wide public was supposed to infuse a new spirit of vitality into its audience. Whereas most elite art and literature of the Wilhelmine era, composed in an epigonal classical tradition, seemed to advocate the cultivation of spiritual values, many products of the Jugendstil movement were sensual and vitalistic. In place of Christian asceticism, the new arts advocated a self-consciously pagan hedonism. Several observers argued that the desire to overcome repression was demonstrated by the shift in theatrical taste: the middle classes were increasingly drawn to vaudeville because of its physicality and sensuality, its eroticism and bodily energy. Eberhard Buchner, author of a study of Berlin's variety shows, noted: "Vaudeville art is above all bodily art, sensual art. Sensuality is expressed more unreservedly and more im-mediately in vaudeville halls than in any other artistic establishment." Bierbaum proclaimed: "We want to raise vaudeville to the sphere of art, but we do not want to make it an institution for the crippling of good and natural instincts. On the contrary: everything that is healthy and vital, every good and joyful thing that emanates from our senses shall find an abode here, shall find straightforward and beautiful expression." Moeller van den Bruck too saw variety shows as an expression of "zest for life" *(Lebenslust)* and asserted: "Vaudeville is everything that Dionysos impels men to do."[23]

This reference to Dionysos was an allusion to the ideas of Friedrich Nietzsche, whose name was frequently invoked by supporters of cabaret. At a time when people of every imaginable persuasion—from anarchists and Social Democrats to anti-Semites and the far Right—were attempting to appropriate Nietzsche to their causes, the incipient cabaretists could hardly refrain from coopting his thought. Nietzsche had called upon his contemporaries to rejuvenate themselves and their culture, a task that would require overcoming Christian asceticism, the work ethic, and bad conscience vis-à-vis the lower classes. According to Nietzsche, humor was an indispensable attribute for revitalization and self-overcoming, a necessary prelude to the appearance of the future "overman." Throughout his works Nietzsche praised the value of laughter and dancing. Zarathustra proclaimed: "Lost be to us the day upon which we have not danced at least once! False be the truth that was not accompanied by a laugh!" Nietzsche espoused a Dionysian world, where everything held sacred would be laughed out of existence, and man's repressed instincts would become a source of joyous exuberance. In *Human, All-Too-Human* (1878) he spoke of the "joy in nonsense" produced by "the overturning of experience into its opposite, the purposeful into the purposeless, the necessary into the arbitrary." In *The Joyful Science* (1882) he called for a commitment to folly: "Nothing is as useful to us as the *fool's cap:* we need it in relation to ourselves—we need every wanton, floating, dancing, mocking, childish, and blissful form of art, in order to preserve that *freedom over things* that our ideal demands from us." Nietzsche concluded that work by evoking "the ideal of a spirit who naively, that is unintentionally and from overflowing abundance and power, plays with everything that has hitherto been deemed holy, good, untouchable, godly." Such a being would appear to be a "parody of all prevailing worldly seriousness, all solemnity in gesture, word, tone, view, and duty."[24]

It is not surprising that Nietzsche was often invoked by the supporters of cabaret. Bierbaum's Stilpe proclaimed: "We will give birth to the overman [*den Übermenschen*] on the stage boards [*auf dem Brettl*]." This statement probably inspired Wolzogen to dub his cabaret the Überbrettl. In any case, Wolzogen noted in his memoirs: "I began to immerse myself in Nietzsche. And just as Nietzsche's dream of an overman colored my catchword about the 'Überbrettl,' so too did Nietzsche's idea of the Dionysian man, the dancer, the joyful science." When Wolzogen opened the second venue of his cabaret in November 1901, a bust of Nietzsche stood in the foyer. Such enthusiasm is understandable, but like most of Nietzsche's self-proclaimed followers, the advocates of cabaret did not read the philosopher very well. Had he lived to witness German cabaret, it is unlikely that he would have expressed approval. After all, Nietzsche specifically attacked the premises upon which it was based. The fragmentation of experience in the modern world, along with its reflection in the arts, was for him a sign of decadence. In *The Case of Wagner* (1888) he proclaimed: "What characterizes every *literary* decadence? The word becomes sovereign and springs forth from the sentence, the sentence spreads out and obscures the meaning of the page, the page takes on life at the expense of the whole—the whole is no longer a whole anymore." Nietzsche attributed such decadence to the same aspects of urban life which the proponents of cabaret would later praise. In *Human, All-Too-Human* he asserted: "When one lacks firm, calm lines on the horizons of one's life, like the lines of mountains and forests, the innermost will of man itself becomes restless, distracted, and covetous, like the essence of a city-dweller: he has no happiness and gives no happiness." In *Joyful Wisdom* he predicted: "Sometime, and probably soon, we will realize what is missing above all in our big cities: peaceful and wide, expansive spaces for reflection." In the meantime citizens have become overly hasty and su-perficial: "Man already is ashamed of resting; prolonged meditation almost gives him pangs of conscience. He thinks with a watch in his hand, as he eats lunch, his eyes glued to the business page—he lives like someone who fears 'missing out on something.'"[25] This attitude led to a loss of form, and of sensitivity to form, which for Nietzsche was the requirement of all truly great art.

Nietzsche denied that it would be possible to heal the psychological fragmentation of modern man with superficial aesthetic remedies. In "Schopenhauer as Educator" (1874) he attacked the current historicist style of architecture and interior design, but his criticisms could have been directed just as well against Jugendstil a generation later: "Truly, it would not be worth lifting a finger for German culture, if the German were to conceive the culture that he lacks and must strive for, as arts and niceties suitable for prettifying life." Nietzsche believed that the "prevailing ten-dency toward 'beautiful form'" was a futile attempt to paper over "that haste, that breathless grabbing at the moment, that excessive hurry, that racing and chasing, which currently chisels wrinkles into men's faces and tattoos everything that they do." Nietzsche would have scorned cabaret's catering to mass taste, its attempt to capture an audience that had suc-cumbed to vaudeville. In *Nietzsche contra Wagner* (1888) he contended: "I am essentially antitheatrical by nature; from the depths of my soul I have a deep disdain for theater, that *mass art* par excellence, which every artist feels today. *Success* in theater—and my admiration sinks permanently out of sight; *failure*—there I prick up my ears and begin to have respect."[26] Perhaps on that basis alone, Nietzsche might have begrudged cabarets, short-lived ventures that they were, some respect after all.

### Berlin Wit: Laughter and Censorship

Joking was one of cabaret's major attributes. One reason why the new ventures took hold in Berlin was the city's long tradition of subversive wit. Various theories have tried to account for the existence of "Berliner Witz."

Most trace its birth to the fact that the city's harsh conditions in the early modern era forced the inhabitants to keep mentally alert in order to survive. Nature was stingy in Berlin, which had arisen "in the sand of the mark of Brandenburg," according to the cliché. The city's heterogeneous population added further elements of difficulty and confusion. After the devastation of the Thirty Years' War the city was hungry for new inhabitants, and its population came to be drawn from all parts of Central Europe, and even further afield. In the seventeenth century Friedrich Wilhelm, the Great Elector, welcomed Jews expelled from Vienna and Huguenots driven out of France. In the 1720s the city greeted Protestant weavers facing persecution in Bohemia. Generally Berlin drew upon the inhabitants of Brandenburg, but it also attracted craftsmen from Holland and the Pfalz and laborers from Silesia, Pomerania, and Poland. The melting down of these groups was never complete, and a fully homogeneous citizenry was never achieved. Nevertheless, there arose (supposedly) a certain Berlin character type, whose pushiness was a product of the struggle to survive in a heterogeneous environment. Even Goethe noted that in Berlin, "you do not get very far with politeness, because such an audacious race of men lives there that you need to have a sharp tongue and also be rather rude in order to keep your head above water."[27]

That "sharp tongue" came to be called "Berliner Schnauze" (literally, "Berlin snout"). The Berliners were believed to have a corresponding style of wit, one marked by disrespect of authority and cynical skepticism toward received values. Whether the average Berliner actually betrayed these characteristics in the early nineteenth century is hard to determine. What is more certain is the fact that this stereotype of the Berliner became accepted by many people as early as 1821, with the performance of Julius von Voss's play *Der Stralauer Fischzug*. This was the first popular farce *(Possenspiel)* that presented local characters speaking *berlinerisch* as a pointed and aggressive argot. The play had numerous imitators during the ensuing decades, both on stage (the skits of David Kalisch) and in illustrated comic pamphlets and journals (such as those of Adolf Glassbrenner). A roster of characters was developed in these media which depicted the average lower-class Berliner as half-educated yet cunning, self-assured, and slyly subversive of authority. Major representatives of this attitude were cabdrivers, hawkers, shoemakers' apprentices, and the *Eckensteher* figure, a man-for-hire who advertised his availability by slouching against street-corners.[28]

It would be difficult to come down on a single side of a chicken-or-egg argument: did the reality shape these images, or did the images shape actual behavior? Nevertheless, over time, the continued presentation of such characters in the popular media led to the type of characterization noted by Ernst Dronke, an observer of the city's manners, in 1846: "From the tendencies and the nature of Berlin wit we can learn about an element of the Berliners, namely the fact that they leave nothing, indiscriminately nothing, unridiculed. If anything is a characteristic of Berlin, then it is such criticism, the negation of every authority." Thirty years later, the popular encyclopedia, *Meyers Konversationslexikon,* noted: "The Berliner is always quick-witted, always ready to find a sharp, spicy, witty formulation for every encounter and event . . . But the Berliner also has the tendency to carp at everything great or profound that confronts him, or to drag it down to the level of illusion or fashion, in order to play with it until it is tossed out in favor of another toy." The encyclopedia conceded that even though Berliners were very proud and defensive of their city vis-à-vis outsiders, they had "the exquisite quality of treating themselves and their weaknesses ironically, and of making all aspects of Berlin the object of their wit."[29]

This image of the Berliner, which had been fashioned in the generation prior to the revolution of 1848, continued to dominate popular farces into the 1870s. Thereafter demographic and economic shifts made the artisans and preindustrial workers who populated those plays obsolete, and the traditional farces disappeared from the repertory. As hawkers, apprentices, and *Eckensteher* gave way to employees of heavy industry and department stores, new images of Berlin had to be fashioned for public consumption. As we shall see, the revues and cabarets of the early twentieth century played an important role in providing updated character types. There one could encounter performers like Claire Waldoff or Paul Graetz, who spoke or sang in an aggressive Berlin dialect about the foibles of their day.

One reason why the Berlin character type could survive into the modern age was because its attributes became even more necessary as time progressed. If anything, the metropolis demanded an even greater agility of mind. Richard Hamann wrote: "In Germany the Berliner is considered especially quick-witted, and in fact, to mention simply something superficial, the crossing of the Potsdamer Platz or even a walk through the Friedrichstrasse in heavy traffic demands a presence of mind that finds ill-defined signals and indirectly perceived images sufficient for directing one's volition." These conditions were obviously the same ones that gave birth to Simmel's conception of the metropolitan psyche. They also had ramifications in the realm of wit, according to Hamann and other observers. The urbanite's detachment from traditional bonds could generate not only a blasé attitude, as Simmel contended, but also a cynicism that mocked all fixed values. Hamann claimed that the "splitting of consciousness" in the big city resulted in a know-it-all attitude, a feeling of detachment from and superiority to all values, persons, and events. In such a situation of perpetual distance, anything could serve as a target for wit: "Big-city society, although much more tolerant than that of the small town since it demands nothing of the individual, is nevertheless much more mocking, because the aesthetic tendency to apply one's wit to phenomena can become the sole interest that one has in other things."[30] The resulting cynicism was one of the outsiders' major complaints about the Berliners. In the Weimar era, it also was a charge leveled against cabaret.

Wit can reveal a negative side, insofar as it expresses some of the least noble of human emotions: malice, hatred, ridicule. But it also can display very idealistic sentiments. Satire, after all, consists most fundamentally in contrasting a person's stated values with his or her actual practices. Underscoring the discrepancy between ideals and realities need not be cynical; it can be pedagogical or even therapeutic. Uncovering hypocrisy can free the body politic from delusion, or warn citizens away from dangerous individuals or ideologies. On a more general level, laughter can loosen mental constraints and make room for innovative thought. Nietzsche certainly had that end in mind when he called for laughter, and similar ideas could be found in quite different camps as well. Speaking of Bertolt Brecht, Walter Benjamin wrote: "there is no better starting point for thought than laughter. And in particular, splitting your sides normally offers better chances for thought than shaking up your soul."[31] Cabaret at its best hoped to engage in such a mentally liberating enterprise.

The emancipatory aspect of wit was highlighted in what was probably the most perceptive account of humor written at the turn of the century: Sigmund Freud's *Jokes and Their Relation to the Unconscious* (1905). Freud contended that the joke was "the most social of all the mental functions that aim at a yield of pleasure." The pleasure derived from joking resulted from the fact that it lifted a repression, be it internal or external, in a public context (that is, in the presence of the joker's audience). Freud was particularly interested in jokes that were *tendenziös,* "tendentious" in the sense of having a sociopolitical goal or focus of attack. Such jokes invariably criticized something that demanded renunciation, such as a political authority, a moral imperative, the institution of marriage, or even reason and logical thought (which were challenged by nonsense jokes). By making fun of such people or values, jokes provided a partial release of the frustrations that they generated: "to the human psyche all renunciation is exceedingly difficult, and so we find that tendentious jokes provide a means of undoing the renunciation and retrieving what was lost."[32] What was lost was, of course, the freedom of thinking, speaking, or acting as one desired.

The more committed and self-conscious cabarets supported such freedom. Consequently, they dealt with the two major taboos of the modern world: sex and politics. But such topics were broached in the face of authorities that espoused renunciation. The most effective censor sat, in fact, in the public's head. Often prevailing norms had been internalized so successfully that audiences were unwilling to hear performers who challenged their political or moral values. The most successful entertainers were those who spoke to people's repressions, but did not call for a major restructuring of thought or action. Ultimately, by the Weimar era, that came to be seen as one of the major pitfalls of cabaret: it could be a safety valve, where the spectators would "let off steam" through laughter, but then proceed to live as they always had. Cabaret thus could sustain the status quo inadvertently, insofar as it defused tensions that otherwise might have been stored up longer and eventually released in much more forceful forms.

The audience was not the only authority that prevented cabaret from getting out of hand. Up until the fall of the monarchy in 1918, the theaters of Wilhelmine Germany were subjected to preliminary censorship. Before a performance, the script of every play, skit, or song had to be submitted in duplicate to the police, who would examine the text and determine its suitability for public presentation. Most scripts were approved, but often cuts were indicated in the texts returned to the theater. The police would retain the duplicate copies and send an observer to the performance to ascertain whether the cuts had been made. He also determined whether any other aspect of the presentation, such as gesture or intonation, might have subversive overtones. Infractions of the rules might result in fines, and a repeat offender could even have his license to perform permanently revoked.

The documentation generated by the police censors is a boon to historians interested in the politics of the stage, but performers subjected to it naturally did not find it so congenial. Cabarets in particular might face difficulties, insofar as they sought to challenge the very values that the police were instituted to uphold. The German Criminal Code provided for prosecution in three areas where cabarets were tempted to tread: obscenity, blasphemy, and lese majesty. These laws covered sexuality, religion, and politics—precisely those areas where renunciation was greatest. Consequently, the censors and the cabaretists struggled to determine how daring one could be in all of those categories. The battle was not, however, straightforward. The police had the legal right to ban all subversive material, and they could have been heavy-handed in withdrawing licences. We shall see that they actually did deny permission to controversial works, and even shut down recalcitrant stages. In general, though, the Berlin police provided surprising leeway, for several reasons. It is very probable that they realized that satire had a safety valve function and could diffuse discontent to a certain extent. Over time they certainly became aware that censorship provided inadvertent advertisement to playwrights or theaters by creating a succès de scandale. The actions of the censor were, after all, reported and debated in the daily press, and the banning of one book or play might increase sales of other works by the same author. Writers such as Hermann Sudermann and Hermann Bahr gleefully acknowledged that fact and used it to their profit. Cabarets could profit from notoriety as well.[33]

Most fundamentally, the police were told by their superiors to respect Berlin's reputation as a *Weltstadt*, a city with aspirations to cosmopolitan allure. One could hardly attract tourists or impress foreigners with a repressive cultural regime. Although the authorities often disliked what cabarets had to say, they were forced to concede that their presence was one more sign that Berlin was an important center of entertainment and artistic innovation. Above all, cabaret was a perfect expression of the city's nature. An urban desire for fragmented forms of diversion, a demand for sensuous modes of entertainment, and a local tradition of biting wit combined to give it form. Although it was to face numerous commercial and political obstacles, once born, Berlin cabaret could not be contained.

# Between Elitism and Entertainment: Wolzogen's Motley Theater

The first German cabaret was founded in Berlin by Ernst von Wolzogen in January 1901. His Motley Theater (Buntes Theater), also known as the Überbrettl, served as a testing ground that revealed many of the problems faced by subsequent cabarets. Critics praised the artistically innovative numbers on opening night, but the audience applauded the more entertaining and risqué songs. Wolzogen cast his lot with the paying public and eliminated experimental works from his stage. Whereas this angered the critics, Wolzogen soon found himself battling competitors as well, since the Motley Theater's initial commercial success inspired other entrepreneurs to found cabarets. Wolzogen attempted to revive his artistic prestige as well as his finances by moving into a specially commissioned theater in November 1901. August Endell's structure was a splendid example of Jugendstil design, but it could not halt the deterioration of Wolzogen's fortunes. The "Überbrettl-Baron" was forced to surrender his Motley Theater in May 1902. Like so many of its successors, this first cabaret proved to be a dynamic but short-lived venture, whose fortune was shaped by a continual negotiation among performers, the public, critics, and competitors.

## The Premiere of the Motley Theater

Ernst Ludwig Freiherr von Wolzogen (1855–1934; fig. 4) was the progeny of an old noble family that had lost its wealth in the course of the seventeenth and eighteenth centuries. By the nineteenth century the Wolzogens began to have familial and professional connections to artistic circles. Ernst von Wolzogen's grandfather had married into the family of Friedrich Schiller. His father, a bureaucrat who became director of the Schwerin court theater in 1867, married a daughter of Friedrich Schinkel, whose buildings had embellished the Prussian capital. Their son, Hans von Wolzogen, became a stalwart of the Wagner circle in Bayreuth. Ernst was the offspring of his father's second marriage, to a wealthy Englishwoman. During the 1890s he lived in Munich as a free-lance writer and became

4. Ernst von Wolzogen in 1902.

known for fashionable novels and plays; he also composed the libretto to
Richard Strauss's *Feuersnot*. Unable to achieve his main goal, the directorship of a court theater, he began to think seriously about founding a
"literary vaudeville," an idea that he had derived from Bierbaum's *Stilpe*.[1]
  On June 9, 1900, Wolzogen reported to the Berlin police his intention

of founding an "artistic variety show." The enterprise, scheduled to open in October, would be financed by a limited liability corporation "consisting of some well-known Berlin aristocrats and financiers." Wolzogen asked the police whether a theater or a vaudeville license would be appropriate for his project. Because he planned "presentations of a dramatic nature, such as pantomimes, marionette plays, dialogues, and so forth, but no actual theater plays," a theater license might seem out of place. However, it would not be a vaudeville hall either: "it will distance itself just as much from the normal conception of a variety show or Tingeltangel, since on the one hand acrobats are out of the question, and on the other hand all presentations will meet high artistic expectations in form and content."[2] Such passages underscored the generic ambiguities that would characterize future cabarets as well.

The letter also betrayed Wolzogen's elitism, a tone of embarrassment at being involved in such an enterprise. He contended that performances would be tailored to "the taste of a small elite audience. I have agreed to direct this artistic vaudeville only on the condition that its refined artistic character be maintained." In accordance with the "exclusive and intimate character of the enterprise," it would open "in a relatively small hall (at most four hundred people)" and would be "attached to a first-class restaurant." The snobbery evident in this passage suffused Wolzogen's published works, which are full of statements castigating the masses and praising refinement, nobility, and other supposedly Nietzschean ideals.[3]

Wolzogen was able to stress the refined and exclusive nature of his project since he believed that he enjoyed strong financial backing. By the beginning of August, however, his major investor had pulled out of the enterprise and the limited liability corporation dissolved. Wolzogen took over financial responsibility for the venture. The fact that he had to scrape together contributions not only delayed the opening until January 1901 but also forced him to adopt a somewhat more populist tone. After all, the project would now have to be a commercial success, or else he would face personal bankruptcy. Wolzogen proceeded to promote his project through articles and interviews, and throughout the fall and winter of 1900 he kept the newspapers buzzing with talk of his upcoming cabaret. In one of these articles he contended that even though "the genuine artist has been at all times an aristocrat of Nietzschean persuasion, a hater of the *profanum vulgus*, a member of the master caste [*Herrenmensch*]," modern times inexorably tended toward breaking down class barriers. Even "aristocratic England" had given birth to the applied arts movement, which brought aesthetic values into daily life. Wolzogen introduced an uncharacteristically democratic note into his discourse by observing: "I find it superfluous to start wailing about leveling and degradation. Aside from the fact that one actually cannot do anything to stop this powerful trend of the times, it really is after all more just and more humane to allow everyone to have a little, instead of the few having everything and the majority nothing." Wolzogen now stated that he too would follow this trend by "seeking out the people in their places of entertainment." He quickly noted that by this he did not mean the people *(Volk)* in the form of the rabble *(Pöbel),* but rather "the people in the form of those hundreds of thousands who possess spiritual desires and who are open to an ennoblement *[Veredelung]* of their taste."[4]

The "ennoblement" of vaudeville became one of Wolzogen's key slogans. The idea was implicit in the neologism that he coined in the fall of 1900: "Überbrettl." Not only did it have overtones of Bierbaum's Nietzschean conception of cabaret ("we will give birth to the *Übermensch* on the *Brettl*"), but it also implied that the popular stage would be raised to something over and above its current standard. In an interview published in October 1900, Wolzogen noted that vaudeville had become more popular than theater, at least for broad sectors of the public. He explained this, as we have seen, by reference to the "nervous" age that sought "aphoristic, terse, and catchy tones." He conceded that people desiring "bodily beauty, power, and skill" could readily turn to the acrobatic numbers in vaudeville shows. Yet if they went there looking for spiritual satisfaction, they would be "horrified" by the "repertory of the chanteuses and the humorists, the pantomime of the eccentric clowns, and the musical offerings." These were the genres that had to be "ennobled," and Wolzogen called upon "genuine artists, poets, composers, actors, and singers" to do for vaudeville what painters and sculptors had done for the applied arts. He envisioned an "artistic variety show," sans acrobatics, where smaller and more intimate genres of the performing arts would find a worthy home.[5]

On the basis of this proposal, Wolzogen persuaded various people to loan him sums of 500 and 1000 marks, payable at 10 percent interest at an unspecified future date. By January 1901 he had collected 10,000 marks. This sum did not permit him to realize his goal of renting a theater at the fashionable corner of Friedrichstrasse and Unter den Linden, a future venue of Max Reinhardt's Sound and Smoke. Instead he leased the somewhat seedy premises of the near-bankrupt Secessionbühne on the Alexanderplatz, at some distance from the entertainment hub of the capital.

The opening of Wolzogen's theater on January 18 was a smashing success. The enterprise was called officially the Buntes Theater. *Bunt* is an adjective that can mean "motley," "colorful," or "full of variety." The first evening of the cabaret, which lasted over three hours, did indeed provide a medley of moods and genres. The very date of the premiere had an ironic touch: it was the two hundredth anniversary of the elevation of the Hohenzollern dynasty to kingship, and the thirtieth anniversary of the proclamation of the Second Reich at Versailles. At the royal opera house that evening, the Imperial family and an audience consisting of "an ocean of uniforms interspersed with a few black tailcoats" attended the premiere of *The Flight of the Eagle (Der Adlerflug)*. This dramatic apotheosis of the Hohenzollern dynasty had been written by Josef Lauff, a retired artillery major who served as unofficial court playwright. Several blocks away, at the Motley Theater, Wolzogen introduced the evening by referring to the historic date and asking the Kaiser to respect the medieval rights of the court jester to speak the truth.[6]

Wolzogen's rather sheepish introduction set the political tone for his cabaret. In October 1900 he had said that his venture would have "political" verses, but these "would have to stand strictly above the parties and adopt a superior tone." A few weeks later, anticipating that censorship would create problems for his enterprise, Wolzogen contended that too much red-penciling would be counterproductive. Indeed, he argued that public satire could be a safety valve for suppressed discontent. Suppression of laughter would cause dissent to fester, while a good side-splitting laugh would vent accumulated frustrations: "the paw with splayed claws that is laughingly slapped on the knee is much less harmful than the fist clenched in the pocket." The argument that satire served to diffuse rather than exacerbate tension would be repeated in the Weimar era. Whereas later satirists deplored the inability of their art to effect significant change, Wolzogen used the stabilizing potential of wit to advocate its free expression. He reiterated these themes in a poem that he published on January 27, the Kaiser's birthday, in which he again begged the monarch not to be angry at those free-speaking court jesters who neither "clench their fists in their pockets" nor blindly shout out their loyalty.[7]

Wolzogen's simultaneous pandering to the Kaiser and his call for free speech put severe limits on the politicization of his cabaret. Naturally the censors also played a role, insofar as they deleted several works from the premiere. Nevertheless, the numbers in question—a poem by Hugo Salus on the erotic escapades of monks, as well as verses by Otto Julius Bierbaum and Alfred Kerr—were excised not for any political reasons, but on account of alleged obscenity. The only work performed at the premiere that even bordered on the political was "Assigned to the Poetry Detachment" (Zur Dichtkunst abkommandirt). The verses recounted the life of an officer named Josef who, upon retirement, took up poetry and proceeded to militarize the muse; he cared little for popular acclaim, as long as the Kaiser liked his works. The poem was, of course, a parody of the career of Josef Lauff, whose Hohenzollern extravaganza was being premiered at the opera house that same evening. This work proved to be one of the most popular pieces that evening. Much of its effectiveness was due to the witty text by the outstanding Bavarian satirist Ludwig Thoma. Some reviewers noted, however, that his verses were hardly as caustic as the political lyrics in the Berlin farces of the 1840s.[8]

Equally important was the music written by the pianist and in-house composer of the Motley Theater, Oscar Straus (1870–1954). A native of Vienna, Straus ("with one 's'," as many early reviewers noted; he was no relative of the famous Viennese waltz dynasty) eventually achieved world fame in 1907 with his operetta, *A Waltz Dream,* followed a year later by *The Chocolate Soldier.* The first step on that path to success came on the opening night of the Motley Theater, when the public and the critics applauded not only his music to Thoma's satirical verses but also the undisputed hit of the evening, Bierbaum's "The Merry Husband" (Der lustige Ehemann). A couple in the dress of the Biedermeier era (Robert Koppel and Bozena Bradsky) sang and danced to words describing their marital bliss (fig. 5). The song began with childish neologisms ("Ringel-ringelrosenkranz," "Klingklanggloribusch"), and described how the husband danced "like a peacock" around a rosebush with his wife. The third stanza had a rather explicitly asocial and escapist message:

> The world is someplace far away,
> Who cares what happens there!
> It hardly is of interest,
> Indeed, if it did not exist,
> There'd still be us somewhere.

> Die Welt, die ist da draussen wo,
> Mag auf dem Kopf sie stehn!
> Sie intressiert uns gar nicht sehr,
> Und wenn sie nicht vorhanden wär'
> Würd's auch noch weiter geh'n.

The words and the dance both depicted a couple quite literally turned in around itself and oblivious to the outside world. Moreover, the singers were distanced historically from the audience by dressing in quaint costumes from the Biedermeier era (1820s–1840s). Far from being an expression of modern times, the number represented a nostalgic looking-back to a supposedly idyllic, cozy, premetropolitan age. It did so in a distinctly antipolitical manner. After all, the Biedermeier years were the *Vormärz* as well, an age of mounting social and political discontent that culminated in the revolution of March 1848. *Vormärz* sentiment had been expressed in the Berlin farces of the 1840s, whose tone was missed by some reviewers

5. A hit is born: Bozena Bradsky and Robert Koppel perform "The Merry Husband."

of the Motley Theater. Preferring Biedermeier to *Vormärz,* Wolzogen presented a historically distanced and *gemütlich* number, whose quaintness was reinforced by the rather antiquated polka rhythms and trills in the accompaniment. Two reviewers used the adjective "allerliebst" (most sweet, most lovely) to describe the effect. It was purely saccharine entertainment.[9]

The first rendition of "The Merry Husband" elicited sustained applause and cries of "da capo!" One reviewer noted that "verse, melody, and dance created such a charming and enchanting harmony, that cheerfulness spread like an electric current throughout the whole house."[10] The work had to be repeated, and it went on to become the season's instantaneous hit (the word "Schlager" was in use already back then). Here finally were the "applied lyrics" that Bierbaum had called for; indeed, the poem had been published at the beginning of his anthology, *Deutsche Chansons.* By adding quaint yet cheerful music, costuming, and dance to what was at best an insipid poem, the Motley Theater had devised a number that could be enjoyed in the theater and sung at home, as Bierbaum had prescribed. Not surprisingly, once the work became famous, advertisements for the sheet music noted that it could also be performed effectively at parties and especially at weddings.

Several other numbers were sung and recited on opening night, more or less erotic works that were partly sentimental, partly risqué. Several reviewers noted that they could have been sung just as easily at the Wintergarten, or even at an average Tingeltangel. As at those institutions, the songs and poems at the Motley Theater were performed by good-looking young women. Olga Destrée and Olga Wohlbrück, who would remain stalwarts of the venture, were described by reviewers as "risqué" *(pikant).* Wolzogen wrote the lyrics for two songs that diverged from this saucy/sentimental model, but they only underscored the ambiguities of the Motley Theater. "Madame Adèle" satirized German vaudeville artists who pretended to be French. The deliberately cliché-ridden text described how a young seamstress had an affair with a poor poet, dumped him for a richer paramour, and ended up as a vaudeville singer and "grande cocotte." The novelty and humor of the work resided in the constant switching between a colloquial Bavarian dialect and some elementary French. Many reviewers noted that this song (performed by Bozena Bradsky) was very popular with the audience. They failed to point out that there was unintended irony in the fact that, even though this work made fun of vaudeville singers, many of Wolzogen's other offerings were little better. "The Errand Girl" (Das Laufmädel) was even more problematic. This song described how an errand girl's constant running up and down staircases and through bad weather made her increasingly ill; while she dreamt about finding a rich suitor, in reality early death was all that awaited her. What might have been a socially critical number was at best, to use the words of a reviewer, "tragic-sentimental." The critical edge was blunted by the text itself—rather Bierbaumesque neologisms with childish onomatopoeia ("Platsche-pitsch-Spagatelregen," "Stöckelstiefel klippeklapp")—and especially by the fact that Olga Destrée sang the piece in "vaudeville dress" *(Variétékostüm)*, a combination of visual flamboyance and décolleté.[11]

Most of the songs were concentrated in the first third of the evening. The second and third segments, following intermissions, saw the presentation of larger works which testified to the diversity of the Motley Theater. The audience witnessed the world premiere of "Episode," a segment from Arthur Schnitzler's *Anatol* cycle about a self-satisfied and self-deluding Viennese bon vivant. It was followed by Christian Morgenstern's "Il pranzo—Das Mittagsmahl," a parody of the works of Gabriele d'Annunzio. The show also included "König Ragnar Lodbrok," Detlev von Liliencron's absurdist ballad about a mythical down-and-out monarch, which was set to music by Wolzogen and performed as a shadow play. The final work was a pantomime in which Pierrot committed suicide after failing to steal the heart of Columbine from another man.

This eclectic selection indicated that Wolzogen was well aware of cabaret's potential ties to other innovative theatrical forms. At least three major trends were reflected in these diverse works. First, they bore witness to the increasing prevalence of small artistic forms *(Kleinkunst)*. The profusion of one-act plays at the turn of the century was one index of the putative "crisis of drama" that also acted as midwife to the cabaret movement, which sought to provide a stage for succinct and fragmented forms of thespian art. Second, two of the numbers reflected a novel theatrical sensibility, one that favored gestural and visual expression over dialogue. Whereas shadow plays eliminated the actor, pantomime obviated the spoken word. Oscar Geller, the creator of the Pierrot number, argued that pantomime was a more natural, instinctive, and atavistic language than any verbal medium.[12] A third sign of new trends was the employment of irony and satire, which questioned the mores and fashions of the fin de siècle. Schnitzler's *Anatol* scenes depicted the self-delusions of the narcissistic bon vivant, and Morgenstern parodied the literary equivalent of such fulsomeness.

Wolzogen's presentation of these works testified to the artistic pretensions of his theater. The audience, however, was less enamored of them than it had been of the songs performed at the beginning of the evening. Liliencron's ballad and the accompanying shadow figures elicited hearty laughter, and the pantomime was well received. The scene from *Anatol*, however, appears to have earned only polite applause. The reviewers noted that it would have been better acted at most conventional theaters, and that it was not humorous enough to please the cabaret public. The critics gave Morgenstern's parody high marks, but almost all of them noted that few members of the audience were familiar with the works of d'Annunzio, and some had never even heard of him.[13] Wolzogen too must have noted that his public was disinterested in innovative numbers, for he kept them out of subsequent shows. It was up to Max Reinhardt's Sound and Smoke cabaret, which premiered five days later, to cater to a select public of true theatrical cognoscenti.

## Critics and Competitors

All in all, the premiere of the Motley Theater was a great success. That was certainly true from the box-office perspective: the theater was sold out for several weeks. Since tickets for the 650 seats were rather expensive, Wolzogen was able to repay his 10,000-mark loan after just ten days, and he reaped the profits thereafter. The critical response was also very positive, albeit somewhat more mixed. All reviewers praised Wolzogen for his versatility. In particular, he proved to be a succesful conferencier—cabaret's equivalent of a master of ceremonies, who introduces numbers and, through his extemporizing, makes the spectators feel that they are being addressed directly and personally. Wolzogen also showed talent as a poet, composer of music, and recitor of others' works. Many observers, though impressed with what they had witnessed, still expressed some disappoint-ment at his failure to attain the level of Parisian cabaret. One reviewer would have preferred "more levity, impudence, self-irony, in short: more saucy humor." Another critic, though generally very pleased, said that it was almost a "family-style Tingeltangel," more variety show than true Überbrettl: "it lacked the grotesque hyperbole, the powerful stamp that had been expressed in the 'Über'-prefix." At best, another critic noted, it was "entertaining and *gemütlich*": "The performers don't make any great demands on the imagination and mental concentration of the audience, and the audience does not demand grand or elevated art, so both are satisfied." This was clearly a type of diversion appropriate to a public which, in Bierbaum's words, "simply wants to be entertained."[14]

The overall atmosphere of the Motley Theater was indeed very different from that of the Parisian cabarets. The latter were, in essence, taverns where the audience could smoke and drink, walk in and out at leisure. Moreover, there was a directness and an intimacy between performer and public. In contrast, Wolzogen's venture was still very much a theater, where the audience sat in rows facing the stage. Consequently, according to one reviewer, the public had to buy tickets in advance, appear punctually, and listen with silent attention; the spontaneity, the to-and-fro of Parisian cabarets was absent. Wolzogen's opposition to such an atmosphere reflected his elitism. He noted in his autobiography that he rejected the Parisian model because "everything in me balked at the idea of playing the bartender and of putting myself on a *frère-et-cochon* footing with my honored guests . . . Such casualness went too much against my taste, and my aristocratic conscience had compelled me since childhood to maintain my distance from the masses. My Parisian experiences and my own sensitivity led me to fashion my cabaret in the following manner: no beer and wine service, no dense smoke, but rather a regular theater. Footlights and a proper orchestra pit between me and the public."[15] Wolzogen preferred to pretend that he was hosting entertainment in a private salon, and the stage was set accordingly: it had the appearance of a room furnished with a concert piano, sofas, and armchairs. As master of ceremonies, Wolzogen introduced the various entertainers, and he took a seat onstage during their performances.

Censorship—which was more severe in Prussia than in France—also played a role in preventing the Motley Theater from displaying the political or erotic audacity of the Parisian cabarets. Not only the critics but also the Berlin censors contended that it was not quite the venture that they had been led to believe it would be. A police report of February 9 noted that, even though Wolzogen had claimed in advance that his venture would "raise vaudeville to a higher artistic level," in practice "this hope must be replaced by the fear that the Motley Theater would perform and depict the most daring things if a watchful eye were not kept over it." The resulting vigilance impeded, but did not hamstring, the venture. Although all critics deplored the existence of censorship, one of them noted: "in general, the censor has given fair consideration to the freedom and the atmosphere of such a cabaret, and has in the end permitted some daring verses and some impudent punch lines." Another observer believed that Wolzogen would be able to speak even more freely if only he had the courage to challenge the censors: "Everyone points to the censor as if to a bogy. But has anyone seriously taken up a fight with censorship? . . . The idol of censorship is not set in bronze, it is only a plaster cast. In the last decade so much of this plaster has been chipped away that little stands in the way of more extensive crumbling." Recent scholarship suggests that intrepid theater directors could indeed get away with quite a bit in Prussia at that time.[16] Wolzogen was not, however, the man to lead the battle against the censor. His elitism, his desire to stand above all parties, and his pandering to the Kaiser on opening night hardly characterized him as a person who desired to challenge the powers that be.

By March 9 Wolzogen's cabaret could look back to fifty sold-out performances. One reviewer summed up: "The Motley Theater is the greatest success of the winter." Wolzogen had built upon the strengths of the premiere. Oscar Straus wrote music for a clone of the "Merry Husband," namely "The Hazelnut" (Die Haselnuss), which was performed by the same pair of singers in Biedermeier outfit. Invariably the audience would then demand that they sing the "Merry Husband" as well. Another new hit was "Here Comes the Music" (Die Musik kommt), Liliencron's poem about a passing military band, likewise set to Straus's music. As this repertory grew, criticism mounted. Already on opening night one reviewer noted that "the music changes everything, and makes even the trivial interesting." As the weeks passed, more critics noted that "such insipid verses as Bierbaum's 'Merry Husband'" would be nothing without the accompanying music. Conversely, other reviewers asserted that the music actually detracted from the virtues of Liliencron's "Here Comes the Music," which used the power of melodic words to evoke the approach, passing, and fading away of a band. While Straus's music might elevate some of Bierbaum's verse, it could obscure the virtues of Liliencron's sound-poetry.[17]

Some critics contended that, far from bringing true poetry to a wider audience, the Motley Theater systematically selected bad works, even from the repertory of otherwise good writers. One observed that the public received a false impression of poets like Richard Dehmel and Liliencron, since it heard only those verses that could be set to "the banal polka and waltz rhythms" of Oscar Straus—"a selection that takes into account melodic trivialities, countless cocotte-biographies with cocotte-aspirations, affairs with sweet young things and sentimentalities." This critic noted that the venture could not be considered an "ennoblement" of vaudeville, since the songs were as sensuous and suggestive, and the women's shoulders as bare as in any variety show. Another observer was appalled by the "Beggar Boy Song" (Bettelbubenlied), which began with a beggar boy's plaintive cry that no one gave him anything, but ended with his looking forward to the fact that a beggar girl "will give me something tonight in the hay." The presentation of this song was even more tasteless: "A woman appears in a state of undress typical of variety shows, decked out with pearls and tinsel and bracelets, and she sings—in such an outfit!—a beggar boy song that is supposed to awake in us sympathy for the dispossessed members of society."[18]

Many critics accused Wolzogen of pandering to an audience that did indeed desire only entertainment. The police report of February 9 noted that the well-educated and culture-hungry clientele which Wolzogen had predicted for his enterprise had failed to materialize: "Without a doubt the public that appears at these shows differs in part from that which usually goes to theaters; one does not see members of the upper educated classes and literary circles attending the performances in great numbers." To be sure, Wolzogen, Bierbaum, and others had stated in advance that they hoped to attract precisely those people who had abandoned theaters in favor of variety shows. But instead of raising this public to a higher plateau of taste, as Wolzogen had proclaimed, he rapidly sank down to its level. One reviewer of the fiftieth performance noted: "The Motley Theater has turned into a family-style vaudeville hall, or at least it is well on the way to becoming one. All that is pleasing, all that lulls one directly to sleep, such as 'The Merry Husband,' or 'Here Comes the Music,' or the new song of the 'Hazelnut' . . . bears without exception the stamp of the good bourgeois."[19]

Some reviewers were caustic in their descriptions of the audience to which Wolzogen catered. In *Die Gesellschaft,* which a decade earlier had been the major journal of the naturalist movement, one critic claimed that the Motley Theater was a stage not against, but rather for philistines. Another writer in that journal said that it appealed to the taste of the "easily satisfied compact majority." Other reviewers noted that Wolzogen, for all his aristocratic pretensions, was no better than the lower-middle-class elements whom he entertained. His pseudo-Biedermeier stage outfit— a brown jacket with gold buttons, gray pants, and shoes with buckles and white spats—"revealingly reminded one of those friendly men who open the doors for you at department stores." This reference to salesmanship and the consumer sphere was not entirely off the mark, inasmuch as Wolzogen, Olga Wohlbrück, and other stalwarts of the Motley Theater would soon allow their names to be used in magazine advertisements for "Javol," a shampoo and hair tonic. One critic contended that by becoming thus a "cuckold of a captain of industry," Wolzogen had prostituted his venture and forfeited his artistic credit.[20]

The harshest criticism was leveled by Maximilian Harden, the self-styled "praeceptor Germaniae" and incisive observer of Wilhelmine politics. In an article provocatively entitled "Tingeltangel," he wrote: "The nobility descends from its ancient castles. In Silesia the wiliest businessman can become a prince, and in Berlin the son of an old aristocratic family every evening dons light-gray pants and a brown coat with gold buttons, applies makeup to his cheeks and eyelashes, and for two hours tells jokes to the assembled host of plebeians in exchange for money. And for all that there are still people who whimper that democracy has not yet prevailed in the north of Germany." According to Harden, the middle classes flocked to the Motley Theater because they enjoyed being attended to by a nobleman: "the petty and especially the grand bourgeoisie, the traveling salesmen and the assessors, the butter vendors and the chamber-of-commerce members who daily fill the hall up to the highest corner, all are flattered that the baron up there exerts himself so much for them."[21] For Harden, Wolzogen's enterprise was but one more example of the socially pretentious bourgeoisie, the degenerate nobility, and the general bad taste that characterized the Wilhelmine era.

The Social Democratic press was also harshly critical of the Motley Theater. For *Vorwärts,* the major socialist newspaper in Berlin, Wolzogen's venture exemplified the German intelligentsia's inability to take a truly radical stand. Expressing mock surprise at seeing two officers in the audience, the reviewer noted: "For me they symbolized the fate of those enraged bourgeois literati, who promptly transform themselves from revolutionary anarchists and nihilists into authors for girls' boarding schools, officers' clubs, and veterans' associations as soon as money starts tinkling in the cashbox." Anticipating an argument that would be made by Kurt Tucholsky and others during the Weimar era, the reviewer contended that self-censorship for the paying public was even more severe than externally imposed police censorship: "Everything of a political or social nature is strictly taboo. Whatever has been let through by the neighboring police headquarters is suppressed by financial success." A writer for *Die neue Zeit,* the theoretical journal of the Social Democrats, likewise speculated that the censors probably did not have to waste too much red ink to ward off "poetic assassination attempts against the state, order, authority, and property." Even in nonsocialist journals like *Das Magasin für Literatur* one could read: "the audience is a much more severe censor than the censorship bureau itself. One can file an appeal against the opinion of the censor, but not against that of the audience." This was due to the fact that the bourgeoisie was "very sensitive" about its "political and social interests."[22] In fact, the archives of the Berlin police indicate that the censors' main concern was the tendency of the Motley Theater to perform erotically suggestive, not politically sensitive material.

Not surprisingly, very few works that could be construed as political or socially critical were performed at the Motley Theater in the spring of 1901. The only scandalous piece of that nature was "The Marshal's Baton" (Der Marschallstab), which alluded to the vanity of Field Marshal Alfred Graf von Waldersee, commander of Germany's China expedition. The song, which was illustrated by shadow figures, described how Waldersee held his marshal's baton "firmly" in his hand everywhere he went—including, the last stanza related, in the lavatory.[23] The song had obvious political dimensions, not only because of the butt of its satire but also because the refrain was set to the tune of the "Watch on the Rhine." Still, whatever humor there was in the punch line resided less in the political overtones of the music than in the genital double entendre of the final image.

Cabaret always has had a tendency to combine the political with the erotic, in accordance with its desire to shock, or to amuse, or to make someone or something look ridiculous. A generation later, some of the best songs of the Weimar era would begin with sexual imagery and end with a political message. Having lured the public's attention with erotic bait, the Weimar chanson would lead its listeners on an unexpected political detour. At Wolzogen's venture, however, songs took the opposite path: verses with a potential social or political statement terminated with sexual imagery, so that their critical message was dissipated. That was true of the "Beggar Boy Song" as well as "The Marshal's Baton." The Waldersee parody was a big hit with audiences, even though some listeners were scandalized. Indeed, it is rather surprising that the censors allowed the song to be performed, and it testifies to their relative leniency.

Despite mounting opposition by the critics, the financial success of the Motley Theater inspired a host of imitators. By the summer of 1901 the Berlin police reported that forty-two requests to open cabarets had been submitted. Wolzogen himself sought to maximize his profits and to publicize his venture by taking part of the troupe on tour. From the beginning of April until the middle of July, the traveling cast of the Motley Theater, which included most of the star performers, appeared in Leipzig, Hamburg, Vienna, Prague, Breslau, Dresden, Frankfurt am Main, Karlsruhe, and Baden Baden. A rump cast under the direction of Hanns Heinz Ewers remained in Berlin. Most observers noted that the quality of the remaining performers was sorely deficient. Heinrich Hart, a respected naturalist writer, reported that the replacement team performed the "The Merry Husband" in precisely the same manner as its predecessors: "Almost automatically precise. And I do not understand why they have not yet recruited machines to perform the 'Husband' and 'Here Comes the Music.' These electronic creations are basically designed for a mechanical rendition. They will be able to achieve their greatest effect once they are powered by electricity."[24]

Despite the poor critical response, Ewers evidently derived gratification (or profit) from having a troupe under his direction. When Wolzogen returned to Berlin, Ewers took his own players on tour, and continued to use the name "Motley Theater." On July 26 Wolzogen published an open letter, warning the public away from traveling shows that paraded under his name: "Without the friendly assistance of the press it is impossible for me to undertake anything against the host of pirates who are becoming more impudent every day, and who tend to damage severely the artistic credit of my enterprise." Ewers replied from Switzerland with an open letter of his own, in which he stated that Wolzogen had allowed him, "against payment," to use the logo and repertory of the Motley Theater.

He noted further that Wolzogen could hardly complain about poor quality, since he had granted the same rights, again in exchange for money, "to an ensemble playing in eastern German cities, which in no way can claim to have any artistic merit." Moreover, Wolzogen had sold the rights to the repertory without providing any additional royalties to the authors and composers of the songs. Ewers recalled further that in the fall of 1900, Wolzogen had published an essay stating that he hoped that his forthcoming cabaret would inspire a host of imitators throughout Germany. But now Wolzogen sought to stifle all competition: "The 'ideal' motives have given way to purely material ones." Having leveled this public blast, Ewers dropped the name "Motley Theater," but he continued to tour throughout eastern Europe for well over a year under different appellations.[25]

Wolzogen would soon have problems of his own, as his greed boomeranged on him. Victor Bausenwein, the proprietor of the building where the Motley Theater performed, decided to found his own cabaret. Wolzogen had to vacate the premises, and on September 1 a new venture, the Motley Stage Boards (Buntes Brettl), had its premiere there. While another venue was being renovated for the Motley Theater, Wolzogen had to take his troupe on tour again. During a stint in Hamburg a major falling-out occurred. Although the facts are hard to ascertain, it seems that while Bozena Bradsky was ill, Olga Destrée performed some of her songs. Bradsky thereupon wrote a highly insulting letter to Destrée, whose husband replied in kind to Bradsky. This resulted in a backstage fistfight between Destrée's husband and Oscar Straus, Bradsky's "protector." In the end, Bradsky, Straus, and Robert Koppel broke their contracts with Wolzogen; they were promptly hired by Bausenwein. This was a major coup for the Motley Stage Boards, which now had the two original singers and the composer of "The Merry Husband."[26]

Bausenwein had made an even bigger catch before the premiere of his Motley Stage Boards. At the end of August a press release announced that Detlev von Liliencron would be its artistic director and a regular performer. Bausenwein had sought a suitable replacement for Wolzogen, and Liliencron seemed to fit the bill; not only was he one of Germany's greatest living poets—much more respected than Wolzogen—but a baron as well. Noting that now there were two cabarets headed by barons, the Social Democratic *Münchener Post* speculated: "Perhaps we will soon witness ousted princes or ex-Reich chancellors serving as cabaret directors." Maximilian Harden's acerbic assertion that the public delighted in being entertained by noblemen seems to have become a business maxim. Wolzogen hired another baron, Karl von Levetzow, to replace Ewers. Moreover, a day after Bausenwein's employment of Liliencron was announced, the *Berliner Lokal-Anzeiger* carried the following listing in its help-wanted section: "*Impoverished count or baron,* who can write some poetry, sought for a cabaret touring company." In less than a week, fourteen counts and barons had applied for the job, which eventually was awarded to a certain Gideon von Stempel. The initial advertisement as well as the ensuing talent search caught the attention of journalists throughout Germany. One popular newspaper asked: "Will there be enough barons for all of the new cabarets, or enough cabarets for all of the literary barons?"[27]

Although the advertisement provoked ridicule, many reviewers were aghast at the fate of Liliencron (1844–1909). One of Germany's preeminent poets, he had been admired along the whole length of the political and artistic spectrum. While conservatives applauded his militaristic verses glorifying his battlefield experiences in the wars against Austria and France, naturalist and other modern writers saw him as their artistic forebear. Breaking with the official tradition of neoclassical verse, Liliencron developed freer poetic forms to evoke more exact and immediate descriptions of his impressions, be they of battles, nature, or amorous encounters. Yet Liliencron's fame and prolific output did not bring fortune in its wake, and he was perpetually in debt. Thus he could not refuse Bausenwein's offer of a thousand marks a month to lend his name to the Motley Stage Boards and to recite his verses there on occasion. Unfortunately, Liliencron's unsteady voice and uncertain demeanor were inadequate to the task, and he often was hissed by Bausenwein's public. This sent shock waves throughout the literary community. A writer for *Die Gesellschaft* stated: "A picture to weep over, this prostitution of genius." Alfred Kerr, Berlin's premier drama critic, wrote: "You dream about something like that for half the night. A gray-haired man who cannot speak has to step forward and recite two poems that nobody understands . . . and as soon as he has, with embarrassment, rattled them off and left the stage, people hiss at him." Kerr was reminded of a poem by Ferdinand von Freiligrath, in which a dispossessed African prince was forced to beat the drum at European carnivals. Liliencron himself wrote to a friend: "A whore sells only her body, but I have to sell in addition my name and my soul."[28]

By September 1901 the cabaret movement had acquired such a bad reputation that Richard Dehmel, another major poet and close friend of Liliencron, circulated an open letter objecting to the fact that some of his verses had been reprinted in Bierbaum's *Deutsche Chansons* and other cabaret anthologies: "I protest publicly against the exploitation of my spiritual property for business machinations, which use the artistic pretext of educating the public in order to cultivate a pseudo-art that corrupts taste, or at best promotes a tinsel-art that might amuse our people for a while, but never can raise them up to a serious appreciation of art."[29] This bad press persuaded Wolzogen to try to improve the quality of his performances when he inaugurated his new theater on November 28.

## New Theater, Rapid Demise

The main attraction on the opening night of Wolzogen's new venue was not any part of the performance, but the building itself. August Endell's structure came to be considered one of Germany's two major theaters designed in the Jugendstil manner, along with Richard Riemerschmid's Munich Schauspielhaus (also 1901). Endell (1871–1925) had grown up in Berlin, where his father was an architect. In 1892 he went to Munich to study philosophy and literature, but he soon fell under the spell of that city's burgeoning Jugendstil movement. Endell never received any formal training in art or architecture, but he was strongly influenced by the abstract crystalline and biomorphic designs of the innovative artist Hermann Obrist. He also was inspired by Theodor Lipps, the professor of aesthetics who developed a theory of empathy *(Einfühlung)*, which attempted to describe the psychological impact of lines, shapes, and other visual stimuli. Endell combined these two influences into an artistic practice which began by copying natural shapes, but then subjected them to a series of free variations that often resulted in abstract patterns. After assessing subjectively the aesthetic or affective impact of the various shapes that he had generated, he applied them as elements of design to objects of everyday use: carpets, wallpaper and hangings, curtains, furniture, rooms, even entire houses.[30]

Endell was a paradigmatic modernist who believed in art as artifice, and as an expression of modern life. In his extended essay *On Beauty (Um die Schönheit)*, he rejected the realist and naturalist precept that art must imitate nature: "It is not a piece of nature viewed through a temperament, it is not at all nature, but something totally different. There is no greater mistake than to believe that the careful representation of nature is art." Instead, nature was useful only insofar as it provided a repository of forms and colors that could be subjected to variations, which then could be utilized according to human needs. In his short book on *The Beauty of the Big City (Die Schönheit der grossen Stadt)*, Endell, who had returned to Berlin in 1901, argued that contemporary sensibilities were being determined by the metropolis. He asserted that "there is only one healthy foundation for all culture, and that is the passionate love for the here and now, for our time, for our country." He contended that the modern city was not only "our home," but also a landscape of sights and sounds at least as fascinating and complex as any "natural" countryside: "In spite of all the ugly buildings, in spite of the noise, in spite of every fault that one can find in it, the big city is, for him who has eyes, a miracle of beauty and poetry, a fairy tale more varied, more colorful, more multiform than any tale told by a poet, a home, a mother who extravagantly lavishes on her children new fortunes every day."[31] The bulk of the book described specific places in Berlin, which at certain times of day or night provided incomparable sounds and sights.

With such attitudes, Endell was an ideal person to design a theater for cabaret performances that also sought to cater to the desires of modern urbanites. Having caused a sensation in Munich with his Elvira photo-atelier of 1897, with an immense, wavelike ornament on its facade, Endell was commissioned by Wolzogen to renovate a vaudeville and dance hall that occupied the courtyard of an apartment block on the Köpenicker-strasse. The conditions were challenging, insofar as he had to retain the outer walls and roof, as well as a performance space that had a wide stage but a shallow auditorium. Nevertheless, Endell savored the opportunity to design a public structure in its entirety: "Every form, every detail was conceived completely anew, any imitation of earlier or foreign forms was deliberately avoided. The entire woodwork, the doors, windows, lights, gratings, the patterned textiles, embroidery, carpets, doorknobs, clothes hangers, even the upholstery tacks were produced according to specially designed drawings . . . It was the first time that I was allowed to fashion and furnish rooms down to the last detail entirely at my own discretion."[32]

Although the theater has since burned down, photographs and descriptions from the time indicate that Endell solved its artistic challenges in stunning fashion. The auditorium, which held some 800 seats (150 more than the Alexanderplatz locale), had two balconies on the back wall. Endell tried to give the broad, shallow space with a seemingly low ceiling a sense of added height by accentuating vertical elements: the sides of the auditorium were decorated with tall treelike designs, and a huge flower burst forth from the top of the stage opening (fig. 6). Vegetative and biomorphic forms pervaded not only the auditorium, but the stairwells, foyers, and dining areas as well. Such novelties of design were matched by new color schemes. In place of the traditional crimson, white, and gold of European theaters, the auditorium had bluish walls, greenish balconies, and a ceiling that evoked mother-of-pearl.

Endell's structure was praised widely. Fritz Stahl, a reviewer present at the opening, observed that "the building was the hit of the evening." He found Endell's designs appropriate for a cabaret, but he contended that "this style would be impossible for rooms in which one sees the forms continuously and at close range. They are downright stabbing and prickly." Karl Scheffler, the respected art critic, noted Endell's proximity to Impres-

6. The stage and auditorium of the Motley Theater, designed by August Endell in 1901.

sionism and said that his works demanded "mental gymnastics" from the observer: "Under the impact of Endell's decorations, your nerves twitch and itch [*zucken und jucken*]." This style was clearly intended to complement cabaret's desire to provide "terse and catchy" numbers for a "nervous" age. Stahl asserted that the building, more than any performance, realized the promises made by the word "Überbrettl": "modern to the point of sensationalism, moody to the point of bizarreness, and, despite its lunacy, tasteful to the point of being high art." On a slightly more critical note, Scheffler too contended that Endell's structure fit the bill perfectly: "Wolzogen needed an interior that provoked serious contemplation on the one hand, and fun on the other, that 'secessionist' mixture wherein revolutionary honesty, blasé self-irony, and bourgeois banality are represented in equal parts."[33]

Whereas praise was lavished on the building, reaction to the opening performance was somewhat more mixed. Wolzogen had spread the word that he would improve the quality of offerings in his new house, whose new pretensions were symbolized by the bust of Nietzsche in the main foyer. In an interview published on the eve of the opening, he noted: "the sitting around in a salon will come to an end. I must confess that the Biedermeier outfits, the blue tailcoats, and the shiny buttons were a lot of very expendable superficialities." Likewise, in an opening statement at the premiere, Wolzogen asserted that he would no longer perform "The Merry Husband," "Here Comes the Music," and other hits of the previous season. He said he would aim in a "higher direction," and that his new stage would be a "theater of surprises." The critics noted, however, that there were very few surprises, and not all of those were welcome. A performance of Ludwig Thoma's *The Medal (Die Medaille)* had been touted in advance as the high point of the evening. It was the satirist's first successful play, a one-act work concerning a provincial official who hoped to use an award ceremony as a forum for promoting himself, but whose plans were foiled when all of his guests drank themselves silly. A humorous send-up of provincial bureaucrats and Bavarian peasants, it had been very well received at the Munich's Residenztheater earlier that year. The performance at the Motley Theater was, however, "bad, terrible, beneath contempt," according to one reviewer; the actors had difficulty mastering the Bavarian dialect, and much of the dialogue was incomprehensible.[34]

The use of Thoma's play for the opening night also gave insight into Wolzogen's business practices and use of publicity. Earlier he had issued several press releases, claiming that he had hired Thoma as a literary consultant. The writer was infuriated by this false assertion; in reality, he had merely signed a contract granting Wolzogen permission to mount the Berlin premiere of *The Medal*, as well as the exclusive right to perform his satirical verses in the capital. Thoma issued his own press releases to set the record straight, and fumed about Wolzogen's "Kitschinstitut" in letters to his friends. He had no desire to "prostitute myself à la Liliencron," but he did look forward to pocketing large sums with a minimum of effort. Within a week of the opening night, with its disastrous performance of *The Medal*, Thoma wrote to a friend: "Wolzogen can lick my ass with his Tingeltangel; I'll collect my monthly salary and not worry about anything else. He has completely messed up the pecuniary success of *The Medal*, and if he keeps waffling along in this manner, he'll be bankrupt before the end of winter."[35] This prediction proved to be essentially correct, even though Wolzogen's venture had a few more months to live than Thoma anticipated.

Somewhat more successful was the recitation of Thoma's "The Protest Meeting" (Die Protestversammlung), a scene that described how a group of German citizens started out wanting to publish an angry protest at their government's failure to defend the Boers, but ended up sending a meek postcard with illegible signatures. There was, however, much unintended irony in presenting that piece at the Motley Theater, since it could have been considered a parody of Wolzogen's own pusillanimous political stance. In his interview he had repeated the assertion that his satire would not imitate that of Parisian cabarets: "The satires on our times and our society that you will hear in my theater will be, so to speak, those of a well-educated man of the world, without any fervent party stance." The new stage did indeed present satirical *Schattenbänkel* (moritats illustrated by shadow figures), yet the critic for the liberal *Berliner Tageblatt* considered these works "political, but harmless."[36]

The Schattenbänkel were retained and updated at future performances, but they left critics of all persuasions dissatisfied. In April 1902, for example, most reviewers found the verses "very weak," no more than "harmless beerhall poetry." Only the ultraconservative *Neue Preussische Zeitung* protested that the moritats took the standpoint of a "Social Democratic newspaper reader": "they showed how the Reichstag president throttled the [socialist] representative Bebel whenever he wanted to speak the truth; how the German commoner has his last piece of bread stolen by the agrarians; how only officers are still allowed to write 'poetry'; how [the Boers'] president Krüger is kicked across the border after a signal from above, and other such stale jokes." Although these themes were just as much liberal as socialist, the few extant examples of the Schattenbänkel force us to concur that the humor was very stale indeed.[37]

The dullness of the political satire pointed to a more general problem— the fact that Wolzogen's stage lacked numbers dealing with local themes. In January 1901, before the opening of his original Buntes Theater on the Alexanderplatz, Wolzogen told the press that authors from Berlin would provide the bulk of his numbers. But the following November one reviewer noted that most of the material came from Bavarian authors, such as Thoma and Hanns von Gumppenberg, who had emerged as an outstanding literary parodist at Munich's venturesome cabaret, the Eleven Executioners (Elf Scharfrichter).[38] Wolzogen's lack of home-grown Berlin talent became increasingly apparent over the ensuing months. From December 10–31 the theater was given over entirely to guest appearances by Sada Yacco's troupe of Japanese actors and Loie Fuller's serpentine dances, both of which attracted great interest for their non-Western or nontraditional sense of movement, color, and theatricality. When Wolzogen's troupe returned, much of the repertory had to be taken from other cabarets. By May the program was dominated almost entirely by works from Munich authors: there were skits by Gumppenberg and Julius Schaumberger, as well as a guest appearance by Frank Wedekind, the biting playwright who had earned great acclaim as a performer of grotesque ballads at the Eleven Executioners.

The borrowing of others' works as well as the increasing shift to skits and one-act plays testified to the general dearth of cabaret material. By April 1902 the Motley Theater was presenting four one-act plays, Sound and Smoke had shifted completely to short dramas, and the Motley Stage Boards announced its intention to do the same. There were two major reasons for this trend. First, very few qualified authors were committed to writing the types of saucy or satirical verses that were the mark of a true cabaret. The lyrics to most of the hits of 1901 had been penned before the cabaret movement was launched, and that stock was depleted rapidly in the first months of that year. Although numerous authors tried to cash in on the fad, very few of them had any competence. Some writers, such as Dehmel, were disgusted by the whole trend and wanted nothing to do with it. The most successful cabaret authors had gravitated to Munich's Eleven Executioners, but even they began to experience artistic burnout from the wearisome task of providing new material for programs that changed every six weeks. Second, there were few entertainers committed to cabaret. Writers who could recite or sing their own works were rare in Berlin; Wolzogen and Ewers were the exception. Aside from the chanteuses, most of the performers were professional actors who felt more secure in plays and dramas. This fact also influenced the shift toward skits.[39]

Wolzogen's problems were compounded by financial pressures. In order to pay for the new building, he reverted to his plan of the previous year to establish a limited liability corporation. He found the necessary investors, but retained only a minority of votes in the corporation, and subsequently blamed the other shareholders for the bad decisions that were made. Be that as it may, it is obvious that the new Motley Theater found itself in a financially untenable situation. The costs of running the cabaret were exceedingly high, averaging 1800 marks a night, which the box office proceeds could not always cover. Some of the star performers commanded exceedingly high salaries. Wolzogen also had a costly policy of signing exclusive contracts with numerous writers and composers, in order to keep them away from competitors. Such contracts were made not only with famous authors like Thoma but also with totally unknown figures like the young Arnold Schoenberg, who had set several Überbrettl-style poems to music. Despite receiving payment, many of these people made few or no contributions to the Motley Theater's repertory; for example, only one of Schoenberg's songs was performed. Another problem was the location of the new theater. The site, which was owned by one of Wolzogen's major investors, was even further removed from Berlin's entertainment center than the Alexanderplatz theater had been. The Motley Theater now found itself situated in a working-class neighborhood, but it depended upon a middle-class clientele. Over time it proved exceedingly difficult to ensure a steady flow of bourgeois spectators to what was to them a godforsaken venue.[40]

Wolzogen's disputes with his investors came to a head in January 1902, when the other shareholders voted to lure Oscar Straus and Bozena Bradsky away from Bausenwein's enterprise. The reappearance of Bradsky and Straus on January 20 was welcomed by the public and the critics, but it infuriated Wolzogen, who left for another cabaret tour from mid-February to mid-April. Given the tensions and state of disarray, it is not surprising that the quality of performances at the Motley Theater rapidly took a turn for the worse. One reviewer of the February program stated flatly that it "wasn't worth the trouble"; another claimed that it was becoming a torture to sit through repeated funerals of the cabaret movement. A third complained that Wolzogen had not only failed to keep his promise to create a "theater of surprises" with a higher literary direction, but had abandoned artistic pretensions altogether: "Wolzogen knows very well that a public with true literary sensibilities no longer comes to him, because that public has it up to here with the cabaret nonsense." Now the theater attracted only "comfort-loving and phlegmatic stragglers," who might be "very respectable bourgeois, but in the theater they want above all to be left in peace." By April the major critics had lost all respect for the enterprise. The reviewer for the *Berliner Tageblatt* wrote: "The old style of theater had the undeniable advantage for authors that only one or at most two of them could suffer a fiasco on a single evening; but the cabaret has become an institution for mass murder." The reviewer then proceeded to "count the dead on last night's field of battle."[41]

May turned out to be a disastrous month for the cabaret movement: the Motley Stage Boards folded, and Wolzogen was forced to resign the directorship of the Motley Theater. Wedekind, who was making his guest appearance then, wrote to a friend: "Poor Wolzogen. Unfortunately I arrived just in time to see him sacked from his own enterprise. The sight of this spectacle was as unedifying as it was pitiable." After the summer break the Motley Theater continued under the direction of Marcel Salzer and Martin Zickel, who produced one-act plays with a small interlude of songs and humorous verse (called the *Bunter Teil*). Even this interlude was dropped in December. In May 1903 the theater was sold to Adolf Philipp, a native of Lübeck who had founded the Germania Theater in New York City in 1893. When that stage was torn down ten years later to make way for a subway station, Philipp returned to Berlin. There he converted En-

dell's structure into the Deutsch-Amerikanisches Theater, which successfully produced farces and light comedies.[42]

Wolzogen was anything but a gracious loser. In an open letter of May
21 he blamed the press for driving him away from the Motley Theater by
"heaping insult, scorn and ridicule" upon him. He accused the critics of
holding him unjustly responsible for his bad imitators, and not showing
enough respect for his literary past and his current endeavors. Wolzogen
vowed not to have anything more to do with the movement he had
inaugurated. However, failure to find other employment kept him on the
road for the next three years, as he hosted cabaret evenings throughout
Central Europe and Scandinavia.[43]

Wolzogen gave vent to his frustration and bitterness through increasingly
open and outspoken anti-Semitism. Already in his essay on the "Ueberbrettl," published in the fall of 1900, he had noted: "Even though the
talent for personal recitation is deplorably rare in our Germanic race, there
are enough other races and mixed-breeds among us who are more talented
in this respect." This sentence appeared in the *Vossische Zeitung,* in the
original version of that essay, but was deleted from some subsequent
reprints (as in *Das literarische Echo*). Eight years later, when it was
republished in a collection of essays, Wolzogen not only reinstated that
line, but added a long epilogue that laid the blame for his failure squarely
on the shoulders of the Jews. He claimed that the idea for the Überbrettl
came from "genuine German poets" such as Bierbaum, Liliencron,
Wedekind, Thoma, and himself. However, most of his "in-house poets and
composers," as well as his most appreciative audience and supporters,
belonged to "that other race which is so far ahead of us in terms of agility
of spirit and the ability to discern future trends. But this aptitude of our
Jewish fellow-citizens, which is so valuable for the tempo of our cultural
progress, is completely surpassed by their talent for commercial exploitation." Wolzogen proceeded to argue that he had been tricked into the move
to the Köpenickerstrasse, with all of the financial problems that it entailed,
by his Jewish investors. That set the stage for the prostitution of his idea:
"I came to regard myself as a father who must live to see his cheerful,
favorite little daughter made drunk, seduced, and bartered away cheaply
by white-slave traders."[44]

This symbolic equation of his Jewish investors with procurers of sweet
Germanic girls completed Wolzogen's compendium of anti-Semitic clichés
in 1908, but in 1921 he augmented them in his autobiography. By then
he had come to regard the whole cabaret movement as a giant miscalcu-
lation, a venture that inevitably had to fall into Jewish hands: "I had found
it strange that my musicians belonged without exception to the Semitic
race. Today I know why that could not have been otherwise. The whole

idea of my Überbrettl was un-Germanic, since the Teuton, and especially the German, creates his best and purest works only in a spirit of deepest solemnity." The Jews, meanwhile, had become the "nearly exclusive managers and profiteers of German spiritual capital." Wolzogen asserted that the Jews considered the spoken and written word a powerful "tool of mass suggestion," and thus they established an almost complete "Jewish monopoly" in the realms of newspaper and book publishing, theater directing, theater agencies, criticism, literary history, art scholarship, playwriting and acting.[45] Such lines, penned in the early 1920s, would become even more prevalent a decade later, as the Nazis' power surged.

In other ways as well, the short history of the Motley Theater presaged issues that would mark the cabaret for the next two generations. Censorship certainly was a problem, but self-censorship, the desire to cater to public taste, put even greater constraints on the repertory. Many other difficulties centered on the fact that cabaret never could define itself very precisely. Ewers noted in 1904: "The press demanded art and drew thick red lines under every banality in the poor Überbrettl, while the public at large insisted on silliness and became very cross at every little scrap of art."[46] Wolzogen opted for the public at large, as would many of his successors. Yet when that happened, both press and public realized that they often could find much better entertainment at the more established vaudeville halls. It would take some years, and much trial and error, for authors, composers, and performers to develop a style more clearly suited to cabaret. Simultaneously, they had to educate the press as well as the public to be connoisseurs of the new genre. In many ways this proved to be a Sisyphean task. Although future ventures enjoyed somewhat more success, cabaret would remain a protean art that failed to find a lasting form.

# CHAPTER THREE

# From Artistic Parody to Theatrical Renewal: Reinhardt's Sound and Smoke

At its inception, cabaret occupied an ill-defined space between variety shows and dramatic theater, and it tended to evolve toward one pole or the other. Wolzogen's Motley Theater at first slid down to the level of vaudeville, then ended as a stage for undistinguished one-act plays. In contrast, Sound and Smoke (Schall und Rauch) never inclined toward variety shows, and when it turned to drama, it proved to be the seedbed of one of the most significant revolutions of theatrical practice in the twentieth century. The guiding spirit behind both the cabaret and the subsequent theatrical reform was Max Reinhardt. In January 1901 his cabaret began to give occasional performances for theater connoisseurs, making light of the various dramatic styles of the day. The following November, when he acquired his own stage and started to perform nightly, he discovered that his formula of theatrical parody was too esoteric for a general audience. For several months he held the public's attention with a series of political satires. Within a year he switched from satiric skits to one-act and full-length plays, but his productions retained the vitality and dynamism of his cabaret numbers. Sound and Smoke thus stood at the beginning of a new theatrical sensibility and practice, which revolutionized the stage by stressing exuberant play.

## Theatrical Parody for Connoisseurs

Max Reinhardt (1873–1943) grew up in Vienna, the son of a small Jewish businessman who was bankrupted by the depression of the 1870s. After acting in various suburban Viennese and provincial Austrian theaters in the early 1890s, he was hired by the municipal theater of Salzburg for the 1893–94 season. There he caught the attention of Otto Brahm, who signed him on to the Deutsches Theater in Berlin, the stronghold of naturalist drama.

During those years Otto Brahm (1856–1912) stood at the cutting edge of German theater. In 1889 this respected critic founded the Freie Bühne (Free Stage), an association for private performances of controversial dramas. Such an organization was needed both to avoid the preliminary censorship to which public performances were subjected and to provide a forum for recent plays that were considered too unprofitable by commercial theaters. Although the Freie Bühne was limited to a relatively small number of connoisseurs, the idea spawned other organizations. In 1890 Bruno Wille founded the Freie Volksbühne as a theater for the working class. Wille stressed the socially critical works of Henrik Ibsen, but his unwillingness to stage more radical plays soon led to a split. When Franz Mehring, the prominent Social Democratic theorist, took over the Freie Volksbühne in 1892, Wille founded the Neue Freie Volksbühne, which soon burgeoned into the largest such theater organization in Germany.[1]

Brahm's Freie Bühne was associated mainly with the works of Gerhart Hauptmann, whose *Before Sunrise (Vor Sonnenaufgang)* received a tumultuous reception at its premiere in 1889. Hauptmann was the first major German dramatist to write works depicting the harsh life of the lower classes in a supposedly realistic style. The graphic descriptions of poverty and disease were considered shocking at the time, and were criticized harshly by conservative critics and politicians. A typical reaction was voiced by the future chancellor, Prince Chlodwig zu Hohenlohe-Schillingsfürst. In a diary entry of December 11, 1893, he noted that he had attended Brahm's production of Hauptmann's *Hannele Goes to Heaven (Hanneles Himmelfahrt),* about a poor girl who dies of tuberculosis: "This evening at *Hannele*. A frightful concoction, Social Democratic-realistic, at the same time full of sickly, sentimental mysticism, uncanny, nerve-rattling, altogether awful. Afterward we went to Borchardt, to put ourselves back into a human state of mind with champagne and caviar." Official attitudes were summed up by Berlin's Police President, who defended a ban on a naturalist play with the argument: "We find the entire movement disagreeable" *(Die janze Richtung passt uns nicht).*[2]

Brahm took over the Deutsches Theater, a commercial theater, in 1894 and turned it into a bastion of naturalist drama. Reinhardt, soon after his arrival in the fall of that year, wrote to a friend: "Berlin is veritably a magnificent city—Vienna multiplied by more than ten. Truly metropolitan character, immense traffic, a tendency toward the grandiose throughout, and at the same time practical and upright." He soon became one of the more noted actors at the Deutsches Theater. Paradoxically, the young man made a name for himself portraying elderly characters, and by November 1900 he was famous enough to be cast in the title role at the world premiere of Hauptmann's *Michael Kramer.* Nevertheless, Reinhardt became increasingly dissatisfied with Brahm's ultrarealist style, which he considered too untheatrical: by attempting slavishly to copy human speech and gesture, naturalism denied the expressive potential of the stage. Reinhardt believed that the purpose of art was to be artistic, even artificial, to create a world different from the reality of mundane existence. He noted in 1901: "What I envision is a theater that gives joy back to humanity. Which leads them past themselves, out of the gray misery of daily existence into the bright and clear air of beauty. I feel that people are fed up with encountering their own troubles in the theater, and that they long for brighter colors and a heightened sense of life."[3]

In order to move beyond naturalism, Reinhardt occasionally acted in modernist plays outside the Deutsches Theater. For example, he took on the role of the old king in the German-language premiere of Maeterlinck's *Pelléas et Mélisande,* staged by Berlin's Academic-Literary Society (Akademisch-Literarischer Verein) in 1899. Reinhardt also desired more independence and influence. Already in 1895 he wrote to a friend about his plan to create an experimental stage for actors: "We would fill the roles with people who have been unknown up to now, yet who would fit these roles so well that exemplary performances would result from numerous rehearsals and sensitive directing . . . Then we naturally would have to choose plays that are interesting and winning. We do not want to be unhealthy by denying our egoism. In every respect the project is infused with the will to power."[4] Reinhardt's "will to power"—he had immersed himself in Nietzsche's works at the time—would create a theatrical empire within the space of a few years.

Reinhardt took his first step toward independence by founding Sound and Smoke. That cabaret evolved from a weekly social gathering at the Café Monopol, consisting mainly of younger actors of the Deutsches Theater: Reinhardt, Friedrich Kayssler, and Richard Vallentin, as well as Josef Kainz, Martin Zickel, Christian Morgenstern, and others. They called their club The Spectacles (Die Brille), a reference to the restricted vision of bourgeois philistines. People newly accepted into the circle would undergo a mock ritual, at the end of which they would be declared to be endowed with sight. Soon the group began to improvise parodies of current theatrical productions. At the end of 1900, they presented some of their skits to a wider audience at a New Year's Eve party. Since Morgenstern had come down with a severe case of tuberculosis, the other members decided to repeat the performance as a charity to raise money for his costly medical treatments. Since they had trouble finding a name for their group, they eventually settled on Schall und Rauch, based upon Goethe's assertion that a name was nothing more than "sound and smoke."

The first performance of Sound and Smoke took place at the Künstlerhaus in the Bellevuestrasse on January 23. The invited literati and theatrical luminaries were asked to contribute 10 marks toward Morgenstern's costs. Unlike the general public at Wolzogen's Motley Theater, which had opened five days earlier, the select audience of Sound and Smoke consisted of what one reviewer called "a whole parterre full of stage royalty."[5] The three main organizers of the event—Max Reinhardt, Friedrich Kayssler, and Martin Zickel—introduced the evening clad in Pierrot outfits (fig. 7). They tailored the show to their public by presenting parodies of the performing arts. There were humorous renditions of violin and piano solos, as well as a takeoff on Wagner's *Walküre*. The highlights of the evening were parodies of theater. The first of these, "L'Intérieur or The Intimate Theater" (L'Intérieur oder Das intime Theater), satirized the general unpopularity of avant-garde drama, in particular the symbolist plays of Maeterlinck. The skit depicted a theater that had become "intimate" because it failed to attract any spectators. While the director, the ticket seller, and the coat-check clerk dozed in the box office, a figure called "The Stranger" appeared and asked a porter whether he dare shock the sleepers by requesting a ticket. After much hesitation the Stranger mustered enough courage to make the request, but he could not awaken the slumberers.

This plot may well have been a form of self-parody, insofar as it might have referred to the fate of Martin Zickel's Secessionsbühne, whose recent failure had allowed Wolzogen to take it over for the Motley Theater. A further level of parody was aimed at the symbolist productions with which Reinhardt had been involved. The entire conversation took place in a mystical, mock-Maeterlinckian mode, as in the porter's opening description of the situation: "They never come here . . . That is the 'Intimate Stage!'—Nobody ever comes there . . . It is a blessing that they do not hear us.—There they sit. They wait for him who is supposed to come." Whereas that skit satirized the providers of theatrical productions, the next number parodied its consumers. "Ten Righteous Ones" (Zehn Gerechte) was a pantomime that portrayed a row of spectators in a theater audience, including a critic, a fop, an artist, an inconsiderate latecomer, and others who were variously hostile, enraptured, and phlegmatic. The actual audience in attendance evidently appreciated this parody of themselves, since a reviewer reported: "The auditorium more or less squirmed with laughter. You see yourself as if in a mirror and laugh yourself out."[6]

The hit of the evening consisted of four renditions of *Don Carlos* in different theatrical styles. The first, billed as "Old School, 1800–1890," was a takeoff on provincial troupes. Schiller's play was reduced to five three-minute acts, and the dramatis personae were cut down to Elisabeth and Philipp, supposedly played by the troupe's director and his wife, as well as Carlos and Posa. All other characters, including "the assembled grandees of Spain," were acted by a single mute supernumerary. The skit made fun of the overly pathetic acting style of the "old school," which also characterized court theaters; it was made even more ridiculous within

7. Introducing Sound and Smoke: Martin Zickel, Friedrich Kayssler, and Max Reinhardt in Pierrot costumes.

the impoverished context of a provincial stage. The next rendition, entitled "Karle: A Comedy of Thieves" (Karle: Diebskomödie), represented the "naturalist school, 1890–1900"; it parodied the dramas of Hauptmann and Arno Holz as well as the acting style of Brahm's troupe, which the founders of Sound and Smoke had come to know so well. It was set among an impoverished Silesian family that displayed typically naturalist propensities such as alcoholism, mental retardation, suicide, and incest. For example, in place of Carlos' love for his stepmother, Elisabeth, Karle lusted after his natural mother. The third version, representing the "symbolist school, September 1900–January 1901," was entitled "Carleas und Elisande" by "Ysidore Mysterlinck." It was a scene of total obfuscation, with no comprehensible plot line and a mystical dialogue much like that in "L'Intérieur." The final rendition, depicting "the Überbrettl school, January 18–31, 1901," may be more accurately described as a takeoff on vaudeville. Elisabeth was portrayed by a man singing variety-show tunes, and Carlos entered juggling oranges and said in the broken, multilingual argot of clowns: "O God, o God, ich lieben meine Mutter!"[7]

These parodies, most of which were written jointly by Reinhardt, Kayssler, and Zickel, were by no means hostile toward the butts of their humor. After all, Reinhardt would be directing Maeterlinck's works in his own theater in the not-too-distant future. They did, however, make light of a situation that Reinhardt had criticized as early as 1895: "Earlier there were good and bad actors. Today there are pathetic, naturalist, declamatory, modern, realist, idealist, pathological, extrovert and introvert actors, etc. etc. etc. Earlier there were actors who portrayed humanity [*Menschendarsteller*]. Today there are Ibsen actors, Hauptmann actors, stylized actors, and so forth. This too is a sign of our times, which has the pettily pedantic need to place everything, even art, into boxes, drawers, crates, or molds."[8] What Reinhardt opposed was not any particular style, but rather the segregation of the theatrical arts into mutually hostile camps. He advocated pluralism, rather than intolerance and exclusion. After all, he himself had felt constrained by Otto Brahm's persistent and monotonous employment of naturalism. His own productions in the near future would adopt whatever manner of performance he considered most appropriate to the given drama. By underscoring the foibles of all styles in his humorous skits, he did not intend to damn the thespian arts in toto, but to suggest that no one school had a monopoly on good taste. The competing theatrical groups, divided against each other by their doctrinaire "isms," were supposed to recognize their respective faults and to congregate in a true community that would celebrate the stage in all its diversity.

By assembling a "parterre full of stage royalty" to witness a program that made it laugh at itself, Reinhardt took the first step toward the realization of his goal. He and his colleagues were very pleased with the response. Kayssler wrote to Morgenstern after the premiere: "The really beautiful thing about the evening was the fact that all of these hard-bitten Berliners turned into children." He concluded that "there still must be opportunities for healthy laughter here after all." The great success of the first evening led to several other performances before invited guests (February 6, March 3, March 16, April 9). Kayssler reported to Morgenstern again in March: "You do not have any idea what a fertile ground for this light art Berlin is at the moment."[9]

Sound and Smoke continued to add new numbers in the style of the opening night. March 3 saw the premiere of "The Stage-Direction Committee" (Das Regiekollegium), in which a playwright attended a rehearsal of his new drama, only to find that the production was being thrown together sloppily by actors and directors who had nothing but contempt for him. The "Diarrhoesteia" (March 16) was considerably more adolescent in its humor, insofar as a series of jokes dealt with the fact that the word *Durchfall* can mean either a theatrical flop or diarrhea. This skit, dealing with the premiere of a work that ends in a fiasco, was written in mock-Greek style. It included a chorus of theater investors who witnessed their capital running down the drain, two competing choruses of spectators (the "moderates" in the parterre and the "radicals" in the gallery), and theater critics dressed as Furies who pursued the hapless playwright in the end.[10]

The Sound and Smoke evenings were so successful that Otto Brahm allowed the troupe, which consisted mainly of his own actors, to stage a public matinee at the Deutsches Theater on May 22. After one more closed performance at the Künstlerhaus (May 28), Sound and Smoke ended its spring season in Berlin. In July the troupe played several times in Vienna, in conjunction with a guest appearance of the Deutsches Theater. Meanwhile Reinhardt and Kayssler planned to found their own company to put on nightly performances. Despite Reinhardt's central role, Hans Oberländer had to function as the official manager of the enterprise. Up to that point Brahm had been happy to see his younger actors engaged in the occasional performance of theatrical parodies, but he was not amused when some of them requested to leave his troupe before their contracts ended. Many of the actors who had taken part in the earlier Sound and Smoke evenings had to forego performing in the new enterprise; even Reinhardt did not gain his freedom from Brahm until January 1903. Nevertheless, he continued to play a commanding role behind the scenes.

Sound and Smoke opened its own theater on October 9 in the Hotel Arnim, near the prestigious corner of Friedrichstrasse and Unter den Linden; coincidentally, it was the same location that Wolzogen had failed to acquire for his Motley Theater the previous fall. Reinhardt commissioned Peter Behrens to redesign a small theater there. At the time, Behrens was making a name for himself as a major contributor to the Jugendstil exhibition at the Darmstadt Artists' Colony. In conjunction with Richard Dehmel and Georg Fuchs, he was also devising a theory of symbolist stage design. The main innovation they proposed was the "relief stage," a shallow proscenium without sets and props, backed only by a solid wall or tapestries, before which actors would perform in relief. This project was not realized until Fuchs opened the Munich Artists' Theater (Münchener Künstlertheater) in 1908, but the idea was widely discussed at the time.[11]

Behrens was also no newcomer to satire. He might well have attended the guest performances of the Eleven Executioners and Wolzogen's Motley Theater at the Darmstadt exhibition in July 1901. More important, he contributed to the Darmstadt "Überdokument" at the end of August. This small exhibition, wherein the Darmstadt artists displayed parodies of their own works, was conceived as an arts-and-crafts equivalent of the cabaret movement. It was fortunate for Reinhardt that Behrens had a sense of humor, because the designer had been the butt of one of the jokes in the Don Carlos parody. The "Carleas und Elisande" segment was subtitled "Eine Gobelinesque," and the stage directions called for all the characters to stand in a row in front of a dark black curtain, which would make them stand out "like a Gobelin tapestry." That was obviously a takeoff on Behrens and Fuchs, whose essays of the previous months had used the same phrase to describe the intended effect of the relief stage.[12]

Behrens' design for the Sound and Smoke theater turned out to be a very uncharacteristic work (fig. 8). It had none of the elements of his proposed relief stage, nor did it betray any of the aspects of industrial design for which he subsequently became famous. Nevertheless, precisely because of its eccentricity, most reviewers found it very suitable as a venue for cabaret. The use of a dark red stage curtain trimmed with gold, and the framing of the proscenium with a Greek temple pediment, provided a parodistic evocation of traditional, classically inspired theater design. The audience was also surrounded by the attributes of the cabaret. "Sound" was suggested by a series of masks with grotesquely opened mouths, which were largely reproductions of some works by Arnold Böcklin; at that time the Swiss artist, regarded as a precursor of symbolist and other modern trends, was at the height of his fame. Between the masks were braziers that seemed to emit clouds of painted "smoke," whose visual effectiveness was heightened by the dimmed electric lighting. Moreover, to one side of the stage was a reproduction of Böcklin's caricature of a critic swinging an enormous pen. The reviewer of the progressive *Freisinnige Zeitung*

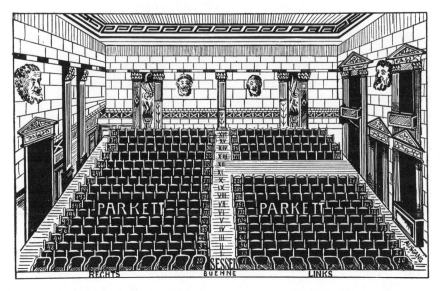

8. The interior of the Sound and Smoke theater, designed by Peter Behrens in 1901.

regarded the total effect as "a very nice parody of willful ceremoniousness," while a writer for the conservative *Kunstwart* complained that it was a "messy lump," which "strikes one directly as a mockery of the most noble ancient stylistic order."[13]

Although most critics were pleased with the theater itself, they were severely disappointed by the opening production. Part of the problem lay with the actors, who did not match the quality of the earlier performers whom Brahm now bound to their contracts. The drop in quality was so evident that a reviewer for the ultramonarchist *Neue Preussische Zeitung*— never too well informed about developments in modern culture—assumed that a totally unrelated group of actors had pirated the name of Sound and Smoke. Other critics deplored the loss of intimacy between actors and audience, as the troupe switched from occasional evenings before cognoscenti to the business of performing for a more general public night after night. Reinhardt and his colleagues now faced an audience similar to that which Wolzogen and Bausenwein entertained. Nevertheless, they continued to present the type of theatrical in-jokes that had been so successful in the spring before their invited audience. For example, one rather long skit about a would-be cabaret director included an "obscene manuscript" personified by a woman in risqué attire, a theater agent costumed as a meat fly, and the public depicted as a frazzled hermaphrodite, plastered over with advertisements and unable to form a critical opinion.[14]

Sound and Smoke's earlier "invited guests," who consisted of theatrical connoisseurs, might have enjoyed such works. But now the critics complained that this self-referential humor concerning the arts was out of place in public performances before a general audience. In January one critic had disapproved of Wolzogen's attempts to introduce literary parody at the Motley Theater: "It always appears to me to be like a cat biting its own tail. And—let's be honest!—in the life of the present, literature occupies a shabby back seat; who cares about literary shadowboxing!" Ten months later, the same accusation was being hurled at Sound and Smoke. In reference to a couple of skits parodying the poets Stefan George, Hugo von Hofmannsthal, and Arno Holz, the reviewer for *Das Kleine Journal* asked: "Do the directors of Sound and Smoke believe that this subject interests a larger public?" The *Norddeutsche Allgemeine Zeitung* echoed this remark by querying: "Who has any inclination or understanding for literary satire, apart from some of the first-nighters?" A whole chorus of critics noted that, for a public theater, such works were too narrowly focused. The *Neue Preussische Zeitung* declared: "The field of vision of most numbers hardly goes beyond the life of the stage. And we have had enough of this petty scoffing at directors, authors, agents, actors, reviewers, censors, etc." The *Berliner Morgenpost* concurred: "What transpires in poets' garrets, in the bedrooms of directors, and in the hearts of actors is well-nigh the sole subject matter of the Sound and Smoke authors. Does that comprise the whole world?" And the *Berliner Börsen Zeitung* complained: "What's insufferable in this whole story is above all the fact that these people speak only to themselves, they mutually engage in tasteless self-irony, and they are ungrateful enough to make fun of modern and contemporary authors, upon whose shoulders they stand, after all."[15]

Most reviewers believed that Sound and Smoke had made a serious mistake by retaining literary satire while giving up its intimate public. Indeed, little more than a month later, Sound and Smoke's original format was adopted by a new group, the Bad Boys (Böse Buben). Rudolf Bernauer (1880–1953)—one of the cofounders of the Bad Boys, along with Carl Meinhard—had taken part in the premiere of Sound and Smoke on January 23, but moved away from Reinhardt's circle thereafter. Like the member of Sound and Smoke, both Bernauer and Meinhard were young actors in Otto Brahm's Deutsches Theater. After the performances of Reinhardt's group became public, Bernauer and Meinhard began to stage their own evenings of theatrical parody before invited audiences of cultural luminaries and connoisseurs. The first of many occasional performances took place on November 16 in the Künstlerhaus, the first venue of Reinhardt's cabaret. The audience received programs in the form of a schoolboy's exercise book in a child's handwriting, and Bernauer and Meinhard appeared on stage dressed as pupils with paper hats. They recited a poem listing the names of all the extant cabarets and their directors ("Überbrettl, Sezession / Wolzogen und Liliencron," and so on). Next the actor Leopold Iwald appeared as the conferencier—or rather, as a parody of one, inasmuch as he adopted the role of a "spoilsport" *(Miesmacher)*, who introduced every number with disparaging words and shrugged his shoulders in disgust whenever the audience applauded. The first musical number consisted of several versions of "The Merry Husband," culminating in one performed by two actors made up to look like Franz von Lenbach and Saharet. At the time, the famous Munich painter and the infamous vaudeville dancer were rumored to be having an affair. The audience roared its approval.[16]

After these initial takeoffs on the Motley Theater's hit, the Bad Boys proceeded to theatrical satires in the manner of Sound and Smoke. These included a performance of four alternate endings for Ibsen's *Doll House.* The actual ending, where Nora slams the door on her husband, never to return, had been considered incredibly shocking when the play was first performed in the 1880s. In fact, in several early productions, the final scene was rewritten so that Nora relented and returned home at the last moment. With that in mind, Bernauer and Meinhard penned several "improved" endings in the style of contemporary playwrights. The Wedekindian version had Nora voluntarily going to an insane asylum, while the Maeterlinckian ending had her seeking out an obscure goal in the Great Beyond. In the final rendition, composed in the manner of Josef Lauff, Nora and her husband shouted their loyalty to the royal sovereign and applauded his aspirations for world power, while a bust that looked suspiciously like Wilhelm II appeared at the back of the stage. That and other parodies made the evening highly successful, and Bernauer and Meinhard staged similar performances at irregular intervals over the course of the next several years. Unlike the Sound and Smoke troupe, they never turned to a larger public. As they told the police at various times, the repertory of the Bad Boys consisted "without exception of satire on theater and journalists," and they performed exclusively for invited "artists and patrons of the arts," for "members of the theater, writers, and the press."[17]

### A Temporary Turn to Political Satire: Serenissimus

The Sound and Smoke troupe could not afford to return to an exclusive format for connoisseurs, owing to its financial investment in Behrens' theater. Condemned to face a wider public, it was forced to augment the scope of its repertory. After the premiere in the new house, the *Freisinnige Zeitung* argued that Sound and Smoke would have to address broader social concerns if it hoped to remain viable: "They remained stuck in literature and theatrical satire, that is, in a rather narrow circle. To repeat: if our cabarets are to have a future like those in France, then they have to seize upon satire of all our political and public life. Timidity here will lead to a dead end." Sound and Smoke took these strictures to heart. The new numbers performed on November 15 led the critic of the liberal *Vossische Zeitung* to note: "This time the jokes stepped out of the narrow circle of self-reflection and demonstrated—at least for the most part—that special characteristic of sharpness and biting social criticism, which one can certainly appreciate as one element in the humor of a metropolis."[18]

The major embodiment of Sound and Smoke's political satire was Serenissimus. He had first appeared on their stage during the public matinee of May 22, in conjunction with a parodistic rendition of Hauptmann's *Weavers (Die Weber)*. That work had been the battle cry of the naturalists several years earlier. The drama dealt with an uprising of starving Silesian weavers in 1844, one of the first major outbreaks of working-class discontent in the age of incipient industrialization. Although closed performances of the play were presented by the Freie Bühne and the Neue Freie Volksbühne in Berlin (February and October 1893), the censors prohibited public performances. Only after persistent appeals through the courts was the ban lifted, and the public premiere took place at the Deutsches Theater on September 25, 1894. It was both a critical success and a succès de scandale, as Reinhardt noted several weeks after the opening: "At the moment our *Weavers* are still creating a tremendous stir and the house is sold out every day. That was a sensational success. More stormy and demonstrative than I have ever witnessed in any theater. And that says a lot, given the cool, impudent, and wise-cracking nature of the Berliners." Wilhelm II did not share in the enthusiasm. Because of the performance of *The Weavers* and other naturalist works, he permanently canceled his subscription to the "Kaiser's Loge," a box to the right of the proscenium at the Deutsches Theater.[19]

Those events provided half of the background for the parody of the *Weavers* at Sound and Smoke on May 22. The other half was derived from a series of jokes about "Serenissimus und Kindermann" that appeared regularly in the pages of the satirical journal *Jugend*. Serenissimus, a fictitious potentate of a petty German principality, was benighted in every sense—politically, culturally, mentally—while Kindermann was his loyal adjutant who had to explain the world to him. These popular caricatures were brought to life at Sound and Smoke, which pretended to present a special performance of *The Weavers* for Serenissimus, carefully edited for His Highness by Kindermann (fig. 9).

At the beginning of the skit, the actor playing Serenissimus (Victor

9. Kindermann (played by Gustav Beaurepaire) explains the world to Serenissimus (Victor Arnold).

Arnold) took a seat in the very loge that the Kaiser had canceled. Kindermann (Gustav Beaurepaire) explained to him from the proscenium that he had "ground down the sharp edges of the work, eliminated the rude and repulsive aspects, and amplified and elaborated the few poetic and moral passages."[20] The curtain then opened to reveal, in place of the hovel of the starving workers in Hauptmann's play, a very cozy bourgeois household, in the center of which stood a dining table whose sparkling white tablecloth was laden with sausages, cakes, and Mosel wines. Hauptmann's old, impoverished Ansorge was transformed into the owner of a basket weaving enterprise. In private Moritz Jäger still pretended to be politically radical, but publicly he bowed and scraped to authority at every opportunity. The notorious Weaver's Song (from 1844) was sung, but only after Serenissimus was told that it dealt with conditions deep in the heart of Africa. Whereas the original play ended with soldiers firing a volley into a crowd attacking the house of the industrialist Dreissinger, the edited version terminated with arriving soldiers singing "Deutschland über Alles," while the rest of the cast toasted Dreissinger as well as Serenissimus. At numerous points throughout the performance the potentate was drawn into the stage action. Often he would interrupt the play to make a comment or ask for an explanation, at which point Kindermann would step out of the wings to provide the needed information. The actresses playing Mother Baumert and Emma, wearing their Sunday best, constantly flirted with Serenissimus from the stage. At the end he descended to the proscenium and awarded medals to the actors and pinched the cheeks of the actresses.

This skit was so successful because it operated on many levels, but primarily because it took some fairly obvious swipes at the Kaiser. Wilhelm II had, after all, opposed naturalism in general and *The Weavers* in particular. Not only had he canceled his loge at the Deutsches Theater; in 1898 he also blocked the jury of the Berlin salon from awarding Käthe Kollwitz a small gold medal for a graphic cycle inspired by Hauptmann's *Weavers.* Moreover, just as Serenissimus constantly interrupted the skit, the Kaiser could not refrain from venting his fatuous opinions on cultural matters. In fact, he would soon make some of his most notorious comments. At the end of 1901, Wilhelm inaugurated the "Avenue of Victory" (Siegesallee), lined with statues of thirty-two of his Hohenzollern ancestors. After arguing that the Greek and Roman style represented immutable artistic laws sanctioned by Nature and by God, he proclaimed: "An art that disregards the laws and limits that I have defined is no longer art." He proceeded to lambast "the so-called modern tendencies" and "the frequently misused word 'freedom.'" For him, critical artists were unpatriotic: "When art, as is often now the case, does nothing more than depict poverty as being more dreadful than it already is, then it commits a sin against the German people." Instead, art should provide inspiration for all classes, a goal it could achieve only when "it lifts up, not when it descends into the gutter."[21]

In general, Reinhardt was not a very political man of the theater; in time he came to see the stage in increasingly apolitical and counterpolitical terms. At the turn of the century, however, he and his colleagues were well aware that they were potential victims of the Kaiser's persistent attacks upon innovative art. Even though Reinhardt was highly critical of naturalist performance, he too would gain fame in 1903 by producing a classic piece of "gutter art," Maxim Gorky's *Lower Depths.* More immediately, Sound and Smoke would soon be engaged in constant skirmishes with the censor. By satirizing Wilhelm and the conservatives, the members of that cabaret were defending their own territory, the cultural sphere, from outside interference.

The issue also had larger civic implications, since many literati believed that art was the ultimate sanctuary of individual freedom. That point was made clear by Heinrich Mann in his novel *Professor Unrat* (upon which the film *The Blue Angel* was very loosely based). Appalled at the vulgar public's taste at a Tingeltangel, the self-righteous and authoritarian teacher became agitated: "But he could not force them to find beautiful, what was beautiful according to his judgment and dictate. This was perhaps the last refuge of their insubordination. Here Unrat's despotic drives struck against the outer limits of human willingness to bend . . . He could hardly stand it. He gasped for air, looked around for an escape from his powerlessness, wriggled with the desire to crack open such a skull and use his crooked fingers to straighten out its sense of beauty."[22] This biting account of an art censor's mentality underscored the need to defend personal aesthetic taste as the last bastion of liberty and individuality.

Sound and Smoke's *Weavers* proved to be a transitional work. While it included heavy doses of the type of theatrical parody that was the troupe's trademark at that time, it also revelled in political satire. Six months later, when parody of the stage was no longer sufficient entertainment for the general public, Sound and Smoke revived Serenissimus. His reappearance was the most heralded event in their new program on November 15. Two days earlier Oberländer informed the police that Serenissimus was the focal character of Sound and Smoke: "The figure of Serenissimus, who sits in the loge and comments on the performance, is now being introduced by us as a regular feature. The Serenissimus scenes actually create the frame for our program and for this reason cannot be absent." At the premiere of the new show the entry of Serenissimus was preceded by an excruciatingly long fanfare, and the audience greeted him with loud applause. He proceeded to make dim-witted comments throughout the show; for example, after two pantomimes he complained about the bad acoustics, because he "could not hear a word." He also descended to the stage to acquire first-hand contact with a fetching soubrette who sang Wolzogen's "Madame Adèle."[23]

Ironically, that same number also attracted the attention of a genuine figure of authority: the policeman in attendance that evening. He reported that although there was nothing improper in the text of the song, and that the performance at the Motley Theater had been perfectly acceptable, the rendition at Sound and Smoke betrayed an "exceedingly indecent manner" and "was very capable of giving offense." Eventually the directors of Sound and Smoke received a cautionary note from the police, who told them that the song would be prohibited if it were not performed with "greater decency." At the same time, the police reported to the Ministry of the Interior: "Although this theatrical enterprise has been in existence only six weeks, it has submitted to the censor no fewer than 500 pages of handwritten poetry, songs, and stories as well as 29 plays and various printed works. The auditing of this extensive material was made even more difficult by the fact that the directors of Sound and Smoke unfortunately have the tendency to overstep the bounds of the morally permissible."[24]

The Serenissimus scenes would soon cause other problems for the police. Toward the end of November an anonymous letter was sent to the Empress, which said: "Gibberish-Wilhelm [*Quassel-Wilhelm*] appears every evening as Serenissimus in Sound and Smoke and amuses the audience with his 'clever' speeches based on a famous model." It is not known whether the Empress actually read this letter, but the Ministry of the Interior took it as an invitation to investigate the cabaret. The police heightened their watchfulness over the performances. On December 3 they sent Oberländer a letter, warning him that "the actor playing Serenissimus has repeatedly spoken words and sentences that have not been submitted to the censor. I hereby notify you that every such transgression will be strictly punished." Within two weeks the police caught an infraction. At the end of three succesive performances, the perpetually clueless Serenissimus had spoken these unapproved lines: "Present the large gold medal for art and science to director Sound and the small gold medal to director Smoke, or vice versa." Although Glasenapp, the head of the censorship department, suggested a stiff penalty, the imposition of 30-mark fines on Oberländer as well as on Victor Arnold, the actor performing Serenissimus, was little more than a slap on the wrist.[25]

Aside from small fines, the censors did not believe that they could forbid the Serenissimus scenes outright. Since the caricatured potentate did not refer directly to any reigning monarch, the skits could not be prohibited on grounds of lese majesty. Of course the censors had the legal authority to prohibit the scenes; but had Sound and Smoke appealed to the courts, then the police would have had to argue that the Serenissimus figure was a passable likeness of the Kaiser. That dilemma had become apparent several years earlier, when the pacifist author Ludwig Quidde published a notorious article entitled "Caligula" (1894). Ostensibly a portrait of the vain, aggressive, and unpredictable Roman emperor, readers recognized it as a thinly disguised portrayal of Wilhelm II. Yet the state could not confiscate the work because it was, word for word, an account of ancient history. Prosecution for lese majesty would have constituted an admission by the judiciary that it was indeed an accurate depiction of the Kaiser as well. The same arguments applied to Serenissimus, and so the censors treated the issue gingerly. Possart, one of the ranking censors (as well as the son of Ernst von Possart, the intendant of the Munich Court Theaters), stated in reply to a query from the Ministry of the Interior: "In my opinion, there is no reason to see in [the Serenissimus scenes] a reference to contemporary or recent circumstances at a German princely court. Especially in cases like this one, it is highly awkward to proceed with a protest, let alone a prohibition, unless there is a compelling reason."[26]

There was no "compelling reason" to censor the scenes inasmuch as they were not, in the last analysis, overly critical. They certainly lacked the bite of, say, Quidde's "Caligula," or of Harden's attacks on the Imperial regime. Only extreme conservatives took offense at Serenissimus. Eduard von Mayer, writing in the monarchist *Deutsche Zeitung,* said: "Politically I find the scenes dangerous in the highest degree. The purpose of these jokes, which have been sent into the world by the Jewish-French *Simplicissimus,* is after all a malicious denigration of sovereign princes. The sovereign as an idiot! . . . One cannot object that only petty princes are implied, or that a not very gifted duke from the historical past is depicted; the principle and the effect remain the same, namely, the denigration of nature's law that rulers are necessary." However, such views were not shared even by some actual sovereigns. Possart noted in his report that "as far as I can tell, the scenes have not caused any offense. I have learned that the performances at Sound and Smoke have been attended by sovereigns of the federal states, such as the Grand Duke of Mecklenburg-Schwerin and members of princely houses, without any of them having been offended by the depiction of Serenissimus."[27]

In fact, monarchical institutions might even have benefited from the safety-valve effect of the Serenissimus scenes. The critic Paul Mahn, writing for the *Tägliche Rundschau,* contended that "there is room here for political satire in the very best manner, because it dissolves everything into a liberating laughter over a blessedly stupid person, who really cannot help himself and who otherwise does quite well personally." Although the Serenissimus scenes were no compliment to princely houses, the general good-naturedness of the character and his endearing foolishness were a much safer option, for all parties concerned, than bitter accusations of incompetence. As might be expected, the Social Democratic press accused Sound and Smoke of political timidity, even after it had reintroduced the Serenissimus scenes: "What one heard and saw was sound without meaning and smoke without fire."[28]

The Serenissimus skits were protected above all by their immense popularity. Numerous reviewers contended that those scenes alone kept Sound and Smoke financially viable through the spring of 1902, when Wolzogen's and Bausenwein's enterprises were going bankrupt. Their appeal resided not only in the comic talent of the actors, the wittiness of the comments, and the indirect political references, but also in their ability to create a cabaretic atmosphere by breaking down the barriers between actors and spectators. One reviewer noted that the scenes established that "cheerful rapport between stage and auditorium, the free and easy gaiety, the improvisation, which make up something like the soul of cabaret. It is no longer as in stiff performances—*here* the stage, *there* the spectators, and between the two, a world. A merrily invigorating bridge is created."[29] The Serenissimus scenes, like the satires on Lauff or Waldersee in the Motley

Theater, proved that Berlin audiences of the Wilhelmine era enjoyed political parody, as long as it was performed in a good-natured, nonaggressive spirit.

Another kind of number was considered more controversial, at least by a few members of the audience: the humorous depiction of Jews. The police reported that on March 20 and 21, 1902, some members of the audience engaged in shouting, whistling, and foot-stamping to interrupt the "Story of the Dead Rabbi" (Geschichte vom toten Rabbi), a series of Jewish anecdotes told by the actor Emanuel Reicher. Although the perpetrators of the disturbance could not be apprehended on the second night, at the first occurrence the theater personnel caught "seven apparently Jewish students," whose names were submitted to the police to be prosecuted for causing a public nuisance. Reicher's stories were but one of many occasions upon which Jews served as the subjects of humor. At the premiere in January 1901, the "Karle" episode of the *Don Carlos* parody contained the figure of Markwitz, who was described in this manner in the published version of the text: "He is doubtlessly a Hebrew, but does not like to admit it. In addition he has had himself baptized several times, but not to any apparent advantage. His nose has the boldly curving line of the Chosen People. It is white and huge and sweats constantly. The moustache under this nose resists being forced to look like that of the Kaiser." Despite the fact that Markwitz spoke in a "gutteral" fashion and walked with a "Jewish" gait, he considered himself "the paradigm of a beautiful Teuton." Obviously this character was a parody of a converted, German-nationalist Jew, but equally obviously, it employed some of the most offensive anti-Semitic clichés. The same can be said of the description of the "Chorus of Investors" in the "Diarrhoesteia": "They are well-fed and well-dressed men with hats and frock coats and intensively Roman noses. They bow and bend, murmur and sigh, as if before the Wailing Wall in Jerusalem."[30]

To be sure, both of these examples are drawn from works that were premiered while Sound and Smoke played before an invited audience. Although there are no extant guest lists for those early performances, in October 1902 Oberländer sent the police the names of people invited to a closed performance of Oscar Wilde's *Salome* by the Sound and Smoke troupe. An accompanying note read: "The enclosed list comprises the names of all people who are allowed in free of charge at all times, and who otherwise always accept our printed invitations."[31] An examination of that list indicates not only a high number of luminaries from the worlds of theater, art, and literature, but also a majority of Jews. Given the predominance of Jews in the Sound and Smoke troupe as well, it is likely that the references to Jews were intended to be another type of in-house joke among actors and audience, much like the prevailing satires on theater.

Such jokes appeared more problematic when Sound and Smoke went public, and took its Jewish scenes before a wider audience. Granted, none of the reviewers in the major newspapers or journals took umbrage at the Jewish caricatures, nor can one ascertain what aspects of these scenes provoked the Jewish students to protest. It may have been a case of offended religious sensibilities. It may also have reflected a more political concern about toying with stereotypes potentially harmful to Jews as German citizens. After all, the heyday of Adolf Stöcker, the anti-Semitic preacher, was not that long gone. Although this incident remained isolated at the time, twenty-five years later Jewish organizations in Berlin would mount massive protests against Jewish cabaretists who told jokes about Jews to general audiences. In the Wilhelmine era most viewers apparently accepted such humor as standard and unproblematic fare on cabaret stages. But by the Weimar period, anti-Semitism had grown to be such a clear political danger that many more people heatedly questioned the wisdom of joking about Jewish stereotypes in public.[32]

### The Path to a New Theatricality

The Serenissimus skits were immensely successful, and they might have laid the basis for a broader movement of political cabaret. But that was not to be, since Reinhardt's long-term interest remained focused on theater. The satirical scenes kept Sound and Smoke financially viable at a time when theatrical parody alone failed to attract an audience. The troupe used these months to shift toward drama. During the winter and spring of 1902, the repertory of Sound and Smoke underwent a significant change, as one-act plays came to dominate the programs. Most of those works were comic skits, but serious modern dramas were performed as well, in particular, plays by Strindberg (The Stronger, The Bond, The Outlaw).

This trend had been plotted already at the outset of Sound and Smoke. On January 30, 1901, Kayssler wrote to Morgenstern about the group's plan to transform the cabaret eventually into a theater for one-act plays, and ultimately to take over the Deutsches Theater: "That can be a path toward the near future, namely the time when Brahm will relinquish the Deutsches Theater, and that will probably happen in two years, when his contract expires. We want to turn this affair into a small theater and eventually cast off all accessories [alles Beiwerk]. A theater for one-act plays is something good . . . We will start with an intimate theater. If a greater theater develops out of it, that's up to us." Considering the fact that Kayssler, Reinhardt, and the others were still very junior actors, one would have been tempted at that time to dismiss this letter as youthful megalomania. Yet it proved to be uncannily prescient, as Reinhardt and his friends systematically realized their stated goals in the ensuing years.

Although the Serenissimus scenes were retained through the summer of 1902, the other cabaretic elements, which Kayssler had dismissed as "accessories," were progressively discarded. By April 15, Oberländer could write to the police: "With the presentation of a Strindberg cycle and several literary novelties by other outstanding authors, the directors of our stage will have completed the transformation of Sound and Smoke into a 'theater' by the end of this season. Our goal is to start off the next season with a repertory that will display a strictly literary tendency."[33]

The troupe drew the logical consequences and gave up the pretense of being a cabaret. It began to call itself Kleines Theater (Schall und Rauch), and by January 1903 it dropped the parenthetical words entirely. This was in keeping with the new repertory, which consisted of serious full-length plays. Predictably, Reinhardt produced a wide variety of dramas. As early as 1901, he wrote: "I do not even think about fixating on a specific literary program, whether naturalism or anything else. Of course I believe that the highest art of our age, that of Tolstoy, has grown far beyond naturalism; abroad, Strindberg, Hamsun, Maeterlinck, Wilde have gone very different ways; in German art, Wedekind and Hofmannsthal are proceeding along other paths." Reinhardt proclaimed: "Whatever new young talents appear in our time, no matter where they come from, I will welcome them all."[34]

Despite this focus on drama, the Kleines Theater did not entirely forget its cabaretic roots. The novelty of its productions lay in a new sense of theatricality, their ability to draw upon visual, gestural, and musical elements that Reinhardt missed on dramatic stages: "I cannot tell you how much I long for music and color." According to Reinhardt, the theater should be a site of play, of experiment, of fantasy. A major fault of nineteenth-century performance was excessive emphasis on the spoken word. In retrospect, Reinhardt wrote about the Vienna Burgtheater, which he had idealized in his youth: "At that time the performance of plays was exclusively focused on the word. The stage was very primitive; only the furniture was absolutely indispensable; everything else was the actor and his word."[35] Reinhardt applauded the centrality of the actor, but he deplored the domination of the word. Words alone left much unsaid, since human expression was musical and visual as well as verbal. Gesture, pantomime, music—all elements of Sound and Smoke—were for Reinhardt inherent parts of theatricality. In his cabaret he made light of the plenitude of dramatic styles, but he also employed a wealth of nonverbal theatrical devices. When he moved on to more serious drama, he suspended the parody but retained the experimentation, the sense of play.

Similar opinions were shared by the more innovative modern playwrights. It came as no surprise that Reinhardt's troupe performed Oscar Wilde's *Salome* (November 15, 1902), Wedekind's *Earth Spirit* (December

17, 1902), and Hofmannsthal's *Elektra* (October 30, 1903). These works demonstrated a movement toward dance, pantomime, and other nonverbal means of expression. *Salome,* at first performed as a closed production for invited guests, culminated in a sensuous and seductive dance. The production was noteworthy also for the collaboration of major visual artists, the sculptor Max Kruse and the painter Lovis Corinth, on the set designs. *Earth Spirit* embodied a new theatrical spirit to an even greater extent. In the 1890s, when he had composed the play, Wedekind already had come to prefer the theatricality of vaudeville and circus to literary drama. *Earth Spirit* deflated the importance of words as means of communication by devising the technique of *Aneinandervorbeireden,* the depiction of the fact that people actually "speak past each other" when they appear to be engaged in conversation. Simultaneously, Wedekind began to emphasize mimic elements drawn from popular theatrical traditions. *Earth Spirit* opened with an animal trainer who introduced the play as an extended circus number, while the third act was set in the dressing room of a vaudeville hall. The heroine, Lulu, was a character beyond the bounds of bourgeois convention and reason, whose "body language" was at least as significant as her spoken words. After the opening of the drama at the Kleines Theater, Kayssler wrote the author: "Do you know what you have done today? You have strangled the naturalistic monster of verisimilitude and brought the element of play to the stage."[36]

In a very different manner, Hugo von Hofmannsthal too wrote scripts that emphasized gestural elements of theater. In the early 1890s, when still in his teens, Hofmannsthal had burst onto the literary scene as one of the outstanding poets of the day. At the same time, though, he seriously questioned the power of words. In a 1895 essay he spoke of people's "profound nausea" in the face of words, "because words have placed themselves in front of things." Humanity was caught in a web of language: "normally words are not under the control of men, but men are under the control of words." Tired of the profusion of "lies" and the inability to empower words in any personal sense, people turned to the popular theatrical arts. "Thus a desperate love has been awakened for all of the arts that are performed mutely: music, dance, and all arts of the acrobat and the clown."[37]

In the ensuing years Hofmannsthal ceased writing lyric poetry and composed theatrical works that emphasized mime and spectacle. Predictably, he and Reinhardt were soon drawn to each other. A conversation with the director in May 1903 led Hofmannsthal to compose a new rendition of the Electra story. This work was also inspired by the outstanding acting of Gertrud Eysoldt, who played Lulu as well as Salome in the Berlin productions. Dance, which had a pivotal function in *Salome,* became the culmination of *Elektra.* At the end of that work the exultant heroine told her sister to "be silent and dance," as she threw herself into "a nameless dance." The play ended with this explicit rejection of words, this refusal to apply limiting names to ineffable acts.[38]

Reinhardt continued to champion the plays of Wedekind and Hofmannsthal in the following years. He also proceeded to build up a theatrical empire. In February 1903 he took over the Neues Theater on the Schiffbauerdamm, which would become Brecht's theater half a century later. He thus had two stages upon which to present his highly acclaimed productions of German classics as well as modern works, such as Gorky's *Lower Depths* (January 23, 1903), Maeterlinck's *Pelléas and Mélisande* (April 3, 1903), Lessing's *Minna von Barnhelm* (January 14, 1904), and Schiller's *Love and Intrigue* (April 22, 1904). The pinnacle of his early productions was *A Midsummer Night's Dream* (Neues Theater, January 31, 1905), a boisterous spectacle of unprecedented visual and mimic vitality. Finally, in the summer of 1905 Reinhardt gave up the Kleines Theater in order to acquire the Deutsches Theater. This not only confirmed Kayssler's prediction but also marked the symbolic end of naturalist stage direction in Berlin.

Reinhardt went on to ever more grandiose theatrical experiments, such as theater-in-the-round productions of classical plays on arena stages and in circus halls, and open-air performances of mystery plays. The roots of these later productions lay in Sound and Smoke. Rudolf Bernauer contended that Reinhardt's cabaret "was his first enterprise, from which all of the others grew." The playwright Max Halbe highlighted the pivotal role of cabaret in the revitalization of modern theater: "Whoever has lived through those times has no doubt that the real revolution came less from above, from high literature, than from below, from the lesser arts, from the *Brettl,* from cabaret." Of course, cabaret alone did not destroy naturalist drama. In October 1901, the noted critic Erich Schlaikjer had contended: "Cabaret attracts audiences and authors. Yet it is not cabaret that is the cause of the decay [of naturalism], but rather that decay is the source of cabaret."[39] Actually, both statements were equally true. Born out of discontent with naturalist drama, Reinhardt's cabaret also contributed to the supercession of narrow realism and the revitalization of the stage.

Sound and Smoke provided a context for Reinhardt to break away from the naturalism of Otto Brahm. At the same time that he joked about the profusion of competing and mutually intolerant theatrical styles, Reinhardt presented pantomimes, songs, and nonverbal elements that became central to his later productions. Above all, he learned to accentuate the fact that *Schauspielkunst,* the art of the theater, dealt primarily with *Schau* and *Spiel,* with spectacle and play. Both at Sound and Smoke and in his later productions, he engaged in "play" in all of its connotations: amusement, performance, experiment.

Reinhardt did not exhaust all of the possibilities of cabaret. It is particularly noteworthy that political parody, so pronounced in Sound and Smoke, disappeared from his later productions. The development of cabaret along critical lines would be the task of other writers and performers. Reinhardt's achievement lay in his ability to sense the theatrical potentialities of cabaret, and to use it as a springboard for a rejuvenation of the stage.

# Cosmopolitan Diversions, Metropolitan Identities

The cabarets of Wolzogen and Reinhardt inspired a host of other ventures, which attempted to cater to a metropolitan public. A number of pub-cabarets on the Parisian model displayed some artistic merit, and they sought to evoke an atmosphere of liberality and openness appropriate to a *Weltstadt*. Most taverns and restaurants offering late-night entertainment could not, however, make such claims, and the police eventually closed them down. The most successful performers and theaters were those that consciously sought not only to reflect but also define the conditions of life in metropolitan Berlin. Claire Waldoff, a feisty singer with a pushy yet upbeat temperament, modernized the image of lower-class character types which had populated nineteenth-century stages; soon she was considered the very embodiment of "the Berliner." The cabarets of Rudolf Nelson and the Metropol-Theater's revues crafted a more elitist image of the city. Whereas Nelson's urbane music catered to a wealthy and urbane clientele, the Metropol's extremely popular shows trumpeted Berlin as a center of fashion and modernity.

## Policing the Pub-Cabarets

In the first months of 1901 many critics and observers of the cultural scene deplored the absence of a truly Parisian cabaret in Berlin. They noted that the improvisation common to the French ventures stood in stark contrast to the Germanic planning of Wolzogen's Motley Theater. The Chat noir of Rodolphe Salis had evolved spontaneously from a private gathering of writers and artists into a forum for public performances, all the while retaining its tavern setting. In contrast, the Motley Theater was conceived as a regular stage with programs planned in advance. One reviewer commented that Wolzogen "overlooked the formless and unconstrained nature of French cabarets, the improvisational element in the artistic performances there, the feeling of camaraderie among the audience—and instead founded, in true German fashion, an Überbrettl based on a system with a fixed program."[1] Wolzogen explicitly rejected the Parisian prototype as being too plebian for his taste. Moreover, censorship laws prohibited improvisation on a public stage. Nevertheless, in the fall of 1901 several Berlin artists' pubs developed into cabarets more or less on the Parisian model.

The first of these was called The Hungry Pegasus (Zum hungrigen Pegasus), which performed every Saturday night beginning on October 2, 1901. The central figure was Max Tilke (b. 1869), a young and unsuccessful painter who had spent some time in Spain as well as in Paris, where he had become acquainted with cabaret. Tilke acted as conferencier; he also played the guitar and sang Andalusian folk songs. Other performers included Ernst Griebel and Charles Horning, two artists who had traveled to the United States. Together they sang what reviewers invariably referred to as "Niggersongs," without any consciously pejorative connotation. They were joined by Georg David Schulz and Hans Hyan, poets who would soon found their own cabarets. Another frequent guest was Maria Eichhorn, who recited erotic and sadomasochistic verses under the pseudonym Dolorosa. One observer described her performance rather charitably: "A young woman in a white gown, with chrysanthemums in her hair, recites her own poems, full of a sultry, perverse sensuality and at the same time a singular profundity. One cannot laugh at the meager vocal ability; it seems as though the monotonous sound of the voice hides an immense anguish and an immense fear that want to cry forth." Dolorosa appeared often at several artists' pubs over the ensuing months. Another habitual performer at such venues was Erich Mühsam, a satirical poet with an anarchist bent who eventually gained fame as a leader of Munich's Soviet Republic in the spring of 1919.[2]

The weekly performances of the Hungry Pegasus took place in a small back room of an Italian restaurant near the Potsdamerbrücke (fig. 10). The walls were decorated with sketches by Tilke and Griebel, and the conferencier never failed to note that they were for sale. The fifteen tables normally seated some sixty people, although often a hundred would be packed in ("sardine-style," one reviewer complained) on any given Saturday. In the words of an observer, the public consisted of "artists and scholars, writers and financiers, ladies of the best society and piquant bohémiennes. One of the best-known gynecologists sits next to one of our best caricaturists; a high-ranking civil servant has a friendly conversation with a journalist who has attacked him often enough in his newspaper." What attracted these people was the sense of "absolute equality" and the "indifference [Wurschtigkeit] toward all conventions."[3] Occasionally members of the audience were invited to perform. Fortunately for the other spectators, professional singers and musicians mainly took advantage of this opportunity.

10. A performance at the Hungry Pegasus cabaret.

The Hungry Pegasus was, in short, a place where middle-class citizens could observe, and even pretend to be, bohemians. The tavern setting provided a more free-and-easy atmosphere than the restaurants frequented by the bourgeoisie. One critic proclaimed that "one laughs and feels happy, an atmosphere of youthful freshness pervades the whole." The same factors that attracted many middle-class citizens and tourists to the Parisian cabarets—light entertainment in an unconstrained environment, the desire to relive one's real or imagined youth—proved equally compelling in Berlin. The setting also was an expression of, as well as diversion from, the stresses of big-city life. Walter Benjamin noted: "One of the most primitive and indispensable diversions of the metropolitan citizen, who day in, day out, is locked into an infinitely variegated social environment—is to plunge into a different environment, the more exotic, the better. Thus the artists' dives, the criminals' bars. In this respect, the two hardly differ from each other." The addition of an "artists' dive" like the Hungry Pegasus added yet another metropolitan note to Berlin's nightlife, and led a reviewer to exclaim, with only partial irony: "Hurrah! Berlin ist Weltstadt!"[4]

Unlike its Parisian counterparts, the Hungry Pegasus was not political or socially critical. The Progressive *Freisinnige Zeitung* complained: "Why is Max Tilke not more forceful, why does he not stick his hands deeper into the caldron of politics and social conditions? . . . Only with great

shyness does a trace of social criticism or a parody of the police state dare
to come foreward." This observation missed the point that the purpose of
the venture was amusement, not politics. Even an otherwise activist poet
like Mühsam shied away from socially critical statements in cabarets,
which he considered inappropriate locations for political enlightenment:
"I never regarded the cabaret, which had become a mercantile institution,
as anything other than a source of income. During the many years that I
appeared for a longer or shorter time as a cabaretist, I never performed
anything other than word games or other innocuous things. Even when it
was requested of me, I always refused to recite serious works before a
paying public."[5] This statement indicated that many, and often contradictory, reasons could account for the generally apolitical nature of German
cabaret. Wolzogen's conservative standpoint made him avoid political satire. Mühsam too refrained from critical statements in cabarets, but he did
so in order not to cheapen the impact of his anarchist beliefs. Sound and
Smoke's Serenissimus had clear political overtones, but the figure was
dropped as Reinhardt's more purely theatrical passions came to the fore.

The police initially were suspicious of the Hungry Pegasus. Tilke recently
had been fined for public insult, and he was rumored to be irresponsible,
debt-ridden, and a Social Democrat to boot.[6] He evaded censorship by
running the Hungry Pegasus as a "closed" club: only people with invitations were admitted, and no entrance fee was charged. Although practically
anyone could receive an invitation, and a plate was circulated for contributions, the police ceased being concerned with the venture because they
concluded that it was harmless. Moreover, they probably had no desire to
provoke needlessly the well-heeled and well-connected clientele. In any
case, the Hungry Pegasus disbanded in May 1902, when Tilke decided to
return to painting full-time.

The Hungry Pegasus was the first of several establishments that came
to be known as *Kneipenbrettl,* or pub-cabarets, to distinguish them from
those Wolzogen-style ventures that were housed in regular theaters. The
*Freisinnige Zeitung* noted that this was the reverse of the course followed
in Paris: whereas the Chat noir had evolved out of informal gatherings in
artists' pubs, the Berlin Kneipenbrettl were inspired by the local cabaret-
theaters. Four months after the Hungry Pegasus opened, Georg David
Schulz split away and founded In Seventh Heaven (Poetenbänkel zum
siebenten Himmel) in a restaurant in the Kantstrasse. A rather mediocre
poet, Schulz (b. 1865) bore the nickname "Schmalz" on account of the
dripping sentimentality of his verse. His pub-cabaret was a clone of the
one he had left; it too appeared once a week (Wednesdays) in a small room
with contemporary graphics on the walls. Schulz acted as conferencier and
performed his own songs. Music also was provided by Bogumil Zepler,

who had composed several works sung at the Motley Theater. The main attraction of this cabaret was a former seamstress who used the stage-name Marietta de Rigardo. The daughter of a Swiss man and an Indian woman, she had been raised in an Ursuline convent in Manila. Her dark complexion and broken German made her seem exotic, and she was considered exceptionally beautiful. She married Schulz in 1902, and later wedded Ludwig Thoma. Like the Hungry Pegasus, the Seventh Heaven gave the police no cause for concern. It had a respectable clientele—anywhere from thirty to sixty people "from artistic and theatrical circles" on any given night—and "did not follow any tendencies that were political, antireligious, and so on." The police concluded that it was "a rather harmless venture."[7]

The police reached very different conclusions about Hans Hyan's Silver Punchbowl (Silberne Punschterrine), which opened on November 26, 1901, in a restaurant in the Steglitzerstrasse. Hyan (1868–1944) was considered the Berlin counterpart to Aristide Bruant. Like his French model, he employed the local argot, sang songs about criminals and the poor, and insulted the people who came to his cabaret on Tuesday evenings. One of his best-known songs, about a murderer's last night before his execution, clearly was modeled on Bruant's "A la Rocquette." Like the Parisian Mirliton, the Silver Punchbowl offered the middle classes an opportunity to pretend they were slumming, while remaining in the secure confines of a bourgeois tavern. Despite this built-in hypocrisy, to Hyan's credit it must be said that he possessed an exceptional ability to imitate the speech of various social groups in Berlin, in particular the slang of the downtrodden and criminal classes. One reviewer wrote that "at the moment there is probably no other author who has such a masterful command of the Berlin dialect and the argot of the criminal world." Twenty years later Kurt Tucholsky claimed that Hyan was incomparable in his ability "to capture phonetically the Berlin manner of thought, the Berlin soul."[8]

From the beginning the police were very concerned with this venture. After all, Hyan knew whereof he spoke, inasmuch as he had a rather impressive criminal record. In 1891 he had been sentenced to three years' imprisonment for aggravated burglary; ten years later he was being investigated for suspected robbery (the case was eventually dropped). He wrote for pornographic publications with names like *Pikanterien* and *Satyr,* and in 1899 he was fined 300 marks for libel. Initially, though, the police did not find much to worry about. A report of December 31, 1901, noted that most of the numbers had "political, satirical contents," yet these works were still quite tame. Hyan's songs about policemen, about the Hohenzollern statues in the new Siegesallee, or about the crooked dealings of bankers had less bite than, say, the weekly jokes and caricatures in *Simplicissimus.* A critic for the Social Democratic *Vorwärts* called attention to one "political" song with satirical references to Bülow's tariffs, Chamberlain's South African policy, and the amorous escapades of King Edward; however, the jokes were "so cheap that no prosecutor would move against them, even if the law permitted him to."[9] Like other cabaretists, Hyan was protected by the ruse of claiming to perform before an invited public.

Within a year the police were showing greater concern with the increasingly daring tone of Hyan's numbers. In August 1902 they cited reports that the works were "very risqué, sometimes even lascivious," and that the venture was concerned "not so much with the cultivation of art as with stimulating and tickling the senses." In addition, Hyan appeared to be generous and indiscriminate in handing out "invitations." By November the police concluded that the Silver Punchbowl was de facto a public stage, but they did not move against the enterprise until a year later. In December 1903 a police report noted that Hyan sang songs concerning a "fat priest" who seduced minors and fathered numerous offspring; a cleaning woman who threw her illegitimate baby into a latrine; and a public prosecutor who hanged himself in a lavatory after confronting in court a prostitute with whom he had an affair. Moreover, Dolorosa had become a regular performer at the Silver Punchbowl, and her numbers were now completely unacceptable: "she presented her own works, which had in part a strongly masochistic streak. Among other things, she sang 'The Song of Songs of Pains and Tortures' and described in erotic poems the joys of whiplashes and slave-chains."[10]

Not only had such numbers become intolerable, but Hyan was now openly flaunting the legal restrictions on closed performances, which prohibited charging admission. Before this time he had financed the venture by "passing the plate," the proceeds of which were "always very considerable," given the "well-off public," according to a police report of August 24, 1902. By December 1903, however, he was demanding a 1.50-mark entrance fee, even from people holding invitations. Moreover, he had hired a woman to send out unsolicited invitations to doctors, dentists, and lawyers whose names were gleaned from the Berlin address book. Since the Silver Punchbowl was now clearly a public and commercial enterprise, and one that speculated on the least noble instincts of its customers, the police decided to move definitively against it, and it ceased operations in 1904.[11]

The police had their reasons for hesitating to move swiftly against the Silver Punchbowl. Like the other cabarets, Hyan's venture might have been protected by the nature of the clientele, described by the police as "belonging to the better circles." One reviewer noted that the public was "very mixed," with "ladies in reform dresses and Cléo de Merode hairdoes, youths . . . with huge secessionist cravats, young jurists and tradesmen, authors, painters, sculptors, honorable gray-haired heads of families with wives and daughters." This was obviously not a disorderly or disreputable audience. The police were concerned that if censorship were too harsh, it might actually create sympathy among such people for the writers or cabarets in question. This dilemma was made explicit in a long report that Kurt von Glasenapp, the head of the theater supervision division of the Berlin police, sent to the Prussian Ministry of the Interior on May 15, 1902. In response to his superiors' query about why he was not moving more forcefully against the cabarets, Glasenapp replied that censorship was often counterproductive. In the 1890s, during the heyday of socially critical naturalist drama, the police had learned that by banning a play, they inadvertently would advertise its author and boost his popularity. Furthermore, a successful appeal to the courts to overturn the censor's order—a not infrequent occurrence—was guaranteed to make the play a hit. Glasenapp contended that this resulted in a situation where "those theater directors and writers who were more interested in sensationalism than art" actively sought police interference, "especially when they were in bad financial straits. In particular, one must count among them the managers of cabarets and their affiliated authors." In this report Glasenapp cited the Motley Stage Boards as an exceptionally egregious case, but his remarks could have been directed just as well against the Silver Punchbowl a few months later. He argued that it would be better to allow the more obnoxious cabarets to die a natural death by bankruptcy, rather than prolong their lives artificially by means of the free publicity provided by censorship.[12]

What eventually persuaded the police to move against cabarets was intensive lobbying by their commercial competitors: variety-show directors as well as restaurant and tavern owners. When a major crackdown on cabarets finally occurred in 1904 and 1905, it was in response to repeated prodding by such groups. Of some seventy-two venues that claimed to be cabarets in 1904, few had any serious artistic aspirations; most were simply restaurants that offered live, late-night entertainment. In his survey of Berlin cabarets published in 1904, Hanns Heinz Ewers complained: "Every pub-proprietor who failed to find customers for his sour beer and bad wine eagerly seized upon this new bait. Dozens of ham actors, who had been running in vain from one agency to another in search of a contract, suddenly felt the calling to direct a cabaret."[13] Consequently, dozens of taverns and restaurants started to offer late-night entertainment by third-rate performers.

Vaudeville directors decried such ventures as unfair competition, since they evaded licensing. It would have been logical to treat pub-cabarets according to article 33a of the Commercial Code, the so-called "Tingeltangel paragraph." This and related regulations stipulated that for-profit performances without "higher artistic interest" required a special permit and were subject to certain limitations: vaudeville halls had to pass fire-safety inspections, submit materials to the censor for prior approval, and terminate their shows by eleven at night. The strict wording of these regulations, however, did not apply to many pubs and restaurants with late-night entertainment, which lacked the outward trappings of a theater or variety show (costumed actors or singers, stage sets and props). Cabarets with such theatrical elements, such as Wolzogen's Motley Theater or Reinhardt's Sound and Smoke, were required to apply for a license and submit to the attendant rules, but pub-cabarets were not. This gave such establishments a competitive advantage, according to variety-show directors. Not being subject to censorship, they could present more risqué numbers. They were not bound to a closing time, and thus could cater to a late-night crowd. The existence of pub-cabarets was also decried by other tavern and restaurant owners, who believed that their colleagues offering entertainment had a marked advantage in attracting customers. In June 1903 the vaudeville artists' association summed up their frustrations with the proclamation: "Away with the Parasitic Weeds!"[14]

The organizers of pub-cabarets responded by claiming that they were not subject to licensing, an assertion that could be argued in two ways. As we have seen, many of the more artistic pub-cabarets claimed to be private clubs for invited guests, and thus were not bound by preliminary censorship or other restrictions. The police could counter that assertion by demonstrating that "invitations" were handed out freely or that admission was collected directly or indirectly. Most owners of pub-cabarets, however, did not use the "private club" ruse; they obviously were public dining establishments with live entertainment. Nevertheless, they tried to avoid licensing under article 33a by claiming that their performances possessed "higher artistic interest," and were not "for-profit" since no admission was charged.

Both assertions were highly questionable. While venues like the Hungry Pegasus, In Seventh Heaven, and the Silver Punchbowl might have possessed some artistic merit, that was hardly the case for dozens of other self-styled cabarets. A writer for the conservative *Deutsche Warte* complained about performances "in the smoked-filled back rooms of wine-taverns, where second- and third-rate actors perform suggestive lyrics and monologues, where wilted female vocalists in very low-cut dresses sing risqué songs, and a couple of young things who know absolutely nothing about art catch the public's eye by displaying their youthful curves in unrestrained dances." Such observations were not limited to conservative critics with moralistic axes to grind. At the other end of the political

spectrum, Erich Mühsam complained about the quality of would-be cabarets: "Tasteless dilettantism, tedious smut, witless humbug."[15] Opponents
of such performances argued that since this could scarcely be called art,
their producers clearly required a Tingeltangel license. The "not-for-profit"
argument was specious as well. Even if no admission was charged, the
owners of pub-cabarets benefited from inflated coat-check fees and jacked-
up wine prices.

The police response to these allegations was not straightforward. On
July 29, 1903, the trade supervision division of the Berlin police issued an
order for neighborhood officers to investigate the cabarets on their beats.
The list of clues to look for—such as availability of "invitations," charging
of admission fees, and inflated coat-check and wine prices—were taken
almost verbatim from the "Parasitic Weeds" protest that had been published six weeks earlier. Although the vaudeville directors' suspicions were
confirmed in many cases, the police were slow to act; they did not an-
nounce a crackdown on cabarets until October 1904. Many shows seem
to have been terminated at this point, and in March 1905 the Berlin police
reported to the Prussian minister of the interior that "all cabarets here
possess a license according to article 33a of the Commercial Code. When
a cabaret without one puts on public performances, it is immediately closed
down by the police." Yet that contention seemed to be somewhat exaggerated, inasmuch as a month later the same minister received protests
from the Berlin restaurant- and pub-owners' association, who complained
that many unlicensed cabarets were still alive and well.[16]

Just as the police were hesitant to censor the more artistic cabarets, they
were cautious about moving against the pubs and restaurants with late-
night entertainment. On rare occasions restaurant owners were able to go
to court and successfully argue that their "cabaret" performances possessed some artistic merit and hence did not require licensing. The greatest
concern, however, derived from Berlin's growing reputation as a *Weltstadt*.
The city competed with other world centers for prestige, as it tried to
portray itself as an equal to London, Paris, and New York. Part of the
reason for this was economic, inasmuch as tourism had become an increasingly important component of Berlin's economy. Sightseers from the
rest of Germany and other parts of Europe, as well as traveling businessmen, sought diversion at night. An entertainment district developed in
Friedrichstadt, the area along Friedrichstrasse between Unter den Linden
and Leipzigerstrasse. This was where most of the cabarets and would-be
cabarets were located, as well as many pubs and restaurants; it also was
one of the centers for prostitution. The nightly goings-on there troubled
the authorities, but the police recognized that such activities were an
unavoidable, indeed expected, aspect of big-city life.

Despite their avoidance of heavy-handed policies, the police faced mounting criticisms from certain circles that their regulations were too severe. The requirement that theaters, variety shows, and staged cabarets cease at eleven at night derived from a police ordinance of the mid-nineteenth century. Writing for the liberal *Berliner Tageblatt,* a lawyer argued in 1905: "The closing-hour—which was imposed on Berlin in the 1860s, when it was a Central European capital with a small-town character—contradicts the very nature of cabaret as a fixture with world-class, cosmopolitan allures that serves a cosmopolitan public." Visitors to the capital, looking forward to a night on the town, were disappointed to see the licensed cabarets close at such an early hour. At best, after eleven they proceeded to dine at restaurants with unregulated entertainment; at worst, they turned to much less wholesome diversions.[17]

The authorities were well aware of this dilemma. In July 1905 Theobald von Bethmann Hollweg, the future chancellor who was then Prussian minister of the interior, sent a letter to Berlin's police chief in which he acknowledged that the lack of regulations for unlicensed cabarets was unfair to "other more or less artistic presentations, from the theater down to the Tingeltangel." Some restrictions were necessary, but Bethmann Hollweg cautioned: "I would not, however, be able to approve of a narrow-minded or puritanical curtailment of those forms of culture, social life, or entertainment that derive from the special character of a metropolis [*Weltstadt*]." The end result was a compromise. On May 5, 1906, the Berlin police chief finally ordered that all cabaret-style performances in restaurants and pubs be treated as Tingeltangel, and hence licensed according to article 33a of the Commercial Code, subjected to preliminary censorship, and bound to the eleven o'clock closing hour. These stipulations forced many restaurants to curtail their entertainment. Nevertheless, to meet the demand for late-night diversions, the police granted special licenses to four cabarets, permitting them to remain open until two in the morning; however, they were prohibited from using costumes or stage sets, to avoid competing with variety shows.[18]

It was not surprising that the cries of jealous competitors kept the police on the alert, since commercial forces were ultimately decisive in making or breaking the dozens of cabarets that appeared after the turn of the century. But despite the new restrictions, Friedrichstadt continued to be a lively center of late-night diversions. It seems that enforcement was not all that strict, since in 1910 Berlin's chief of police again had to promise the restaurant owners and vaudeville directors that he would take more severe steps against unlicensed, would-be cabarets in pubs and restaurants. When vaudeville directors accused cabarets of being "parasitic weeds" back in

1903, they probably did not suspect that their commercial rivals would be as tenacious and hard to eradicate as the refractory plants.[19]

### Two Sides of Metropolitan Cabaret: Rudolf Nelson and Claire Waldoff

Given the competitive nature of the entertainment business, few cabarets proved to be viable for any length of time. Those with the longest life span were founded and guided by Rudolf Nelson, who would continue to be a commanding presence on the German cabaret scene until the middle of the century. Whereas Nelson catered to an upper-class audience, Claire Waldoff's portrayals of lower-class Berlin characters made her one of the most popular entertainers on Berlin stages well into the thirties. The urbane cabaret of Nelson and the plebeian persona of Waldoff marked two different images of metropolitan life.

Born Rudolf Lewysohn into an impecunious Jewish family, Rudolf Nelson (1878–1960) demonstrated musical talent as a very young child. For pragmatic reasons, however, his parents steered him toward a career in the textile trade. After several miserable teenage years as an underling in that business, he finally was awarded a scholarship to study composition at the prestigious Stern Conservatory. Yet there too he was unhappy, since his taste ran toward popular music, not classical composition. According to his own (not always reliable) memoirs, Nelson managed to slip in to the opening night of Wolzogen's Motley Theater, and immediately he was captivated by the new genre. He terminated his studies and signed up with a succession of cabarets: the post-Wolzogen Motley Theater, the Silver Punchbowl, In Seventh Heaven, as well as others with names like Charivari, The Merry Faun (Zum fröhlichen Faun), and The Big Surprise (Zum blauen Wunder). He demonstrated exceptional capabilities as a composer and improviser, and as a pianist and musical director. His big financial break came when he was recommended to Joachim Albert, a Prussian prince and an enthusiast of popular music who needed live entertainment at an evening party. Nelson's success there led to a string of invitations to appear at similar occasions. He thereby became well-known among "the leading circles of the Berlin and Potsdam court society," as well as among "prominent people in industry and banking."[20]

Even though Nelson's performances at private gatherings in these circles could earn him a thousand marks in a single evening, he decided to set up independently. Together with Paul Schneider-Duncker, an actor, he persuaded the owner of the Roland von Berlin, a near-bankrupt restaurant on Potsdamerstrasse, to convert part of the premises into a cabaret. After extensive remodeling, 150 people could be seated in a small room around tables or in rows of seats. From the very beginning, Nelson aimed at attracting a wealthy clientele. The first performances were sold out, despite an exceedingly steep entrance fee of 20 goldmarks. In the ensuing years Nelson continued to enjoy a packed house, though he had to reduce ticket prices to 3 marks.

This prolonged success was the reward for the fact that Nelson and Schneider-Duncker consciously sought a style of entertainment that Berliners called *mondän* (fig. 11). It was supposed to generate an ambience of carefree metropolitan glamour. Unlike other cabarets, which presented works by a number of composers, almost all of the songs in the Roland von Berlin were written by Nelson, who had a genial ability to imitate and elaborate on a variety of musical styles. Part of the entertainment was "international," inasmuch as Nelson was one of the first musicians in Germany who was able to compose ragtime, the cakewalk, and the two-step. Schneider-Duncker provided the appropriate dance movements while singing such numbers. Most of Nelson's compositions, however, remained in the style of Central European popular tunes, and took their themes from daily life in Berlin. Many of the songs scripted by O. A. Alberts, the in-house lyricist, made light of current fashions; the most popular of such works was entitled "Frightfully Chic Kid-Leather Shoes" (Scheusslich chike Chevreauxschuh'). On rare occasions, the songs even took good-natured jabs at Imperial culture. "Dummies on the Right, Dummies on the Left!" (Rechts ein Puppchen, links ein Puppchen!) recounted how a policeman, speaking a thick Berlin dialect, proudly showed off the Hohenzollern statues on the Siegesallee to a tourist.[21]

The most common theme was sex. In 1913 Kurt Tucholsky wrote: "If you analyze these cabaret songs, then you find that the bottom line confirms the existence of extramarital sexual relations." Tucholsky allowed, however, that Nelson's works were a cut above the rest: "At the piano: Rudolf Nelson. The rocking, flowing, coquettish refrains of these songs purl over the keys, his fingers hardly move, but there where the refrain sets in (ritardando—the printed score says fermate), you sense that he takes pleasure in the hit, in his engaging, light rhythm. He sits at the piano, and one understands the significance and the importance of a chanson refrain."[22] Tucholsky had reason to underscore the importance of the refrain in Nelson's oeuvre, since it embodied not only the musical heart of a piece, but also the key to its punch line. A typical song would have an unchanging refrain that sounded innocent enough after the first stanza, but would acquire obvious erotic implications by the last stanza.

A classic example of that format was the popular "Jacques Manasse." Set in the milieu of the Jewish textile business that Nelson had come to know as a youth, it recounted how a young woman showed up at her first

11. Urbane cabaret: the performers of the Roland von Berlin, with Rudolf Nelson and Paul Schneider-Duncker standing in front (1906).

job (fig. 12). The refrain listed the people to whom she was introduced: "First the apprentice Jacques Manasse, / the young man with the petty cash box, / then the severe managing clerk, / the firm's token Christian [*Reklamechrist*], / and next the silent shareholder, / over fifty and still a bachelor, / and then in person, / the head of the company, I. S. Cohn." The next stanza described how she turned the heads of all of these men, and arranged to have a rendezvous with each one of them. This time the refrain was used to list the order of the assignations. The last stanza described how she had a baby a year later, and when her mother asked who would support it, she replied that its father was a limited-liability corporation ("G.m.b.H") formed by her lovers. The final rendition of the refrain described how she made the monthly rounds to collect paternity payments, starting with Jacques Manasse. It concluded with a slight twist, however, since "the head of the company, I. S. Cohn" refused to contribute.[23] In addition to illustrating a model use of refrain, the song may also be regarded as a compendium of themes common to *mondän* cabaret numbers: the belief that women on the lower rungs of the occupational

12. The perils of female employment: cover of the sheet music for Nelson's hit "Jacques Manasse" (1912).

ladder were readily "available"; the notion that Eros was the great social leveler (in this case, of an office hierarchy); and the idea that whenever sex appeared, a monetary demand was sure to follow.

Despite the success of the Roland von Berlin, personal differences caused Nelson and Schneider-Duncker to separate in 1907. Schneider-Duncker retained the original venue, and Nelson proceeded to open a cabaret in an arcade on the corner of Friedrichstrasse and Unter den Linden. The new venture, which seated 220, was named the "Chat noir," in honor of the world's first cabaret, and in recognition of the fact that Nelson was trying to provide Berlin with some of the metropolitan glamour of Paris. Nelson flourished in the new locale, and he fiercely defended his financial opportunities against competitors. In 1910, when the Chat noir was one of the very few cabarets permitted to perform later than eleven o'clock, he informed the police of another venture that was doing so illegally. He also squealed on a cabaret that performed a song which had been censored from the Chat noir's repertory.[24] Nelson might have sought to evoke an atmosphere of metropolitan suavity, but behind the scenes, it remained a dog-eat-dog world in the Big City.

Nelson continued to attract his favored clientele. A police report of 1912 noted that the audience consisted of "a better class of people, officers in civilian clothing, members of financial circles and the fast set, tourists and ladies of the upper demimonde." The circle of Nelson's admirers reached to the very apex of German society, inasmuch as he was summoned to a private performance for the Kaiser. At the beginning of November 1908, Wilhelm II and his hunting entourage were staying in Donaueschingen at the castle of Prince Egon zu Fürstenberg. The Prince arranged for entertainment by Nelson as well as two other members of the Chat noir ensemble, the baritone Jean Moreau and Theodor Francke, a comedian. The high point of the evening was Moreau's rendition of Nelson's popular song, "The Shopgirl" (Das Ladenmädel), one more case of a sexually available female employee. Once again the refrain initially appeared in an innocuous context. The baritone recounted how he had to go to the back of a women's fashion store in order to meet a young shopgirl: past the blouses and the dresses, past the petticoats, past the undergarments—"and then, and then came she" (und dann, und dann kam sie). Predictably, the last stanza set the action in a *chambre separée,* and the same refrain was used to relate the order in which the shopgirl divested herself of her clothes. The song was very much to the liking of the Kaiser, whose puritanical public persona did not prevent him from enjoying dirty jokes in private. Indeed, Wilhelm was so amused by the piece that he requested Moreau to sing it five times. Nelson profited not only from his 1500-mark honorarium but also from the fact that the next day's newspapers reported the Kaiser's "lively applause" for the evening's entertainment.[25]

Whereas Nelson gained publicity from this event, the Kaiser garnered notoriety. The Nelson soiree took place a few days after Wilhelm's infamous interview had been published in the London *Daily Telegraph.* His fantastic claim to have provided decisive aid to the British in the Boer War (by suggesting military plans of action and keeping other powers out of the conflict), as well as other profusely pro-British statements, provoked a public outcry in Germany. Although the Kaiser was facing the greatest crisis of his regime, he seemed impervious to its implications. Rather than remain in Berlin to reassert his legitimacy, he proceeded with his scheduled hunting trip. The national newspapers reported with increasing dismay the official accounts of his activities, which repeatedly related his "good spirits" and tallied the number of bucks he had shot. This insouciance seemed doubly grotesque, inasmuch as a mining disaster in Hamm, where over three hundred men lost their lives, occurred in the same week. The report that the Kaiser and his entourage had spent an evening being entertained by Berlin cabaretists was the last straw. His distraction by such frivolous activities, in the face of the political crisis and the workers' tragedy, seemed to accentuate even more the blindness and lack of judgment that afflicted him and his advisers.[26]

Because Wilhelm II eventually weathered the storm, the *Daily Telegraph* affair usually is portrayed as another case where Germany's political parties failed to take advantage of a situation that would have allowed them to shift some power from the crown to the parliament. On a less lofty level, the incident also underscored a prevalent yet disturbing feature of German cabaret: a form of entertainment that could have been critical and satirical was used to distract its audience—in this case, even the head of state—from political responsibilities and realities. The perception that cabaret ultimately depoliticized its audience was to provoke heated debates during the Weimar era. The incident also highlighted the degree to which cabaret, or a certain type of cabaret, had become acceptable in the very highest reaches of society.

While Nelson's urbane cabaret catered to the wealthy and privileged, another type of performance, epitomized by Claire Waldoff, sought to evoke the nature of the common citizen of Berlin. Defining civic identity was particularly problematic in Berlin, which underwent rapid growth throughout the nineteenth and early twentieth centuries. Every year tens of thousands of immigrants were attracted to a city that was the capital of Prussia and the Reich, as well as the major center of German commerce, finance, and industry. For much of the modern era Berlin had a primarily non-native population. Censuses from the 1870s on generally revealed that only 40 percent of its inhabitants had been born within its boundaries. According to the prevailing cliché, the "true Berliner" came from Posen, or from Breslau. In 1899 Walter Rathenau declared: "As far as the Berliners are concerned, I do not know exactly whether they do not exist anymore, or not yet."[27]

Given the shortage of a native population and the predominance of immigrants, the residents of the capital were faced with the question: What

13. Berlin's spunky new star: Claire Waldoff at the beginning of her long career.

does it mean to be a Berliner? One person who attempted to answer that question was Claire Waldoff (1884–1957; fig. 13). Like all "true Berliners," she came from elsewhere. The daughter of a former miner who opened a pub, Waldoff grew up in Gelsenkirchen, in the Rhine-Ruhr industrial basin. Her family had higher ambitions for her, and sent her to a girls' high school *(Mädchengymnasium)* in Hanover; this was a highly unusual move for a child of her class. Waldoff proved to be exceptionally bright. She would have gone on to study medicine upon graduation, but her father's desertion of the family made this financially impossible. Having long been fascinated by theater, she now had the opportunity to change careers. Starting in 1903, she acquired roles with various provincial stages and touring companies. After three years she landed a position in Berlin.

Although Waldoff's autobiography, written late in her life (1953), is not reliable in every detail, there is no reason to doubt the gist of her account of her arrival in the capital: "Then I saw the giant city Berlin and was overwhelmed. I immediately sensed the special character of this city, its unheard-of tempo, its temperament, its incredible brio . . . I fell passionately in love with Berlin. Not because the city was beautiful or the Imperial capital, but because it was Berlin, with its special atmosphere, its vivacious and curt character." In the ensuing months Waldoff became a keen observer of the city's manners, and she gained perfect mastery of its brash dialect.[28]

This new identity soon paid off. In the fall of 1907 Waldoff was brought to the attention of Schneider-Duncker, who was searching for new performers after Nelson and several others had left the Roland von Berlin. Though somewhat skeptical of her potential, Schneider-Duncker was willing to give her a chance. Her debut at the cabaret, toward the end of 1907, was a tremendous success, in particular her rendition of the new "Song of the Marsh-Reed" (Schmackeduzchen-Lied). Walter Kollo, who replaced Nelson as in-house composer, and Hermann Frey, the author of numerous popular lyrics in Berlin dialect, teamed up to write this self-consciously silly ditty about a drake and a tufted marsh-reed. The audience was surprised and delighted by the totally novel manner of Waldoff's performance. Unlike cabaret's other chanteuses and soubrettes, she was anything but *mondän:* her short, stocky build, bushy red hair, and simple dress were in marked contrast to the corseted figures, stylish coiffures, and haute couture sported by the other cabaret divas. While these women utilized a conventional repertory of hand, arm, and body gestures while singing, Waldoff stood absolutely still; at most she would move her head, roll her eyes, and use her rather harsh, guttural voice for expressive purposes. Only between the stanzas of the marsh-reed song did she perform a little dance, in which she waddled in a circle like a duck.

This number struck a totally new note for an upper-class cabaret. Its content and manner of presentation might even have seemed a parody, a total inversion of the conventional style of cabaret performance. Yet it was firmly rooted in the Berliner's traditional mode of joke-telling. A commentator on the city's manners wrote in 1892: "No gestures, no wry faces, no smirks: the Berliner is dry and cold-blooded when he jokes. He displays an intentionally deadpan countenance, which stands in such contrast to his words that it never fails to provoke laughter." Otto Reutter, the tremendously popular satiric singer and comedian at the Wintergarten, stood absolutely still while performing. Waldoff did the same. A reviewer for *Der Sturm* noted in 1911: "This little girl stands on stage with the correct manner of a pure German maiden, motionless, arms hanging down, hands modestly folded, with an incredibly harmless expression; only the eyes occasionally roll to their corners in horror, as she bawls ribald, sexually observant songs in a Berlin dialect. The whole expression, the fashioning of the Berliner's erotic character, lies completely in the intonation." Two years later Kurt Tucholsky took note of Waldoff's "impossible and inimitable technique," and claimed that the unexpected modulations of her voice left him disconcerted and speechless.[29]

The reviewer for *Der Sturm* correctly emphasized the sexuality of Waldoff's songs. Here too, in this most prevalent of themes, she struck new notes for the cabaret. Other chanteuses employed double-entendres and similar indirect means of expression to evoke amorous affairs, in which the men were invariably wealthy bons vivants, while the women ranged across all strata of society, from the seemingly proper upper-class wife to the loose shopgirl. Waldoff, in contrast, employed straightforward expressions to describe relations exclusively among the lower classes. She would employ a thick Berlin dialect, and take on the role of either the "boy" or the "girl" (it was well-known that she was a lesbian in private life). In her most famous song, "Hermann heesst er!" (He's Called Hermann, 1913), she sang of her love for a man who was unambiguously physical: "I've known he-men before, / But no one ever reached his goal / As fast as he." The song was a hymn of praise for his ability to neck *(knutschen)*, squeeze, and kiss her, and to leave her with a wrinkled blouse and a crushed skirt. Describing his moves on the dance floor, she crooned: "sometimes he nudges me with his knee" (mit de Knie manchmal stösst er). "Stossen" (to nudge, knock, poke) was also a colloquial word for sexual intercourse, and Waldoff highlighted it by employing a ritardando and drawing out the vowel—*stöööööst*. Nothing was left to the imagination. There were times, of course, when the directness of Waldoff's songs provoked cuts by the police. Yet Tucholsky noted that, even here, she succeeded in subverting the censor: in place of the excised lines, she would sing some nonsense sounds, and her intonation would give the audience a clear idea of what was omitted.[30]

Waldoff rapidly gained tremendous popularity. After several months at the Roland von Berlin, she was lured away by a lucrative offer from Nelson. In the years before the outbreak of war, she appeared nightly at the Chat noir as well as other, less expensive venues. By limiting her performances to three songs, with no encores, she could easily appear on two or more different stages in an evening. This gave her great public exposure among various social classes, and allowed her rapidly to become an icon of Berlin. Describing her employment of the local dialect and mannerisms, she noted: "I began to become *the* Berliner, a prototype of the Berliner, a representative of modern Berlin." By the 1920s Tucholsky was equating her with the statue of Berolina on the Alexanderplatz.[31]

Waldoff provided an up-to-date image of the Berliner with which people from all classes could identify. For most of the nineteenth century the stage persona of the Berliner was self-confident and antiauthoritarian, yet it was embodied in figures representing preindustrial occupations, such as fishwives, street hawkers, and apprentices. The popular musical farces which were populated by such characters died out in the 1870s, since those figures no longer corresponded to the reality of industrial Berlin. Waldoff's achievement was to modernize the stage persona of the Berliner, to bring it up to date. Although she rarely penned her own lyrics or music, she worked closely with writers and composers to fashion a specific image. Like the earlier figures, her character was spunky, pushy, and quite definitely unrefined. Yet now it was firmly rooted in modernity, since she touted the opportunities that the metropolis offered even to its poorer citizens. She rarely mentioned the harsh working and grim housing conditions of Berlin's proletariat. Instead, she portrayed what purported to be the leisure-time activities of the lower-middle and working classes. In her songs, the metropolis in all its modernity was there to be enjoyed by one and all: its sexual freedom, its new recreations (such as bicycling), and the novel mass-cultural entertainments (cinema or the Lunapark, a vast amusement park that opened in 1910). Even an expedition into the countryside had a metropolitan flavor: one rode the crowded suburban train and reached fields and forests littered with paper left by picnickers (see "'ne dufte Stadt ist mein Berlin!" and "Wenn der Bräutigam mit der Braut," both prewar songs). Alternatively, "nature" might be represented by an allotment garden on the edge of the city ("Die Laubenkolonie").

Such touches gave a distinctly contemporary and urban note to Waldoff's performances. Up to the end of the Weimar era she would continually update her themes and her repertory, to keep abreast of the latest popular practices and entertainments. Although she invariably portrayed lower-class characters, she appealed to all social strata. Over time she came to perform in mass-cultural vaudevilles and revues as well as the most expensive cabarets. She probably can be accused of trivializing social issues before middle-class audiences, since she gave the impression that after hours, life was a ball for the lower classes. Her major function, though, was to establish a sense of community among Berliners of all social levels, to foster pride in their city and its modernity, and to sustain an image of assertiveness and self-confidence which all citizens could emulate.

### Fashioning Berlin: The Metropol Revues

While Waldoff was recreating and updating the persona of the Berliner, the multifaceted life of the city was reflected in the ten revues presented annually at the Metropol-Theater from 1903 until 1913. By the turn of the century there were clear indications that a parodistic treatment of Berlin themes would score a great public success. The *Vossische Zeitung* chastised Sound and Smoke for limiting its satire to the world of the stage, instead of taking on the city at large: "a parody theater could perhaps provide a permanent home for the self-irony of a giant city . . . But of course the irony would have to reflect the large corpus of the city, of this fascinating, vitally pulsating center." Reinhardt did not take up that challenge, but others were in the process of doing so. Although the old tradition of popular musical farces had died in the 1870s, the turn of the century saw the emergence of Berlin operetta. This new genre was quite literally an offspring of the variety show. The first Berlin operettas, composed by Paul Lincke (1866–1946), were one-act works that provided part of an evening's entertainment at the Apollotheater, a vaudeville hall. His first hit was *Frau Luna,* which premiered on May 1, 1899. The audience was attracted not only by the liveliness of Lincke's music but also by the humor of the plot. The script, written by Heinrich Bolten-Baeckers, called for a group of Berliners to fly to the moon. This not only allowed a revival of some of the Berlin character-types that had died along with the musical farces, but it also gave the set designers opportunities to create eye-catching decors. Moreover, the work adopted vaudeville's propensity to feature production numbers with women in tights and outlandish costumes. The success of this combination induced Lincke to compose a string of popular works (most notably *Berliner Luft,* 1904). Other composers and scriptwriters followed suit, as they cranked out a number of spectacular, evening-length "production-number operettas" *(Ausstattungsoperetten).*[32]

Although these operettas included Berlin characters and themes, the city itself did not become a central focus of shows until the Metropol-Theater began staging its annual revues on January 6, 1903, with the premiere of *"Get the Latest!! The Very Latest!!!"* ("Neuestes!! Allerneuestes!!!"). The theater building where these productions took place had been opened in 1892 (and is now the Komische Oper). It originally bore the misleading name "Theater Unter den Linden," since it was actually located on Behrenstrasse, in the central entertainment district. After going bankrupt under its first manager, it was taken over in 1898 by Richard Schultz (1863–1928). Originally an actor with the prestigious and innovative Meiningen court theater, Schultz had organized touring companies and managed Berlin's Central-Theater before acquiring the new venture. He immediately renamed it, significantly, the Metropol-Theater, and he began to search for a style of popular metropolitan entertainment. He had the good fortune to engage a talented composer and a witty librettist. Viktor Hollaender (1866–1940) grew up in Berlin, but went abroad in the 1890s to work as a conductor (and occasionally composer) in musical theaters in Milwaukee, Chicago, and London. In 1901 he returned to his home city, where Schultz hired him as the Metropol's resident conductor and composer. Hollaender also wrote cabaret songs on occasion. One of his works, the music to Bierbaum's "Roses," was performed at the opening night of Wolzogen's Motley Theater. Julius Freund (1862–1914), who scripted all of the Metropol revues, had abandoned his acting career at the prestigious Vienna Burgtheater in order to write comic verse. Throughout the 1890s he penned lyrics for performers and shows at various variety stages and musical theaters in Berlin, including Schultz's Central-Theater.[33]

After producing a number of relatively successful musicals in which dance numbers featuring women in tights played a prominent role, Schultz finally scored a tremendous hit with *Get the Latest,* composed by Hollaender and scripted by Freund. Annually updated "revues" of the year's events had been seen on Parisian stages Like the Folies Bergère. Schultz was encouraged to import the genre by the relative success of cabarets in Berlin after the turn of the century. From them, the Metropol revues adopted the parody of current fads and fashions (and occasionally politics); from the new operettas, they took the Berlin characters, the dressed-down women, the production numbers, and the spectacular stage effects. When they focused these elements on Berlin itself, it proved to be a winning combination.

The impact of cabaret could be seen from the very beginning of *Get the Latest,* because the loose plot centered around a visit to Berlin by Serenissimus, of Sound and Smoke fame. By giving the petty potentate a tour of Berlin, the revue could underscore the city's modernity; it sought to project an image of a city constantly on the move, perpetually changing its visage. It presented the newest sights, such as the Wertheim department store, the elevated train, and the Siegesallee. The revue further celebrated the latest inventions that touched everyday life, such as the coin-operated vending machine or the Kodak hand-held camera. The latter gave rise to a burgeoning breed of photojournalists, who sought to capture the sights and faces of the city for the illustrated newspapers (fig. 14). The Metropol mocked reporters and news photographers for their pushiness and indiscretion, but emulated them as well. As its title suggested, *Get the Latest* considered itself an up-to-the-minute chronicle of metropolitan life, a sort of *Berliner Illustrirte Zeitung* brought to life on stage. Moreover, by focusing on the capital's new embellishments, it touted Berlin as a city of which one could be proud, a true *Weltstadt* on par with the best. The "Linden Song" (Lindenlied) pointedly contended that Unter den Linden could hold its own with the Parisian boulevards and Vienna's Ringstrasse.[34]

Berlin's modernity was the major new theme introduced by the Metropol

14. *Get the Latest!!* The "Kodak-Song" is performed by women posing as photojournalists and reporters.

to the city's theatergoers. Other aspects of the revue had been seen elsewhere in other forms. The fourth act was cribbed in spirit from Sound and Smoke and the Bad Boys, inasmuch as it consisted of parodies of recent plays by Maeterlinck, Wedekind, Hauptmann, and Sudermann. It also included a short scene with an actor imitating Wolzogen, introduced as the director of the "Vorüberbrettl," who proceeded to blame the press for his misfortunes. One element of theater that was not parodied, however, was the production number, which Schultz had mounted so successfully in the past. The revue was replete with women in tights and outlandish costumes who posed and danced on all conceivable occasions. They marched as well, since the Metropol introduced groups of women in military uniforms, an image that was to persist on revue stages until 1940. The final act of the evening was one big production number entitled "Wine, Women, and Song."

If theatrical parodies and production numbers had been seen before on Berlin stages, reviewers were pleasantly surprised by the degree to which the Metropol employed political satire. Part of the third act was set at the Reichstag, where tariff measures were being fought out. Some rather lame jokes were made about actors representing politicians of all stripes, from the Social Democrats (Bebel, Singer) and the Progressives (Richter) to the Center (Gröber) and the Free Conservatives (Kardorff). Suddenly, however, the spirits of Bismarck and Windthorst, his Centrist opponent, rose up from their graves and admonished the representatives for the current pettiness and mediocrity of parliamentary debate. The most pointedly political scene came toward the end of that act, with the appearance of the leaders of the defeated Boers (Botha, Dewet, and Delarey). In what counted back then as a tear-jerker, they sang about British atrocities and deplored the fact that the Kaiser had spurned them. They concluded by appealing to the audience, that is, to the German people. In the ensuing act, which consisted of theatrical parodies, a policeman kept interrupting the action to censor dubious lines.

Such scenes evoked praise from the critics. The *Vossische Zeitung* surmised that "the satire went as far as the higher authorities allowed." The reviewer at the *Berliner Tageblatt* contended that "a fresh wind, with an impudence hitherto unseen in Berlin, dares to touch excellencies and other high persons over whom the censor used to hold his protecting pen. A little more sharpness, a little more grace, a little more understanding for the freedom of humor on the part of the authorities—and we will be on the road to political satire, which has long sought to find a place on stage, to no avail." Over time that reviewer must have been disappointed, because the Metropol never exceeded the limits defined by its first revue. Its politics were clearly middle-of-the-road, perhaps National Liberal. The revue made fun of the Reichstag, but it was careful to spread its weak jokes among members of several different parties. The Boer number certainly criticized the Kaiser, but would hardly have been considered radical; their cause was popular among Germany's liberals, who believed the English had perpetrated unjustifiably brutal atrocities in that war. Moreover, to underscore its basically nationalist orientation, the "political" third act of the revue concluded with a military production number, complete with waving flags and marching soldiers, who sang of their willingness "to die gladly in the hour of danger" to defend their banners.[35]

*Get the Latest* was, in short, a genuine "revue," with something for everyone: up-beat images of Berlin, theatrical parody, political satire balanced by blatant chauvinism, and (in the words of the *Berliner Tageblatt*) "colorful ballet-girls displaying waists of every size." Having been rewarded with frequent applause and rave reviews, it was performed over three hundred times, an exceptionally long run for a show at that time. The nine ensuing revues were equally successful. Schultz never failed to provide lavish production numbers, and every season Freund scripted his witty texts. As for music, though Schultz continued to draw mainly on the services of Viktor Hollaender, he also turned to Paul Lincke for two revues (*Donnerwetter—tadellos!*, 1908; *Halloh! Die grosse Revue!*, 1909), and to Rudolf Nelson for the last one (*Chauffeur—in's Metropol!!*, 1912). With such consistent high quality, the Metropol became a major tourist attraction, and opening night became de rigueur for Berlin's high society. The title of the 1907 revue proclaimed smugly: *You Gotta See It!* (*Das muss man seh'n!*).

Much of the attraction of the revues could be attributed to their up-beat image of Berlin. To be sure, there were occasional songs or dances portraying Biedermeier idylls, suggesting that life was perhaps more *gemütlich* before the Empire. In Wolzogen's Motley Theater, the Biedermeier "Merry Husband" clearly had a nostalgic message. That might have been true of similar numbers in the Metropol, were it not for the fact that images of the "good old days" were juxtaposed with equally positive scenes of present-day Berlin. Depictions of the past served to accentuate the modernity of the present. The majority of the Metropol's numbers welcomed with open arms the city's immensity, its hectic tempo, its commercialism and consumerism. Responding to the great number of tourists in the audience, the Metropol stressed Berlin's importance as a capital of entertainment. The Lunapark, cinemas, and the newly opened beach facilities on the Wannsee were all advertised on stage, as were the growing number of spectator sports, such as boxing and the six-day bicycle race.

The Metropol revues touted Berlin's nightlife in particular. Those "bigots" (*Mucker*) who attempted to curtail late-night entertainments were taken to task in *You Gotta See It*. Even by making good-natured fun of "high cultural" performances, such as Reinhardt's production of Wedekind's *Spring Awakening*, the revues could advertise, in a backhanded way, Berlin's up-to-date repertories. Indeed, the Metropol claimed that the city's nightlife placed it ahead of other capitals. It was better to live in Berlin than in Vienna or, heaven forbid, London: "As soon as day has turned to night, / all of London's shut up tight!" (Doch in London bei der Nacht / Wird die Grossstadt zugemacht; *Hurra! Wir leben noch!*, 1910). That was, of course, also an implicit warning to the authorities against imposing an early closing hour on Berlin. According to the Metropol revues, only Paris could compete with Berlin as a true metropolis.

In the face of a large body of literature (and not merely "provincial" literature) condemning the "German Chicago," the Metropol exhorted Berliners to be proud of their modernity, and tourists were told that they should marvel at and enjoy the novelties of the capital. They were treated to an image of the metropolis that was lively, lavish, liberally open-minded, self-assured, *mondän*. If certain aspects seemed crass or excessive, that was because Berlin was still very new to its role. "Metropolinchen" sang in *You Gotta See It*: "I have the foibles of my youth, / I'm still a young metropolis!" This was an image that municipal and Imperial officials were delighted to have projected. Julius Freund maintained extremely friendly personal relations with Glasenapp, the head of the theater censorship department. When Traugott von Jagow was named Berlin's chief of police in 1909, he summoned Freund into his office to tell him: "I have asked you to see me so that you can hear from my own mouth: With me you can do whatever you like."[36] This statement suggests not only that the police were willing to give the Metropol freer rein than other theaters and cabarets but also that social prestige was attached to being portrayed, even if satirically, in the immensely popular revues.

Although the shows continued to include references to political affairs, the authorities did not have to worry, since the Metropol maintained its generally nonpartisan, nationalistic stance. In 1907 a number showed representatives of all factions in the Reichtag, which had been dissolved, bidding farewell to women who represented their respective parties, as well as their amours in the capital (fig. 15). Granted, some works seemed to criticize official culture. The Kaiser's aesthetic penchants, as manifested in the Siegesallee and other works, were parodied in a song entitled "Shut your Monumouths!" (Haltet euer Denkmäuler!; from *Das tolle Jahr*, 1904):

> Too many times we've had to see enshrined
> Musicians, poets, riffraff of that kind!
> No marble now for masters of the pen,
> It's all for gods and military men!
> For every statue there is now the norm:
> If not naked, then in uniform.
> But no civilians! Officers alone
> Shall have the honor to be hewn in stone!

> Uns machen zuviel Konkurrenz die Dichter,
> Die Musici und ähnliches Gelichter!
> Gestattet sei der Marmor drum nunmehr
> Nur noch für Götter oder Militär!
> Für jedes Bildwerk gelte streng die Norm:
> Entweder Nacktheit oder Uniform.
> Nur kein Civil! Es soll der Mensch allein
> Vom Leutnant aufwärts marmorfähig sein!

A similar satire on the social role of the military was to be found in what was perhaps the most famous song of the Metropol revues, "Donnerwetter—tadellos!" (from the revue of that name, 1908). "Goddam—perfect, not a flaw!" was known to be one of the Kaiser's favorite expressions. In the revue, a singer sporting a monocle and the uniform of the Imperial Guard expressed his disdain for civilians and boasted of his prowess as a gambler and a lover. The accounts of his escapades were punctuated by the refrain:

15. The Metropol's view of the dissolved Reichstag in 1907: the couples represent various political parties.

> Goddam, dammit, if we aren't the greatest guys!
> His Majesty can't help but say in awe:
> Goddam, ev'ry single one of you's a prize!
> Now really: goddam—perfect, not a flaw!
>
> Donnerwetter, Donnerwetter, wir sind Kerle!
> Bei Kritik sagt Majestät: Famos, famos!
> Donnerwetter, jeder einzelne 'ne Perle!
> Also wirklich: Donnerwetter, tadellos!

The Kaiser was so incensed at this number that he prohibited officers from attending the revue. That was an overreaction, however, because the song's potential bite was weakened by Paul Lincke's snappy music and the fetching performance of Joseph Giampietro, one of the best-loved stars of the Metropol. Ostensibly a caricature of aristocratic and military hauteur, the actual performance made the figure sympathetic, and constituted an indirect compliment to the "feudal" class portrayed.

As in the first revue, subsequent shows engaged in some rather blatant nationalism. In reference to the various diplomatic crises of those years, the Metropol invariably portrayed the French as revanchist, and the English as big-mouthed bullies who let other people do their fighting for them. The revues showed especially marked support for colonialism. In 1907, in the wake of a fiercely jingoistic parliamentary election focused on Germany's African presence, *You Gotta See It* opened with a scene of German troops in Southwest Africa. A soldier sang a tear-jerker, in which he pined for his "Annemarie" back home, while conceding the necessity of fighting "fierce battles" with the "black rabble" *(mit dem schwarzen Pack)*. Another figure then turned to the audience and asked whether one could possibly abandon these "pioneers of culture." "Annemarie" would be revived in future years, for it became one of the most popular troop songs in both world wars. The Nazis, however, claimed that it had been written by a common soldier in World War I, since they could not attribute it to its Jewish authors, Hollaender and Freund.[37]

For all the optimism, indeed braggadocio of these revues, it is hard to avoid detecting a defensive tone underneath. The French might have been revanchist and the British perfidious, but the revue's authors were clearly disturbed by the fact that, by 1912, Germany had no friends aside from Austria (see the "Zankensemble" in *Chaffeur—in's Metropol*). On another level, there was clearly some concern about the status of Berlin. It would hardly have been necessary to provide constant comparisons with Paris, London, and Vienna if the Metropol had been confident of Berlin's rank. The revue's excessive desire to impress and its underlying defensive tone corroborated a charge frequently made at the time: that Germany was an upstart Empire, with Berlin its parvenu capital. Many contemporaries took note of the difficulties faced by Berliners in dealing with their sudden power, wealth, and modernity. Arthur Eloesser, an essayist and outstanding observer of prewar Berlin, wrote in 1912: "What belongs to a metropolis? Anything amusing, surprising, exciting, sensational, intensified stimulation, temptation renewed daily." Yet in order to acquire its own, genuine character, a city required "a broad, powerful stratum, which takes things in slowly and suspiciously, which has the noble task of refusal and rejection." Eloesser claimed that Berlin had no such integrative caste; instead, the city's inhabitants blindly consumed whatever came their way. "The Berliner of today does not know where he belongs and where he does not belong; he is the most greedy metropolitan in the world, and he devours all tidbits without ever digesting them."[38]

Eloesser believed that Berliners were above all concerned with maintaining their metropolitan image, and hence turned to London and Paris for inspiration. "We take from both provisionally, but not always the things appropriate to making the new metropolitan person . . . We have a Moulin rouge [a Berlin dancehall] where a windmill never stood, and we imitate the cabarets of Montmartre, as if Kreuzberg [a working-class district of Berlin] had sprouted its own artistic bohemia to enliven our nights." For Berliners, the importation of cabaret and other metropolitan features was but a first step; more fundamentally, they desired to be better than their mentors, to surpass them with all possible speed. This mentality was simultaneously competitive, braggardly, and defensive: "the Berliner looks every tourist in the eye with avid inquisitiveness, to find out if he is impressed by the new city's tasteful expenditures, its most sumptuous hotels, and its best automobiles. And if his eyes still don't blank out from all of the wonders of technology, the bid is doubled. Is a corso missing, or a fabulous variety theater? It will be supplied immediately."[39] This could just as well have been a plausible account of the Metropol revues, which bombarded the audience with the latest sights and wonders of the city. The shows sought to dazzle the tourists, and to assure the Berliners that they did indeed reside at the hub of the world.

Eloesser deplored the fact that Berliners were more concerned with impressing others than fulfilling their own, more genuine needs. Another type of argument could be made, however, which contended that Berlin had found its authentic expression in the types of images presented in the revues. A major theme of the Metropol—perhaps the dominant one, in the final analysis—was fashion. The revues not only presented seasonal fads but also underscored the importance of fashion more generally. Granted, that concept was parodied on all conceivable occasions. *Goddam—perfect* began with a scene wherein Venus, representing authentic beauty, was supplanted by "Madame Chic." Nevertheless, the whole concept of the revue was based upon the notion that certain clothes, venues, shows, events, even appliances, were the talk of the town during a given season. The title of another show, *You Gotta See It,* referred not only to the revue itself but to the sights and trends that it depicted on stage. For all its mockery of such fads, the Metropol implied that the totality of those fashions constituted the image, and perhaps the reality, of Berlin.

This belief was not limited to revues. Many contemporary observers argued that Berlin, as a constantly changing city that balked at traditions, found evanescent structures of cohesion in its passing fashions. Metropolis implied movement, and that motion was given form by fashion. Whereas Eloesser deplored the lack of a long-standing discretionary caste, others argued that its function had been taken over by short-term tastemakers. Georg Simmel contended that fashion performed the dual function of unification and segregation. In situations where the upper class was porous (as among Berlin's parvenus), fashion coalesced its adherents into an elite of connoisseurs, at the same time that it excluded those who lacked the taste, or more often the money, to adopt the latest styles or to attend the "must-see" events. Simmel contended further that the "field of fashion" consisted of "externals—clothing, social conduct, amusements," that is, the same themes depicted on the Metropol's stage. Fashion was embodied in such "externals" because they could be modified easily and rapidly. This was necessary in order for the "fashionable" caste to stay ahead of those subelite classes which sought to imitate their betters: "Just as soon as the lower classes begin to copy their style, thereby crossing the line of demarcation the upper classes have drawn and destroying the uniformity of their coherence, the upper classes turn away from this style and adopt a new one, which in turn differentiates them from the masses; and thus the game goes merrily on."[40]

From this perspective, it appears that the Metropol revues were channelers of fashion. They could not claim to be its arbiters, inasmuch as a show would depict events and styles that had appeared over the previous season. Indeed, inasmuch as a revue would promote yesteryear's fashions before a wider public—many of whom were middle-class Berliners, or tourists and other "provincials"—it contributed to the trickle-down "game" that forced the "fashionable" classes to innovate in order to stay ahead of the rest. While the Metropol did not create specific fashions, it did promote the importance of fashion in a general sense. By bolstering the belief that it was socially important to stay "in style," the Metropol reflected as well as shaped its audience. One reviewer noted that "the parquet, the loges, and the galleries of the Metropoltheater" displayed "the piquant, original, metropolitan social portrait, which Julius Freund and Richard Schultz have created anew for Berlin."[41]

The promotion of fashion was not simply a means of touting Berlin's metropolitan qualifications; it also mirrored the city's economic core. For the new metropolis, being fashionable was good, but becoming wealthy from fashion was better. Much of its prosperity was based upon services and industries which depended on changing styles. In turn-of-the-century Berlin, garment-working was the largest occupational sector after the civil service. Much of the retail trade, and especially the department stores, were geared to selling clothing and other fashionable commodities. Thus the Metropol did its best to promote the latest trends in outer- and underwear (fig. 16). A song like "What the Fashionable Lady Needs" (Was die Modedame braucht; from *Halloh! Die grosse Revue!*), was not just a tentative strip-tease number, which showed the type of shoes, stockings, garters, chemises, and corsets that "a woman of the world" and "a woman of today" was expected to have. It also promoted the types of commodities that were manufactured and retailed in Berlin.

The refrain of that song contained the old saying, "Clothes make the person" (Kleider machen Leute). But there were people who made the clothes, and they remained in the shadows. Berlin harbored a large and discontented working class, which produced the commodities that fueled the economy. Needless to say, the proletariat never sat in the auditorium

16. Touting fashionable undergarments at the Metropol (1909).

of the Metropol, but representations of it did occasionally appear on stage. Some three-quarters of Berlin's garmentworkers were women, who were engaged in piecework at home for appallingly low wages. This point was made straightforwardly in the "Song of the Home-Laborer" (Lied der Heimarbeiterin, in *Die Nacht von Berlin*, 1911), where a woman toiled through the night for a paltry 50 pfennings. That was, however, only one in a series of images of "Berlin at night," the remainder of which consisted of vignettes of amorous encounters or amusements. The glimmer of social conscience was quickly swallowed up by other, more entertaining images; in fact, it was followed by a "Song of the Old Roué." An even more egregious juxtaposition appeared in *The Devil Laughs* (*Der Teufel lacht dazu*, 1906), which included "a supposedly serious song about the sufferings of home-laborers, during which six silk-clad legs, which peek enticingly out of a box, beat the measure."[42] Perhaps that image was supposed to make a connection between the purchase of silk stockings and the exploitation of labor, but other ideas certainly entered the minds of the gentlemen in the audience.

The most hypocritical number at the Metropol was arguably the "Prostitute's Song" (Dirnenlied) in *Halloh! Die grosse Revue.* One could scarcely argue with the song's message, dealing with the sad lot of prostitutes. It was, however, disingenuous to present such a theme at the Metropol, which was itself a sponsor of prostitution. Like its prototype, the Folies Bergère, the Metropol admitted prostitutes to the theater, for 1 mark, one hour after the performance started. As in Paris, they would promenade in the lobbies and wait for clients to approach them.[43]

Such duplicities were perhaps just one more example of the jumbled juxtaposition of values that marked the Metropol's shows, which catered to as many attitudes and tastes as commercially possible. The revues consciously incorporated and capitalized on many images that were generated by Berlin's cabarets. The theme of upper-class flirtation had been prominent in Wolzogen's Motley Theater and could be seen in Nelson's contemporaneous ventures. Reinhardt's parodies of artistic trends and fads also had their place on the Metropol stage. Above all, the theme of Berlin and the Berliners contributed to the popularity of the revues. That subject, which had been regenerated in a vaudeville context by Lincke's short operettas, soon would account for Waldoff's spectacular success. The singer's up-beat depiction of lower-class loves and leisure-time activities complemented rather than challenged the Metropol's presentation of upper-class diversions.

In the final analysis, the Metropol's success was based upon the fact that it embodied the fundamental formal principle of the metropolitan psyche: "Variété." The display of diverse commodities in department stores and the juxtaposition of numbers in vaudeville were combined triumphantly in the revue. In fact, the last of the Metropol's prewar shows included a scene that presented Berlin as one big department store—for material goods, as well as for culture and politics:

> Customer:  Politics!
> Employee:  To the right, please!
> Customer:  Municipal affairs!
> Employee:  To the left, please!
> Customer:  Something dramatic!
> Employee:  Right here, please!
> Customer:  Something literary!
> Employee:  Over there, please!
> Customer:  Fashion and sports!
> Employee:  Proceed to the first floor, please.
> Customer:  Courtroom!
> Employee:  Second floor.
> Customer:  City gossip!
> Employee:  Third floor.

This exchange was followed by a chorus asserting that the revue itself was a department store that collected and displayed the year's fashions and events. The equation of modern Berlin with the form of both the *Warenhaus* and the revue was thus made explicit. The Metropol inadvertently corroborated Simmel's assertion that numerous variegated objects, attractively packaged and put on display, constituted the entertainment most appropriate to the modern urbanite. The Metropol both reflected and fashioned the image of what it dubbed the *Warenhaus Gross-Berlin*.[44]

# CHAPTER FIVE

# Political Satire
# in the Early
# Weimar Republic

The outbreak of war in August 1914 marked a caesura in the development of German cabaret. Satire and parody were discouraged as censorship came under the control of military authorities and the country's political tone turned virulently nationalistic. In December 1921 Max Herrmann-Neisse, the outstanding cabaret critic of the Weimar Republic, noted in reference to the war years: "Cut off from contact with European neighbors, German cabaret sank to the lowest capabilities of the genre. Incompetence justified itself by means of inflammatory orgies of patriotism, and the conferencier garnered cheap applause with German nationalist editorials." He concluded: "German cabaret today still has trouble recovering from this ugly state."[1] Much popular entertainment in the Weimar era was marked by the aggressive nationalism that commenced in 1914. Within that context, writers and performers who espoused liberal and democratic values had great difficulty finding a proper voice and an appreciative public. That was evident in the works of Kurt Tucholsky and Walter Mehring, who provided politically ambiguous lyrics for the major cabarets of the early Weimar Republic: Max Reinhardt's revived Sound and Smoke, Rudolf Nelson's Theater am Kurfürstendamm, and the Wild Stage of Trude Hesterberg.

## Nationalism in Wartime and Postwar Entertainment

During the first weeks of hostilities most theaters in Berlin closed, out of respect for the gravity of the situation. It was assumed that Paris would be captured and the war terminated within a couple of months. When the German advance ground to a halt, however, the theaters, cinemas, variety shows, revues, and cabarets reopened. It had become obvious that those performers who had not volunteered or been drafted needed their former venues of employment. More important, the authorities realized that during prolonged hostilities, diversions for the civilian population would be necessary.

Previously many writers had contended that the stress of big-city life created the desire for diverse and light-hearted entertainments. Now it was argued that the emotional dislocations of war required a continuation of such amusements. In November 1914 the author of an article in the *Berliner Börsen-Courier* on "The Wintergarten in the War" contended: "Variety-show treats in wartime are perhaps not to every person's taste. God knows, there is so much preaching about the seriousness of our times, that the carefree singsong of the dance troupes and the dizzying agility of the acrobats do not seem to fit in. On the other hand: many people believe that occasional diversion is needed precisely for nerves that have been stretched to their limits, that are hounded from one excitement to another." In November 1915 another observer explained the popularity of wartime cabaret: "In this time of buffeting events, restless expectation, and continual impatience, people do not like to tie themselves down to the fixed time and place of a dramatic performance . . . Particularly in the cabarets of western Berlin, the consummate informality of the performances corresponds to the public's disposition, which at present is not always inclined toward long-winded entertainments."[2]

The same observer noted further that cabarets were easily able to keep up-to-date with the latest wartime events. Variety shows, revues, and cabarets did indeed reflect on Germany's situation. Of course, as in all belligerent countries, the tone was one-sidedly nationalistic. A favored number on all stages was Ernst Lissauer's "Song of Hate against England" (Hassgesang gegen England): "We love as one, we hate as one, / We have one enemy alone: / England!" (Wir lieben vereint, wir hassen vereint, / Wir haben alle nur einen Feind: / England!). Ferdinand Bonn, an acclaimed dramatic actor in Berlin, recited those verses "with many theatrical gestures and articulations" at the Wintergarten in December 1914.[3] But despite Lissauer's invective, England was not Germany's only enemy. Those aspects of German entertainment that once had sought to evoke Parisian suavity were quickly teutonified. The Chat noir cabaret was rebaptized as the Schwarzer Kater, and a new term, "Ansager," was created for the person who had previously called himself a "Conférencier." Needless to say, the international star-circuit had collapsed with the outbreak of hostilities, and no French, English, Russian, or other enemy performers could appear on Berlin's variety show or cabaret stages. That fact, along with military conscription, contributed to a rapid fall in the quality of performances.

The older style of revue, which made light of political, social, and commercial fashions, was no longer tenable. The director of the Metropol-Theater in the 1920s wrote retrospectively: "The war brought about an upheaval. We were forced to discontinue revues that were based effectively on politics and local events . . . and turn to operetta."[4] Many of the operettas performed during the war were pure entertainment and diversion, with no contemporary allusions. There were, however, a number of very topical musicals. In the first winter of the war, the Metropol performed *Where Our Thoughts Are: Scenes from a Great Age (Woran wir denken: Bilder aus grosser Zeit)*, whose cast included Claire Waldoff. The music was written by a popular Berlin operetta composer who had previously called himself Jean Gilbert; now that gallicisms were unpopular, he resumed his real name, Max Winterfeld. Walter Kollo, who had composed many of Waldoff's songs, was an even more prolific contributor to the musical war effort. In the fall of 1914 he churned out two musicals, *Get the Extra! Humorous Scenes in Serious Times* and *Keep Hittin' 'Em! (Extrablätter: Heitere Bilder aus Ernster Zeit* and *Immer feste druff!)*. A cowriter of the former script was Rudolf Bernauer, previously of the Bad Boys; the latter libretto was written by Willi Wolff, author of "The Shopgirl," which had entertained the Kaiser six years earlier. Nelson composed two musicals that fall: *The Kaiser Called* and *At the Outskirts of Paris (Der Kaiser rief* and *Krümel vor Paris)*. His major contribution to the wartime stage came in 1916, when *Boys in Blue (Blaue Jungens)* glorified Germany's naval and submarine prowess.

Some of the topical shows were scripted by Otto Reutter, one of Berlin's most popular humorists, who regularly recited satirical verses at the Wintergarten. After the outbreak of hostilities he took a lease on the Palast-Theater and produced wartime musicals such as *1914, Berlin in the War* and *Don't Dare Go to Berlin (Berlin im Krieg* and *Geh'n Sie bloss nicht nach Berlin)*. Reutter attempted to put humor at the service of the war effort. In *Berlin in the War* the chorus intoned: "Laughter too is a civilian service obligation" (Auch lachen ist Zivildienstpflicht). His musicals, like those of the other writers and composers, continually assured their audiences that Germany would win the war. Reutter underscored the positive aspects of the conflict, in particular the fact that it united all Germans: conservative burgher and socialist worker, Prussian and Bavarian, were depicted fighting side by side in the trenches. Simultaneously, many didactic messages were aimed at the home front, that is, the actual audience. It was continually exhorted to subscribe to war loans, to contribute time and possessions to the war effort, and to follow the regulations on rationing. Even food and fuel shortages initially were treated in a joking, light-hearted manner, until conditions worsened with the passing years. Despite the generally upbeat tone, certain topics clearly were off limits to humor. Already in *1914,* Reutter included a song which contended that it was no longer appropriate to caricature Prussian officers on the level of "Goddam—perfect," now that those men were dying on the battlefields.[5]

Musicals being what they are, the shows included heavy doses of romantic sentimentality. The young women invariably married soldiers and spurned suitors, however rich, who remained civilians. Some of the musicals written in the first months of the war even suggested romantic attachments at the front. In Kollo's *Get the Extra,* a German soldier sang to "Ninette," the "pearl of the Ardennes":

> Mad'moiselle! Oh, mad'moiselle!
> I'll annex you, if you please.
> We're in Belgium, after all,
> Where such things are done with ease.

> Mamsellchen! Ach, Mamsellchen!
> Komm lass dich annektier'n.
> Wir sind ja doch in Belgien,
> Da kann so was passier'n.[6]

Such scenes soon disappeared from the stage, not on account of their incredible tastelessness, but because it was feared that the image of soldiers engaging in frontline flings might demoralize wives and fiancées at home. Fidelity became a major motif in the later wartime musicals, as faithfulness to one's spouse and to one's nation became intertwined themes.

Understandably, entertainers had to strain ever harder to make the best of an increasingly bad situation. At a time when textiles were rationed and the government tried to encourage the purchase of paper clothing, one number featured a woman in a chic cellulose dress who sang: "Miss Fashion now wears a completely different dress, / Miss Fashion accommodates herself to the seriousness of the times. / And the gentlemen murmur with enthusiasm: / That paper dress, oh no, how modern it is" (fig. 17). The prewar linkage of flirtation, fashion, and Berlin's modernity was thus alive and well on stage, although one doubts that many in the audience were convinced. An especially poignant, or perhaps horrific, employment of popular entertainment for the war effort was embodied in Carl Hermann Unthan. Born without arms, Unthan became known in the prewar years for vaudeville appearances in which he played the violin and demonstrated other skills with his feet. In May 1915 the illustrated insert of the *Berliner Tageblatt* reported that he had offered his services to the German army to assist soldiers who lost their arms in the war. He was supposed to show them "not only how one can perfectly substitute use of one's feet for one's hands, he will also give them back their self-confidence and prove to them that they will not be dependent upon the support of their fellow citizens." The article was accompanied by pictures of Unthan lighting a cigarette, playing the violin, shaving, typing, tying a necktie, and playing cards—all by means of his dextrous feet.[7]

Like musical theaters and variety shows, wartime cabarets faced major obstacles. They had to struggle with tightened censorship, the limitations

Die ist richtig...!
(National-Theater, Berlin.)

Frau Mode trägt jetzt ein ganz
anderes Kleid.
Frau Mode paßt an sich
dem Ernste der Zeit.
Und es murmeln
begeistert die Herren,
Solch' ein Papierkleid.
Nein, wie modern.

Anni Wenkhaus

17. "Miss Fashion" promotes "modern" paper clothing during the Great War.

on hiring imposed by military conscription, and an audience that dwindled with the mounting inflation. As usual, Rudolf Nelson ran the most successful ventures. Although he lost his lease for the Chat noir in 1914, he managed to run two other cabarets concurrently for the first two years of the war, despite the difficulties of the day. Police observers present in February and April 1915 repeatedly noted that attendance at Nelson's locales was "moderate" and the audience respectable; it consisted primarily of members of the middle classes as well as a small number of officers, NCOs, and enlisted personnel. There were also "better women of the demimonde, who, however, did not stand out especially."[8]

Like the musical stages, Nelson's Metropol-Cabaret and his Cabaret Sanssouci presented patriotic numbers. A police observer noted that Lissauer's "Song of Hate against England" was performed with "vehement passion" on January 13, 1915, and received much applause. A month later, a skit about the war of 1871 was greeted "with great enthusiasm," as was a song about the German Empress. Another type of patriotic number featured tableaux of actors made up to resemble great historic personages or current allies and war heroes. Frederick the Great, Blücher, and Bismarck reappeared from the past, while contemporaries included Field Marshal Hindenburg, Admiral Tirpitz, Zeppelin, Chancellor Bethmann Hollweg, King Ludwig III of Bavaria, Emperor Franz Joseph of Austria, and the Sultan of Turkey. The police noted that Hindenburg and Franz Joseph received especially hearty applause. However, they banned the representation of Frederick the Great and Bethmann Hollweg, since Prussia's wartime regulations prohibited the depiction of any member of the Hohenzollern family, dead or alive, as well as any of Prussia's governing politicians. Of course, there were other, permissible ways to pay homage to the Kaiser. At the Metropol-Cabaret in April 1915, Willy Prager even sang a new rendition of "The Shopgirl." In this patriotically updated and cleaned-up version, it was the Kaiser who appeared at the end of the refrain: "and then, and then came he" (und dann, und dann kam er).[9]

The nationalistic tone of Nelson's shows undoubtedly conformed to his own viewpoint, but even so the censors kept a close watch on his performers. In January 1915, according to a police observer, Claire Waldoff complained to the audience that many of the songs she had planned to present had been prohibited. She thus performed only one of her innocuous Berlin songs, as well as a patriotic "Soldiers' Song" (Soldatenlied), which she delivered "in her own pert manner, which the audience seemed to love and for which she received ample applause." Two months later Willy Prager complained to the audience about censorship. Still, some unauthorized material slipped by, and in April 1915 the police wrote Nelson protesting the delivery of unapproved songs and even lines that had been explicitly forbidden. He was warned that he would be subjected to "further stringent controls, and should any more irregularities be detected, you can reckon with the strictest measures and possibly the closing of the locale by the High Command for the duration of the war."[10]

Nelson not only was chastised by the police, he even irritated members of the audience on occasion. Although his public was generally appreciative, there were times when a spectator might take offense at certain numbers and notify the authorities. In January 1915 an anonymous letter, signed only by "a decent Jewish woman" (eine anständige Jüdin), complained about a performance in Nelson's Cabaret Sanssouci: "At a time when hundreds of Jewish soldiers are earning the Iron Cross, is it fitting that filthy Jewish tales [*jüdische Unflätigkeiten*] are told—unfortunately by a person who is himself Jewish? Words like *tineff* (translated: human feces), *chuzpe, ponim,* as well as repulsive Jewish jokes may well please the *well-dressed* Jewish Kurfürstendamm *plebians* [*Pöbel*], but are a severe insult for decent Jewish women, who have husbands on the field of battle."[11] The police ordered Nelson to have the performer cut these words, since they had not been approved by the censor; otherwise they did not seem perturbed by the incident. Indeed, most people would not have been disturbed by Yiddish words that were innocuous (such as chutzpah), or at worst somewhat vulgar (although the woman's translation of "tineff" was technically correct, the word was used freely in colloquial language to refer to shoddy goods or nonsensical remarks).

It is impossible to know who wrote the letter, but it does bring out some of the social tensions that had surfaced by the fifth month of the war, as well as problems of Jewish self-identity. Obviously the woman was concerned about maintaining an image of Jewishness that was patriotically German, morally decent, and financially modest. She protested the use of Yiddish expressions, which she clearly considered vulgar. Like many members of Berlin's long-standing Jewish community, she might have been expressing disdain for the *Ostjuden,* the more recent Jewish immigrants from eastern Europe. She also might have sought to oppose the use of a lower-class, non-"high"-German dialect, which typecast Jews as being not fully integrated into German culture and society. At the same time, she deplored the appearance of "well-dressed" Jews in the audience. It is possible that she had suffered a decline in her own fortunes since the outbreak of the war, and hence was expressing the irritation of a *déclassée.* But it is also conceivable that she was concerned by public displays of Jewish well-being, since charges of Jewish war profiteering were arising in anti-Semitic circles. In any case, the letter's author must have been unduly sensitive to this issue, since the police, who were also on the lookout for excessive ostentation, made no such observations. To them, the audience simply belonged to the *Mittelstand,* the not especially well-off middle classes.

Similar concerns about excessive wealth, as well as the threat of anti-Semitism, became apparent a year and a half later in a widely noted incident concerning Nelson's new venture, the Künstler-Spiele on the Kurfürstendamm. He inaugurated the cabaret on August 25, 1916, with a program entitled "When the Night Begins" (Wenn die Nacht beginnt). Soon after the opening a popular newspaper, *BZ am Mittag,* reported that the show had "twelve amusing scenes concerning a stroll on the Tauentzienstrasse, the rationing of fabrics, a butter line, and the shortage of automobiles," all set to music by Nelson. It noted that this took place in front of "overcrowded tables loaded with champagne." The article related further: "On the skillfully erected stage there are a number of lovely women in high spirits, who sing their songs and swing their legs." It said of one actress in particular: "The less she wears, the prettier she gets—and sometimes she is very pretty indeed!"[12]

This article alarmed the police, who sent observers to several perform-ances. All reports indicated that the show was perfectly decent, even with respect to the actresses and their costumes. The police concluded that the article was a publicity notice inserted by Nelson or one of his agents, in order to attract "well-heeled members of the fast set." Many newspapers regularly published such publicity statements, disguised as reviews, in exchange for a run of paid advertisements from theaters and cabarets. Most readers could easily distinguish them from genuine criticism, since their tone was thoroughly positive and laudatory. In this case, however, the ploy backfired on Nelson, since it provoked a storm of protest. The image of champagne-swigging bons vivants listening to jokes about food rationing and gawking at half-naked women infuriated many readers—es-pecially since the battle of the Somme was raging at that very time. Other newspapers reprinted the notice with scathing commentary, and soon the Berlin police were receiving complaints "almost daily from diverse sectors of the population (officers, Reichstag delegates, reservists, etc.)."[13]

Letters also arrived from the front lines. One, signed by several soldiers on the Western front, complained: "We come from the battlefield, where we experience nothing but sorrow, pain, and death, and in the big cities they party into the night . . . Our wives hardly know how to scrape by with their children, while the others dissipate their money with whores and champagne." A Bavarian soldier concluded that "that pack of sows deserves to be hanged, if they're that well off, those unpatriotic bastards." One complaint from the home front was more ominous. A Bavarian from Berchtesgaden, referring to the article, lambasted the extravagances of Jewish "war profiteers," while "German" women froze and starved and "German" men fought bloody battles. Those comments, which implied that Jews caroused while "Germans" suffered, were obviously the type of accusations feared by the German-Jewish woman who had complained to the police eighteen months earlier. Furthermore, the letter of the Bavarian anti-Semite concluded with comments that presaged the right-wing ideol-ogy of the Weimar Republic: he deplored "the revolutionary agitation among Jewish students," which aimed at "abolishing the Hohenzollern dynasty after the war and establishing a republic under Jewish leader-ship."[14]

The old dictum that the Muses remain silent during war certainly held true for cabaret, whose artistic quality was negligible for the duration of hostilities. Unfortunately, that condition did not generally improve after the signing of the armistice. The tenor of wartime entertainment cast a pall over popular amusements during the Weimar era. Many variety shows, musicals, and would-be cabarets of the early 1920s continued to propound the radical nationalism that had dominated the stage after 1914.

If anything, the tone was even more chauvinistic after the Empire's collapse. Several factors pushed many German citizens into a bitterly antirepublican, anti-internationalist stance. They believed the lie, consciously put forth by Erich Ludendorff and other generals, that their armies had not been defeated on the battlefield, but had been "stabbed in the back" on the home front by striking socialist workers and mutinous "red" sailors. The antileftist implications of this attitude were fortified by the uprisings during the winter and spring of 1918–19. Many citizens feared that Germany might share the fate of Lenin's Russia, where the Bolshevik Revolution had given way to a bloody civil war. Outrage at foreign powers was inflamed by the Treaty of Versailles, the agreement "dictated" by the victorious Allies, which forced Germany to accept full moral responsibility for the war and imposed an impossibly steep reparations bill. Whereas England was viewed as Germany's most perfidious enemy during the war, now France was deemed the major foe, especially after its occupation of the Ruhr valley in January 1923. By that time the hyperinflation had eradicated middle-class savings, a fact that cemented opposition to the new republican order.

It was not only the middle classes who were hurt. In March 1921 Erzherzog Leopold Ferdinand von Habsburg, whose fixed income had been wiped out by the Austrian inflation, found himself compelled to accept a role in a skit performed in a Berlin cabaret. A Habsburg archduke was, of course, an immensely greater catch than any of the turn-of-the-century *Brettl*-barons. Liberal newspapers gloated, conservatives were horrified, but after a mediocre attempt at acting, the aristocrat disappeared from the cabaret scene.[15]

While a genuine Habsburg was an anomalous attraction, standard fare on postwar popular stages consisted of reciting the litany of nationalist grievances. Writers and performers who tried to sustain prorepublican, antinationalist cabarets in the postwar era often complained about the attitudes of their conservative competitors, who attracted much larger audiences. That was due in part to the economics of the day. With mounting inflation, the only people who could afford more costly forms of live entertainment were those with fixed capital or the new class of "profiteers," who were unlikely to have liberal sympathies. Max Herrmann-Neisse wrote in December 1921: "The low standard of Berlin cabarets depends to no small degree on their milieu. Fleece-joints that require a minimum consumption of champagne have to respect the people who fill the cash register, and the worse the audience, the more ominous the program." He concluded four months later: "In accordance with the cash and class of their patrons, the cabarets are pleased to spread and solidify reactionary attitudes."[16]

Several writers and performers from Berlin's liberal cabarets wrote articles criticizing the "political humorists" who appeared at chauvinist cabarets and variety shows. A liberal entertainer who used the moniker "Dr. Allos" wrote: "What is important in these patriotic recitations is the fact that the word 'German' must appear twice in every line. One also must avoid mentioning unpleasant truths: everything must be rosy, especially the past and the future, and one may end with a powerful admonition to get back to work." Tucholsky noted that such "humorists" talked about the "good old days," when beer and breakfast rolls had been cheap, coal and ham plentiful, and taxes low or nonexistent. What he found ominous was the listing of complaints without clear analysis: "But *who* made the breakfast rolls so expensive, that is not said. *Who* drove the country into the war, *who* sustained the war for two years longer, when it could have been ended, *who* lived in daily luxury the whole time, when women and children suffered privations at home and stood in line: the humorist with his sweaty collar sings nothing about that."[17] The right-wing entertainers encouraged unfocused feelings of discontent that rebounded against the republican politicians in power, despite the fact that the forces of reaction ultimately had been responsible for Germany's misery.

Other observers claimed that rightist cabaret performances were not only bad politics, but also bad art. Fritz Grünbaum, a Viennese conferencier who appeared at many of Berlin's liberal cabarets in the 1920s, noted that an actor could garner thunderous applause by reciting denunciations of Germany's "enslavement" and curses at her enemies. Such applause, however, was directed "only at the tendency of his poem, but had absolutely nothing to do with the personality or accomplishment of the declaimer." Herrmann-Neisse concurred: "Whoever has no artistic ability can achieve a cheap triumph with hurrah-songs and black-white-red clichés" (a reference to the colors of the old Imperial flag, which had been superseded by the republican banner's black, red, and gold). He gave a concrete example: "At the moment Frederick the Great is fashionable on film and stage as the idol of nationalist, agitational propaganda: in the cabaret 'Potpourri' he is evoked not only in a feeble musical . . . but also in a bombastically declaimed horror-poem as an apparition threatening the non-German powers of the peace conference." Kurt Tucholsky even wrote a song that poked fun at the nostalgia for Frederick in cabarets and revues.[18] Needless to say, such parodies and criticisms did not put a halt to nationalist entertainment. The strictures of Tucholsky, Herrmann-Neisse, Grünbaum, and others merely underscored their realization that the market for entertainment was not well disposed to democratic ideas. That difficulty was brought home to them when they tried to voice their own political values in postwar cabarets.

## Limitations of Republican Satire: Kurt Tucholsky

Nationalist "political humorists" reacted to Germany's military defeat, the onerous demands of the Allies, and the social and economic disruptions following the collapse of the monarchy. By contrast, liberal and prorepublican cabaretists had a different set of concerns. Their discontent dated back to the war years, which had brought unprecedented and needless suffering. Nearly two million Germans had been killed and over four million wounded; one out of every eleven Germans was a casualty of the fighting. To be sure, an overwhelming number of citizens had supported the war at the outset, when it was believed that Russia had attacked first. Even the Social Democratic (SPD) delegation in the Reichstag, which in previous years had claimed that it would block hostilities with a general strike, voted for war credits. Yet as the conflict dragged on, casualties mounted and privations at the home front become increasingly harsh, owing to the Allied blockade. A growing number of citizens with leftist or liberal sympathies began to question the reasons for continuing the fighting. They were horrified by rightist calls for a "peace through victory" *(Siegfrieden)* and territorial expansion. This blatantly repudiated the war's initial justification as a defensive struggle, and obviously was an unattainable goal as well.

Discontent on the leftist end of the political spectrum crystallized in the pacifist Independant Social Democratic Party (USPD), which split off from the SPD in April 1917. An even more radical "Spartacus" faction formed around Karl Liebknecht and Rosa Luxemburg. The popularity of pacifist views was made manifest during the massive, albeit short-lived, strikes in January 1918, in which over a million workers took part. The military collapse that began at the front in August 1918 culminated in the strikes and naval mutinies that brought down the monarchy in early November. Public hostility toward officers and aristocrats was very high during the ensuing weeks, and workers' and soldiers' councils were formed in numerous cities. Nevertheless, by the spring of 1919 it was clear that many adherents of the old regime had managed to maintain their influence, to the detriment of the new republican order.

The persistence of the old elites was abetted, paradoxically, by the cautious policies of Germany's new socialist leaders. On November 9, the Kaiser's abdication and the proclamation of the republic were followed by the appointment of Friedrich Ebert, chairman of the SPD, as chancellor. A bureaucrat to the core, Ebert epitomized the revisionist and, in practice, antirevolutionary spirit of the SPD, which strove for a gradual democratization of German politics and a slow but steady growth of the trade union movement. He had hoped that a constitutional monarchy with a strong parliament would follow the end of war, and he was surprised by the proclamation of a republic. Moreover, he was horrified by the councils and the far-left parties, which demanded a thoroughgoing democratization of politics and socialization of major industries. He believed that too rapid social change would lead to chaos and civil strife, as events in Russia seemed to prove. Furthermore, he feared that a civil war in Germany, unlike Russia, would terminate with a victory of counterrevolution and an abrogation of the few social gains that the SPD had acquired painstakingly over the course of half a century. The theologian Ernst Troeltsch, an observer of those events, concluded that the Social Democratic leaders had "adopted the [November] revolution to appease the masses; it was a revolution that the socialist leaders had not made and that, from their perspective, was an abortion, but which they pretended to accept as their own long-sought child."[19]

To keep that child in line, the Wilhelmine military, so long the enemy of republicanism and social reform, was called in as guardian. On the evening following his appointment as chancellor, Ebert held a secret telephone conversation with Wilhelm Groener of the German General Staff. Groener agreed to support the new republic if Ebert promised to use the army to maintain social order against the leftist demands of the council movement, the USPD, and the Spartacists. Although this agreement remained secret, its implications were soon revealed. Gustav Noske, the Social Democrat who became minister of defense, declared himself the "bloodhound of the revolution," and he called upon the army and the extreme right-wing Freikorps units to put down all leftist disturbances. In early January a small uprising of Spartacists in the capital was suppressed, leaving a hundred dead; their radical leaders, Luxemburg and Liebknecht, were murdered while in custody. The quelling of even larger disturbances in Berlin in March cost the lives of over a thousand citizens, many of them shot on mere suspicion. At the same time, the old order reasserted itself in other areas. Most notably, the civil service and judiciary continued to be manned by prewar bureaucrats and judges, still thoroughly imbued with antirepublican values.

Liberal and leftist writers and performers were shocked by the seeming hypocrisy of the Social Democrats. Ostensibly socialist, even Marxist,

Germany's new leaders had allied themselves with elements of the old regime in order to quell leftist disturbances. Since the essence of satire consists in highlighting the discrepancies between ideals and realities, that contradiction offered a field that humorists cultivated with ease. Much of the harvesting took place in cabarets.

Berlin's first major postwar cabaret was Max Reinhardt's revived Sound and Smoke. During the war Reinhardt had continued to be a successful theater director; he expanded his empire by taking over the Berlin Volksbühne and laying the groundwork for the Salzburg festival. A character in Otto Reutter's *Don't Dare Go to Berlin* (1917) even suggested that Reinhardt should be made a military commander, because his organizational abilities would lead to victory.[20] Following the war, Reinhardt acquired the Schumann Circus on the Schiffbauerdamm, and commissioned the expressionist architect Hans Poelzig to redesign the interior for an arena stage. The new venture, dubbed the Grosses Schauspielhaus, was inaugurated on November 29, 1919, with a production of Aeschylus' *Oresteia*. Reinhardt also decided to resurrect the cabaret that had marked the commencement of his independent career. He did not, however, have any direct control over the performances; his role was one of benign sponsorship, rather than hands-on management. The Grosses Schauspielhaus thus acquired a double function: while Aeschylus was presented upstairs, in the former circus ring, the performances of Sound and Smoke took place in the underground cellars where the wild animals had been encaged.

The new Sound and Smoke opened on December 8, 1919, and the premiere received very mixed reviews. A major problem seems to have been the poor acoustics and sightlines of the cellar, which was broken up by numerous thick pillars; many spectators and critics simply could not hear or see much of the performance. Other troubles resided in the show itself. A revived Serenissimus, the trademark of the earlier venture, commented on the program as he had a generation earlier. The critics, however, found him totally passé, now that the Kaiser and the various German princes had been deposed for over a year. The *Berliner Tageblatt* noted: "We have encountered Serenissimus and his faithful Kindermann all too often. For now we have had enough of princely potentates, even of such a harmless nature." The *Berliner Börsen-Zeitung*, which said that "the dead man" should be "left in his grave," issued a challenge: "Let a [SPD] party secretary, the president, or the minister for foreign affairs make fitting comments on events, if you have any courage." Another irritating number consisted of two songs written and performed by Gustav von Wangenheim. Dressed in a Pierrot costume, he deplored the demise of the "Bohème": in the prewar era literati and intellectuals had filled Berlin's cafés, but now their seats were taken by the *Schieber*, the notorious black marketeers. Critics considered the Pierrot figure, like Serenissimus, frightfully outdated, and were uncomfortable with the nostalgic looking back to the antebellum years.[21]

The critics were much more amused by a cartoon film, sketched with childish stick-figures by Walter Trier, entitled "A Day in the Life of the Reich President." It began as a takeoff on a notorious photograph of Ebert and Noske in swimsuits that had graced a recent cover of the *Berliner Illustrirte Zeitung*. For generations the German citizenry had been accustomed to seeing its leaders in military uniform or formal civilian dress; hence the publication of a snapshot of the new, hardly photogenic rulers in shorts was considered scandalous, and it certainly deflated the aura of republican leadership. Perhaps the most successful number of the evening was by Paul Graetz, who soon would become one of the most popular cabaret performers. Dressed as a street vendor and employing a thick Berlin accent (fig. 18), he belted out a song that included a few swipes at Noske. Obviously, by December 1919 it had become de rigueur among satirists to attack the Social Democratic minister of defense, who repeatedly called in troops to suppress leftist demonstrations.

Graetz's song was scripted by Kurt Tucholsky (1890–1935), who contributed numerous lyrics to republican cabarets in the immediate postwar years. He had become known as a critic for the journal *Die Schaubühne*, where he even reviewed performances at the Wintergarten and other variety stages, since he believed that popular entertainment should be treated as seriously as "high" art. Tucholsky also perfected his talents as a writer of satirical stories and verse. His first publication, at age seventeen, was a short allegory critical of the Kaiser that appeared in *Ulk*, the satirical supplement of the *Berliner Tageblatt*. He eventually served as editor of *Ulk* from 1918 to 1920. By that time he had grown much more politicized, due to the war and the suppression of rebellions in the spring of 1919. His views on current events appeared with increasing frequency in *Die Schaubühne*, which was renamed *Die Weltbühne* in 1918. That year Tucholsky also joined the USPD, and remained a member until its dissolution in September 1922.

Strongly committed to democratic and republican values, Tucholsky was an implacable foe of reactionary tendencies, whether in government, the military, the civil service, the judiciary, or the church. Perhaps more consistently than any other person, he contrasted the ideals of the Weimar Republic with its social and political realities; thus he became the premier satirist of the age. He was committed in particular to pacifism. Although he had not seen the worst of the war—in 1915 and 1916 he was stationed along the static Eastern front, and thereafter was assigned to a desk

18. Paul Graetz performed Kurt Tucholsky's irreverent monologues and songs in the postwar Sound and Smoke.

job—he was well aware of the senseless suffering and loss of life that the conflict had entailed. He hoped to ensure that it never would be repeated.[22]

Given Tucholsky's values, it is surprising that some of his cabaret songs overlapped thematically with those of the nationalist variety shows that he deplored. That became especially clear in the song performed by Graetz at the opening night of Sound and Smoke. "When the Old Motor Beats in Time Again" (Wenn der alte Motor wieder tackt) contained a compendium of complaints that easily could have been enunciated by a conservative "political humorist." It deplored black marketeering, the weakness of the mark, the high cost of public transport, and the spotty performance of public services like mail, water, and electricity. Granted, the song made some points that placed it clearly in the antinationalist camp: it called for the dismissal of Noske and the disbanding of militarist organizations, and it claimed that economic production should be geared to civilian, not military needs. Every stanza concluded, however, with a refrain that prescribed how to restore health to Berlin: by getting workers back to work. Only when "the lathe operator spits into his hands," "the welder swings his hammer," and "the salesgirl respects us again," will a "rebirth" of Berlin take place.[23]

This call to work harder—in the face of strikes, slowdowns, and the shortening of the workday to eight hours—was a common theme in conservative variety shows. It was a demand that middle-class audiences, who blamed the proletariat for Germany's domestic troubles, liked to hear. The connection between Tucholsky's song and the conservative agenda was made explicit in March 1922, when Herrmann-Neisse deplored "the fad of critical verses that in the last analysis represent the vilest official slogans and drone on about events from the standpoint of the nationalist bourgeoisie. Graetz's hit 'When the Old Motor Beats in Time Again' was the fanfare to these hymns, which carp at social struggles from the standpoint of the beerhall." Herrmann-Neisse considered appeals for "the settlement of antagonisms and the necessity of a new joy in work" to be "totally reactionary and dangerous." In fact, "settlement of antagonisms" might well have referred to another song scripted by Tucholsky, "That Is the Heartbeat" (Das ist der Herzschlag; 1920), which deplored the fighting among SPD, USPD, Bolsheviks, and militarists. It placed equal blame on agents of leftist "rebellion" and the right-wing putschists, "Kapp and his gang." The solution proffered was: "Children, extend to each other again the old fraternal hand!" (Kinder, reicht euch wieder mal die alte Bruderhand!). That would restore "the heartbeat that holds us together" (der Herzschlag, der zusammenhält).[24]

One might well ask why Tucholsky penned such lines. His political essays in *Die Weltbühne* and other left-liberal journals indicated that he was well aware that class contradictions and political hostilities were deeply rooted in German society, and would not have been amenable to any facile, "handshake" solutions. It appears that Tucholsky was less aggressive and more conciliatory when he adopted the persona of the cabaret lyricist. He was more sensitive than most writers to the different contexts and audiences of his trade. His works appeared under his real name—and also under four different pseudonyms, each geared to varying aspects of his output (Ignaz Wrobel, Kaspar Hauser, Theobald Tiger, and Peter Panter). Theobald Tiger was the lyrical, satirical persona. Like the others, it clung firmly to pacifism: "That Is the Heartbeat," like "When the Old Motor," included lines that damned Noske as well as the revival of militarism. On social issues, however, Tiger's songs could be less clearly committed to left-liberal viewpoints. That resulted from Tucholsky's authorial strategy, the fact that he hoped to gain a broad audience through his poems and cabaret songs. Several weeks before the opening of Sound and Smoke he confided in a letter: "I think that it will provide good publicity." That goal could be achieved only if he took account of the attitudes of his audience, and the onlookers at Sound and Smoke were a mixed bag. The BZ am Mittag noted approvingly that "the nouveaux riches are in the minority," but leftist newspapers considered the public still too conservative to appreciate critical cabaretic art. The SPD's Vorwärts contended that "to a large extent the public was certainly well dressed, but less well disposed." It concluded: "What cannot be changed is the audience, but that's just the way things are." Predictably, the USPD's Freiheit did not believe that such resignation to public taste was in order: "You have to start out differently, *against* this audience, *against* these times, if you want to triumph with your cabaret."[25]

Tucholsky himself was well aware of the problematic nature of the postwar German audience. His initial goal was a type of ruthless satire that made no concessions. In January 1919, in response to the question "What is satire allowed to do?," he answered: "Everything." For Tucholsky, the satirist was "an offended idealist: he wants the world to be good, but it is bad, and so he runs full tilt against it." Two months later he answered the charge that he and other political commentators were too negative by contending that there was precious little in Germany that they could affirm: "Are we soiling our own nest? But you cannot soil an Augean stable." The German bourgeoisie was so thoroughly antidemocratic that conditions would be incapable of improvement without the spread of "decent convictions": "We are well aware that you cannot realize ideals, but we also know that nothing in the world has occurred, changed, or taken effect without the flame of ideals." These precepts, which saw "no salvation in compromise," informed Tucholsky's political contributions to Die Welbühne and other journals.[26]

Tucholsky was less principled in his works performed before a live audience, in a milieu dominated by the desire for entertainment. In an article for the Sound and Smoke program booklet of June 1920, he wrote: "In Germany it is not considered tactful to conduct politics in a cabaret. The audience gets angry, because it wants to be amused and does not want to hear any editorials, and the politicians get angry, because the sacred, serious business of politics is dragged down to the level of cabaret." The German unwillingness to conflate politics and cabaret was surprising to Tucholsky, who believed that such satire could have a useful political function—the same function, in fact, that Wolzogen had attributed to it a generation earlier. Before the opening of Sound and Smoke, in an essay on "Political Satire," Tucholsky had written that the Germans "still do not know that a well-aimed joke is a better lighting rod for public anger than an ugly riot that cannot be brought under control." Another article on "Political Verses" contended that "a song is a good safety valve, through which powerful emotions dissipate in a harmless manner, whenever the boiler is bursting with pressure, as it is today."[27]

Tucholsky evidently wanted his satirical songs to discharge the political animosities of both left and right, animosities that he explicitly condemned in those same songs. Under any circumstances, that would have been a mighty task for chansons that reached a limited cabaret public. But in the postwar years, Tucholsky conceded that it was well-nigh impossible. Even before the opening of Sound and Smoke he concluded:

> Everything has stayed the same.
> That's because the harshest and most pitiless German censor does not sit in a bureaucratic office, but in the parquet. Round and fat he sits in the middle of the parquet and prevents any performer singing a song onstage from deviating even a hairbreadth from the accepted line.
> Now that is a sad state of affairs: the middle class, the bourgeois, is indignant and feels his most sacred values attacked if ever someone on stage should dare to express an opinion different from his own—he will not stand for radicalism in a variety show and will never forgive a singer for it.

That opinion was largely confirmed by Tucholsky's experiences at Sound and Smoke, where the audience gave at best a tepid reception to political satire. Consequently, that cabaret soon cut down on its political numbers. Three months after the opening of the venture Tucholsky wrote to a friend: "Everything is so sad: even here pandering to the consumer, that is, the audience, which is mostly loathesome. A truly literary cabaret would not work. It is very, very sad."[28]

In 1929 Tucholsky wrote: "the cabarets are gripped by the strange ambition of wanting to be aggressive without offending anyone." Yet that same charge could have been leveled against his own lyrics at the beginning of the decade. Despite his strictures against political passivity, Tucholsky rapidly depoliticized his contributions to Sound and Smoke. One song for the cabaret's second program, in January 1920, still contained satirical elements, but it avoided taking a firm stand on any substantive issue. "Around the Litfass Column" (Immer um die Litfasssäule rum) referred to Berlin's large, cylindrical drums covered with political posters and commercial advertisements. Sung by a woman, the song complained about the various inanities displayed, ranging from politics (Noske, of course) to film stars and theater directors; even Max Reinhardt received some jabs. The woman concluded that her poodle had discovered the only proper use of the Litfass column: "Now and then my pup / lifts his leggy up" (Und es hebt das Kleinchen / ab und zu ein Beinchen). The song suggested, in other words, that one should ignore or dismiss entirely the political and commercial spheres. Indeed, in the ensuing months Tucholsky generally limited himself to rather witty, but basically innocuous love songs, such as "Lady in White," "The Song of the Dickey-Bird," "The Girl of the Tauentzienstrasse," and "Oh, Rest your Cheek" (Dame in Weiss, Das Lied vom Piepmatz, Das Tauentzienmädel, and Ach, lege deine Wange). Another number, "Take It Off, Petronella!" (Zieh dich aus, Petronella!), parodied the postwar vogue of nude shows.[29]

The fortunes of Sound and Smoke dwindled along with the critical bite of Tucholsky's songs. The first director of the cabaret, Rudolf Kurtz, was replaced in the fall of 1920 by Hans von Wolzogen, who had acted occasionally as conferencier in the earlier programs. The son of the founder of Berlin's first cabaret could not, however, rescue the revival of its second cabaret. In March 1921 the basement was leased to new managers, who announced that they would not continue it as a "literary cabaret." Instead, they turned it into a vaudeville hall, and by January 1922 Herrmann-Neisse exclaimed: "Soubrettes as in a provincial Tingeltangel, trained dogs and doves in an establishment that bears the respectable name of Sound and Smoke!" Two months later he noted that the venue was advertising itself as a "Bier-Variété-Kabarett." The final indignity came with the appearance of the type of nude show that Tucholsky had mocked in "Petronella." Already in October 1921, the notorious "Ballet Celly de Rheidt" (to be discussed in the next chapter) had made a guest appearance, while in May 1923, the locale was taken over by Erna Offeney, another well-known provider of stripped-down entertainment.[30]

As Sound and Smoke proved unamenable to satirical verse, Tucholsky sought other stages for his works. One option was provided by Rosa Valetti (1869–1937). Best known as a character actress, Valetti also performed in cabarets after the war. On December 23, 1920, she opened her own venture, the Cabaret Megalomania (Cabaret Grössenwahn). It was located on the Kurfürstendamm, in the premises of the Café des Westens (itself nicknamed Café Grössenwahn, since aspiring writers tended to congregate there). Valetti's Megalomania was in many ways a throwback to some of the pub-cabarets of the turn of the century, which had evoked the milieux of Berlin's poor as well as its criminal elements. Valetti had experienced the great Parisian cabarets in the 1890s, and her own venture was modeled after that of Aristide Bruant. She performed some of his songs on opening night, but most of the numbers dealt with Berlin's own down-and-out population.

In future performances the most successful songs of this type were written by Friedrich Hollaender (1896–1976). The son of the composer of the prewar Metropol revues, Hollaender already had made a name for himself by providing the music to numerous songs at Sound and Smoke (such as Tucholsky's "When the Old Motor" and "Around the Litfass Column"). He came into his own as both composer and lyricist at Megalomania. His "Songs of a Poor Girl" (Lieder eines armen Mädchen) were written for Blandine Ebinger (b. 1902), the waif-like chanteuse he married in 1919. In a series of numbers—"The Dime Song," "When I'm Dead," "Oh, Moon" (Das Jroschenlied, Wenn ick mal tot bin, Oh, Mond)—she portrayed a frail, sickly, barely adolescent girl from the Berlin working class. Highly sentimental and full of pathos, the songs mingled feelings of sexual awakening with a longing for death as the sole escape from poverty.[31] These numbers were extremely successful, even though several critics questioned the appropriateness of entertaining well-to-do spectators with scenes from the life of the poor.

In Valetti's defense it can be said that she actually did show genuine concern for the pressing social and political issues of the day. One indication of that was her frequent performance of "The Red Melody" (Die Rote Melodie), which Tucholsky wrote explicitly for her. This, his most hard-hitting antiwar song, with music by Hollaender, was addressed directly at Erich Ludendorff. Having enjoyed almost dictatorial powers during the World War, Ludendorff staunchly opposed democracy and repeatedly tried to sabotage the Republic in its early years. In performing the song, Valetti played the role of a mother who lost her only son in the war. She warned the general: "Don't dare try it once again" (General! General! Wagt es nur nicht noch einmal!). The song concluded with an image of the battalions of the dead, both soldiers and slaughtered political radicals, arising from their graves and marching against Ludendorff.[32] Within Tucholsky's cabaretic oeuvre the "Red Melody" stood out for the pointedness and forcefulness of its attack. Valetti could not, however, present such numbers for long. Like Sound and Smoke, Megalomania was able to remain an artistically respectable cabaret for less than two seasons. In 1922 Valetti relinquished her management and returned to acting, and the venue became an undistinguished nightclub.

By then Tucholsky had found another stage that seemed more promising, at least initially: Rudolf Nelson's Theater am Kurfürstendamm. Nelson's latest venture, inaugurated in 1917, had survived the war intact, but the composer realized that conditions in postwar Berlin were quite unlike the good old days. In 1919 one of his songs lamented how different everything was, including the entertainment scene:

> Berlin, Berlin, you just aren't what you were.
> Where is your humor, levity, and wit?

Where are the good old songs we used to hear?
Friedrichstadt now looks like Myslowitz!

Berlin, Berlin, ich kenne dich nicht wieder.
Wo ist dein Leichtsinn, dein Humor, dein Witz?
Wo sind die lieben guten alten Lieder?
Die Friedrichstadt sieht aus wie Myslowitz!

Now that the entertainment district of prewar Berlin (Friedrichstadt) looked like the provinces (Myslowitz), the city seemed to have lost even its characteristic wit. But as always, Nelson adapted well to the new situation. He even had something of a vested interest in disparaging Friedrichstadt, since he had already moved his base of operations west, to the Kurfürstendamm, which in the 1920s replaced the Friedrichstrasse–Unter den Linden axis as the new center of fashionable shopping and entertainment. One reason for the failure of the postwar Sound and Smoke was its location in the "old" entertainment district, which now attracted only tourists and townspeople seeking mindless distraction. Nelson was much better situated for the new times. In October 1920 a police report confirmed that his patrons came from the elite western ("WW") districts, such as Charlottenburg and Grunewald: "The theater was almost completely sold out and attended by an audience mainly from WW, which heartily applauded the performance."[33]

The work that they applauded was *Totally Crazy (Total Manoli)*. Already in 1919, Nelson had begun to switch from cabaret to loose revue-type works, and *Totally Crazy* was his first major production of that nature. The dialogue and some of the songs were scripted by Fritz Grünbaum, the Viennese conferencier whom Nelson had hired for the prewar Chat noir. Although Grünbaum served in the Austrian army during the war and spent most of the 1920s in Viennese cabarets, he still maintained his connections with Berlin. That was evident from the flimsy plot, in which the devil introduced a demimondaine to the "crazy" life of the German capital. The work made fun of various prominent people, sights, and fads of the city, much like the prewar Metropol revues. Indeed, a police observer compared the two, but noted that Nelson's productions were, understandably, much less opulent than the Metropol's had been. Numbers included a parody of Reinhardt's Grosses Schauspielhaus; a takeoff on the postwar foxtrot craze; a song claiming that one could keep warm only by kissing, since all German coal was being taken by the French; a scene entitled "Hell on Earth," depicting the treatment of citizens by government bureaucrats; and an assembly of "black marketeers of the world" (Schieber aller Länder). That latter group included politicians who supposedly had profited from Germany's travails: Ebert, who had been elected president in 1919; Philipp Scheidemann, his first chancellor; and wartime finance minister Karl Helfferich. The police were particularly displeased with that scene, but since censorship had been abolished, the most that they could do was to plead with Nelson and the performers to drop the reference to Ebert, which they considered unseemly and inappropriate.[34]

Although it displeased the police, the scene with the profiteers included what the critics considered the best song of the show, "Under the El-Train Arch" (Unterm Stadtbahnbogen). That was one of several songs in the revue scripted by Tucholsky. Sung by Willi Schaeffers, who later would become a prominent cabaret director in the Nazi and Adenauer eras, the number described the exploits of a black marketeer. The first stanza listed what he offered for sale "under the el-train arch": everything from butter and sausage to gold and stocks. The second stanza recounted what he received under the arch: the sexual favors of a deposed princess-turned-prostitute. The third and last stanza became political, as the singer declared what he would like to see disappear under the arch: "the pile of bureaucrats," "the dear Soviets," and the "Entente commission." Once all of them were gone, "things would be better in Berlin."[35]

The song demonstrated one of the strengths of Weimar chansons compared to those of the Wilhelmine era. Whereas the latter ("The Shopgirl," for example) tended to terminate with sexual punch lines, the songs of the twenties often passed through sexual allusions and ended with political statements. By 1928 a critic could note: "The three-stanza-system—whereby the first stanza explains the occasion and situation, the second stanza turns erotic, and the third stanza moves into politics—has become a routine practice."[36] The "El-Train Arch" displayed precisely this structure. But it was a model song in another way as well, since the political note on which it ended revealed a failure to take a clear stand; that too was an all-too-common characteristic of the Weimar chanson. After all, an attack on bureaucrats, Bolsheviks, and the Allied commission enforcing the Treaty of Versailles would have been applauded by all parties except the Communists. Indeed, by placing much of the blame for current problems on leftists and the Entente, the song betrayed a somewhat conservative standpoint. Whatever the intent, "Under the El-Train Arch," despite its political veneer, would not have challenged or revised the opinion of any member of Nelson's well-heeled audience.

Tucholsky also wrote the lyrics for Nelson's next two revues, *Please Pay!* and *We're Standing Backward* (*Bitte zahlen!*, 1921; *Wir steh'n verkehrt*, 1922), but as at Sound and Smoke, their political tendency was unfocused. A critic for the liberal *Tagebuch* said of the 1922 revue: "Here politics is mocked in an affable, light manner that offends no one." One of the show's hit songs, entitled "Raffke," portrayed a fictitious black marketeer of that name (derived from the verb *raffen,* to grab or snatch up), who was a comic feature in the *Berliner Illustrirte Zeitung.* The program listed the character, in bold letters, as "His Majesty Raffke," and critics noted that the figure was a worthy up-to-date successor to Serenissimus. The two characters shared many attributes: not only were both uncultured, unedu-cated, and promiscuous, but they were presented in a comical and almost affable manner. According to the *Vossische Zeitung,* even that attenuated degree of caricature required some courage, because Nelson had real Raffkes sitting in his theater. In contrast, the *Berliner Börsen Zeitung* reported that "the nouveaux riches were not obtrusive," at least not at the premiere.[37] Whatever the composition of the audience, the song could hardly have been deemed critical or offensive, and it was a great success.

The other hit of *We're Standing Backward* was equally problematic. "I'd Like so Much to Have a Tamerlane Today" (Mir ist heut so nach Tamerlan) described a woman's desire to have a man like the Asiatic despot: "A little bit of Tamerlane, yes Tamerlane would be nice" (Ein kleines bisschen Tamerlan, ja Tamerlan wär gut).[38] Since the song went on to contend that all the men in the theater were sexual weaklings, it was, on the surface, another number that combined an erotic message with a kidding of the audience. But the reference to Tamerlane, a strongman par excellence, gave the song a political dimension as well, albeit an attenuated one. The number obviously parodied the right-wing demand for authori-tarian leadership at a time of political vacillation and surging inflation. Equating that desire with a love-starved woman's craving for a he-man produced wonderful satire, but its joking tone and erotic veneer down-played the seriousness of the threat. Once again, Tucholsky had scripted humorous, prorepublican lyrics that did not tread too harshly on conser-vative customers.

Herrmann-Neisse provided perhaps the most accurate assessment of Tucholsky's songs when he wrote: "They are usually aggressive within a certain middle range, not out-and-out radical, but also not philistine-domesticated. That is why he is able to supply texts to such widely divergent venues as a Nelson revue and a combative cabaret." For Nelson, as at Sound and Smoke, Tucholsky evidently believed that he had to make concessions within the context of public entertainment, especially since he needed the income it generated. In September 1922 he wrote a friend that "Nelson has improved my financial condition not unappreciably." Conse-quently, he was dismayed the following spring, when it became apparent that Nelson would not require his services any longer. To ride out the raging inflation, Tucholsky was forced to take a job as a bank secretary for several months in 1923—something of an embarrassment to the frequent critic of commercialism, finance, and capitalism. At the same time, he was well aware that he had always been dependent upon such circles. In a fictitious, parodistic obituary that he wrote for himself that year, he envisioned his own funeral, with Nelson conducting a chorus that sang the Tamerlane song. The obituary continued: "That was one of the innumerable chansons of the deceased, created for circles that he pretended to despise so much; with one hand he criticized them, and with the other he siphoned off their champagne. He was quite a problematic character."[39]

## Dada and Metropolitan Tempo: Walter Mehring

Tucholsky's "Motor," sung by Graetz at the premiere of the new Sound and Smoke, embodied some of the dilemmas and concessions that would plague Weimar cabaretists. Another set of problems was embedded in the culminating number of the show, a political puppet play entitled *Simply Classical! An Oresteia with a Happy Ending (Einfach klassisch! Eine Orestie mit glücklichem Ausgang)*. Just as a tragic trilogy in ancient Athens had concluded with a bawdy satyr play, Reinhardt's production of the *Oresteia* was given a comic counterpart. The puppet play contained many takeoffs on the performance "upstairs," as well as on other cultural fads of the day, such as film stars and jazz. Primarily, though, it was a parody of current political events. At the beginning of the play Agamemnon, dressed up as a Prussian general, was deposed by Aegisthus, who proclaimed a republic with himself as president. Described as a pacifist, a "man of letters and professional moralist," this Aegisthus was much like Kurt Eisner, the USPD prime minister of Bavaria who had been assassinated in February 1919. The same fate awaited Aegisthus, who was killed in the second act by Orestes, described as "an officer of the Attic Freikorps" who desired "to reestablish the old order." The third act threatened a return to democracy at the prompting of Woodrow Apollon, described as "perpetually in Yankee-dress, lives only in higher spheres" (fig. 19). However, the good-natured naiveté and political ineffectiveness of the American allowed Orestes to reassert himself. At the end of the play he led his Freikorps units to the Baltic, where the Allies had in fact permitted German troops to remain armed in order to ward off the Bolshevik threat. Secondary figures included a trio of conservative, liberal, and socialist newspaper editors, representing the modern equivalent of the Greek chorus. There also was a rather tasteless "Electra from the Salvation Army," who collected money for "starving anti-Semites" and sold "contraptions that some people use / In cultured nations to roast Jews" ([Ich] handle nebenbei mit Apparaten / Für Kulturnationen zum Judenbraten).[40]

In this puppet play all major actors in postwar Germany—the Kaiser,

19. "Woodrow Apollon" in Walter Mehring's *Simply Classical!* The puppet was designed by George Grosz and crafted by John Heartfield.

the General Staff, the Freikorps, and anti-Semites, as well as idealists like Eisner and Wilson—were reduced to a common level of ludicrousness. This disparagement, indeed trivialization of politics and politicians was made obvious in a monologue of Aegisthus, which he delivered while practicing with a punching-ball:

> It's easy to laugh at me, ladies and gents!
> But do *you* have any more competence?
> Do you think that ruling is such a delight?
> Attacks from the left, attacks from the right,
> The morning papers add blood to the fight,
> The satirists make fun of your plight,

With outright spite, they incite and indict.
The whole thing's lost every trace of romance,
The hero's pose, the stately stance.
There's no more crown and no more throne,
In short, it's just not worth a bone.
Werfel or Rolland might be your name,
But brains won't win you points in this game.
If you try to hang out with intellectual men,
The Dadaists stage a putsch right then.
. . .
In the end you say with a hang-dog face:
There's just no good in the human race.


Meine Herren und Damen! Sehr einfach zu lachen.
Aber besser machen! besser machen!
Überhaupt, haben Sie schon mal regiert?
Bald wird man von links, bald von rechts sekkiert,
Bald steht man im Morgenblatt blutbeschmiert,
Im Beiblatt von Zille karikiert,
Wird visitiert, persifliert, ausspioniert.
Und dabei fehlt der Sache jede Romantik,
Die Heldenpose, die Iambengigantik.
Man krönt nicht mehr und man thront micht mehr.
Mit einem Worte: es lohnt nicht mehr.
Ob man Werfel oder Romain Rolland heisst,
Sicher ist, das auf Geist keine Katze mehr anbeisst.
Hält man's mit den Intellektuellen,
Gleich putschen die Dadaisten-Rebellen.
. . .
Schliesslich merkt man betrübten Angesichts:
Mit der Güte der Menschen war's wieder mal nichts.[41]

The reference to Dadaists was very appropriate, inasmuch as Dada embodied the quintessential deflation of German politics. Indeed, *Simply Classical!* was itself a Dadaist performance of sorts. The text was written by Walter Mehring, the puppets were designed by George Grosz and executed by John Heartfield, and the music was composed by Friedrich Hollaender. Each one has become firmly identified with Weimar culture: Mehring as a prolific writer of cabaret lyrics; Grosz as a bitter caricaturist of Weimar politics and bourgeois society; Heartfield as a pioneer in leftist political photomontage; and Hollaender as the inspired composer and performer of music for cabaret, revue, and film.

Of these four, all but Hollaender had been associated closely with the Berlin Dada movement since the closing months of World War I. Dada had been launched in Zurich in 1916 at the Cabaret Voltaire, where avant-garde numbers were performed by an international group of radical and pacifist artists. When Richard Huelsenbeck, a participant in the Zurich group, returned to Berlin in January 1917, he soon found adherents to Dada's antiwar ideals, men such as George Grosz and the brothers Helmut and Wieland Herzfelde. To protest the blindly anti-English sentiments of the day, Georg Grosz had anglicized his first name, and Helmut Herzfelde started calling himself John Heartfield. They also succeeded in minimizing their personal involvement in the war effort. Although Grosz had volunteered for service in November 1914, his attitude changed rapidly, and he was discharged several months later for medical reasons. Soon after being redrafted in 1917, he was committed to the psychiatric ward of a hospital. Heartfield had avoided service altogether by faking a mental breakdown on the day he was to have been sent to the front. After several months in an asylum, he was assigned to postal duties in Berlin's Grunewald neighborhood, where he made a point of tossing out much of the mail he was supposed to deliver.

Berlin's Dadaists were appalled by the senseless slaughter of the war, as well as the complicity of artists and intellectuals, who either glorified the fighting or retreated into purely aesthetic concerns. Grosz and Wieland Herzfelde wrote in retrospect: "Dada was not an ideological movement, but an organic product that arose as a reaction to the head-in-the-clouds tendencies of so-called holy art which sought inspiration in cubes and gothic, while the field commanders painted in blood." Berlin Dada attacked not only all artistic traditions, but also every political tendency, including republicanism. For Berlin's Dadaists, the absurdity of modern politics was compounded by postwar events, as the putatively socialist regime conspired with the prewar military elites to suppress workers demanding genuine socialist reforms. In March 1919, during the bloody quelling of the disturbances in Berlin, Wieland Herzfelde was arrested for having published a magazine critical of the military; he feared for his life during his harrowing two weeks in custody. Such experiences alienated him as well as many other artists and intellectuals from the new republican regime. The resulting opposition to all existing artistic and political trends was summarized by Raoul Hausmann, one of the leading Berlin Dadaists, who proclaimed in 1919: "I am not only against the spirit of Potsdam—I am above all against Weimar."[42] For him and his fellow Dadaists, Weimar implied not only the classical literary tradition of Goethe and Schiller, but above all the party-politics and parliamentarism of the new republic.

The Dadaists' mocking of all political trends was visible in Mehring's *Simply Classical!* They also vented their opposition by staging what future generations would call "happenings." They held processions through Berlin, wearing skull-masks and huge Iron Crosses, and mounted inflammatory shows, such as the First International Dada Exhibition of June 1920. That event included a Prussian officer's uniform topped with a pig's head, which resulted in prosecution for defamation of the Reichswehr. Many of the dozen public evenings of Berlin's Club Dada held between January 1918 and March 1920 included quasi-cabaretic numbers. Johannes Baader, known for disrupting a church service as well as the Weimar National Assembly, proclaimed at a Dada evening in 1919: "Dada is the cabaret of the world, just as it, the world, is the cabaret DADA." One absurdist performance was the "race between a sewing machine and a typewriter." For half an hour Huelsenbeck pounded at a typewriter, filling up page after page, while Raoul Hausmann stitched away uninterruptedly at a circular band of mourning crepe. Herzfelde recalled: "George Grosz was the emcee and referee. When he finally declared the sewing machine the victor, Huelsenbeck, the loser, smashed the typewriter against the floor of the stage. The victor, Raoul Hausmann, did not let himself be disturbed. He continued to stitch the endless mourning crepe with undiminished doggedness." Given the Dadaists' antics, it was no wonder that some critics greeted their appearance at the opening of Sound and Smoke. The reviewer for the Social Democratic *Vorwärts* reported: "The Dadaists were also there, and with reason, since it cannot be denied that the Dadaists are almost the only people left who have madness in their joints, and some spirit as well."[43]

Dada was not, however, an undisputed affair. Even one of Wangenheim's Pierrot songs, performed earlier that same evening at Sound and Smoke, had a line that proclaimed: "Dadaism is the bitter end, / an artists' hoax for any entrance-fee" (Der Dadaismus ist das bitt're Ende, / der Künstlerulk um jeden Eintrittspreis). What many people objected to was Dada's totally oppositional stance, which seemed to represent a negativism that could result only in "the bitter end" of cynicism. Granted, Dada could be artistically innovative and productive, but its political stance was highly problematic, since it found no basis of support in the party spectrum of the time. The Dadaists had great sympathies for the new Communist Party of Germany (KPD). Grosz, Heartfield, and Herzfelde even may have joined the Party at its founding congress at the end of December 1918. Nevertheless, the KPD itself had little sympathy for Dada's clowning around, which contributed nothing to the betterment of the proletariat and hardly disturbed the prevailing order. In a highly critical review of the First International Dada Exhibition, Gertrud Alexander wrote in the KPD's *Rote Fahne:* "Do these gentlemen really believe that they can harm the bourgeoisie with that? The bourgeoisie laughs at it."[44] That laughter was at times appreciative, at times dismissive, but it failed to inspire a radical reformulation of values. The political ineffectiveness of Berlin Dada was one reason for the movement's collapse over the course of 1920. Some participants, like Heartfield and Herzfelde, adopted a committed communist stance; others, like Grosz, remained socially critical, but could not concur fully with KPD practice; and still others, like Mehring, retained a completely nonpartisan, satirical attitude toward the events of the day.

Walter Mehring (1896–1981) was the person who carried into cabaret not only Dada's unfocused combativeness but also its artistic innovations. He had been born into a family that was both cultured and political. His mother, Hedwig Stein, was an opera singer; his father, Sigmar Mehring, was a member of the SPD and the editor of *Ulk* until his death in 1914. In that capacity he had been sentenced to three months' fortress confinement in 1900 for publishing a poem critical of the Kaiser. His son held pacifist sentiments during the war, and although trained as a gunner, he never saw front-line action. From 1918 to 1920 he was part of Berlin's Dada scene and published lyrics in their journals. One issue of *Jedermann sein eigener Fussball* (Everyman His Own Football) was confiscated on account of Mehring's allegedly obscene poem, "Der Coitus im Dreimäderlhaus" (the latter being the name of a popular operetta). Mehring was brought to trial, but, unlike his father a generation earlier, he was acquitted.[45]

Mehring's *Simply Classical* provided a clear illustration of his distrust of all political persuasions, which could be seen in his other works as well. In 1920 several of his lyrics were set to music and performed at Sound and Smoke. The January program included "The Saucy Song" (Das kesse Lied), which was something of an antichanson, since the performer pretended to forget the refrain: "But the refrain—the refrain—the refrain / Oh miss, there is something about Noske in it, / And something about making love" (Doch der Refrain—der Refrain—der Refrain / Ach Fräulein, da is was von Noske drin, / Und was vom Lieben).[46] Already in January 1920, Mehring realized that the postwar cabaret song could be reduced to this recipe: a little bit of sex, a little bit of Noske. Although that was certainly true of Tucholsky's works, Mehring tried to break out of the formula. To be sure, he too combined sex and politics, but his juxtapositions were much more startling and unsettling than those of Tucholsky or any other cabaret lyricist of the day.

By October 1920 Mehring's works were attracting the most attention at Sound and Smoke. Critics took special note of Paul Graetz's performance of a trio of Mehring's works entitled, collectively, "Berliner Tempo." The first song, "Attention Gleisdreieck!" (Achtung Gleisdreieck!), referred to one of Berlin's nodal points of commuter rail traffic. It was almost a simultaneous poem: the published version appeared as two side-by-side columns, and in performance, the singer skipped from one to the other and back. The sequence was almost immaterial, since the work consisted of juxtapositions of single words, or at most two- or three-word phrases. They evoked various types of people ("Jedermann, Lebemann, Biedermann, . . . Ehemann," that is, everyman, man of the world, philistine, husband); different entertainments (cinema, theater, fairground, cabaret); several modes of transportation; and a melange of political standpoints (socialist, republican, militarist, racist). Nothing bound these terms together, except for their simultaneity in the big city. In fact, they were always tending apart, as the refrain asserted: "Everyone in / Different / Direction and / Attention! The / *Gleis-drei-eck!*" (Jeder in / Anderer / Richtung und / Achtung! Das / *Gleis-drei-eck!*).[47]

In formal and stylistic terms, the poem was very much in the Dadaist mode. Berlin Dada emphasized montage in both the visual arts and literature. Its collages, photomontages, and free-verse lyrics consisted of snippets drawn from a variety of media: advertisements for commodities, political slogans, newspaper reports, manifestos, handbills, posters, postcards, telegrams. By juxtaposing such sources the Dadaists sought to evoke the hectic nature of modern metropolitan life, a perception that had given birth to cabaret a generation earlier. Beyond that, they sought to question the veracity of such media. After all, each advertisement and every political speech was a self-contained whole that sought to coax the reader/viewer/listener to make a purchase or cast a vote. By fragmenting such statements and placing them alongside other ones making contradictory claims, the Dadaists hoped to reveal the illogicality, not to mention the mendacities, embedded in the commercial and political spheres. *Simply Classical* had made fun of all of the political trends and many of the cultural fashions of the day, but had done so by employing traditional forms of rhymed verse. A work like "Gleisdreieck" went much further: by adopting the staccato tempo, paratactic antigrammar, and iterative structure of Dada verse, it evoked a society in a state of rapid fragmentation. Both works ultimately dissolved any ground upon which they might have stood, but the Dadaist verse made that dissolution more forceful and apparent.

The other two parts of "Berliner Tempo" displayed similar formal properties. On the surface, the "Flying-Trapeze Song of the Contortionist Ellen T" (Couplet en Voltige der Contorsionistin Ellen T) represented trapeze artists in a circus or vaudeville act. It had, however, a deeper message. The first two stanzas introduced "Ellen" and "Ellen's husband," both of whom proclaimed themselves "international." The cosmopolitan nature of prewar circus and variety shows was evoked by mixing together snippets of German, Berlin dialect, Americanisms, and French. The third and last stanza, however, featured the "patriotic number" *(Hurranummer)* with

"Ellen's baby," who proclaimed in her broken Anglo-German argot: "Ich bin sehr for national." The stanza mocked postwar American patriotism as well as German chauvinism, with references to the Imperial colors and the troops stationed in the Baltic region.[48] In short, the number portrayed the shift from prewar cosmopolitanism to postwar chauvinism against which Tucholsky, Mehring, and other critical cabaretists had to contend.

The last song of the trio was entitled "Berlin Our Home" (Heimat Berlin), but it gave a hectic twist to the normally cozy associations of *Heimat*. What it portrayed was the tempo of the city:

> Giddy-up! Down the Linden! Don't act dead!
> On horse, on foot, in twos!
> Got a watch in my hand, and a hat on my head
> No time! No time to lose!

> Die Linden lang! Galopp! Galopp!
> Zu Fuss, zu Pferd, zu zweit!
> Mit der Uhr in der Hand, mit'm Hut auf'm Kopp
> Keine Zeit! Keine Zeit! Keine Zeit!

The song continued at that breathless pace. Although it too consisted of a concatenation of clichés and slogans shouted in Berlin dialect, its use of a regular metric and rhyme scheme made it formally less innovative than the other two songs, with their short, staccato lines. The somewhat more conventional style might have made the work more accessible to the public and the critics; in any case, it was a major hit. The reviewer for the *Berliner Tageblatt* praised Mehring and singled out that song as "the pinnacle." According to the *Berliner Börsen-Zeitung,* "the audience went wild." A decade later, Tucholsky still could look back on Graetz's performance of the song and proclaim: "That is the most Berlin-ish poem that I know."[49]

Friedrich Hollaender, who composed the music for many of Mehring's works, contributed an essay entitled "The New Chanson" to the October program booklet of Sound and Smoke. In it he wrote: "No longer should the audience be simply amused. It should think and, if it does not want that, it should be bowled over by the rhythm!—The new chanson is a matter of suggestion, it is the mastering of the masses. There is only one name for it, a life-giving concept: 'Berlin Tempo.'" He went on to contend that that song worked by means of the "suggestive potency" of "rhythm and verbal power." Hollaender's driving music and Graetz's forceful performance undoubtedly contributed to the success of the number as well, but it was above all the verbal cascades and rhythmic drive of Mehring's text that reflected the rush of the metropolis and carried the audience along. Assessing Mehring's work in 1920, Tucholsky wrote: "Never has there been anything like such rhythm." Significantly, he faulted Mehring only for neglecting the "idyllic" aspects of Berlin, for seeing the city as too "hard-mouthed" *(hartmäulig)*. That said as much about Tucholsky's tendency toward sentimentality, often apparent in his love songs, as it did about Mehring's focus on Berlin's metropolitan brio. In general, though, Tucholsky expressed enthusiasm for Mehring, and he concluded: "If the new age has brought forth a new poet: here he is."[50]

Tucholsky regretted that "Mehring does not have it easy. There is no cabaret adequate for him." At that time the only alternative to Sound and Smoke was Rosa Valetti's Megalomania, which featured some of Mehring's works. Just as Valetti sang Tucholsky's most radical song, the "Red Melody," her repertory included Mehring's most aggressive political poem, "Simultaneous Berlin" (Berlin simultan). It began with an image of Ebert as a self-made man who had profited from the revolution: "In auto-dress a self-made-gent / Make way! For it's the President!" (Im Autodress ein self-made-gent / Passage frei! Der Präsident!). Short, clipped lines then evoked various scenes of postwar Berlin: an "academic proletarian" dying in the dirt, a man accosting prostitutes, black marketeers plying their trades. Soon the major theme of the poem appeared—the rise of violent anti-Semitic forces:

> An Ufa film
> Hails Kaiser Wil'm.
> Cathedrals wag reaction's flag,
> With swastikas and poison gas,
> Monocles won't let hooked noses pass.
> On to the pogrom
> In the hippodrome!
>
> Im Ufafilm
> Hoch Kaiser Wil'm.
> Die Reaktion flaggt schon am Dom,
> Mit Hakenkreuz und Blaukreuzgas,
> Monokel kontra Hakennas'
> Auf zum Pogrom
> Beim Hippodrom![51]

By 1920 Mehring, himself of Jewish descent, saw more than wordplay in the juxtaposition of swastikas, poison gas, and "hook-nosed" Jews (Hakenkreuz, Blaukreuzgas, Hakennas'). The Ufa film company had been founded during the war with government funding as a medium of war propaganda, and the film industry continued to spout nationalist sentiments in the Weimar era. Mehring warned that such nationalistic entertainment could incite actual anti-Semitic violence, which might be staged as a public spectacle: the "pogrom" in the "hippodrome." By suggesting that a violent, politicized mass art could inspire a violent, aestheticized mass politics, Mehring anticipated some of the theories of fascism later developed by Ernst Bloch, Siegfried Kracauer, and Walter Benjamin.

Mehring had difficulty finding a cabaret, let alone a hippodrome, appropriate to his own art. Sound and Smoke soon was given over to variety shows, and Valetti's stage eventually turned into a theater for one-act plays. Yet in the fall of 1921 a new locale proved hospitable to Mehring's works. Trude Hesterberg (1892–1967) had attended Reinhardt's acting school and had made a name for herself as an operetta singer. She performed at Nelson's Künstlerspiele during the war, and thereafter she appeared occasionally at Sound and Smoke. At that point she apparently caught the cabaret bug. Inspired by Valetti's management of Megalomania, Hesterberg borrowed some money and opened her own cabaret, the Wild Stage (Wilde Bühne) in the basement of the Theater des Westens on September 11, 1921.

Hesterberg managed to hire, and at times discover, some of the very best cabaret talent of the twenties. One very popular new number on her stage was presented by Wilhelm Bendow, who appeared as "Lydia Smith, the Tattooed Lady." Wearing an illustrated body cast, "she" pointed to various pictures on "her" body, and made comments with sexual overtones about political figures ("the assembled impotentates of Europe") and other celebrities of the day. Other prominent members of the troupe were Marcellus Schiffer, who wrote lyrics, and the composer Mischa Spoliansky. As we shall see, by the end of the decade that team would be writing some of the most successful cabaret-revues. The Wild Stage was the first cabaret to perform a song by Erich Kästner, who likewise would write some of the best cabaret lyrics in the waning years of the Weimar Republic. Moreover, the only time that Bertolt Brecht personally performed his songs in a Berlin cabaret was in January 1922, on Hesterberg's stage. For six days he sang "Jakob Apfelböck," about a boy who murdered his parents, and the "Ballad of the Dead Soldier" (Die Ballade vom toten Soldaten). This grotesque song described how the German army, short on manpower in the waning months of the war, dug up a soldier who had already been killed once in battle and sent him back to fight at the front. The bitter work, which also attacked military doctors, churchmen, and chauvinist citizens, caused a scandal at its first performance, and Hesterberg had to drop the curtain until the audience quieted down.[52]

Hesterberg was helped in her talent search by Walter Mehring, whose works held a central place on the Wild Stage. In May 1922, when exhaustion forced Hesterberg to leave the venture for several months, he became artistic director of the cabaret. Hesterberg personally sang many of his

20. Trude Hesterberg sings Mehring's "Song of the Stock Exchange."

lyrics, such as the "Song of the Stock Exchange" (Börsenlied; fig. 20). The number was a satirical pastiche of business clichés ("time is money," "no risk, no gain") as well as patriotic songs and religious hymns, slightly varied to acquire a capitalist bent. Mehring had another worthy interpreter of his works in Kurt Gerron (1897–1944). Hailed by many critics as an equal to Paul Graetz, Gerron threw Mehring's verses at the audience in a manner that was, according to Herrmann-Neisse, "striking, concentrated, threatening, hitting, at times resounding." Two of Gerron's most successful numbers were Mehring's "Pied Piper of Hamelin" (Der Rattenfänger von Hameln) and "Breaking-In" (Dressur). The "Pied Piper" ("Rat-Catcher" in German) called together a long list of contemporary characters, including politicians, black marketeers, pseudo-educated bourgeois, and literati. They were addressed as an assortment of vermin, capable only of crawling: "Groveling has won the day" (Heute siegt die Kriecherei). For "Breaking-In," Gerron dressed as a whip-wielding circus trainer who tried to tame "the beast humanity." It portrayed a man-eat-man world of anti-Semites hungering after Jews, capitalists thirsting for their competitors, and politicians panting for putsches. In a world calling for violence and war, the tamer claimed to have brought all of these animals to heel.[53]

But who was breaking in whom? What was Mehring really saying? On the surface it might seem that he was calling for an authoritarian, Hobbesian solution: since men naturally tore themselves apart, they needed a strong leader to keep them docile and pacific. That cannot have been the intended message, however, since Mehring was no supporter of a dictatorial state, in spite of his belief that *homo homini lupus*. An alternative was proposed within the refrain, but it was hardly a happy solution. "Everyone—drilled in liberty" (Alles—in Freiheit dressiert) implied that social peace could be achieved by "training" people to "be free." The choice of words suggested, however, that socialization for a republican democracy was just one more form of breaking-in; it masked the fact that someone somewhere was still cracking the whip. Mehring apparently saw no resolution to the paradoxes he presented. Violence and power seemed to be facts of life. Even freedom, as defined by the state, was suspect.

Unlike Tucholsky, Mehring could not bring himself to write idealistic or sentimental works that held out hope for a fraternal handshake among Germany's contending parties and classes. Like Tucholsky, he failed to turn cabaretic satire into an instrument for focused political criticism. Both men took a bleak view of postwar German developments, which seemed to be aggravated with every passing year. Significantly, they felt increasingly attracted to France, a country that had nurtured a genuine revolutionary tradition and developed a firm republican system. Mehring took trips to Paris regularly as of 1921, and lived there from 1924 to 1928, before returning to Berlin. Tucholsky's emigration was more definite: he moved to Paris in 1924, as correspondent for the *Weltbühne* and *Vossische Zeitung*, then to Sweden in 1929. Even when abroad, both men maintained close ties to Berlin and continued to write lyrics and essays commenting on German conditions. Still, they had reached a point where they despaired of Germany's becoming a stable republican polity.

Tucholsky and Mehring may have succumbed to political despondency, but that did not prevent them from becoming outstanding satirists. Cabaret remained a questionable political tool, but it offered wide opportunities for political entertainment. Both men were masters at underscoring the contradictions that plagued the early Weimar Republic and at capturing the spirit of postwar Berlin. In October 1920, Karl Wilcynski, himself a cabaret performer, had said of Mehring's and Tucholsky's works, as performed by Graetz and backed by Hollaender's music: "They are Berlin." That same month, the author Alfred Richard Meyer said of the work of those four men: "Here is a completely new style of song. Current events are raised to a literary height." This new style was so influential that it even was appropriated by the outspokenly conservative cabarets. In March 1922 Herrmann-Neisse wrote of right-wing "political humorists": "Of course the recent tendency is to have intonation and presentation freely based on Paul Graetz, verse form freely based on Mehring, and as content the fondly heard preaching of [right-wing] editorials."[54] The style, but not the politics, of Tucholsky and Mehring had made inroads among the antirepublican competition. That was paltry compensation for the fact that the public's muted enthusiasm for republican values had attenuated Tucholsky's and Mehring's own political engagement, beginning with Sound and Smoke.

The year 1923 marked the end of the postwar political cabarets. Audience attitudes, as well as the political paradoxes that tied up the satirists, had been recurrent stumbling blocks. Now the rampant hyperinflation dealt a crushing blow, and the Wild Stage was forced to close. No other cabarets with serious political or literary aspirations survived that year. Herrmann-Neisse lamented in the fall of 1924: "In place of an intellectual, fighting cabaret, Berlin now has long been dominated by all types of cabaret surrogates." A year later he could only repeat himself: "A decisively independent, purposefully intellectual and fighting cabaret no longer exists, only amusement locales on approximately the same level, each of which has its own method of acceding to the wishes of the public."[55] What the public of the mid-twenties wanted was not critical cabaret, but spectacular revue.

# The Weimar Revue

The most popular form of live entertainment in Weimar Berlin was the revue. Although revues tended to avoid overt political statements, they revealed some prevailing assumptions about gender as well as race. Immediately after the war the abolition of preliminary censorship allowed nude dancing *(Nackttanz)* to flourish. In a series of actions in 1922, such as the trial of Celly de Rheidt, the police and the courts were able to establish some control over the public display of women's bodies. These cases set guidelines for presenting the live female form, which became the major attraction of the revues. Such stages also performed "Americanized" music and entertainment. Their conception of the United States was influenced by what Germans perceived to be black culture, which they considered a form of vital "primitivism" appropriate to modern urban life. This characterization of blacks, however well-meaning in intent, underscored prevailing racial stereotypes. Similarly, reactions to the kicklines of "Girls" revealed attitudes toward gender and sexuality. Superficially, the Girls seemed to embody a vital new image of womanhood. More fundamentally, however, they represented deeper structures of order and control in the modern world.

## Nude Dancing on the Early Weimar Stage

In the early years of the Weimar Republic numerous entrepreneurs took advantage of the abolition of preliminary censorship and staged shows featuring naked or nearly naked women. Before 1918 the police could prohibit, in advance of a performance, any presentation that they believed would offend public morals or religious sensibilities. In Prussia, producers could appeal to the courts to overturn such bans; they often were successful in cases where works by respectable playwrights had been proscribed. Yet for "minor" genres, such as cabaret or dance, court cases would have been too costly and their outcome too unpredictable; thus managers of such shows were forced to abide by the decisions of the police. After the war this situation changed dramatically, as no stage performance was required

21. "Beauty in its purest and most original form": young members of the Ballet Celly de Rheidt.

to receive prior approval. That did not mean, however, that everything was permissible. The public prosecutor still could bring producers and performers to trial for violating articles 183 or 184 of the Penal Code, which prohibited public obscenity, or article 166, concerning blasphemy. Nevertheless, in the early years of the Weimar Republic, Berlin stages enjoyed considerable freedom of a rather unwholesome sort. Social and political dislocations, the strained resources of the police, and liberalized definitions of obscenity often permitted public displays of nudity to pass unchallenged.

One of the most notorious groups in those years was the Ballet Celly de Rheidt. The eponymous dancer was in fact named Cäcilie Funk (born 1889), and was married to Alfred Seweloh (born 1887), a demobilized first lieutenant. Times were difficult for officers following the war, but Seweloh realized that his wife might generate the needed income. During the course of 1919 he began to arrange for "beauty evenings" *(Schönheitsabende),* a code word for nude dancing, featuring his wife and other women in various states of undress (fig. 21). In order to justify these presentations, Seweloh claimed that they were inspired by classical art, and that they served to rejuvenate the shattered German nation. In a program booklet for the Celly de Rheidt ensemble circulated in December

1919, he wrote: "To our destitute people, broken and martyred by the most terrible of all wars, sunk into the grayness of everyday existence, we hope to bring beauty in its purest and most original form, in the shape of woman, God's creation, and to revive the sublime art of Praxiteles and blessed, marble-rich Hellas—that is the high goal and inspired aspiration of Celly de Rheidt." Acting as conferencier, Seweloh used similar words to introduce the performances in March 1920: "Our most fundamental goal is to bring the ideal of beauty to our shattered people, and to raise it up from its misery."[1]

Such statements did not fool anyone as to the true nature of the performance. As one reviewer noted, "the shattered German people could not possibly have appeared in great numbers. The high ticket prices are affordable only by that part of the people that has not been completely shattered." A police report of December 1919 reported that a performance of the Ballet Celly de Rheidt at the Babijou Bar, on the Potsdamerstrasse, was attended by "ca. 250 people of both sexes, belonging to the better circles." By August 1920 the police noted that although the ticket prices initially had ranged from 15 to 25 marks, the top price was now 100 marks. Indeed, there were rumors that during the Agricultural Week (Landwirtschaftswoche), when rich estate owners from the provinces would be in town, tickets had been sold for up to a thousand marks. In any case, it was true that the Ballet Celly de Rheidt had increased its advertising space in local newspapers for that week. Significantly, "women of the demimonde" could attend for a token fee, indicating that the shows also served as markets for prostitution.[2]

The well-heeled spectators were able to see quite a bit for their money. Sometimes Celly's dancers appeared with their pelvises thinly veiled, but little else in the way of clothing. On their upper bodies they might wear transparent scarves or strings of wooden beads, though these merely surrounded and "accentuated" their breasts, at least according to the police. Stefan Grossmann, the editor of the liberal Tagebuch, concluded that "breast-baring was actually one, if not the center of attraction of the performance." In any case, there was no question of aesthetic contemplation, since none of the women had received any formal training in dance, as a subsequent trial revealed. Critics and observers often used the word Hopserei (hopping around) to describe their movements. Their performances were, in essence, short pantomimes, lasting several minutes at most, on a variety of themes: "The Vampyr," "Salome," "Opium Intoxication," "Dance of the Gladiators," "Czardas." Herrmann-Neisse considered it an "extremely boring, untalented gesticulation." Grossmann found the dances "not immoral, but boring," and contended: "What is irritating is not the nakedness, but rather the fuss over it."[3]

Such opinions were not universally shared, however, since that "fuss" proved to be very profitable for Celly and her husband. Over the course of 1920 and 1921 they appeared at some of the more fashionable venues, often to sold-out houses. They were a frequent attraction at Nelson's Künstlerspiele, as well as at his former locale, the Schwarzer Kater; they even appeared at the nonliterary Sound and Smoke in October 1921. In 1920 they rented their own stage for some months and dubbed it the Celly de Rheidt Theater. Since performances lasted only a couple of hours and required little physical strain, mental concentration, or artistic skill, the troupe could easily appear at two different venues every evening.

The financial success of the venture did not mean that it was uncontroversial. One problem had to do with the performers: not only did they appear nearly naked, but many of them were underage. Celly was in her thirties, "somewhat rounded, equipped with a considerable layer of fat, and past her first springtime," according to Grossmann. He found that unproblematic: "If Frau Celly de Rheidt wants to display her body, that is her own business." He was horrified, however, that a girl who seemed to be only twelve years old performed with the troupe. The police later ascertained that several girls aged fourteen to sixteen were employed by the ballet. Other observers were shocked by some of the show's content. Two numbers in particular had a tendency to disturb more sensitive spectators. The inappropriately named "Danse de Paraguay" featured many belly-dance movements that seemed to imitate the motions of sexual intercourse. Even more provocative was a pantomime about a nun, danced by Celly. Falsely accused of breach of chastity and facing expulsion from her convent, the nun fell down before a statue of the Virgin Mary and tossed off her clothing. At that moment the statue, posed by another dancer, came to life and extended its arms in blessing. Thereafter the nun (still naked) ran to an altar and threw her arms around a crucifix. Seweloh prefaced the pantomime with the contention that "here nakedness is a divine revelation of chastity." For some observers, such comments only accentuated the offensiveness of the number.[4]

Throughout 1920 the police and the public prosecutor considered taking steps against the Ballet Celly de Rheidt. Yet they refrained, because some officers and prosecutors did not consider the performances obscene enough to guarantee a conviction, given current standards, which had become laxer since the abolition of preventive censorship. Occasionally they would send notes to the managers of theaters hosting the performances and request that the women be more fully clothed. Such missives could meet with stern rebuffs, unthinkable in the Wilhelmine era. In August 1921 Rudolf Nelson replied indignantly: "Competent experts in such matters have determined incontestably that the dance performances in my theater are presented with highest artistic perfection and only as a form of art, so that it is completely impossible that a person capable of distinguishing art from eroticism could experience even the slightest injury to his sense of decency." Nelson offered to hold two seats free every evening for the police, so that they could ascertain the veracity of his statement. Some reponses were even ruder. When an engineer denounced Celly's perform-ances in the Schwarzer Kater to the police, the manager of that theater wrote to the informant: "Apparently you became sexually aroused by the dances, and now you want to impute that to others. Why don't you just drive to Steinach [a clinic for sexual dysfunctions] and let them implant some new glands in you, then you won't need to seek artificial sexual arousal at so-called beauty evenings." That went too far, and in a civil trial the director was fined 600 marks for having written the insulting letter.[5]

Despite the defensiveness of the cabaret managers, protests about nude dancing kept reaching the police. The issue also was debated in the press. Liberals like Grossmann and Herrmann-Neisse believed that Celly's self-display was silly, but within her rights. Conservatives, however, were concerned about the moral fiber of the nation, especially in the wake of military defeat (a symbolic castration, if ever there was one). In May 1920 the journal of the Society for Combating Public Immorality declared: "We have lost many things in the past years, the war, our markets, our political prestige, our credit . . . As long as we retain our self-respect, everything is not yet lost. We are ripe for total decay only at the moment where we must admit to ourselves that we have also lost our self-respect." The article suggested that the success of Celly de Rheidt might indicate that such a moment had come. At the very least, it shamed Germany in the eyes of other nations: "Foreign countries already call us a dying person, rolling in the mire." The authorities too seemed concerned about the perceptions of foreigners. In an account of another show in March 1922, a policeman noted: "Americans also supposedly attended these nude dances, and are reported to have said that after having seen such things there and at other venues, they had to conclude that Germany was not as badly off as it was trying to claim."[6] At a time when Germany was attempting to prove its inability to meet reparations payments, it was unwise to have foreigners believe that Germans were squandering their money in immoral pursuits.

Despite repeated complaints by the conservative press and private citi-zens, the prosecutors could not legally move against the Ballet Celly de Rheidt until they received a formal denunciation from an offended member of the audience who was willing to press charges in court. In 1921 such a person finally stepped forward: Hoppe, a Protestant pastor motivated by moral as well as nationalistic concerns. During the trial, which lasted for a week in January 1922, he testified that he was devoted to the task of "raising the moral level of the German people, which has fallen deeply because of war and revolution." He attended Celly's performance at the Linden Cabaret in order to "ascertain that in our cabarets, things are presented which the majority of the German people, who do not belong to the ranks of champagne-swigging war-profiteers and similar cabaret patrons, decisively reject." On the basis of Hoppe's complaint the public prosecutor accused Celly, her husband, various members of her troupe, and the manager of the Linden Cabaret of violating various provisions of articles 183 and 184 of the Penal Code. The infractions included not only the dance performances but also the public screening of a "Celly de Rheidt" film, and the sale of postcards depicting her and other scantily clad members of the troupe.[7]

The judges eventually imposed stiff fines totaling 37,000 marks on Celly and her husband, as well as a token fine on the cabaret director. Mercifully, they exonerated the underage dancers of conscious criminal wrongdoing. In order to attain that conviction for obscenity, the prosecutor needed to prove that Celly's performances, film, and postcards had no artistic merit, and that they "had the tendency to injure in a sexual connection the sense of shame and morality of an impartial and reasonable person with natural thoughts and feelings." Aesthetic value and "natural" sexual sensitivity are, of course, impossible to determine objectively, so the trial brought to light the officially acceptable boundaries of those spheres. Indeed, it indicated that sexuality and aesthetics were intimately connected, since what was permissible in one cultural context was punishable in another.

On the surface, the case was clear-cut. Several expert witnesses, including a ballerina from the Berlin State Opera, testified that there was nothing artistic in the performances of Celly de Rheidt. More important, the Sewelohs' defense was seriously undermined by the fact that before an appearance of the troupe, which was slightly delayed, the director of the Linden Cabaret had told the audience: "Be patient a few minutes, the women dancers are not yet completely undressed." On another occasion he announced their entry on stage with the comment: "The reason why you came here at all—will now appear."[8] In legal terms those were damning statements, since they conceded (for anyone who needed convincing) that the performance was presented as nude dancing, without any artistic aspirations. With such evidence, conviction was not too difficult. Nevertheless, in their thirty-page summary of the case, the judges had to provide a detailed justification of why the major defendants were convicted on certain counts but not others. Those arguments revealed the niceties of judicial thought on sexual and artistic issues.

In the postwar period German courts had ruled that nudity was not in and of itself obscene, and that it was permissible in certain artistic contexts. The judges thus had to argue that those conditions did not apply in the case of Celly's stage appearances, film, and postcards. They contended that her performances might have been considered more artistic in the context of a regular theater, where the darkened auditorium and spotlighted stage would have kept the dancers at some physical and aesthetic distance from the audience. The context of a locale like the Linden Cabaret was, however, very different. The small space meant that the audience, except for those in the cheapest seats, "finds itself in almost immediate contact with the performers." The fact that house lights were kept on and the patrons consumed drinks and tobacco negated the possibility of any aesthetic distance between performers and spectators. By drawing that distinction, the judges made clear that, in the eyes of the law, a cabaret was by nature a more suspicious, and certainly less artistic, venue than a more conventional stage.[9]

Similar differentiations were made in the realm of photography. Some ten thousand postcards had been printed, depicting Celly and other members of her troupe in more memorable poses: "On the fourth postcard Cäcilie Seweloh kneels completely naked in a church before the crucifix, which she touches with her hands. Above all the swelling breasts catch the eye of the beholder." The judges concluded: "The postcards are faulty reproductions of original photographs. They lack any and all technical perfection and artistic value. The grossly sensual nature of the cards is not mitigated by any artistic execution. The cards are objectively obscene." In contrast, the defendants were not held criminally responsible for two larger photographs (18 by 24 centimeters) that were displayed in the Linden Cabaret: "The gaze of the beholder is directed to the breasts of the women dancers. It cannot be denied that something sensual resides in the pictures. Yet the photographs display such technical perfection and artistic execution that the sensual aspects of the pictures are mitigated. These photographs thus do not have the tendency to injure in a sexual connection the sense of shame and morality of an impartial person with reasonable thoughts and feelings."[10] Although the judges contended that both sets of pictures directed the gaze of the spectator toward the women's bared bosoms, the lower artistic status of the postcard medium made it criminally liable, while the larger photographs were protected by their supposedly higher artistic quality.

The judges thereby reinforced aesthetic distinctions dating to the nineteenth century, which were social distinctions as well. Academic nudes had been highly respected and cherished as long as they conformed to certain conventions: they had to look "finished," and their subject matter had to be located in a mythologically or historically distant past, or in a geographically distant and "exotic" country. Works like Edouard Manet's naked *Olympia* (1865), which was both contemporary in theme and unfinished in appearance, were considered beyond the pale. Yet even "acceptable" nudes were considered unacceptable possessions for certain social groups. Before the mid-nineteenth century academic nudes were accessible only to the wealthy and educated classes, who could afford to buy the originals or expensive reproductions or view them in museums. In the last half of the century, however, technological developments gave rise to new media such as lithographs and photographic postcards, which allowed cheap, mass reproduction of images. The German police, who had permitted the sale of expensive reproductions of nudes by, say, Ingres or Bouguereau, confiscated those same images if they happened to be distributed as postcards. The justification for this distinction was both moral and social: the authorities feared that the more affordable pictures of nudes might fall into the hands of "uneducated" youths or the equally "uneducated" poor, who did not have the proper aesthetic training to view such pictures in a "disinterested," that is, nonsexual, manner. Needless to say, that was a sham argument. The pictures in question were often very provocative, but it was assumed that while the middle-class man could control his sexual urges, the youth or the worker could not.[11]

That manner of reasoning, which first appeared in Germany in the 1860s, continued to be upheld by Celly's judges three generations later. Ironically, Alfred Seweloh tried to counteract it on its own terms. He argued that the image of the naked nun clasping the crucifix was inspired by a well-known painting: *Renunciation* (1891), by the respected British artist Philip Calderon. That work had itself been a focus of controversy. Originally entitled *Saint Elizabeth of Hungary,* the painting purported to illustrate the legend, according to which the young and beautiful princess cast off her expensive garments and became a Franciscan tertiary, devoting her life to aiding the poor. Since it depicted a naked woman kneeling before an altar, the painting scandalized many Catholics when it was shown at London's Royal Academy. Critics immediately pointed out the obvious: to say that Elizabeth cast off her *expensive* raiments did not mean that she cast off *all* of her clothes. Calderon, admitting that he had misinterpreted the legend, renamed his work *Renunciation.* Seweloh's claim that he was inspired by Calderon did not impress the judges, who were also skeptical of the painting. They argued that although the subject matter seemed similar, the difference in media determined that while the academic painting "might" be considered artistic, the postcard was definitely obscene.[12]

The judges of the Ballet Celly de Rheidt went even further: they updated such arguments to the detriment of the new medium of film. They ruled that whatever might have been "pleasing" *(das Gefällige)* in a live performance of the dances was totally negated by its transfer to celluloid: "Here the dances are impaired every time by the flickering light, so that the dance movements are less gracious in the film. Furthermore, the film 'Celly de Rheidt' utilizes only black and white. [Quality films tended to have color tinting.] Through all of these defects of the film the pleasing aspects of the dance movements recede and the grossly sensual aspects of the presentation come that much more to the fore. The film produces an even more obscene impression than the dances of the ballet on the stage."[13] Obviously no fans of cinema, the judges here used specious arguments to condemn the medium. After all, they could have argued that the poor quality of the black-and-white film, by negating the plasticity and flesh tones of the nude dancers, seriously undercut the erotic potential of the performance. Did they really believe that a poorly shot film was more obscene than the show at the Linden Cabaret, performed with house lights brightly illuminated? It is more likely that they, like many other conservative and educated citizens, were simply venting their prejudices against the new mass medium. After all, just as inexpensive postcards allowed academic nudes to be purchased by the "wrong" groups, the cheap prices of sensationalistic films threatened to corrupt youths and the poorer classes.

After the trial the Ballet Celly de Rheidt continued to perform, but conviction allowed the police to impose strict regulations on the dancers' attire. The women were ordered to have their breasts and pelvic areas fully covered, otherwise the troupe would be banned permanently from Berlin. The owners of cabarets where Celly appeared were told that if they did not enforce the regulations, they would be shut down. The resulting reduction of exposed skin evidently reduced attendance as well. In April 1922 Herrmann-Neisse referred to appearances of the Ballet Celly de Rheidt, "which does not know how to dance, and whose only means of making an impact is being killed off by official guardians of morality." The economic consequences of such enforced coverups were made clear in the case of the Lola Bach Ballet, which likewise was brought to trial in December 1921, and even resulted in a month's imprisonment for its founder. A police report on a later performance, which operated under the same restrictions as Celly's troupe, revealed a sad financial state of affairs: "During all of these dances the clothing was such that all women dancers had their private parts, breasts, buttocks, and navels completely covered with opaque fabrics. At the end of the performance I presented myself to the business manager [of the Cabaret Potpourri]. He explained to me that because of the decent apparel of the women dancers, attendance at the locality has dropped off sharply, and thus an entrance fee is no longer charged." Celly's situation was equally discouraging. By 1923 the founding couple had divorced and their troupe had split in two, and Alfred and

Cäcilie Seweloh were engaged in a legal battle over the right to use the name Ballet Celly de Rheidt for their respective companies. Cäcilie Funk won the case, but little was heard of her again.[14]

The trials of Lola Bach and Celly de Rheidt crippled two of the more prominent promoters of nude dancing, but they could not halt the wave of prurient entertainment. It was not until the beginning of 1923 that a general crackdown was legally possible. In the wake of the French and Belgian occupation of the Ruhr, Prussia, like most of Germany, declared a state of emergency based on article 48 of the Constitution; this allowed the executive branch to promulgate emergency legislation *(Notstandsgesetze)*. As the weeks passed, Carl Severing, the minister of the interior, used the situation to regulate those aspects of nighttime entertainment that had gotten out of hand. On February 24 he issued a decree that permitted the police to restrict or prohibit any entertainments which merely raised their "doubts" *(Bedenken)*. Severing argued that "now more than ever" it was necessary to uphold law and order, and he ordered that especially severe measures should be taken against "plays which, by their choice of subject matter or by the nature and impact of their presentation, challenge and injure the legitimate feelings of all decent people in a wanton, frivolous, or offensive manner."[15] This decree gave the Berlin police the authority they needed to ban all nude shows.

The eventual lifting of the state of emergency took away the power of the Berlin police summarily to shut down offending locales. By that time, however, they had developed guidelines for public performances that remained in effect for the remainder of the Weimar period. These strictures, though more liberal than the total ban on nudity under the emergency decrees, were slightly more severe than the conditions that had prevailed in the early Weimar years. They were spelled out in a letter of Berlin's chief of police to his counterpart in Dresden: "Women dancers must cover completely their posterior, private parts, and navel with opaque fabrics, so that during dance movements these body parts cannot be revealed in a naked state. Furthermore, the breasts must be covered at least to the extent that the nipples cannot be seen during dance movements."[16] Since these restrictions applied only to women in motion, it was permissible to display fully naked women as long as they remained immobile. As we shall see, these guidelines determined the presentation of women in the Weimar revues.

These guidelines also underscored a curious paradox in the policing of nude dancing. Although the authorities were supposed to restrain obscenity, they were simultaneously complicit in shaping and sustaining it. Coupling nudity with immobility reinforced a traditional pattern of objectification. The naked woman, the woman most open to the gaze of others, was compelled by law to remain totally passive. As soon as she moved, she was required to adopt a series of coverings which defined—again, by law—her erogenous zones. The uncovering and covering of these parts, according to the immobility or activity of the woman, equated female sexual exposure with a passive female stance.

While searching out obscenity, the police were simultaneously opponents and guardians of the obscene. In a curious act of conflation, the policeman's gaze was confounded with that of the lewdest conceivable spectator. The internal police reports on dancers focused exclusively on the anatomical details of the performers. A typical account dealt with Anita Berber, one of the more controversial dancers of the twenties. Notorious for bisexuality and cocaine addiction in her private life, but respected for the artistry, passion, and intensity of her performances, Berber garnered praise from serious critics like Herrmann-Neisse. Nevertheless, the tone of police reports can be gleaned from the following account of her performance in 1926: "The sexual parts, around which the pubic hairs seem to have been shaved off, are clearly visible and are so imperfectly covered by the band between the thighs, that the labia bulge out to the left and the right of the band. The posterior is uncovered." In order to make such observations, the policeman must have adopted the pose of those leering spectators described by another gendarme, at a performance of the Lola Bach ballet in 1921: "If the men in the audience had desired to appreciate the dances and tableaux as a form of art, then they definitely would have to have viewed the presentations as a whole. But this is completely out of the question, since the spectators gazed with opera glasses at a distance of 5 to 10 meters, whereby they could see only individual parts of the body, or could scrutinize at most a single person."[17]

Of course, the police would have argued that the only way to ascertain obscene sights was to go out and see them. There was, however, a self-fulfilling element to their endeavors, insofar as they assumed that the spectators would view the show in the most prurient manner possible. Simultaneously, the authorities could plead their own innocence by adopting a grammatically passive voice. The judges' statements on Celly's postcards and photographs, cited above, did precisely that: "The gaze of the beholder is directed to the breasts of the women dancers" (Der Blick des Beschauers wird auf die Brüste der Tänzerinnen gelenkt), or "the swelling breasts catch the gaze of the beholder" (Dem Blick des Beschauers fallen vor allem die schwellenden Brüste ins Auge). The syntax of those sentences makes the "breasts" the active agents of the visual exchange. Such circumlocutions translate as: "I gazed at these women's breasts—but I was seduced into doing so." Even Weimar judges could not resist the charms of Celly and her troupe, which was all the more reason to punish her.

Naturally, the police and the courts were not wrong to assume that lascivious gazing was a primary ingredient in the success of nude dancing in the early Weimar years. The practitioners of literary and political cabaret might make fun of prurient entertainment, as Tucholsky did in "Take it Off, Petronella," or Mehring in his satirical evocation of the "Swallow's Nest Cabaret:"

> Though films might offer competition,
> We bank on lustful dispositions.
> The legs are still the very best
> At the Swallow's Nest!
>
> Droht auch das Kino Konkurrenz,
> Wir bauen auf die Lusttendenz
> Die Waden bleiben doch das Beste
> Im Schwalbenneste![18]

Such parodies could not stem the commercial appeal of troupes like the Ballet Celly de Rheidt, which even appeared at such respectable venues as Sound and Smoke and Nelson's cabaret. It took intervention by the courts and the police to bring some order to the presentations, and the guidelines they established shaped the parameters of Weimar revues.

## The Americanization of Entertainment: Jazz and Black Performers

The years of so-called "relative stabilization" (1924–1929), between the end of the German inflation and the beginning of the global depression, were the golden age of the Weimar revue. This distinctive form of entertainment was associated primarily with three men: Herman Haller (Hermann Freund, 1871–1943), Erik Charell (Erich Karl Löwenberg, 1894–1973), and James Klein (1886–early 1940s; assumed to have been killed in the Holocaust). Klein, who had mounted variety shows in the prewar era, produced revues for the longest time span (1921–1929). He was considered the least respectable of these directors, given his excessive penchant for staging female nudity. Charell, a dancer, was known for his extravagant choreography and expensive sets and costumes, but he created only three revues in as many years (1924–1926). The most esteemed of the three was Haller, formerly an operetta director, whose six annual revues mounted between 1923 and 1929 epitomized the genre in the minds of contemporary observers, not least because they featured the famous Tiller Girls.[19]

The Klein, Charell, and Haller revues differed greatly from those presented by Nelson in the early Weimar years. Nelson addressed the "Kurfürstendamm public," a rather select, elite audience from the western neighborhoods of Berlin. His works pretended to a degree of sophistication, inasmuch as their effect was based upon a witty and intelligent combination of music and text, performed by exceptional entertainers. In contrast, the other revues were mounted in enormous theaters, seating up to three thousand spectators. Klein managed the Komische Oper, Haller directed the Theater am Admiralspalast, and Charell took over the Grosses Schauspielhaus after the financial failure of Reinhardt's monster spectacles. Unlike Nelson's new venue, these theaters were located on or near the Friedrichstrasse, the traditional entertainment district which continued to attract German and foreign tourists. The size and linguistic mix of the audience necessitated a type of performance that emphasized "show." It featured extravagant costumes, exotic sets, and what the parlance of the day called "Girls, Girls, Girls." If there was a point of comparison for the Weimar revues, it would have been the prewar performances at the Metropol-Theater, which likewise staged extravagant spectacles for a large and mixed public. In fact, the two were frequently contrasted, and always to the detriment of the later shows. Leaving questions of quality aside, a comparison of the Metropol revues with those of Klein, Charell, and Haller provides a means of assessing the tremendous changes that occurred in the realm of German popular entertainment after the Great War.

In both form and content the prewar Metropol revues had been considered ideal expressions of Berlin's metropolitan modernity. Formally, they replicated the fragmented diversity of urban experience; thematically, they exuded the self-confidence of the Imperial capital, the hub of the greatest power on the European continent as well as the world's second greatest industrial nation. This particular combination obviously could not survive the war. Germany's defeat and the economic catastrophy brought about by the blockade and the inflation meant that Berlin could no longer claim to be a model of modernity, at least not in any positive sense. We have seen that in 1919 Rudolf Nelson composed a song that deplored the provincialization of Berlin. That same year, Tucholsky's "Old Motor," sung by Graetz, no longer considered Paris and London worthy of emulation: people there "danced around golden calves," but the singer disdained such activities and told Berliners to remain true to their better natures.[20] Of course, it was rhetorically easy to reject a fashionable lifestyle that many citizens could no longer afford. Tucholsky was clearly trying to make the best of a bad situation.

Given such circumstances, it was to be expected that the early Weimar revues had no upbeat numbers about contemporary Berlin. Instead, they harked back to the "good old days" before the military and economic traumas. Walter Kollo, who composed much of the music featured in the

Haller revues, was perhaps the major cultivator of that theme. His famous "Linden-March" in *Under and Over (Drunter und Drüber),* which premiered in September 1923, at the height of the inflation, remains the epitome of Berlin nostalgia:

> As long as lindens greet us
> There where they've always been,
> Then nothing can defeat us.
> Berlin, you're still Berlin.

> So lang noch Untern Linden
> Die alten Bäume blüh'n,
> Kann nichts uns überwinden,
> Berlin, du bleibst Berlin.[21]

Marlene Dietrich was to revive that song after 1945. By then, it was the 1920s that seemed like the Golden Years.

Although the shows of the early- and mid-twenties could not portray Berlin in a positive light, revues were even more popular after the war than before. The 1926–27 Berlin theater season saw no less than nine revues, playing to nightly audiences totaling eleven thousand spectators. Faced with such statistics, social theorists continued to contend that the variegated form of revues was most appropriate to that city, whose mutability was even more pronounced owing to the postwar dislocations. Siegfried Kracauer and Ernst Bloch noted the congruence between Berlin and the formal aspects of revue. For Bloch, that metropolis appeared to be "a city that is perennially new, a city built around a hollow space, in which not even the mortar becomes or remains hard." Revues seemed to correspond to Berlin's protean nature, since they were "one of the most open and unintentionally honest forms of the present, a cast of that hollow space . . . The appeal of the revues comes precisely from the sensual power and turbulence of scenes strung loosely together, from their ability to change and to transform themselves into one another." Kracauer praised the ability of revues (as well as cinema) to convey "precisely and openly the *disorder* of society . . . In the streets of Berlin one is, not infrequently, struck by the realization that all of a sudden everything might split apart one day. The amusements to which the public throngs also should have that effect." He believed that "the Berlin public behaves in a profoundly truthful manner when it increasingly shuns [conventional forms of high art] . . . and shows its preference for the superficial luster of stars, films, revues, and production numbers. Here, in pure externality, it finds itself; the dismembered succession of splendid sensory perceptions brings to light its own reality."[22]

Just as Bloch's and Kracauer's comments echoed those of Simmel a generation earlier, spokesmen for the Weimar revues updated the assertions of Wolzogen and Bierbaum. Writing in the program book for Charell's *For Everyone!* (*An Alle!*, 1924), Maximilian Sladek, the manager of the Grosses Schauspielhaus, contended that "the life of the big-city dweller is a multifarious interlacing of surfaces. And every life demands the art in which it recognizes itself." Predictably, Sladek concluded that the revue, along with film, was the art most adequate to the urbanite's condition. Whereas variety shows and cabaret had been linked in the discourse of the fin de siècle, now the pairing was film and revue. Cinema had replaced vaudeville as the major form of popular entertainment. This was paradoxical, inasmuch as the first film had been screened in the Wintergarten in 1895, and short films had been part of many variety shows in the ensuing decade. Thereafter, however, the rapid spread of cinemas devoted exclusively to film screenings drove hundreds of vaudevilles out of business in neighborhoods throughout Germany. By the twenties, even managers of regular theaters were worried that they were losing customers to cinema, just as they had complained about vaudeville in the 1890s. In 1924 Monty Jacobs, a respected drama critic of the Weimar era, suggested that the postwar proliferation of revues was an attempt to halt that hemorrhage: "At the moment nothing merits closer attention from theater critics than the development of revue. For with this art form the directors are trying to intercept the departing audience, which is streaming from the stage to the cinema."[23]

Weimar revues tried to compete with cinema by mounting increasingly longer and more spectacular shows. Consequently, the revues of the twenties were distinctly more heterogenous than those of the Wilhelmine era. The visual effects were not only more stunning but more numerous: there could be up to sixty different scenes or numbers in an evening. To mount such excessive shows, the directors had to draw upon a wide assortment of genres. Frank Warschauer, a writer for the *Weltbühne*, noted that the revue "lived in wanton, truly wanton concubinage with variety shows, waxworks, cabaret, operetta, also film, in short, with everything that could possibly come into question for its purposes." Such wild couplings required a wide assortment of partners. Whereas each Metropol revue had been scripted by a single author (Julius Freund) and composed by a single musician (Viktor Hollaender, Nelson, or Lincke), several people contributed texts and music to each of the revues produced by Klein, Charell, and Haller. In addition, a broad assortment of actors, comedians, singers, dancers, and vaudeville performers had to be assembled. Since Germany, let alone Berlin, could not provide enough talent to fill the evenings of three major and several minor revue stages, many entertainers and much music had to be imported from abroad. Reviewing *For Everyone,* War-schauer noted that Charell had brought together talent "from Russia, Scandinavia, England, France, and America. And from Berlin. The result is a cosy confusion of languages, which gives the gaping spectator the impression (or the illusion, I don't know for sure) that we are living in a cosmopolis [*Weltstadt*]."[24]

In the 1920s Berlin was still very concerned with maintaining its world-city image. Before the war it could lay claim to this distinction by touting its own qualifications as a capital of modernity, a global leader in industry, commerce, and consumerism. The disasters of the war and the inflation deprived the city of this distinction, and popular entertainment was forced to reformulate its metropolitan image. In the Weimar era the revues dem-onstrated their cosmopolitan allures not by touting Berlin, but rather by presenting an array of foreign numbers. This accounted for the major difference between prewar and postwar revues. In both the Wilhelmine and the Weimar eras, the revue form was deemed appropriate to the hectic and ever-changing nature of Berlin life. In terms of content, however, postwar revues could no longer turn to Berlin itself for positive thematic images of modernity. They had to look abroad for such icons, and more often than not they turned to the United States. What Berlin claimed to be before the war, New York seemed to be thereafter: a hectic and mighty metropolis, a global center of production, finance, commerce, and con-sumerism.

The 1920s witnessed an Americanization of popular entertainment in Berlin. The music of the prewar revues had derived from waltzes, polkas, mazurkas, folk songs, and marches. Only occasionally would the tango, the Boston, the two-step, the cakewalk, or ragtime be added as exotic interludes. Paul Lincke, for example, wrote an "American Cake-Walk" with the unfortunate title, "Coon's Birthday" (1903), and it will be recalled that "Niggersongs" were performed at the Hungry Pegasus in 1901. Such works were inspired by the occasional appearance of black American troupes in Berlin variety shows at the turn of the century. After the war, however, American music flooded the stages. The specifically Central Euro-pean musical elements receded, and the melodies of revues came to be dominated increasingly by fox trot and jazz rhythms. Even successful popular composers like Nelson had to adopt the new idiom. An observer noted in 1926: "Just as operetta is defined musically by the three-quarter time of the waltz, the revue is characterized by two-quarter time, and more precisely by syncopation. A revue without syncopation seems almost un-thinkable to us today."[25]

Although musical purists might dispute the degree to which Germany produced any true jazz, the shift in popular musical style was radically apparent. A reactionary composer like Hans Pfitzner contended that the "jazz–fox trot flood" represented "the American tanks in the spiritual assault against European culture." The shrill sound of the clarinet and the trumpet, the wailing of the saxophone, and the syncopated rhythms of the drums, banjo, and piano all seemed to portend a breakdown of cultural order. The apparent wantonness of the dances that came with such music—the shimmy in the early twenties, the Charleston later in the decade— threatened to destroy the moral order as well. Yet what appalled the conservatives garnered applause from other circles. Writing in the *Weltbühne* in 1921, Hans Siemsen applauded jazz for being "so completely undignified. It knocks down every hint of dignity, correct posture, and starched collars. Whoever fears making himself laughable cannot dance it. The German high-school teacher cannot dance it. The Prussian reserve officer cannot dance it." Given the ability of jazz dance to promote humanity, kindness, and humor and to destroy "stupidity, haughtiness, and dignity," Siemsen wanted to prescribe it for all public officials. Indeed, had it been introduced earlier, it might have saved Germany from the war: "If only the Kaiser had danced jazz—then all of that never would have come to pass!"[26]

For enthusiasts of jazz, and of American culture in general, blacks became symbols of a radically new cultural sensibility. Although various forms of jazz and pseudo-jazz had been heard in dance halls and on records since the end of the war, Berliners had few opportunities to experience live performances by Americans until after 1924, since there was no financial incentive to perform in Germany until its currency had been stabilized. Two revues featuring American blacks made an especially big impression. The "Chocolate Kiddies" troupe, featuring Sam Wooding playing music by Duke Ellington, appeared at Haller's Admiralspalast in May 1925. Josephine Baker and Louis Douglas staged a show at Nelson's theater the following January. The critical reception of these performances reflected the prevailing view that the United States was both the most modern and the most "primitive" of nations. Modernity was embodied in its technology; primitiveness was incorporated in its black population. Many reviewers did not regard the latter supposition as insulting, since they imputed to blacks a vital energy lacking in decadent and war-weary Europeans. Nevertheless, the discourse of writers putatively sympathetic to blacks was full of racial prejudices.

Since the turn of the century, it had been common for Germans to refer to American blacks as "coons" and "niggers." Even the Dadaist verse of George Grosz and Walter Mehring was replete with those words, albeit apparently without any ill intent, since the terms were used in contexts that approved of blacks and their culture. Not only were seemingly well-meaning Germans insensitive to the denigration and abuse embedded in those words; they also failed to note the more fundamental problems in their disquisitions on the "Africanness" of American blacks. Many liberal German observers attributed a primitive spontaneity to blacks, whose blood supposedly boiled from the heat of the ancestral jungle. A reviewer for the *Berliner Tageblatt,* who applauded the "victory of negroid dance culture over the Viennese waltz," said of Josephine Baker: "In her the wildness of her forefathers, who were transplanted from the Congo Basin to the Mississippi, is preserved most authentically; she breathes life, the power of nature, a wantonness that can hardly be contained." Oscar Bie, the respected dance critic of the *Berliner Börsen-Courier,* saw in her troupe "the remains of genuine paganism, of idol worship, of grotesque orgies." He imputed a similar chthonic feeling to the Chocolate Kiddies, who expressed a "true joy of the earth in drumming, shouting, dancing, singing, and jumping, totally devoid of a message, just as the earth itself." He considered their music "barbarically beautiful, full of primitive improvisations."[27]

At the same time that the black entertainers were considered primevally primitive, they somehow seemed to be paradigmatically modern. Bie believed that their performances could serve as a model for the revitalization of Germany: "They have brought us our culture. Humanity has returned to its origins in the niggersteps, in the shaking and loosened bodies. Only that can help us, we who have become too erratic. It is the deepest expression of our innermost longing." Such words echoed the works of the Expressionist artists a generation earlier, who had displayed their desire for primitive authenticity by painting imaginary scenes of African dancers. While Bie imputed to blacks a vitality that Germans lacked, Fred Hildenbrandt, a noted critic for the *Berliner Tageblatt,* contended that their performances gave perfect expression to the actual condition of European civilization: "What is it other than the tempo of our times, these fast-paced, wild times, whose symbol is truly embodied best of all in a rollicking negro theater." Hildenbrandt here echoed another cliché: that industrial and metropolitan civilization had stripped away cultural constraints and returned its citizens to a primitive wantonness. Count Harry Kessler, whose diaries provide one of the most perceptive accounts of Weimar Berlin, imagined a connection between "Africanness" and modernity. After seeing Baker's troupe at Nelson's theater on February 17, 1926, he wrote: "They are a cross between primeval forests and skyscrapers; likewise their music, jazz, in its color and rhythms. Ultramodern and ultraprimitive."[28]

Josephine Baker was nonchalant about such verbiage. In her memoirs of 1928, she wrote: "In Berlin's journals and newspapers they wrote that I was the embodiment of the German 'Expressionism' of today, of German

'Primitivism' etc. . . . . Why not? And anyway, what is the meaning of all that?"[29] Despite such dismissive words, black entertainers were at least partially complicit in sustaining the belief that they represented primitive vitality. In the United States generations of black performers had been forced to conform to comic stereotypes expected by white audiences. When black troupes crossed the Atlantic, they had to take prevailing prejudices there into account. The Chocolate Kiddies and the Baker-Douglas revue were commercial ventures that toured Europe and presented clichés about America in general, and American blacks in particular. The show starring Baker and Douglas, for example, featured scenes entitled "Steamboat Race on the Mississippi," "New York Skyscrapers," "Wedding in Charleston," "Florida Cabaret," "The Strutting Babies," and "Shake, Rattle, and Roll." The Chocolate Kiddies also exhibited cliché-ridden scenes of black American life (fig. 22).

While the black performers may have reinforced some stereotypes about their race, at times they succeeded in subverting those same images. Iwan Goll, a talented Expressionist writer, took note of the self-parody involved in Baker's "African" numbers. He believed that there was something intentionally ludicrous in the fact that an urban black woman performed a "Dance of Savages" while wearing a loincloth. Baker's most obvious send-

22. A performance of the Chocolate Kiddies in 1927.

23. Josephine Baker shakes her banana skirt at Berlin's Theater des Westens (1928). The curtain was drawn by Benno von Arent, who had no further use for such "degenerate Negro art" after becoming the official Reich Set Designer *(Reichsbühnenbildner)* and a Hitler protégé during the Nazi years.

up of African clichés was also her most famous number: the dance in a banana skirt, which she performed during an appearance at the Theater des Westens in 1928 (fig. 23). At the same time that black entertainers exploded stereotyped images of Africa, they also parodied European society and culture. Douglas performed what he considered "German" ways of talking and walking, to the delight of his audience. He also danced a number that parodied Pavlova's rendition of Tchaikovsky's dying swan. Such acts underscored the stiffness of Europeans and the artificiality of their culture.[30]

Not all responses to black culture were sympathetic. Conservative defenders of European high culture like Pfitzner were horrified by Americanization in general and "negrification" in particular. Right-wing hostility to blacks dated back to Imperial times, when the Reich had large colonial holdings in Africa. German rule was particularly harsh and provoked the Herero and Hottentot uprising in German Southwest Africa and the Maui-Maui revolt in German East Africa. Both were suppressed with tremendous bloodshed; tens of thousands of Hereros were massacred in what became the first instance of genocide in modern German history. Complaints in the Reichstag about such brutalities led to the furious parliamentary campaign of 1907, the so-called Hottentot election, in which Chancellor Bülow rallied nationalist support behind the colonial policies. It will be recalled that the popular soldiers' song, "Annemarie," was written for the Metropol revue in the wake of that campaign.

The colonial experience generated a discourse on the necessity of protecting German culture from black barbarism. That ideology was resurrected in World War I, when German illustrated newspapers mocked the French use of black colonial troops. Photographs of African soldiers on the Western front were accompanied by captions implying that the French were importing barbarism onto European soil. After the war, hostility to those colonial troops burst forth with a vengeance when the French stationed Senegalese and other black soldiers in the occupied Rhineland. Conservative Germans regarded that as an impossible humiliation, and spread rumors that the African troops were systematically seducing, even raping German women. This story, dubbed the "black outrage" (die schwarze Schmach), gained credence in many circles.[31]

Rumors of the "black outrage" even affected the cabaret stage. In early 1922 the police banned two nude-show numbers involving black men with white women. The Lola Bach Ballet, appearing in the Potpourri and Weisse Maus cabarets, included a dance duet with a black man and a white woman. Although the police conceded that the number was not sexually indecent, they prohibited it because they feared it might provoke disturbances. The police took passing note of the private travails of the black dancer, who was born in Cameroon, married to a German woman, and father of a three-year-old girl: "In light of the conditions in the western parts of our country, he has already been subjected to the most unpleasant molestations when he has taken his wife on trips and gone out with her. In Dresden he and his wife were literally spit upon, even by workers." The police also prohibited the performance of a dance entitled "Erotik" by the

Erna Offeney Ballet, because it involved a scene in which four black men forced a white woman to dance herself to death. Again, this number was not banned on account of obscenity, but because the police feared for "public order." Rather disingenuously, the lawyer for the troupe argued that the work should be permitted precisely because it presented "to the German people, in an eye-catching and frightening manner, the black outrage [*schwarze Schmach*]." The USPD's *Freiheit* called that assertion a piece of "impudence," inasmuch as "well-known members of the bourgeois parties and doctors in the occupied territories have reported repeatedly in the press that one cannot speak of a black outrage."[32]

Against such a background, it is understandable why opinion was so polarized over the spread of jazz and the appearance of black revues in the capital. For the right-wing mindset, black arts (or what passed for black arts) became a primary symbol of cultural degeneration. When Wilhelm Frick became the Thuringian minister of education in 1930—the first time a Nazi was appointed to a state cabinet—he promulgated a law entitled "Against Negro Culture," which was used to suppress all forms of avant-garde art. Likewise, when the Nazis mounted a "Degenerate Music" exhibition in 1938, the poster featured a caricature of a black saxophonist sporting a star of David. Paradoxically, however, the Nazis who equated "Negro art" with degeneration shared some of the assumptions of liberal and avant-garde artists, who envisioned black culture as a form of healthy primitivism. Both Nazis and their opponents made ideological statements about black culture, and in both cases, blackness was equated with barbarism—a racially degenerate and corrupt barbarism for the Nazis, a humane and liberating barbarism for the avant-garde.

### "Girls and Crisis"

Whereas the image of blacks on Weimar stages was controversial, another supposedly American icon garnered nearly unanimous praise: the kickline of "Girls." They usually consisted of some ten to twenty young women who performed fast, perfectly coordinated dance steps, as the Rockettes of Radio City Music Hall do to this day. In the 1920s the most famous of such troupes was that of the Tiller Girls, who in fact were English. John Tiller had been a cotton magnate in Manchester until he went bankrupt in the 1880s. Seeking a new vocation, he began to drill young women in perfectly synchronized movements. The number drew great attention in the 1890s, and by the 1920s several Tiller troupes were performing in major cities of various nations.[33] Haller hired one of them, the so-called Empire Girls, away from the Ziegfeld Follies in New York. This created some confusion about their nationality, and throughout the twenties many observers believed that they were an American troupe. The Empire Girls, renamed the Lawrence-Tiller-Girls (after the founder's son) in future seasons, were such a hit in the Haller revues that Charell saw himself compelled to hire his own troupe, the John-Tiller-Girls. Soon other troupes were formed, including the Hoffmann Girls and the Jackson Girls. To proclaim their originality and superiority, Haller's Tiller Girls adopted the slogan: "Often copied—never equaled!" (Oft kopiert—nie erreicht!).

Lineups of pretty women were nothing new. They had been a staple of numerous variety shows, as well as the prewar Metropol. What was novel was the dynamism and precision of the Tiller Girls. From their first performance, in Haller's *More and More* (*Noch und noch*, 1924), they garnered rave reviews. Herbert Ihering, arguably the outstanding theater critic of the Weimar era, immediately concluded that they, like the revue form itself, were a perfect expression of the age: "The revue accords with the needs of the modern metropolis . . . For the audience reacts to movement, to tempo. The applause for comedians is often weak, but for the Empire Girls it thunders right on into the intermissions. The rhythm, the lightness, the exactness are electrifying. The American [sic] Girls are a sight worth seeing and a standard to follow." Ihering concluded: "Beauty on stage, not through nakedness, but through motion."[34]

This dichotomy—in essence, between nude shows and kicklines—was apparent to many observers. We have seen that nudity played a prominent role in many postwar cabarets as well as revues. James Klein was particularly notorious in that regard. The titles of many of his revues attest to the prevalence of nudity: *The World without Veils, Berlin without a Shirt, Strictly Prohibited, Everyone's Naked, Goddam—1000 Naked Women!* *(Die Welt ohne Schleier, Berlin ohne Hemd, Streng verboten, Alles nackt, Donnerwetter—1000 nackte Frauen!)*. At the Komische Oper and similar venues, such as the Theater des Westens, naked women would be arranged in "artful" tableaux, which made them appear like parts of oversized flowers, jewels, or feathered fans. Not only critics but also the spokesmen for Haller and Charell often made fun of the "meat show" *(Fleischschau)* at Klein's theater, yet the more respectable revues were not wholly innocent.[35] Although nude tableaux were less common at the Admiralspalast and the Grosses Schauspielhaus, they still had a role to play. One of the most egregious illustrations of the traditional voyeuristic gaze appeared in Charell's *For You* (*Für Dich*, 1925). In a scene entitled "What Sailors Dream Of" (Wovon Matrosen träumen), a number of nude women were suspended in hammocks directly above a chorus of men dressed as sailors (fig. 24). The gentlemen in the audience were thus treated to sights about which seamen proverbially fantasized.

Within that context, it is understandable that numerous male critics of

24. Voyeurism and a cliché brought to life: "What Sailors Dream Of," in Eric Charell's revue of 1925.

the day noted approvingly that the Tiller Girls and similar troupes appeared to be sexless. Their short hair, slim build, and athletic performance differed radically from the more prurient displays, where naked women appeared in total passivity. In contrast, the Girls performed vigorous athletic motions. The Tiller Girls were known for their coordinated kicklines, often moving up and down stairs (fig. 25). The Hoffmann Girls specialized in even more athletic, circuslike stunts, such as synchronized climbing of ropes suspended from the stage ceiling. This radically new image of womanhood, full of strength and energy, negated the picture of passive sexual receptivity that had prevailed until then, and made the Girls seem asexual. Fritz Giese, a professor of "psychotechnics" at the University of Stuttgart and the author of a book entitled *Girlkultur,* referred to the Girls' "neutralization of the sexes, the exclusion of the feminine." Theater critics wrote of their "absolutely unerotic dance," which resided "beyond sexuality." Even Kracauer argued that they were not primarily sexual, but rather "a system of lines which no longer has an erotic meaning, but at

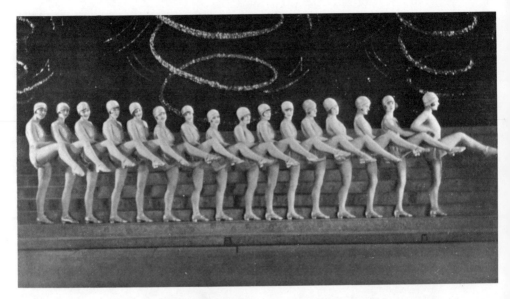

25. The Tiller Girls: "Often copied—never equaled!"

best signifies the place where the erotic may be found." The sexual inap-
proachability of troupes like the Tiller Girls was underscored by publicity
reports which stressed that they were constantly chaperoned, roomed in
pairs, and even traveled with their own pastor. The novelist Joseph Roth
complained ironically about the "well-behaved puritanism" and "provocative moral purity" of the Girls.[36]

One may question whether the Girls' appeal was as asexual as some
contemporary observers claimed. Coy publicity shots certainly gave the lie
to such contentions. Alfred Polgar, an outstanding critic of the day, admitted that he did not understand "why *women* actually go to revue
theaters . . . In revues the primacy of the male reveals itself still unshaken.
There is nothing there for women." Fred Hildenbrandt wondered what
the women in the audience must have thought about the fact that "it is
always members of their sex that run around on stage with hardly anything
on." They must have concluded the obvious: "that's the way the world is,
one has to cater to men, since they pay for the whole racket."[37]

Nevertheless, the persistence of claims that the Girls were asexual suggests that they could not be appropriated easily by more traditional voyeurism. After all, the conventional male gaze continued to be fortified by
the persistence of tableaux featuring naked women. Paul Morgan, a comedian who often appeared both in cabarets and at the Haller revue, wrote
a supposedly humorous vignette that contrasted the two options offered

by the stage: "Olive is an Original-Tiller-Girl, Gerti is a German 'Girl.' Please do not confuse the two. Both are parts of the '300 cast members' in the revue, but the one young woman is a little cog in the 'often copied—never equaled' precision-dance–machine, the other is only capable of displaying a well-shaped bosom. And, as a 'living flower vase,' a bit of ass as well."[38] The same dichotomy appeared on the printed page, in the program booklets of the revues. Whereas the Tiller Girls were invariably photographed in costume, the second string of women performers, such as the Haller Girls, would often be shot in the nude. The reproduction of such pictures turned the revues' program books into a form of soft-core pornography.

Given the Tiller Girls' active demonstration of skills, Fritz Giese as well as many commentators in the popular media believed they represented a more general *Girlkultur*. In this wider sense, a "Girl"—also called, with more respect, the "New Woman"—was paradigmatically young (in her late teens or early twenties) and employed, usually as a secretary, typist, or department-store salesperson. These white-collar jobs had seen an influx of women, and the presence of female employees in what traditionally had been male preserves caused a flurry of speculation—some of it serious and informed, much of it not. On screen, in popular literature, and in advertisements, the employed "New Woman" was touted as being self-assured, "matter-of-fact" *(sachlich)*, and possessing a large degree of independence in her professional and personal life. That image, however, was all too often belied by reality. Sociological inquiries at the time uncovered great discontent among white-collar women, who received low pay, worked long hours at repetitive tasks, had no chance for career advancement, and often were subjected to sexual harassment in the office. Many of them laughed bitterly at the media image of *Girlkultur*.[39]

As for the Girls on stage, it is impossible to know how they experienced their own work. In "interviews" for the popular press, Tiller Girls stressed the combination of dedicated work and glamour that their occupation entailed. Simultaneously, however, they claimed that they had become dancers mainly in order to attract wealthy spectators who would lead them to the altar. Since the same cliché saturated popular literature and films dealing with the "office girl" (who invariably ended up marrying her boss), one may surmise that many statements by the dancers were fictitious, or at least dictated according to a prearranged pattern.[40]

The fact that the stage Girls were rigorously choreographed, worked long hours, and lacked a true career—they often were terminated in their early twenties—belies the notion of independence and individuality that Giese attributed to them. The same holds true for their visual impact. After all, the main impression was that of deindividualized performers submerged into a larger mass. Just as the supposedly independent professional woman in reality was buried in the lower reaches of a rigid office hierarchy, the stage Girl performed in lockstep with numerous clones. Polgar contended that "Girls are a so-called *plurale tantum*. That means that the concept appears linguistically only in the plural." A row of women became Girls only with "the smelting of each individual entity into a collectivity." Walter Benjamin contended that the trademark of the Girls was their quantity, which increased every season: "The revue caters to the bourgeois desire for diversity, more in terms of number than in the nature and arrangement of its presentations. It will soon exhaust its store of inspiration. Ever since it undressed the female body to the point of total nudity, its only available mode of variation was quantity, and soon there will be more Girls than spectators." The lengthening of the kickline entailed a progressive diminution of the individual performer. As the dancer lost her personality, something new resulted—a creation whose allure resided in its precise movements and formal configurations. Oscar Bie spoke of the Tiller Girls' "uncanny appeal of absolute body-motion." Kracauer too suggested that the meaning of such displays resided in their form: "The ornament is an end in itself," and "the constellations have no meaning beyond themselves."[41]

Although the Girls' kickline did not refer directly to anything beyond its own abstract configurations, indirectly it seemed to reflect a modern aesthetic—one derived not from the individual body but from the machine. Many writers resorted to mechanistic images: the various Girl troupes appeared to them as a "precision machine," a "motion machine," or a "Girl machine" *(Präzisionsmaschine, Bewegungsmaschine, Girlmaschine)*. One reviewer wrote approvingly: "The Girls function well" (Die Girls funktionieren gut). Kracauer contended that if the Girls did have a metaphorical meaning after all, it would be "the functioning of a flourishing economy," namely, that of the United States: "When they formed a line that moved up and down, they radiantly represented the superiority of the conveyor belt; when they step-danced at a rapid pace, it sounded like 'business, business'; when they tossed their legs into the air with mathematical precision, they joyfully approved the progress of rationalization; and when they continually repeated the same motions, without breaking their line, one imagined an uninterrupted chain of automobiles streaming from the factories of the world."[42]

German observers conflated the kicklines with images of the United States as a land of technological wonders. Whereas the black entertainers embodied one aspect of America—something spontaneous, wild, uncivilized, unencumbered by European culture—the Girls represented the flip side of the dollar: energy, efficiency, productivity. In the Weimar era, the heated, often caustic debates about "Americanism" focused not only on mass cultural phenomena like jazz, revues, and Hollywood films (which flooded German cinemas after the stabilization of the mark), but also on new ways of organizing production. "Taylorism" and "Fordism" were the buzzwords of the day. Charles Taylor's notions of scientific management, based on time/motion studies of workers and piece-rate incentives, were highly controversial, since they entailed rigid labor discipline and (frequently) low pay. In contrast, Henry Ford—who also had a better knack for self-promotion—received much more positive press. His highly efficient moving assembly line, as well as his desire to create a mass market of low-priced commodities for well-paid workers, were generally admired. A mythology about the productive wonders of American industry gained hold among German intellectuals, and invaded the popular press as well.[43] Since America came to be equated with dynamic energy, mechanical precision, and infinite replicability, it was no wonder that many viewers believed that the English Tiller Girls were American products. Paul Simmel, the premier cartoonist of the *Berliner Illustrirte Zeitung* in the Weimar era, even sketched the Tiller Girls coming off a Ford assembly line (fig. 26).

Whereas the mechanistic overtones of the kicklines gave them an American aura, another aspect appeared to be more distinctly German. The precision of the Girls evoked images not only of machinery but of the military as well. The word "revue" had, after all, originated in the martial sphere, as a designation for the inspection of parading soldiers. The Girls themselves evoked that association on those occasions when they shouldered arms onstage (fig. 27). This aspect of their appeal was especially clear to Polgar: "Another magic besides that of the erotic emanates from the appearance and the actions of the Girls: the magic of the military. Drilled, parallel, in step, correctly executing handholds and manoeuvres, obeying an unseen but inescapable command . . .—it provides the same appeal that makes soldiers' play so palatable to the spectator; but of course only as a spectator." Another critic repeated the common, but erroneous belief that John Tiller had been an officer before becoming a capitalist: "Everything clicks as on a barracks drill-ground . . . Not for nothing was the old Tiller, who first trained the Girls, a sergeant in the English army. However, they no longer appear in the military parade march, but in the rhythm of modern work, to the beat of the machine age."[44]

In the eyes of contemporaries, the Girls performed a fantastic masquerade: they were cheerful and dynamic signs that signified fundamental forces of order and control. The kickline represented both military precision and economic rationalization, the two keys to domination in the modern world. Moreover, the attenuated femininity—the "magic of the erotic"—obscured, indeed sweetened, the powerful forces of order that the Girls

Ford übernimmt die Herstellung von Tillergirls.

26. "Ford undertakes the production of Tiller Girls" in Paul Simmel's 1926 cartoon.

embodied. They were a form of sexual bait, with a hidden hook: whoever consumed their image also internalized an appreciation for mass production, replicability, and military discipline.

The Girls themselves, as individuals and performers, were subjected directly to these same forces. While they might have been freed from some of the cruder forms of voyeuristic eroticism, they were depersonalized in a more fundamental manner. Not only was the individual subsumed into the collective, but she also was dissected into her constituent appendages. In the kicklines, the unit of composition was no longer the whole person, but the body part. According to Kracauer: "The Tiller Girls cannot be reassembled retrospectively into human beings; the mass gymnastics are never undertaken by total and complete bodies, whose contortions defy rational understanding. Arms, thighs, and other parts are the smallest components of the composition." Just as the structure of the revue replicated the fragmentation of sensation in the metropolis, the depersonalization of the dancer paralleled the reduction of the worker's body to economically useful attributes: "the legs of the Tiller Girls correspond to the hands in the factories." To be sure, the most obvious fragmentation of the body took place among the tableaux of naked women, whose overtly sexual attributes (breasts and pelvis) were emphasized. Nevertheless, the Tiller Girls were equally dismembered, though the knife cut along different lines: arms and especially legs seemed to take on a mass life of their own. The performance of the Girls was marked, in Erich Kästner's words, by *das ewig gleiche Beinerlei*.[45]

Not surprisingly, there were women artists and performers who took issue with the Girl troupes. Unfortunately, an "antirevue" planned in 1925 by Hannah Höch, an outstanding Dadaist artist, never was realized. It had been inspired by a Berlin revue that was, in Höch's words, "one of the kitsch-presentations that is geared only to sexual impact by brutal means."[46] Six years later, at Friedrich Hollaender's "Tingel-Tangel" cabaret, the sisters Grit and Ina van Elben staged a dance parody of the

27. The Tiller Girls shoulder arms at the Wintergarten variety theater.

28. Grit and Ina van Elben as the "Tingel-Tangel-Girls" (1931).

Girl troupes. They employed a series of cut-out figures to mock the replicability of women in the kicklines (fig. 28).

The most effective means of criticism was the provision of countermodels. The dancer Valeska Gert (1892–1978), who performed at Sound and Smoke in 1920 and various other venues in ensuing years, was diametrically opposed to the Girl troupes. On the one hand, she danced solo, and her performances often sought to express her own personality. As Hildenbrandt noted, she spoke "only of herself," and performed "autobiographical dances"—the opposite, in short, of the Girls, who subsumed their personalities into the kickline. On the other hand, Gert also parodied the various popular dance fads of the day, which people imitated unthinkingly (fig. 29). One appreciative critic noted that one might consider her dances obscene, inasmuch as they consisted of "uncovering": "Yet Valeska Gert does not uncover herself, but rather the sexuality of dance, and it is understandable that when she puts on the cloak of the tango, the Charleston, or the waltz, nothing but shreds remain in the end. It is not simply a parody or travesty of conventional dances, but rather a proof that bourgeois dance is not an expression of dancelike rhythm, but rhythmic nonsense." Predictably, Gert also performed a parody of the Girl troupes, which "annihilated the Tiller nonsense," according to Herrmann-Neisse. Another critic noted that it "tore the American patent mask" off of "the dissemblers of *Girlkultur.*"[47] But despite critical acclaim, parodies like those of the ván Elben sisters or Valeska Gert were seen by the limited audience of cabaret, not the masses in the revues.

The Great Depression marked the end of the great era of Weimar revues, but it did not spell the end of the Girls. In his article on "Girls and Crisis," penned in May 1931, Kracauer questioned whether the Girls had anything more to say, now that the economic system that they appeared to represent lay in shambles. Speaking of the appearance of a troupe in the Scala variety

29. Valeska Gert demolishes the Charleston.

theater, he exclaimed: "One doesn't believe them anymore, those rosy Jackson-Girls! . . . Their smiles are those of masks; their confidence, a leftover from better days; their accuracy, a mockery of the difficulties faced by the powers that they represent. As much as they snake and undulate, as if nothing had happened, the crisis, to which so many enterprises have fallen victim, has also silently liquidated these Girl-machines." In this case, at least, Kracauer's predictions proved false. Granted, some major revue directors had departed from the scene. James Klein had lost ownership of the Komische Oper through bankruptcy as early as 1926, but he continued to direct revues there until 1929, when he was dismissed. That same year witnessed the last performance of a Haller revue. Nevertheless, Girl troupes could still be found on the stages of variety theaters like the Scala and the Wintergarten, and they migrated to other media as well.

By 1927 Charell had ceased staging revues and mounted, instead, "revue-operettas." Since the competition in the revue market had become fierce, with several shows playing simultaneously, Charell developed a new genre that combined the saccharine sentimentality of musicals with the "jazzy" and risqué qualities of revues. He ransacked and rewrote popular operettas, plays, and stories from the past: *The Mikado, Casanova, The Three Musketeers, The White Horse Inn, The Merry Widow.* Often he arranged for new or "updated" music to be added, and, most incongruously of all, he interspersed kicklines throughout the plots. In *Casanova,* Girls could even be seen parading as Prussian guards of Frederick the Great. By the end of the twenties, with the advent of sound film, Girl troupes became staples in the cinematic versions of musicals. Charell directed one of the most spectacular of the revue-films, *The Congress Dances (Der Kongress tanzt,* 1931).

Embedded in musicals and operettas, the kicklines of the Girls could hide more completely their subliminal messages, the paradoxes at the heart of popular distractions. In Weimar Berlin, revues were the most popular form of live entertainment, and the Girls were the highlight of the revues. Yet both the Girls and the revues were products of human destructuring and dehumanized restructuring. The revue sacrificed dramatic unity in favor, as Kracauer said, of "the dismembered succession of splendid sensory perceptions." In turn, the kickline sacrificed bodily wholeness in favor of a dismembered succession of bodily parts. The human fragments were reordered into dynamic visual forms which, on the surface, appeared vital and progressive, a symbol of rational management and achievement. But more fundamentally, they revealed—or perhaps disguised?—an underlying sense of economic and military order that demanded the dissolution of all personality and the dismemberment of the person. The bodies of the Girls embodied a critique of the modernity that they ostensibly represented.

# Political Cabaret
# at the End
# of the Republic

The closing years of the Weimar Republic, marked by mounting economic catastrophes and a breakdown of parliamentary government, witnessed a limited revival of political cabaret. Popular entertainment had been generally apolitical during the preceding years of "relative stabilization." The spectacular revues were politically noncommittal, with a tendency toward conservative stances. Concurrently, a new breed of cabaret-revues engaged in liberal criticism of the republic, but they betrayed the type of nonpartisan cynicism reflected in the earlier Weimar cabarets. The onset of the Great Depression led to the formation of smaller, more aggressive stages, but, like the economy at large, they collapsed after several months. The electoral success of the Nazis from 1930 on added a new and threatening element to the political equation. Some stages, like Kurt Robitschek's Cabaret of Comedians, opted for silence; others, like Friedrich Hollaender's Tingel-Tangel, underestimated the danger by portraying Hitler as a political buffoon who could not be taken seriously. In the closing years of the republic, the most consistently aggressive cabarets were those of the Communist Party—the Red Revues and the agitprop troupes. Although they showed a much clearer political commitment than any of the bourgeois stages, they were crippled by their Communist ideology, which in its own way failed to assess the true nature of the National Socialist threat.

## The Politics of Revues and Cabaret-Revues

Although the major revues of the Weimar era tended to eschew politics, they betrayed a conservative bent. The prewar Metropol revues had cast critical but good-natured barbs at all political parties, at the same time that they emphasized their nationalism with patriotic tableaux featuring great moments in Prussian and German history. The same formula carried over into many postwar shows. In the new political context, however, such scenes, far from supporting the status quo, could be construed as antirepublican. A satire on the Reichstag could now be interpreted as a denigration of parliamentary democracy, and evocations of the German past could be equated with monarchist sympathies. A balance of political satire with prorepublican sentiments was difficult to achieve.

The most blatantly conservative revue director was James Klein. In *The World without Veils* (*Die Welt ohne Schleier,* 1923), the minister of "Pleitanien"—"Bankrupcia," alias Germany—had a Bolshevik companion, which suggested that leftist radicalism had brought the nation to collapse. Other culprits were foreigners, especially the French occupiers of the Rhine and Ruhr. The same revue concluded with a "patriotic homage to Father Rhine," which made a "gripping impression," according to the reviewer for the conservative *Berliner Lokal-Anzeiger.* Like the reactionary cabarets, Klein's revues repeatedly stressed the need for hard work on the part of the proletariat to pull Germany out of its slump.[1]

The other revue directors were more balanced and cautious in their political statements, in order to avoid offending ticket-buyers of any political persuasion. One critic, deploring the lack of true satire in revues, observed: "Quivering with fear before every paying spectator, the directors appeal to everyone and offend no one." Herbert Ihering wrote in reaction to Haller's *On and Off* (*An und Aus,* 1926): "Even the Metropol revues of the Kaiser's day allowed for more political and contemporary material than the revue of republican Germany." Monty Jacobs too complained about Haller's pusillanimous *Attention! Wavelength 505!* (*Achtung! Welle 505!,* 1925): "Apparently the Haller directors are scared of an age like ours, which is filled to bursting with conflicts. They consciously want to produce an article for mass consumption; they do not want to lose anybody to the left or to the right. Thus they appeal to everyone, that is, to no one." In fact, that revue included a song that specifically told the audience to forget about their differences and return to earlier, less divisive attitudes: "Back then, nobody would ask you, / Are you an Aryan, or a Jew?" (Früher fragt' keen Mensch Dich: Biste / Völkisch oder Zioniste?). That call to overcome race-hatred was certainly laudable, and it clearly placed the revue outside the right-wing camp. But instead of pursuing that line, the song retreated from any further confrontations, as it proceeded to dismiss the political sphere altogether: "forget that nonsense, politics" (Lasst den Quatsch, die Politike).[2]

A similar neglect of current topics and lack of political focus could be attributed to Charell. A linkage to contemporary Berlin might have been suggested by the appearance of Claire Waldoff, who sang two songs in *For Everyone!* (*An Alle!,* 1924). Jacobs contended, however, that these sentimental tunes about dating were "contemplations about human life in general. In Berlin dialect, to be sure. But what about Berlin, what about Germany, what about 1924?" Jacobs saw a similar lack of contemporaneity in Charell's *From Mouth to Mouth* (*Von Mund zu Mund,* 1926), and he speculated that the director was "terrorized" by "fear of the great masses." For example, the Reichstag was parodied only indirectly, in a "bland and timid" scene depicting the senate of ancient Rome. The most striking part of that number was an insert scripted and composed by Friedrich Hollaender and performed by Claire Waldoff. Mounted on a chariot, she barged into the senate and sang: "Toss the Men out of the Reichstag!" (Raus mit den Männern aus dem Reichstag!). The peppy and hilarious number, still performed occasionally to this day, was both a spoof of feminist rhetoric and a criticism of all man-made politics. Like the songs at Sound and Smoke six years earlier, the piece dismissed the political arena as hopelessly incompetent.[3]

Jacobs conceded that "in a country with two national flags, it is perhaps harder than elsewhere to gloss the problems of the day on an entertainment stage." The Haller revue's *Under and Over* (*Drunter und Drüber*, 1923) solved that dilemma, according to a reviewer in the *Berliner Tageblatt*, by creating a program that was "75 percent black-white-red, 25 percent black-red-gold." The predominance of conservative tendencies was made manifest not only in tableaux featuring soldiers from the time of Frederick the Great, but also in the depiction of contemporary conditions: "The republic itself is not ridiculed, one is one-quarter republican after all. But its misery is mocked." At the same time, "Poincaré gets a swipe, as do the English and Wilson. Everything is taken care of. Everyone gets his money's worth." Given the weakness of the gibes, the political tone seemed nonpartisan and inoffensive. The conservative *Lokal-Anzeiger* concluded that "our conditions and problems are presented in such a humorous manner that the tragedy of our time was given a conciliatory, even hopeful air." *Under and Over* was, after all, the revue featuring the hit song that proclaimed: "Berlin, you're still Berlin." Yet that very song revealed the conservative basis of the Haller revue's ideology, since it suggested that traditional military symbols could still unite all Germans. It described how a parade of the ceremonial guard through the Brandenburg Gate appealed to both socialists and reactionaries ("Ob Sozie, ob Reaktionär"), and even coaxed Raffke away from the stock exchange. By indirectly evoking the *Burgfrieden,* the unity of contending parties during the Great War, it did little service to the new republican regime.[4]

We have seen that the kicklines of Girls had military overtones, especially when they shouldered arms onstage; but even there, the revue directors tried to cover all bases. In reference to Charell's *For Everyone,* which had a major production number featuring Girls dressed as toy soldiers, Fritz Engel of the *Berliner Tageblatt* wrote: "The public clucked with delight, and if one were to accuse Sladek [the producer] of doing something with his box of toy soldiers that he had better leave alone, he would answer, with an eye toward the right and an eye toward the left, militaristically-pacifistically, that he also has a couple of angels of peace floating around. Well, it turns out that they disappear after two seconds, and the children's cannons keep shooting, and a fire starts to spread, the fire of enthusiasm in the audience." Oscar Bie, writing in the program book of Haller's *Attention! Wavelength 505!,* noted the Girls' ability to transcend political divisions while maintaining a martial spirit: "The Girls are a solution to the problem. They have linked military memories with the modern love of dance in such an inimitable fashion, that hearts on the right and on the left beat equally for them."[5]

Fortunately there was room for more unequivocally democratic sentiments in Berlin's amusement spots. Although the great commercial revues remained the most popular form of live entertainment in Berlin until the Great Depression, after 1926 a counterbalance appeared in the form of the cabaret-revue. These shows, usually scripted by Friedrich Hollaender or Marcellus Schiffer, and composed by Hollaender or Mischa Spoliansky, offered two perspectives lacking in the Haller, Charell, or Klein revues: they focused on Berlin, as the prewar Metropol revues had done, and they supported decidedly prorepublican and antimilitarist viewpoints. The ground for the new shows had been laid by Rudolf Nelson, who had turned to cabaret-revues as early as 1920. Nelson also was one of the first directors to suggest that Berlin was again becoming a *Weltstadt* in the wake of the economic upturn that began in 1924. His revue of 1926 was entitled, significantly, *It's Getting Better (Es geht schon besser)*. The loose plot concerned a discouraged young Berliner who was about to emigrate to the United States, until a woman took him (and the audience) on a tour that opened his eyes to the rebirth of Berlin. The show displayed, in the words of one critic, "such a reasonable standpoint, since not once did Prussian grenadiers or other military types show up on stage."[6]

Nelson was overtaken in this genre by Friedrich Hollaender, who had increased his skills and his fame ever since writing songs for the postwar Sound and Smoke. The first cabaret-revue that Hollaender scripted, composed, and directed was *Laterna magica,* which premiered in February 1926. Max Herrmann-Neisse, who had proclaimed the death of serious cabaret in 1925, was thrilled by the performance. In an article entitled "Finally a Revue-Parody," he praised the fact that the show demonstrated the satirical skills that cabarets had lost. In particular he was pleased by the send-ups of the spectacular revues: Valeska Gert performed her parody of the Tiller Girls, while a man did a takeoff on American tap dancing. Local themes were given their due by Blandine Ebinger, who personified Berlin women from various social classes. *Laterna magica* inaugurated a series of parodistic revues that were performed until the end of the Weimar

30. A scene from the revue *That's You!*, with Weintraub's Syncopators at left and Friedrich Hollaender at the piano (1927).

Republic, for which Hollaender often provided both lyrics and music. The most successful of these were *That's You* (*Das bist Du*, 1927), *With Us around the Memorial Church* (*Bei uns um die Gedächtniskirche rum*, 1927), *Everyone Gets a Turn* (*Es kommt jeder dran*, 1928), and *Ghosts in the Villa Stern* (*Spuk in der Villa Stern*, 1931). In most of these productions Hollaender's music was performed by Weintraub's Syncopators, the best German jazz band of the day. Sitting at a piano to the side of the stage, Hollaender often played with them (fig. 30). Both Hollaender and the Weintraub group eventually gained international fame for the music to *The Blue Angel*, which was set in a sailors' dive most unlike the upscale cabaret-revue that Hollaender directed.[7]

Some of the lyrics for Hollaender's second revue, *Hetaira-Talk (Hetärengespräche)*, were written by Marcellus Schiffer (1892–1932), whose songs had been performed at the Wild Stage by his wife, the singer Margo Lion. Schiffer became, along with Hollaender, the most prolific scriptwriter and lyricist for cabaret-revues in the later Weimar era. He was especially known for his parodies of the mass media and consumerism. *The Avid Lady Reader* (*Die fleissige Leserin*, 1926; music by Paul Strasser and Allan Gray), his first complete revue script, was a takeoff on the various rubrics of magazines, from how-to articles to gossip columns, from serialized novels to advertisements. The following year Schiffer continued to parody the mass media in *What You Want (Was Sie wollen)*, with music by Hollaender. Herbert Ihering was delighted by that revue as well, but he noted its limitations: "Here lies Marcellus Schiffer's talent: in the parody of things already formed. He approaches contemporary issues by means of a detour through things already written. He makes fun not so much of the events themselves, but rather their reproduction in newspapers and magazines. That gives his revues their levity, but also a touch of snobbery."[8]

Schiffer scripted works for several composers, but his most famous collaborator was Mischa Spoliansky (1899–1985), whose music had been heard at both Sound and Smoke and the Wild Stage. The most successful show of the Schiffer-Spoliansky team was *It's in the Air (Es liegt in der Luft*, 1928). This revue was set in a department store, an image that harked back to the Metropol's prewar evocation of the *Warenhaus Gross-Berlin*. Schiffer's characterization of employees, shoppers, and products constituted a send-up of the consumerism of the day. Shopping had become a mania—sometimes literally, when it took the form of kleptomania, a rather common theme of cabaret songs of the twenties. But consumerism was also unmasked as a pointless and hollow ideal, since at the end of the show all of the shoppers converged at the consumer service desk, where they sought to exchange the purchases that had failed to bring them the expected joys and satisfactions. Customer complaints lay at the heart of another famous work by Schiffer and Spoliansky, *Get Mister Plim! (Rufen Sie Herrn Plim!)*, which was coauthored by Kurt Robitschek and performed at his Cabaret of Comedians in 1932. That takeoff on grand opera was set in a department store, where the owner and chief of personnel, faced with a constant barrage of shoppers' complaints, decided to hire a man to take the blame for everything. Hence anytime an enraged customer came to their office, they turned to the secretary and yelled, "Get Mr. Plim!" Invariably that employee was blamed for the mishap and "fired," to satisfy the shoppers' thirst for revenge.[9]

The cabaret-revues tried to capture what they considered the new spirit of individualism. Herrmann-Neisse wrote in 1925: "It is significant that current hits can express bluntly the purely commercial, egoistical nature [of love affairs], whereas ten years ago the hits romantically, sentimentally transfigured and obscured the matter." In keeping with the new attitude, the title song of *It's in the Air* proclaimed: "There's something objective in the air, there's something prickly in the air" (Es liegt in der Luft eine Sachlichkeit, es liegt in der Luft eine Stachlichkeit). The song's catchword derived from the current wave of *Neue Sachlichkeit*, the "New Objectivity" or "New Matter-of-Factness" in the arts that had replaced the Expression-

31. Margo Lion and Marlene Dietrich as "best girl friends," and something more, in *It's in the Air* (1928).

ism and utopianism of the early Weimar years. The revue maintained that this "objectivity" had invaded all attitudes and relations. No longer was there room for tradition, nostalgia, or old-fashioned sentiments, as individuals reassessed their personal needs and inclinations. That attitude was expressed in a duet sung by Margo Lion and Marlene Dietrich, in her first major stage role (fig. 31). Entitled "When My Best Girl Friend" (Wenn die beste Freundin), it ostensibly described two women on a shopping excursion. It made clear, however, that they were dissatisfied with their husbands and had a very intimate relationship with each other. The song became an unofficial anthem for German lesbians in the late twenties.[10]

Most reviewers agreed that the best number in that show was "I Know That Is Not So" (Ich weiss, das ist nicht so), sung by Willy Prager dressed as an elevator operator. In a slow and resigned manner, the character

HAVE

described his hopes, only to admit in the refrain that he knew they would never be realized. In the first stanza he dreamt of being rich, in the second he envisioned himself as the angel Gabriel. The third stanza turned cultural and political: he imagined that Erwin Piscator, the famous director of leftist plays, would act like a true communist and distribute the profits from his productions. The final stanza made the most explicitly political statement. The elevator operator's hopeful assertion of democracy—"I lean back proudly and tell myself contentedly: Now we have a republic"—was dismissed as an illusion in the final refrain of "I know that is not so." This number was similar to a song performed a year earlier in Hollaender's *Hetaira-Talk,* entitled "Perhaps It's True, Perhaps It's Not!" (Vielleicht, kann sein, vielleicht auch nicht!). The first few stanzas dealt with artistic matters, including the question of whether or not Piscator's production of *The Robbers* had anything to do with Schiller. The penultimate stanza then pondered whether Germany was a republic: "It's possible! Perhaps! Perhaps! Who knows? Perhaps not! But perhaps after all! Maybe not? Perhaps, who knows?" The last stanza asked whether the deposed Kaiser might even become the Reich president, and came to the same nonconclusion.[11]

Just as the early Weimar cabarets questioned whether the ruling Social Democrats were truly socialist, the satirists of the late twenties asked whether Germany really was a republic, since the conservative, antidemocratic forces remained influential. Although some liberal reviewers agreed with the satirists' caveats, they questioned the advisability of stating them publicly. Writing in the *Berliner Tageblatt,* Fritz Engel said of *It's in the Air:* "Willy Prager dreams, in an otherwise brilliant song, about the happy future of the republic, only to add in the refrain: 'I know that is not so! I know that that won't come about!' The purpose of this might be to stimulate weak republicans. But the result? Every supporter of the good old days will nod his head with glee."[12] In other words, the number was probably conceived as a takeoff on would-be liberals who were resigned to the demise of republican values. In practice, however, it also could have been interpreted as a song suggesting that little could be done for the republic after all. It was just as likely that a poor man would become rich, or turn into the angel Gabriel, as it was that Germany would become truly democratic. That was a standpoint that conservative opponents of the Weimar polity would have been happy to hear.

Engel believed that liberal entertainers should leave republican politicians alone. At a time when Gustav Stresemann was trying to negotiate friendly relations with Germany's erstwhile enemies, over the objections of the conservatives, Engel wrote about Hollaender's *That's You:* "His political barbs are actually rather blunt, when he ridicules the republic—out of love for it—and when he makes fun of Stresemann, the hard-struggling representative of German foreign policy whom one would do better to leave alone for now."[13] Engel's standpoint was understandable, but problematic in its own way. He believed that at a time when republican values continued to be challenged by strong antidemocratic minorities, it was important for supporters of the Weimar system to rally around the appropriate politicians. In contrast, satirists believed that no officials were above criticism: one had the right, indeed the duty, to make light of their foibles, even if one basically concurred with them. Engel conceded that Hollaender made fun of the republic "out of love for it," but he believed that such parodies inadvertently provided ammunition to those who would be glad to see it dead.

Liberal critics did not desire an end to political satire, but rather a sharper focus. They believed that the cabarets and cabaret-revues should be more decidedly prorepublican and more explicitly antireactionary. In his review of *It's in the Air,* Engel asked: "Why is a revue opening in the week of the fateful elections so stale and flat when it comes to politics? Because its producers want to be neutral—as in a department store, which forms the background to this revue—so that no customer will leave without buying and paying." He thus suggested that the cabaret-revues faced the same pressures to depoliticize as the more spectacular revues. Be that as it may, other reviewers likewise called for a more aggressive form of satire. The *Weltbühne* review of Hollaender's *That's You* contended: "They act tame, obliging, genial, where they could be daring, aggressive, biting. In the songs there are two or three verses of conventional cabaret before political satire comes as the punchline. But they do not show their claws, instead they offer their paws." Writing in the same journal, Arthur Eloesser said of *With Us around the Memorial Church:* "Granted, you are for the republic, as is fitting for the Kurfürstendamm. You make fun of the illegal Reichswehr troops [*schwarze Reichswehr*] and the reactionary courts . . ., but you are not biting enough to be able to kill anyone with laughter."[14]

One might doubt whether it is ever possible to "kill" a political enemy "with laughter"; that might be demanding more of satire than it can deliver. In any case, some of Hollaender's best songs were explicitly antimilitarist and antimonarchist. One particularly successful number from *That's You,* entitled "The Last Hairpin" (Die letzte Haarnadel), was sung by Annemarie Hase representing an aristocratic old lady from Potsdam. Ostensibly it deplored the passing of women's long tresses in favor of the short, boyish haircut *(Bubikopf)*. But since "Wilhelm" could mean either a hair switch or the deposed Kaiser, it also ridiculed hopes for a monarchist restoration: "No, no, the 'Wilhelm' won't come again" (Nee, nee, der Wilhelm kommt nicht wieder). The song sought to put reactionary aspirations to rest:

> I hear that secret groups again are stirring,
> Who still believe in abject fealty
> And hope to see a monarchy recurring.
> But I know that will never be.

> Zwar sollen sich geheime Kräfte rühren,
> Die ihm noch immer heftig untertan,
> Ihn doch in Deutschland wieder einzuführen.
> Ich glaube aber nicht daran.

Whereas the idea of a monarchist restoration could be dismissed, the threat of renewed German militarism and revanchism was more real. Probably the most successful number from Hollaender's revues was "The Drummer Girl" (Die Trommlerin), first performed by Blandine Ebinger in *Everyone Gets a Turn*. She represented a mechanical figure in a fairground shooting gallery, who would beat her drum if struck in her chest by a bullet:

> I bear a clockwork deep within my core.
> Whoever shoots me, doesn't shoot me dead.
> Instead, he shoots me back to life once more.

> Ein Uhrwerk trage ich in mir inwendig.
> Wer nach mir schiesst, der schiesst mich gar nicht tot.
> Im Gegenteil, er schiesst mich nur lebendig.

What got "shot back to life" was, of course, the hopes of those who thirsted for another war. Many different people took aim at the figure: the student imagined he was shooting his teacher; the husband killed the man cuckolding him; the thief gunned down the policeman. The most common customers were, however, "the men for whom the war was too short" (Die Herrn, für die der Krieg zu kurz gewesen); they used her to keep alive the prospect of renewed battles. Sung in a dry manner with a hint of poignancy, by a figure that was literally the object of attack, the number was a forceful condemnation of aggression. Karl Kraus, the irascible Viennese critic, called it the most powerful antiwar statement of recent memory, more effective than Erich Maria Remarque's pacifist novel, *All Quiet on the Western Front*.[15] It was picked up by other performers, such as Trude Hesterberg, and performed at many liberal and leftist cabarets in the closing years of the Weimar Republic.

## Cabaret and the Crises of the Late Republic

Whereas Hollaender deplored the aggressions latent in society, one of the most disturbing cabarets of the later twenties specialized in bringing them to the fore. Erwin Lowinsky, who adopted the pseudonym Elow, was a largely undistinguished conferencier until he hit upon a novel idea in 1926. He placed advertisements in Berlin newspapers, encouraging amateurs to try out their talents at the (equally undistinguished) Monbijou cabaret. A typical announcement read: "The experimental stage. We seek young talents, whom we will give the opportunity of performing before the metropolitan public every Monday night. We request applications for this 'Cabaret of the Nameless' [*Kabarett der Namenlosen*]." The first announcement received 187 inquiries. Since Elow accepted everyone who applied, and only 15 could perform on any given Monday, he was assured of a steady stream of "entertainment." What awaited these performers was a trap, since invariably they would be insulted by Elow and laughed off stage by the audience. The victims of this enterprise were unfortunate people, dissatisfied with their jobs or their daily lives, who believed that the Cabaret of the Nameless might offer them the "big break" that was touted repeatedly in the rags-to-riches accounts of star entertainers. Lower-level employees, shop assistants, housewives, the unemployed, even mentally handicapped and schizophrenic people would appear. The amateurs were usually scared, their performances were invariably bad—and any signs of weakness would draw loud laughter or rude insults from the audience. Many performers left the stage in tears, and the only ones impervious to the commotion were the schizophrenics, who could not comprehend what was happening to them.[16]

Numerous critics expressed outrage and disgust at Elow's venture. They were particularly horrified by the behavior of the audience. A Viennese critic, for whom the venture represented "typical Berlin bad taste," noted that "the public was whipped up to a degree of self-revelation that is rarely seen"; twenty pictures by George Grosz could not do justice to the face of that public. What was unmasked was the audience's "sadism," a word used by other critics as well. A reviewer for the *Welt am Montag* conceded that the audience represented Berlin, inasmuch as the pent-up aggressions generated by the hectic life of the metropolis found an outlet in Elow's cabaret: "All of the wildness comes alive again, all of the malice, the joy in murder and flaying satiates itself on the defenseless amateurs." Evoking indirectly the "jungle of cities" imagery, many observers believed that primeval, indestructable instincts of aggression were brought forth by Elow. Erich Kästner contended: "Here the public satisfies an instinct that is stimulated elsewhere by executions, insane asylums, and bullfights. Since the combats of the Roman gladiators with slaves and Christians, nothing has changed . . . The arena has become a cabaret." Although horrified by the spectacle, he suggested that it might be necessary. Since the big city was an "inhuman place of residence," it required "inhuman means to endure it." Elow's cabaret was a form of "psychoanalytic cure. One rids oneself of normal instincts by activating them in safe surroundings. Elow is thus a modern doctor for Berliners' nervousness . . . Here is a padded cell for the metropolis." Kästner implied that it was better to have controlled outlets for aggression than uncontrolled ones—murder, say, or war. He was so fascinated by the symptomatic character of the Cabaret of the Nameless that he included a long description of it in *Fabian,* his "moralistic" novel of Berlin, where Elow was renamed "Caligula."[17]

Fortunately, Elow's venture remained unique in Berlin's cabaret scene. As in the early twenties, most ventures were nondescript, and short-lived as well. The major exception was the Cabaret of Comedians or Kadeko (Kabarett der Komiker), the most successful cabaret of the later Weimar era. It was founded in December 1924 by Kurt Robitschek and Paul Morgan in the premises of the Rocket (Rakete), a stage in the Kantstrasse that had hosted appearances by Rosa Valetti and others in the early twenties. The new cabaret drew immediate attention with "Quo Vadis," a mock operetta scripted by Robitschek and Morgan and composed by Willy Rosen. The skit parodied not only the film of that name, but Hitler's "beerhall putsch" of the previous fall as well. By May 1926 it had been performed over three hundred times. In October 1927 the troupe had a similar success with "You Winsome Girl of the Rhine" (Du holdes Kind vom Rhein), with music by Spoliansky. That work satirized the glut of novels and films depicting sentimental love stories in kitschy vineyard settings, as well as the nationalist fervor generated by the continued occupation of the Rhineland by French troops. The usually critical Herrmann-Neisse wrote rave reviews of the Hitler and the Rhine parodies, and he generally welcomed the Kadeko as a lively exception in the otherwise bland cabaret scene.[18]

With growing critical recognition and audience appeal, the Kadeko needed larger quarters. In December 1925 the troupe moved from the Kantstrasse to a theater on the Kurfürstendamm that seated four hundred. By September 1928 it was so successful that it could occupy a new theater designed by Erich Mendelsohn, an outstanding modernist architect. Mendelsohn's recasting of Lehniner Platz was capped by the construction of the splendid Universum movie theater, which today houses the Schaubühne. Robitschek commissioned him to include a theater in a housing block adjacent to the cinema. The auditorium, a model of contemporary design, could seat over nine hundred spectators, either around tables in the parquet or in rows in the balcony (fig. 32).[19]

32. The newly opened Kadeko, designed by Erich Mendelsohn (1928).

Unfortunately, the necessity of filling that many seats night after night forced Robitschek to adopt a more cautious stance. To be sure, he regularly espoused pacificist views, a product of his horrid experiences on the eastern front. He also was willing to take on Hitler and other egregious proponents of nationalism. Such views were not unusually risky, however, since in the mid-twenties Hitler seemed to have little hope of success, and there were few chauvinists in the conventional Kurfürstendamm audience. In general, though, Robitschek avoided political outspokenness on his stage. In April 1926 he asserted that Tucholsky, Mehring, and the leftist poet Erich Weinert were "too political" for his purposes. By 1929, after moving into Mendelsohn's theater, he claimed: "My dream was a cabaret full of aggression, a cabaret of topical satire. But how many people would show understanding for such an ideal cabaret? Twenty journalists and three hundred schnorrers of free tickets. The Cabaret of Comedians has 950 chairs, they seat people of all political persuasions, all social classes, all Weltanschauungen. Try to cook up a sauce that all of them will find tasty!"[20]

Robitschek's recipe was a combination of "cabaret plus vaudeville plus theater." Political jokes became the purview of the conferencier, Paul

Nikolaus, but the bulk of the performance—songs, vaudeville stunts, and comic one-act plays—remained largely apolitical. When longer numbers addressed contemporary affairs, Robitschek, like the directors of the spectacular revues, made sure that all parties were satirized equally. In 1929 a classic example of this policy appeared in *Die Frechheit,* the Kadeko's program book and monthly "magazine of humor." Robitschek described how Berlin's politicized newspapers would report a minor incident: a collision between a bicyclist and a dog. The optimistically liberal *Berliner Tageblatt* claimed that "dog and bicyclist race along the Kurfürstendamm, they hurry—despite a little scratch here and there—toward the brilliant future of the German republic." The pessimistically liberal *Vossische Zeitung* complained that the appearance of *red* blood on a *black* dog with *white* spots turned the incident into an expression of reactionary politics; it called for more laws to defend the republic. The nationalist *Lokal-Anzeiger* claimed that "a foreign bicyclist ran over the dog of a retired general. Fifteen years ago the German people would have stood up as one body and would have swept the bicyclist away with ringing manly fury, but today our faithful dogs lie limply on the ground, shattered by the Treaty of Versailles." The Communist *Rote Fahne* reported: "On the Kurfürstendamm, that pompous boulevard of satiated capitalism on which the proletarian revolution will march against the imperialists in the very near future, a dog attacked a simple proletarian bicyclist!!!!! That's how it starts! First one dog attacks a single bicyclist, then all dogs unite against the Soviet Union!" Finally, the Nazi *Völkischer Beobachter* asserted: "Once more one of our party comrades has been attacked from behind in the dark of night by a bow-legged, flat-footed dachshund. Bow-legged— that betrays the true race of these eastern Jewish pets, with their sagging ears and curls, who suck the marrow of our countrymen and steal the bones from under the noses of our German shepherds. Tomorrow our Führer Adolf Hitler will speak in the sports palace about this national affair. Party comrades should appear in simple battle dress, with hand grenades and flamethrowers."[21]

Like so many other contemporaries, the Cabaret of Comedians severely misjudged the severity of the threat posed by Hitler. Since many of its performers and much of its audience were Jewish, it was understandable that the stage would take swipes at the Nazis' anti-Semitic rhetoric. In January 1926, in a series of parodies describing how various newspapers would review Robitschek's venture, Paul Morgan imputed the following lines to the *Völkischer Beobachter:* "In the [Cabaret of Comedians] there was an un-German, racially alien to-do for a public that consisted almost exclusively of sons and daughters of Israel, which greatly offended the few Aryans in attendance . . . Disgusting hooked noses, the most prominent of which belonged to the Galicians Robitschek and Arno . . . It is high time that our Hitler and our savior Ludendorff appear, in order to make some fundamental changes in the area of entertainment as well! These pigs must be killed!!!"[22] That might have sounded funny in 1926. Hitler's putsch of 1923 had failed miserably, and although he was out of jail, his party had not yet made any inroads into Berlin and was politically insignificant on the national level. To Morgan and Robitschek, Hitler seemed an easy target, an anti-Semitic buffoon.

That very same year, however, other Jews voiced the opinion, in no uncertain terms, that anti-Semitism was not to be taken lightly. At issue was the fact that many cabarets and revues employed comedians who imitated the dialects of eastern European Jews, and told jokes about Jewish practices. Previously, such numbers rarely provoked protests by Jewish spectators: some students disrupted Sound and Smoke in 1902, and a Jewish woman was disturbed by the Yiddish jargon employed at Nelson's venture in 1915. Ten years later such protests were no longer isolated, as anti-Semitism became a much more palpable threat. Verbal and, occasionally, physical attacks against Jews had grown in the immediate postwar years. They reached their climax in November 1923, at the height of the inflation, when a virtual pogrom took place in Berlin's *Scheunenviertel,* a poor neighborhood that was home to many eastern European Jews. Thousands of anti-Semites looted shops and beat up Jews for three days before the police managed to restore order. The return to economic stability in 1924 seemed to take the steam out of radical right-wing parties, but many Jews still urged caution and vigilance.

The Central Association of German Citizens of Jewish Faith (Centralverein deutscher Staatsbürger jüdischen Glaubens), the largest organization that defended the legal rights of German Jews, regularly protested against Jewish comedians who told Jewish jokes on stage. By 1924 Kurt Robitschek and Paul Morgan felt compelled to include defensive words in their introduction to a collection of (often crude) jokes: "The predominant type of humor in this collection as well is Jewish. There always will be a few people up in arms, people who detect derision of the [Jewish] nation and religion in these harmless jokes." Such feeble attempts to downplay the problem were to no avail. Two years later many hundreds of Jewish citizens were "up in arms" about such "harmless jokes." Matters came to a head on April 22, 1926, when the Central Association staged two massive protest meetings simultaneously. Several hundred people listened to speakers representing Jewish youth groups, Jewish women's organizations, and the association of Jewish war veterans. All of them attacked the cabarets' employment of Jewish dialect humor and parodies of Jewish religious practices. As one sympathetic observer noted in the *Berliner Börsen-Cou-*

*rier,* the exaggerated caricature of certain forms of Jewish speech and
practice by Jews themselves only played into the hands of anti-Semites,
who could say: "That's the way they are, and they're even proud of it!"
The assemblies passed strongly worded resolutions stating that no honorable Jew should support such forms of entertainment. Kurt Robitschek
and Kurt Gerron (as well as the director of the Charlott-Casino, another
cabaret) appeared before one of the assemblies and promised that such
numbers would be banished from their stages.[23]

In reporting the meeting, the correspondant for the ultraconservative
*Tägliche Rundschau* agreed with the protest, while noting that "we others"
did not like to hear jokes about the "national and religious sentiments and
practices of Christians and Germans." He added: "According to our observations, the conferencier Robitschek holds the record in both areas."
There is no indication that Robitschek made fun of Christian practices,
but he certainly continued to parody right-wing "national sentiments," as
in the Rhineland numbers of 1927. Moreover, on occasion he continued
to ridicule Nazi rhetoric. By 1930, however, Hitler could no longer be
taken lightly. In the elections of September 1930, the first since the onset
of the Great Depression, the National Socialists polled 6,400,000 votes
and won 107 Reichstag seats, up from 800,000 votes and 12 seats in 1928.
On October 13, the opening day of the new Reichstag, the Nazis made
clear that they would not limit their political activity to parliament. Harry
Kessler noted in his diary: "The whole afternoon and evening there were
great masses of demonstrating Nazis; in the afternoon on Leipziger Strasse
they smashed the windows of Wertheim, Grünfeld, and other department
stores. In the evening they assembled on Potsdamer Platz, chanting 'Germany Awake,' 'Kill the Jews,' 'Heil, Heil' . . . The destruction in Leipziger
Strasse indicated that the disturbances were organized, since only stores
with Jewish names were hit and the stores that appeared to be Christian
were spared in a very demonstrative manner." Two months later, Joseph
Goebbels, the Nazi leader in Berlin, organized massive demonstrations on
Nollendorfplatz to protest the opening of the Hollywood film based on
*All Quiet on the Western Front.* For several days there were standoffs and
occasional skirmishes between thousands of Nazi protesters and hundreds
of Berlin policemen in front of the cinema.[24]

The worst anti-Semitic disturbances before the Nazi takeover occurred
in September 1931 on Kurfürstendamm. As early as January 1928 Goebbels had branded the area a center of Jewish corruption. In an article
entitled "Around the Memorial Church"—an indirect reference to Hollaender's revue, which was playing at the time—he wrote: "That is Berlin
W! The heart of the city turned to stone. Here the spiritual leaders of the
asphalt democracy sit together in the nooks and crannies of cafés, in

cabarets and bars, in the Soviet theaters and fancy apartments . . . One would like to think that it is the elite of the people . . . [but] it is only the Israelites." Goebbels went on to claim that Kurfürstendamm lived off the work of the other Berliners: "What the people in the [proletarian] North create is squandered in the West. Four million people produce life and bread in this desert of stone, and above them sit a hundred thousand drones who dissipate the products of their industry and convert it into sin, vice, and corruption." The "true Berlin," he claimed, was waiting for the day when it could "demolish the site of corruption around the Memorial Church, transform it, and reintegrate it into a resurrected nation." One such day came three years later. On September 12, 1931, Kurfürstendamm was full of Jewish worshipers, coming out of Rosh Hashanah services at the synagogues in Fasanenstrasse and at Lehniner Platz. They were met by over 1500 Nazi youths who taunted them with shouts of "Kill the Jews." Several dozen citizens were severely beaten, and the Café Reimann, known to have a largely Jewish clientele, was devastated.[25]

The Nazi actions directly affected the Kadeko. Attendance had declined somewhat after the onset of the economic depression, but the Nazi intimidation caused a marked drop in box-office receipts as patrons became afraid of walking the streets. In January 1931 Robitschek reported: "The broken windows in Leipziger Strasse, the heroic deeds on Nollendorfplatz have caused the theater losses of thousands and thousands of marks. The box office has become a seismograph of political earthquakes." In order to boost attendance, Robitschek reduced ticket prices by 30 percent in March 1931. An even greater concession to the times was made not at the box office, but on stage. Because of the increased street violence, Robitschek promised to banish all politics from his cabaret. Against critics like Siegfried Kraucauer, who expected more aggressive numbers, the director argued that the public was fed up with political rhetoric. "The sharply politicized times have had other consequences: the public fundamentally rejects every form of politics, be it of the left or the right, in a cabaret. The public also rejects every type of art that tries to be serious. Only laughter can still entice people to terminate a day of discontent with three short hours in a theater." What the audience wanted was "entertainment, diversion, freedom from thinking serious thoughts" (Unterhaltung, Ablenkung, Nichtnachdenkenmüssen). In a public discussion on the state of cabaret in September 1930, Robitschek's assertion that politics did not belong in cabaret was seconded not only by Paul Nikolaus, his "political" conferencier, but also by the loud applause of his Kurfürstendamm public. If further proof were needed, Robitschek could point to the fact that, two months later, a special evening of political satire, including works by Tucholsky and a personal appearance by Kästner, sold barely half of the available tickets. Pressure to depoliticize was felt by other cabarets as well. In February 1930 the managers of the Charlott-Casino announced that they did not wish to address political issues, that they simply wanted to encourage laughter through noncritical, nonpartisan, and inoffensive jokes.[26]

While the larger commercial cabarets became increasingly apolitical, the late twenties witnessed the appearance of smaller, informal ventures that sought to revive the type of political cabaret attempted earlier in the decade. Troupes like Larifari, founded by Rosa Valetti in 1928, and Anti, created in 1929 by a group of young actors and writers, hoped to inject critical polemics from a left-liberal perspective into the cabaret scene. The Artists' Café or Küka (Künstler-Café), which had provided a space for young performers to test their talents on an irregular basis since 1920, also became more political toward the end of the twenties. Yet all three of these ventures collapsed in the spring of 1930, in what the *Berliner Börsen-Zeitung* called the "mass death of the literary cabarets." As the depression worsened, they were unable to hold onto their politically interested middle-class audiences, which had been limited even in the last months of relative prosperity. Of the smaller ventures founded in 1929, only The Wasps (Die Wespen) managed to survive until 1933. Conceived as a "flying cabaret," with distinctly leftist tendencies, it had no fixed base, and it tended to avoid the commercial theaters of western Berlin. Instead, it appeared at irregular intervals at various locales in the proletarian (usually northern and eastern) sections of the city.[27]

The only major new cabaret that was not abandoned by its bourgeois public in the wake of the depression was the Catacombs (Katakombe), founded in October 1929 by Werner Finck (1902–1978). A conferencier and writer of humorous poems, Finck had performed in the Küka and Anti cabarets. His new venture opened in an auspicious locale—the Künstlerhaus, where Sound and Smoke had been launched at the turn of the century. Although Finck's own recitations were politically inoffensive, his initial ensemble comprised people deeply committed to leftist performance. They included Ernst Busch (1900–1980), who was rapidly gaining fame as a singer and as a stage and film actor. Like other left-leaning performers of the day, he crossed the commercial and political divides of the entertainment world: he appeared in revues, but also in leftist films like Pabst's *Comradeship* and his version of *The Threepenny Opera* (both 1931). Increasingly, Busch performed for Communist rallies as well. At the Catacombs, he sang works like the "Song of the Unemployed" (Stempellied), a bitter number in Berlin dialect about the primary social problem of the day. The music was by Hanns Eisler, who became the major composer of pro-Communist music at the end of the Weimar Republic. The lyrics were written by Robert Gilbert, like Busch a "crossover" artist. The son of operetta composer Jean Gilbert, Robert was best known for writing lyrics to popular musicals like *Im Weissen Rössl (The White Horse Inn)*. But under the pseudonym David Weber, he also wrote many socially critical songs performed at leftist and Communist cabarets.[28]

In the beginning, reviewers took note of the high quality and occasional political bite of the Catacombs. By the end of 1930, however, Busch and four other leftists resigned from the ensemble owing to political and financial differences. Finck wanted to tone down the aggressiveness on his stage, and his style of management became more capitalist as well. Whereas the ensemble previously had divided the box-office receipts collectively, Finck now substituted individual contracts, paying himself a significantly larger salary than the others. After the exodus of the leftists, reviewers immediately noticed a more moderate tone in the Catacombs' productions. In March 1931 the critic for *Berlin am Morgen* claimed that "they have lost their character," and by September the reviewer of the *Berliner Tageblatt* could write: "Again there is much droll humor, jokes without much depth. Only rarely do the people of the Catacombs advance from pure harmlessness to aggressive impudence."[29]

Even if political cabarets had proven more viable, they probably would have faced considerable problems in defining their purpose. Those short-lived cabarets that sought to revive the spirit of the early twenties encountered many of the dilemmas of their predecessors. This was hardly surprising, since they mainly performed lyrics by Kurt Tucholsky and Walter Mehring, as well as those by a newcomer to the field, Erich Kästner (1899–1974). Best known for his immensely popular children's book, *Emil and the Detectives* (1928), Kästner also had a large readership among adults for his volumes of poetry: *Herz auf Taille* (1928), *Lärm im Spiegel* (1929), *Ein Mann gibt Auskunft* (1930). He popularized the notion of "poetry for everyday use" *(Gebrauchslyrik)*. In an "Incidental Remark in Prose" inserted into *Lärm im Spiegel*, Kästner said of his verses: "they can be used for the soul [*seelisch verwendbar*]. They were jotted down in company with the joys and sorrows of the present; and they are meant for everyone who has business dealings with the present." At the beginning of the century Otto Julius Bierbaum had called for "applied lyrics" that could be read or performed for the enjoyment of a wide bourgeois audience. Likewise, Kästner's "poetry for everyday use" addressed a broad public, but of a new social background. His paradigmatic reader was a young or mid-career member of the white-collar class, whether man or woman. The tone was often elegaic, as the verses voiced the disappointments of such people: the death of their classmates in the war, their parents' loss of savings in the inflation, the difficulties of starting a career and climbing the office ladder. Their joys were few and most often to be found in love; but there too disappointments abounded. Kästner's mastery of straightforward, four-line rhymed stanzas, which employed everyday language to create striking images, guaranteed the accessibility of his works to a large public.[30]

Like Tucholsky and Mehring, Kästner expressed nonpartisan left-liberal opinions. He was outspokenly pacifist, and he showed great compassion for employees—secretaries, typists, clerks—condemned to remain forever on the lowest levels of the office hierarchy. He was critical of the mass culture that they consumed, and he warned them against the false hopes raised by films, magazines, and revues. Nor did he offer any counterhopes of his own. In a poem entitled "And Where Is the Positive, Mr. Kästner?" (Und wo bleibt das Positive, Herr Kästner?), he exclaimed: "The times are dark, I will not whitewash them for you." Again like Tucholsky and Mehring, he did not suggest any clear way out of the commercial-capitalist cage. His tone was the most resigned of the three, since he seemed to imply that consolation could be found only in close, interpersonal relations. Significantly, his most popular lyrics were nonpolitical. In the Kadeko, Blandine Ebinger performed "A Mother Takes Account" (Eine Mutter zieht Bilanz), about a son's neglect of his parent. Annemarie Hase's rendition of "Introduction of a Chanteuse" (Ankündigung einer Chansonette) in the Küka praised the type of woman who, though not beautiful, could pour her life and soul into a song. While these two works were highly sentimental, another hit was a raucous sex parody. Trude Hesterberg sang "Particularly Refined Ladies" (Ganz besonders feine Damen), which described how women who appeared prim and proper in public became lustful animals in bed.[31]

Some of the smaller cabarets of the late twenties performed the more political works by Tucholsky, Mehring, and Kästner. Yet they encountered the same criticisms, voiced earlier in the decade, which contended that these satirists lacked focused and responsible political convictions. The *Berliner Börsen-Zeitung* complained of the Küka's excessive reliance on Tucholsky in August 1929: "Tucholsky is very entertaining, but rather cheap and ultimately less consequential than he might appear." The *Berliner Tageblatt* was more pointed in its criticism of that program: "The evening was characterized by songs, moritats, aggressive lyrics and satirical prose by Kurt Tucholsky . . . and others, all contemporary and political . . . What we hear is rarely pleasant. Everything deals with the depravity of life in a philistine republic. Explicit assertions are made; but instead of the specifics, we are more likely to remember the general atmosphere in which everything must inevitably follow a dreadfully laughable, lapidary descent to a pitiful demise . . . You laugh, but you don't feel good about it." August

1929: the Great Depression and the final agony of democracy were not yet on the horizon, but the republic was already painted gray on gray and dismissed as moribund.[32]

Some cabaret artists addressed the growing strength of the Nazi party, but they continued to misjudge the magnitude of the threat. Despite the brutality of the street violence in 1931, some responded by continuing to dismiss Hitler as a buffoon who had little chance of success. Friedrich Hollaender founded the Tingel-Tangel cabaret in January 1931, at the spot where Hesterberg's Wild Stage had been located several years earlier. His revue *Ghosts in the Villa Stern* premiered in September of that year. Although it opened only a few days after the Rosh Hashanah violence on the Kufürstendamm, it included a number that denigrated "the little Hitler" as a small-time ghost who should not scare anyone, despite his ferocious appearance. The same show included what was perhaps the best parody of anti-Semites on any Weimar stage. Sung to the music of the habanera from Bizet's *Carmen,* it began:

> If it's raining or it's hailing,
> If there's lightning, if it's wet,
> If it's dark or if there's thunder,
> If you freeze or if you sweat,
> If it's warm or if it's cloudy,
> If it thaws, if there's a breeze,
> If it drizzles, if it sizzles,
> If you cough or if you sneeze:
> It's all the fault of all those Jews!
> The Jews are all at fault for that!
>
> Ob es regnet, ob es hagelt,
> ob es schneit, oder ob es blitzt,
> ob es dämmert, ob es donnert,
> ob es friert oder ob du schwitzt,
> ob es schön ist, ob's bewölkt ist,
> ob es taut oder ob es giesst,
> ob es nieselt, ob es rieselt,
> ob du hustest, ob du niesst:
> An allem sind die Juden schuld!
> Die Juden sind an allem schuld![33]

In the next three stanzas the piece proceeded to pile on ridiculous incidents that one could blame on the Jews.

These two songs parodying Hitler and anti-Semitism adopted the standpoint of the educated and rational citizen. From that angle, the arguments of the anti-Semites were indeed ludicrous, and Hitler really was a little spook who could not be taken seriously by any intelligent voter. The problem with that position was that the number of "intelligent" voters was diminishing rapidly. What made "the little Hitler" great, as well as dangerous, was the fact that many voters, not to mention men committed to street violence, were willing to take seriously the type of totally irrational and absurd statements parodied in the habanera. The two numbers may have reinforced a sense of intellectual and political superiority among Hollaender's audience, but that also might have encouraged a false sense of security by belittling the severity of the threat. Moreover, the songs could have fostered passivity among a public that thought: if one cannot deal with politics rationally, how can one deal with it at all?

A sense of resignation was certainly encouraged, however unwittingly, by a third song in Hollaender's *Ghosts in the Villa Stern*. Sung by a character portraying the inveterate liar Baron Münchhausen, it described a German state where films were pacifist, judges treated Christians and Jews equally, nobody displayed a swastika or black-white-red flag, abortion was legal, and the defense budget was rerouted toward social needs. Each stanza was met with the refrain: "Lies, lies, lies, lies, lies! But clearly it would be nice if it were only a little bit true." The fact that Münchhausen's visions were dismissed as an "illusion" did little to encourage the audience to fight for republican ideals.[34]

Kurt Robitschek, whose finances had been hurt by the street violence, had a better understanding of the irrational basis of the Nazis' appeal. Although he increasingly depoliticized his numbers on stage, he published an article in July 1931 that attributed Hitler's success to his theatrical skills: "What Hitler does, what he trumpets and stages, is political Charell. An old political comedy is refurbished and equipped with Girls, which in this case are called storm troopers." Robitschek suggested that the Weimar system would need better producers if it wanted to succeed: "Why is the democratic republic failing? The stage directors are bad. They are not theatrical enough. The decor is miserable, serious, artificial. Too little color, not enough silk, not enough use of the revolving stage." This was hardly a profound analysis of the Nazi phenomenon, but at least it conceded that Hitler was not using rational means to make his points: what he presented was a spectacle of strength and determination, rather than a logical plan to heal the polity. That being the case, Robitschek claimed that satire was ineffective against him. "If you use irony to pounce on Hitler, in case one of his theses collapses, then you have forgotten: his revolving stage is rolling!"[35]

Satire works only when one can confront a system of ideals with reality, or if one can demonstrate contradictions among the ideals. If the goals are nebulous or changing, then it is hard to get a grip on them. Weimar satirists could highlight the logical inconsistencies of Hitler's thought, but that was irrelevant to Nazi voters, for whom logic was not a virtue. After all, a Nazi speaker once told a group of farmers: "We don't want higher bread prices! We don't want lower bread prices! We don't want unchanged bread prices! We want National Socialist bread prices!" It would have been hard for any cabaretist to top that line. When satirists did try to reduce Nazi ideas to absurdity, they unwittingly forecast the absurd horror of things to come. In December 1931, three months after the violence on the Kurfürstendamm, Werner Finck told the following "joke" in the Catacombs: "In the first weeks of the Third Reich, parades will be staged. Should the parades be hindered by rain, hail, or snow, all Jews in the vicinity will be shot."[36] In 1931 that was still considered funny. Erich Burger, a critic for the *Berliner Tageblatt,* cited it approvingly. It would become much less humorous as the decade progressed.

## Red Revues and Agitprop

Erich Burger noted that in Hollaender's *Ghosts in the Villa Stern,* "a bitter incident can be quickly transformed into a comic effect." This ability of bourgeois satirists to squeeze humor out of the increasingly morbid state of the republic drew the fire of Marxist critics, who saw little occasion to laugh. In an essay of 1931 entitled "Leftist Melancholia," Walter Benjamin accused Mehring, Tucholsky, and Kästner of a "grotesque underestimation of the enemy." He contended that "their political significance exhausts itself by turning revolutionary reflexes, to the extent that they exist among the bourgeoisie, into objects of diversion and amusement that are capable of being consumed . . . In short, this leftist radicalism is precisely that stance that no longer corresponds to any political action . . . From the outset it seeks nothing more than to enjoy itself in negativistic peace. The transformation of the political struggle from a compulsion toward commitment to an object of enjoyment, from a means of production to an article of consumption—that is the ultimate hit of this literature."[37] Benjamin resurrected the contention that satire was nothing more than a safety valve for letting off political steam, a form of (literally) play-acting at politics. The audience might believe that it was participating in some form of collective statement, but it was merely consuming entertainment. In place of such self-duping, Benjamin supported a type of performance that was more focused, aggressive, and uncompromising. One of its embodiments was the agitprop movement of the Communist Party of Germany.

Some of the Dadaist writers and artists associated with the early Weimar cabarets had sympathized with the KPD, especially after the Social Democratic government suppressed the Spartacus uprising and the March Days in Berlin. The subsequent works of John Heartfield, Wieland Herzfelde, and George Grosz depicted the misery and exploitation of the working classes. Significantly, though, in the early years of the Weimar Republic, they rarely depicted the positive aspects of the proletarian struggle. They did not glorify the achievements of the workers' movement, nor did they praise the promised Communist land of the future. Writing in the KPD's *Rote Fahne* in 1925, Gertrud Alexander lamented Grosz's inability to "juxtapose to his caustic criticism of the bourgeois mug [*Fratze*] *the positive element of today's society,* namely the struggle and the heroism of the proletariat—a fault, incidentally, which is shared not only by George Grosz, but by the manifestations of German revolutionary artists in general."[38]

The KPD's attacks on the "negative," unconstructive criticism of Grosz and the others forced them to opt either for or against serious political commitment. Heartfield and Herzfelde chose to toe the party line throughout the 1920s, and they devoted their efforts to political photomontage and journalism in Communist and working-class newspapers. Another convert to the KPD was Gustav von Wangenheim. He had sung excessively nostalgic Pierrot songs on the opening night of Sound and Smoke; he also appeared in films, and played the role of Jonathan Harker in Murnau's *Nosferatu* (1922), the original Dracula movie. But in 1923 Wangenheim joined the Communist Party, and he became a leader of the workers' choral movement.

Erich Weinert (1890–1953) chose to devote his talent to Communist cabaret. Having started out as a satirist in bourgeois cabarets, after 1924 he heeded a call by the editors of the *Rote Fahne* to perform for workers' meetings. In 1926 he repudiated his former "bourgeois" and "negativistic" stance in an article entitled "Political Satire, Political Cabaret":

> Much mischief is being made these days with the word satire. Ever since it has become fashionable, a certain type of writer flits through bourgeois cabarets, pompously bills himself a political satirist, tosses souped-up punchlines into the audience, and like the dear Lord looks down from on high and pastes together conflicting worldviews in such a manner that nobody is hurt.
>
> These petty jokesters simply do not realize that the vocation of the satirist in no way consists of creating a balance by means of conciliatory niceties aimed in all directions. On the contrary, it requires depicting social contradictions as explicitly as possible, by positing nature against the unnatural, oppressed against oppressor, forward against backward. The cabaret-humorists with a "satirical" bent occasionally tickle the rudimentary revolutionary nerves of the good bourgeois, but they do not topple anything.

In short, Weinert critized the above-the-fray stance best exemplified by Walter Mehring when he contended: "I stand neither to the left nor to the right. I have always stood vertically." Those satirists like Mehring and

Tucholsky who continued to write for bourgeois cabarets were, for Weinert, "political clowns of the ruling class."[39] Weinert sought a different audience, and he became one of the major performers in Communist revues, agitprop performances, and political demonstrations until the end of the Weimar Republic.

A more far-reaching innovation was made by Erwin Piscator (1893–1966), who adapted cabaretic forms for political agitation. After associating with Berlin's postwar Dada movement, in 1920 he founded the Proletarian Theater, which performed radical plays in various workers' neighborhoods. Although that venture lasted only several months, Piscator continued to mount socially critical productions. Thus the KPD called upon him to write an agitational revue in anticipation of the Reichstag elections of December 1924. The result was the *Red Revel Revue (Revue Roter Rummel)*, which used short numbers derived from cabaret and variety shows to promote Communist ideals. In his book on political theater, published in 1929, Piscator recalled that he did not want "a revue like those of Haller, Charell, and Klein," but rather a "political-proletarian revue," a "revolutionary revue." He was dissatisfied with the full-length plays that he was used to directing, since their "cumbersome construction and the accompanying problems, which tempted you to sink into psychologizing, constantly reimposed a wall between the stage and the spectator." The revue, in contrast, was "incredibly naive in the directness of its presentation," and thus potentially more powerful. Piscator fashioned a political revue employing all of the possibilities of the stage: "music, song, acrobatics, speed-drawing, sports, slides, film, statistics, skits, speeches."[40]

The *Red Revel Revue* presented fifteen numbers that were loosely connected by two figures—one proletarian, the other bourgeois—who commented on the performance from their respective class standpoints. Some skits were straightforward indictments, such as that dealing with the imprisonment of a Communist propagandist, and another depicting the execution of workers at Noske's behest. Other numbers drew upon various forms of popular theatricality to make their points. Bourgeois election campaigns were depicted as a circus act; a juggler mocked the attempts of the industrialist Hugo Stinnes to stretch the eight-hour workday; and some acrobats evoked the strength and determination of the working class. A further scene consisted of a boxing match among actors made up to resemble Ludendorff, Stresemann, Noske, and Wilhelm Marx, until the Communist hero, Max Hölz, socked them out of the ring. Near the end a "revue within the revue" was presented: a bourgeois cabaret was recreated in order to illustrate the tastelessness and decadence of middle-class entertainment (fig. 33). Piscator thus simultaneously presented and rejected his bourgeois prototype.[41]

Between November 22 and December 7 the *Red Revel Revue* was

33. A decadent cabaret show entertains the bourgeoisie while a war cripple suffers, in Erwin Piscator's *Red Revel Revue* (1924).

performed fourteen times in various workers' neighborhoods of Berlin, and it proved immensely popular. Surprisingly, Piscator did not stage another contemporary revue for a proletarian audience. *In Spite of Everything! (Trotz alledem!)* was a historical revue, a montage of skits and films about events between 1914 and 1919; but it was performed only once, at the opening of the tenth party congress of the KPD in 1925. Thereafter Piscator continued to mount radical productions, but they played mainly to bourgeois audiences. That fact provided the occasion for jokes by Schiffer and Hollaender, as we have seen, but it dismayed leftist critics. Nevertheless, Piscator's *Red Revel Revue* inspired imitators within the Communist movement.

Members of the Communist Youth League of Germany (KJVD) were the first to realize that they could attract much larger audiences if they presented their ideas in the form of "Red Revues," instead of the more traditional didactic speeches. Just as the cabaret movement had been founded a generation earlier as a concession to the bourgeois public's taste for variety shows, Red Revues were a concession to young workers' hunger for entertainment. One Communist wrote in retrospect: "'Public Youth Meeting'—every party functionary knew in advance that that would be a flop . . . Unless there was a very special event, the youths would run right past us and go instead to dances, to the movies, or to the amusement park [*Rummel*] next door . . . Thus some comrades hit upon the idea: What the amusement park can do, we can too. We have to try to clothe our political agitation in a shape as lively as that of the amusement park." Another leader of the KJVD noted: "Of what use were the best and longest political speeches, when only a small portion of working-class youths attended? But tens of thousands went to dances or to amusement parks. Thus we had to elaborate these forms of mass entertainment, we had to give them a political content."[42]

The attraction of such entertaining forms of political agitation was confirmed by the first Red Revel (Roter Rummel) of the KJVD, performed in various working-class areas of Berlin from August 25 to September 5, 1925. The show was part of a series of events in conjunction with the Communists' International Youth Week. An internal report of the Berlin political police noted that the week as a whole "passed without significant success for the sponsors. The major means of agitation were the political-satirical evenings, designated as 'Red Revels.'" The Communist press bore out that summary. Whereas lectures drew anywhere from 45 to 120 listeners, the sixteen Red Revel performances attracted a total attendance of 15,000, nearly a thousand people for every appearance. The KJVD officials estimated that 30 percent of those present were not members of any of the Communist organizations. That was of major importance to the organizers, since they hoped to use the new medium to attract politically "indifferent" youths and adults to the Communist cause.[43]

The purpose of the Red Revels and Red Revues was not only to spread Communist ideas, but to encourage more active political participation. One of the major functions of the performances was to persuade the viewers to subscribe to publications like the *Rote Fahne*, to collect money for specific causes, or to join one of the Communist organizations, such as the KPD, the KJVD, the International Workers' Aid (Internationaler Arbeiterhilfe, or IAH, designed to aid the Soviet Union), and the Red Front Fighting League (Roter Frontkämpfer Bund, or RFB, a more militant group that protected Communist gatherings). These organizations sometimes founded or sponsored their own troupes. In 1926 the Communist Youth League promoted a theater group from Berlin-Wedding to the "First Agit-prop Troupe of the KJVD." Under the direction of Maxim Vallentin, the son of one of Max Reinhardt's early associates, it enjoyed great success, and it was renamed The Red Megaphone (Das rote Sprachrohr) in 1928. That year the RFB as well as the *Rote Fahne* financed the Red Rockets (Rote Raketen). They were given a truck to enable them to travel and perform throughout Germany, where they sought out new members and subscribers for their sponsors. Convoy Left (Kolonne Links), founded by a workers' sports club in Berlin-Steglitz in 1928, was taken over by the IAH a year later and likewise equipped with a truck. As a reward for recruiting sixteen thousand new IAH members throughout Germany in little over a year, it was sent on a trip to the Soviet Union in the spring of 1931.

By the end of the twenties these groups were but the tip of an iceberg; there were dozens of workers' performance groups that presented Communist cabaret and variety shows. The trend blossomed after 1927, encouraged in part by the very successful appearances of Moscow's Blue Workshirts troupe throughout Germany that fall. At the same time there was a move away from Red Revues, which focused on a single theme, to more diverse "agitprop" shows. These consisted of short numbers on a wide selection of themes, and they provided "agitation" and "propaganda" for the KPD's issues of the day. Whereas the longer revues demanded greater skills in composition and presentation, the short agitprop numbers could be scripted and memorized more easily. Moreover, they readily could be brought up-to-date: the day's headlines could be converted into a five-minute insert. Since agitprop numbers required fewer stage properties than the more elaborate Red Revues, they also could be performed more cheaply—an important consideration for workers who were strapped for income, and who were expected to turn all proceeds over to the various Communist organizations.

The highly mobile agitprop troupes performed everywhere imaginable—at indoor assemblies, open-air rallies, or the back courtyards of workers' housing blocks (fig. 34). By June 1931 the Berlin political police could report in an internal memorandum: "There is hardly a single Communist event at which one or another agitprop troupe does not perform. Statements of prominent leaders of the KPD confirm that the agitprop troupes have caused a considerable increase in rally attendance as well as a considerable growth in membership. That is understandable, when one considers the manner whereby the agitprop troupes promote their 'agitation' and 'propaganda' in the shape of short cabaret numbers, skits, one-act plays, and so forth. In comparison even with the most effective speeches, such performances are much better suited for persuading the listeners of the truth of Communist theses."[44]

What was the "truth" that agitprop propounded? Since a major purpose of the shows was to lure the spectators away from bourgeois entertainment, one important subtheme was criticism of commercial mass culture. In 1929 the Red Megaphone performed a long skit entitled "The Wondrous World of the German Philistine" (Des deutschen Spiessers Wunderwelt), which made fun not only of nationalist works like Wagner's operas

34. Prior to the Reichstag elections of September 1930, the Red Wedding agit-prop troupe brings the Communist message to workers in the inner courtyard of a Berlin "rental barrack."

and the patriotic films about Frederick the Great, but also *All Quiet on the Western Front*. At the time, the Communist press argued that a genuinely pacifist novel would have to show that war is caused by capitalism, and that a Communist revolution alone could prevent future conflagrations. The skit ended by criticizing workers who spent their after-work hours listening to the state radio stations, reading books by the liberal Ullstein or the reactionary Hugenberg presses, or attending commercial films. Instead of being lulled by such "kitsch" and "stupefaction works," workers should engage in political activities and limit their cultural diet to works approved by the Communist organizations. Another skit by the Red Megaphone, "At the Bosom of the Republic" (Am Busen der Republik), likewise warned against mass culture. The program booklet for that show asserted: "Whoever finds reading too strenuous goes to the movies. The bourgeois film promotes the idiocy of the masses even better than the press. There the cultural slime of art-kitsch [*kunstverkitschte Kulturschleim*] is even greasier and more pleasurable, and thus it diverts the working class from its misery and from the necessity of revolutionary class struggle." Other agitprop troupes gave concrete examples of mass-cultural obfuscation. In 1928 the Red Rockets had a "Niggersong" in their repertory, which began by describing a black dancer entertaining a bourgeois public. The number then proposed what it considered a more appropriate context for depicting blacks: colonial exploitation and consequent rebellion. It ended with a call for international, interracial solidarity.[45]

Many numbers were directed against Christianity. Although the conservative parties complained about the rampant secularization of the working class, the prevalence of antireligious works indicated that the Communists regarded the churches as a persisting competitor for the proletarian mind. The agitprop songs and skits attacked both Protestantism, with its traditional ties to Prussian conservatism, and Catholicism, which was backed politically by the Center Party, keystone to all of the Weimar coalitions. The KJVD went so far as to propose the celebration of winter solstice in place of Christmas. In an advisory pamphlet for agitprop groups to celebrate the 1928 solstice, the Central Committee of the Communist Youth League noted that Christmas was an especially auspicious time to underscore bourgeois hypocrisy. It suggested juxtaposing the precept "love your neighbor" with scenes of the lockout in the Ruhr, and "peace on earth" or "Silent Night" with the danger of new imperialist wars. A year later a children's agitprop group in Berlin-Moabit performed a skit that showed how proletarian children had to work on Christmas Eve, delivering newspapers or toys, while bourgeois children received all the presents.[46]

The 1928 pamphlet reprinted various skits, including some that protested the persistence of religious instruction in public schools. There also was a bit of adolescent humor, especially in one song by Theobald Tiger, alias Tucholsky. His "Gesang der englischen Chorknaben" (Song of the Angelic Choirboys) began with a blasphemous children's ditty: "Praise be to God, Lord of Pea-ea-eace! / Who's got the lice and the flea-ea-eas?" (Ehre sei Gott in der Hö-hö-he! / Wer hat die Wanzen und Flö-hö-he?). The song continued, in that style, to portray the church as a bulwark of exploitative capitalism, and religion as a means of stupefying the proletariat. The number must have been immensely popular, since it was performed by numerous agitprop groups in the ensuing years. The *Rote Fahne* reported in April 1930 that "the 'Red Hammer,' a well-known Berlin troupe, always receives a great storm of applause with Tucholsky's 'Song of the Angelic Choirboys,' which reaches its apex when the fat priest, with eyes screwed up in rapture, kisses his crucifix." The article then reported that the troupe was about to be prosecuted for blasphemy.[47]

Predictably, the majority of agitprop numbers dealt with political topics. The troupes conducted coordinated campaigns to promote Communist viewpoints before state or national elections, and during debates on emotional issues like the expropriation of the deposed German sovereigns (1926) and the construction of a battle cruiser (1928). They mobilized support and collected funds for striking workers, such as those of the 1928 Ruhr lockout. In addition, there were campaigns to support international revolutionary movements, especially that in China. Not surprisingly, the greatest attention was paid to developments in the USSR, whose supposed proletarian democracy and economic miracles were praised. The agitprop troupes also voiced opposition to measures seemingly aimed against the Soviet Union. In particular, the Locarno Treaty of 1925—which pledged peace with Germany's western neighbors but failed to ratify its eastern borders—was regarded as a capitalist anti-Soviet alliance. The First Agitprop Troupe of the KJVD even employed a Girls number to make the point. During their performance of "Hands Off China!" (Hände weg von China!), the Locarno Girls made an appearance. In the skit, Chamberlain and various "imperialist generals" plotting the division of China were treated to the following entertainment, according to a Berlin police report: "Ten young girls with extremely short skirts dance ballet. Each one has a letter on her chest and on her back, such that they spell 'Locarno' in front and 'anti-Soviet' in back. The generals are exceedingly pleased with this performance." So too was the reviewer for the *Rote Fahne*, who described them as "pretty, sympathetic young comrades."[48]

Numerous skits made fun of the other political parties. Occasionally the Catholic Center and the more right-wing groups were attacked, but the overwhelming majority of numbers was aimed against the Social Democrats. The Communists never forgot the actions of Noske during the early years of the republic. More important, the SPD was obviously their major—and invariably more successful—competitor for working-class votes. To counter those socialist sympathies, the agitprop skits portrayed the SPD as a de facto supporter of capitalism and opponent of revolutionary change. That was not too difficult, since the SPD's Hermann Müller became Reich chancellor in June 1928, and Social Democrats led the Prussian government until Papen's coup of 1932. With such powerful positions, political expediency—as well as the party's genuinely antirevolutionary temperament—sometimes led the SPD to cast rather unsocialist votes. This allowed the KPD, which did not have to worry about coalition-building or governmental responsibility, to take some easy swipes.

According to a police report, one scene of the KJVD's Red Revel of 1925 involved a dialogue between Stresemann and "Mr. Sam," in which they agreed that "the German Social Democrats never left us in the lurch when we needed them to support capitalist interests." A typical anti-SPD performance was that of The Heretics (Die Ketzer), recorded by the police in Berlin-Reinickendorf in November 1928. The revue included a depiction of Friedrich Ebert and the industrialist Hugo Stinnes in heaven, where they embraced and confessed that they always had been of one mind; a scene depicting the murder of Liebknecht and Luxemburg by Reichswehr officers at the behest of the SPD; and a number showing how Socialist delegates increased the tax burden on the working class. All skits were glossed by a figure personifying *Vorwärts*, the SPD newspaper, who recited sentences from that paper in order to damn the Social Democrats with their own words. On other occasions such political didacticism gave way to outright ridicule. The Red Rockets performed a song to the melody of a traditional lullaby, describing the SPD's desire to put the working class to sleep in a black-red-gold bed watched over by Hindenburg. Especially amusing was their song set to the tune of a current, internationally famous hit: it presented the SPD as "Just a Gigolo" (Armer Gigolo), who had to dance to the music of Krupp, Germany's major weapons manufacturer.[49]

The SPD, fearful of the Communists since the first days of the republic, was no less hostile toward the KPD, and it had the firepower to back its ire. Matters came to the head on May 1, 1929. Although Karl Zörgiebel, Berlin's Socialist police chief, had banned all open-air demonstrations, Communist workers in proletarian neighborhoods like Wedding and Neukölln held May Day processions. The police responded to the unarmed demonstrators not only with truncheons but also with bullets, and thirty-three workers were dead by the end of the day. The Communists regarded these incidents as a repeat of 1919, with Zörgiebel as the new Noske, and the split between the two leftist parties was sealed irreparably.

At the twelfth party congress in June 1929 the KPD declared that the

Social Democrats had become "social fascists." This doctrine was to define and cripple the Communist movement until Hitler's coming to power. It held that the growth of the KPD led to a consolidation of procapitalist forces, including the Social Democrats, who eventually would establish a military dictatorship to avert a proletarian uprising. Insofar as the SPD was the party that diverted the most working-class support away from the KPD, it was "objectively" the bulwark of the "fascist" coalition, and hence the greatest obstacle to revolution. In June 1929 *Das rote Sprachrohr*, one of the two major journals of the agitprop movement, devoted a special issue to "the fight against social fascism," in which Erich Weinert declared that "Social Democrats—have now become fascists!"[50]

The Communists believed that their prognosis was confirmed by events in the ensuing months. The global depression that broke out that fall hurt Germany especially severely. Its economic recovery had been aided by short-term loans from American banks, but these were now recalled. Inability to agree on solutions to the crisis led to parliamentary deadlock, and in March 1930 Müller's cabinet was replaced by one headed by the conservative Centrist politician Heinrich Brüning. The new chancellor dissolved the Reichstag and ruled through emergency decrees, promulgated by President Hindenburg according to article 48 of the Weimar Constitution. Following elections, the reconvened Reichstag of September 1930 saw tremendous gains for the Communists (now with 77 seats) and especially the Nazis (107 seats); but despite small losses, the SPD still had the largest parliamentary delegation (143).

Persistent inability to form a governing majority induced Brüning to continue ruling by emergency decree, a fact which effectively spelled the end of parliamentary democracy. Brüning could have been ousted by a vote of no-confidence, but the Social Democrats refused to back such a measure. According to the Communists, that made the SPD the prime supporter of the "Brüning dictatorship" and its economic austerity measures, which hit the working class unusually hard. In June 1931 a report of the Communist-dominated International Workers' Theater League asserted that the Social Democrats "put the Brüning government in the saddle; they rejected all motions in parliament to remove the emergency decrees and the Brüning government, and their government in Prussia puts Brüning's Reich laws into effect in an even more brutal and reactionary fashion."[51]

The emergency decrees soon affected the agitprop troupes directly. Earlier little could be done against Communist performances, as much as the authorities might try. In November 1926 the internal correspondence of the Berlin political police noted that the lenient free-speech laws did not give the courts much chance of prosecuting the KPD's shows. At most, a performance could be terminated if it took place in an auditorium that did not conform to fire-safety regulations.[52] That situation changed radically after March 28, 1931, when a new set of emergency decrees was promulgated. Aimed at the increasing violence associated with Nazi as well as Communist demonstrations, it allowed the prohibition in advance of any public political meetings and marches if the authorities feared that speakers might urge disrespect for the law, insult leading politicians or state institutions, or defame religious organizations.

The Berlin police used the decree as a basis for a total ban on agitprop performances. A memorandum dated April 2 noted: "According to our experience, it is precisely the agitprop troupes which pursue a boundless smear campaign against the state and the religious institutions in the meetings of the KPD and its affiliated organizations. Yet until now there has not been the possibility of moving against the agitprop performances in an effective manner. Now the emergency decree fills that vulnerable gap." The memorandum went on to report that since Communist publications had advised the agitprop groups to mount a large antireligious offensive around Easter, the police were empowered to ban all assemblies at which such troupes were scheduled to perform. That same day Albert Grzesinski, Zörgiebel's successor as Berlin's chief of police, ordered that "assemblies in which agitprop troupes appear are to be forbidden until further notice." Four weeks later the police raided the Berlin offices of the Communist-dominated German Workers' Theater League and confiscated all documents. For the *Rote Fahne,* the police decree and the raid constituted "irrefutable proof that the Social Democratic leaders have only waited for Brüning's emergency decrees in order to take widespread actions against the proletarian agitprop groups . . . With this emergency decree the SPD treads underfoot all freedom of speech, agitation, and proletarian performance."[53]

The *Rote Fahne* attributed the prohibition of agitprop to its political success: over the previous nine months, the troupes had performed 1,400 times before half a million spectators in Berlin and its vicinity, and had succeeded in recruiting six thousand new members to Communist organizations. Such statistics alarmed the authorities, who were disturbed even more by the increasingly aggressive tone of the performances. Originally, calls to violence had been symbolic. In February 1930, for example, the Red Hammer (Rote Hammer) troupe sang its signature song: they struck the ground with large red hammers after every stanza and shouted "hit hard!" (schlagt zu!). Soon other numbers were calling for direct violence. The Left Curve (Kurve links), a KJVD troupe from Berlin, gave a performance in Bochum in July 1930, wherein a young woman took aim and shot at target figures representing the SPD, capitalism, militarism, the Nazis, and the police. The Communist emcee said that because of the presence of an actual policeman, he could not place personal names on the figures. That was not the case in March 1931 at a performance of the KJVD's Red Pioneers (Rote Pioniere) in Berlin. A journalist for the conservative *Reichsbote* reported that in the performance, "Red Pioneers attack armed policemen, beat them to the ground, and kick them with mocking laughter while the audience applauds wildly." According to the observer, "the highpoint of this blood-orgy" was reached when a young Red Pioneer woman led chants calling for the shooting of Hitler, Goebbels, Brüning, Severing, and Grzesinski. We might be tempted to attribute such scenes to the adolescent mentality of the youthful audience. But that same month the police reported that the Red Megaphone, addressing an adult audience, performed a number in which three shots were fired at a bull's-eye held before Severing's head.[54] The type of right-wing, shooting-gallery amusement criticized in Hollaender's "Little Drummer Girl" was becoming a staple on Communist stages as well.

Such violent agitprop numbers were capable of generating strong emotions in working-class audiences. Performing before seven thousand spectators in Berlin in November 1930, the Red Torches (Rote Fackeln) staged a mock trial of figures representing capitalism, the church, the police, the judiciary, and an SPD big shot. The audience was asked to deliver the verdicts. The constable in attendance reported with dismay: "At the appearance of the armed police lieutenant, there was already such anger in the assembly that the speaker hardly could make himself heard. The crowd made the most nauseating suggestions about how to punish him. In the end it was decided to throw all of the armed police into the room where the thirty-three [revolutionary] sailors had been shot [in 1919], and to toss a grenade in after them." The understandably discomfited police observer noted further that "the skillful stage direction was able to whip up the audience's bloodlust. At times many of those in attendance believed that they really were witnessing an actual revolutionary tribunal. Medics repeatedly had to carry out those who were seized by cramps or had collapsed due to their strong emotions." The policeman concluded: "The entire manner of the presentation is certainly capable of sweeping an infected crowd on to all possible spontaneous actions."[55]

While it is understandable that the police wanted to keep such performances under control in the highly volatile political climate of 1931, it is also obvious that the KPD was loathe to give up such a potent medium. After March 1931 the agitprop troupes existed in a state of quasi-illegality, but they nevertheless managed to perform. The police in Berlin and throughout Germany were overtaxed and could not monitor all political rallies. For example, the Communists complained that the authorities had been able to prohibit twenty of the fifty Berlin assemblies that had planned to host agitprop troupes on May 1, 1931. From the police perspective, however, one could argue that the Communists had been very successful in evading the total ban. By November 1931 the Communists circulated a flyer saying that workers' assemblies should not be fearful of inviting agitprop troupes, because "in four-fifths of all cases in which the troupes had not been reported to the police in advance, they were able to perform without any difficulties!"[56]

The troupes devised various other tricks to outsmart the police. They often performed unannounced in the courtyards of workers' housing blocks or at outdoor assemblies. They also attempted (with less success) the old ploy, dating to Wilhelmine times, of declaring an assembly a closed meeting "for members only." One of the most ingenious tricks consisted in using incognito agitprop actors or Communist youths to start political discussions in public spaces. In its guidelines for the "summer agitation" of July 1931, the KJVD suggested that youths should arrive inconspicuously at squares, parks, and especially ice cream parlors, where they would start seemingly spontaneous political discussions with other Communist youths who had arrived earlier. Some of the youths could even pretend to be Nazis, Social Democrats, or Christians. It was hoped that the bystanders would become involved in the debates and won over to the Communist cause. Slatan Dudow's film *Kuhle Wampe* (1932), scripted by Brecht, included a dramatization of such public debates, in this case during a commuter train ride.[57]

The political difficulties faced by the agitprop troupes were not merely of an external nature. Officials of the KPD tried to coordinate agitprop activities and guarantee their political correctness and efficacy. In 1928 Communist delegates packed the annual convention of the German Workers' Theater League, which until then had been under Social Democratic guidance, and took over its organizational apparatus. In the ensuing years the Workers' Theater League tried to have all agitprop troupes join its ranks, a goal it never achieved. The League hoped to control the performance style and ideological statements of its members; to that end it used newsletters and journals. But despite persistent efforts by the central leadership, it never was able to assert extensive control even over those troupes that officially belonged to the League.

The KPD, the KJVD, and the Workers' Theater League repeatedly had to assert the primacy of politics vis-à-vis the proletarian players, who experienced some of the same dilemmas faced by bourgeois satirists. Just as cabarets had been founded to lure middle-class spectators away from variety shows, Red Revues had been created to draw proletarian youths and adults away from mass-cultural diversions. The Communists hoped to use the entertaining format to indoctrinate the working-class public, but they soon discovered that the humor could outweigh the political message. At the turn of the century Sigmund Freud had noted that "with tendentious jokes we are not in a position to distinguish by our feeling what part of the pleasure arises from the sources of their technique and what part from those of their purpose. Thus, strictly speaking, we do not know what we are laughing at."[58] Neither did the spectators of agitprop. The KPD hoped that they would walk away with the political "purpose" in mind, but many viewers remembered only the entertaining "technique" of agitprop's "tendentious jokes." Workers could swallow the bait of amusement without getting hooked on the political line.

Many observers, police as well as Communists, reported that most spectators seemed to attend agitprop performances merely for the free diversion. At a performance by Berlin's Red Rockets in Stuttgart in September 1928, a policeman noted that the audience seemed more taken by the "burlesque" *Nigger-Tanz* performed during the the the anticolonial "Nigger-Song," than by "the serious text." The report continued: "Under the rubric of 'The Political Jazz-band,' all six members sang satirical songs with accompanying jazz music. Here too the political content of the songs took a back seat, because the comic nature of the presentation grabbed the spectators' attention above all." At a meeting of the RFB in Berlin-Spandau four months later, a policeman noted that the political speaker "could barely be heard owing to the prevailing chattering in the hall." More attention was paid to the ensuing performance of the Red Workshirts (Rote Blusen), but for many in attendance, the highlight seemed to be the dance at the conclusion of the show—a product of the fact that agitprop troupes often doubled as dance bands after rallies: "It must be noted that among the public there were many non-Party people, especially youths, who came simply for the ensuing dance. In general the KPD-comrades, especially the women, were dressed for a fete."[59]

Such observations were made as well by Communist critics, who repeatedly cautioned the performers to give priority to the political message. Communist officials wanted to counter a situation where the agitprop troupes were turning into the political clowns of the proletariat, to paraphrase Weinert. They also wanted to avoid the dilemma of bourgeois satire, where laughter could vent frustrations and thus detract from further action. Although party officials were pleased that rallies with agitprop troupes could draw bigger crowds than those with speeches alone, the KVJD journal observed in 1928: "in various assemblies the importance of agitprop troupes was overestimated and the speech regarded as secondary. *Now as before the political speaker must be the most important aspect of our assemblies.*" Other writers argued that agitprop troops should not merely employ humorous satire but also depict serious scenes. Maxim Vallentin, the director of the Red Megaphone, wrote that "satire, the best method of agitation, does not embrace a person completely," and thus propagandistic pathos was important as well: "We must be able to shock, 'electrify and shake into action' (as Potemkin-director Eisenstein said), in order to win human resources."[60]

Since humor was getting in the way of the political message, it would have to be attenuated. Georg Pijet, a Communist writer, argued that to treat certain serious themes satirically would be "simply impossible"; strikebreaking or the uprisings of 1919 were off limits to humor. In 1929 a writer for *Das rote Sprachrohr* argued that satire itself should be made more serious: "All satire is bitterly earnest, and the spectators must realize that." Two years later the same journal still had to warn against exclusive reliance on humor: "Some people believed that 'laughter kills'—and that was correct—but they went further and believed: 'Laughter alone kills—laughter can achieve everything!' and that was false!" At a national meeting of the Workers' Theater League in April 1930 a speaker had to remind the audience that increased support for the KPD was the criterion of theatrical success: "'Ye shall know them by their electoral results'—not by the laughter, applause, or enthusiasm that they achieve."[61]

Some agitprop groups took these strictures to heart. Already in 1925, at one of the Red Revels of the KJVD, the audience was warned not to treat the entertainment as a safety valve for discontent, but rather as a spur to action. After making various jokes about capitalist, militarist, and Social Democratic practices, an actor turned to the audience and said: "And you laugh at that. You know, when I look at you from up here, it makes me want to puke. You laugh and laugh. You even laugh at your own stupidity. Instead of banding together, going to the [reformist] trade unions and beating them to shit—you let this rubbish happen every day—and you even laugh about it!" In 1930 the Red Megaphone began a number with a choric introduction that intoned: "If you / seek diversion—amusement—relaxation—peace / . . . then / you will / cry bitter tears / for—/ your price of admission! / Our jokes / are political—Our seriousness / is political—Our play / is political!"[62]

To ensure that all affiliated agitprop troupes saw their work in a correct ideological context, at the end of December 1930 the Workers' Theater League commenced a series of courses for performers. The schooling, which lasted several days, was purely political and sought "to give the German comrades of the Workers' Theater League a foundation for their work." As the political and economic situation worsened, the agitprop groups were ordered to engage in more direct shop-floor agitation and propaganda, and to become more closely associated with workers in specific factories. Finally, at the national meeting of the Workers' Theater League in April 1931, the delegates voted to institute a "more strict and thorough organization of the Workers' Theater League," and to turn the affiliated performance groups into "political cadres, that is, battle units with responsible functions."[63]

The military metaphor was appropriate, since the KPD believed that it was gearing up for the final revolutionary assault against Germany's "fascist" system. Incredibly, at that late date the Communist leaders still saw the Social Democrats as their major enemy, despite the Nazis' tremendous gains at the polls, and the almost daily battles in Berlin between storm troopers and members of the Red Front Fighting League. At the same national meeting of the Workers' Theater League, the delegates' resolution claimed that the German bourgeoisie "had left the ground of sham democracy and ordered the Brüning regime to establish a fascist dictatorship. In this endeavor it is actively supported by the stance of the SPD and the NSDAP, which increasingly are unmasked as lackeys for the suppression of the working class." For the Communists, the Social Democrats and the Nazis were but two sides of the fascist coin. That idea was spelled out in a political training course for new members of the KJVD in the fall of 1931. The course depicted the SPD as the party of "social fascists," and the NSDAP as that of "national fascists." It branded Nazi propaganda as "social demagoguery," which by using "sham radical phrases" succeeded in "winning over great segments of the working class." Both parties, in short, diverted the proletariat away from supporting the Communists. That meant that "the battle between social fascists and national fascists is only fictitious. It is merely a fight over the state coffers." In the final revolutionary battle the Social Democrats would unite with the Nazis to back a fascist dictatorship against the Communist working class. As late as September 1932 a secret conference of agitprop functionaries was told by a representative of the Central Committee of the KPD: "the ADGB [socialist trade unions] and the SPD are the greatest brakes on our revolutionary policies. If we do not succeed in smashing them, we will never attain the revolution."[64]

This fixation on the Social Democrats blinded the Communists to the magnitude of the Nazi threat. Their inability to see the true nature of National Socialism was made manifest in the agitprop skits. Granted, the Communists correctly surmised that the Nazis did not have the workers' best interests at heart, despite the proletarian rhetoric of men like Otto Strasser, who broke with Hitler in the summer of 1930 and formed the "Revolutionary National Socialists." In anticipation of the Reichstag elections of September 1930, one Red Revel showed that the Nazis could not be considered friends of the proletariat, since their leaders lived too well, they opposed strikes, and they included in their ranks men who had gunned down workers in 1919. One scene described a squabble between Hitler and Strasser, in which the latter threatened to break away: "I'll found the national revolutionary socialists, the revolutionary social nationalists, the revolutionary national socialists, the national social revolutionaries, the social revolutionary nationalists!"[65]

After the September elections the Nazis appeared much less funny. Whereas the KPD leadership remained fixated on the "social fascist" SPD, the Communist rank and file learned that their actual enemies were in the Nazi camp. In his memoirs about the activities of the Left Column agitprop group, Helmut Damerius recalled that political reality was spelled out for them by their working-class audience. Following the party line, the troupe attacked the SPD as the workers' greatest enemy. As for the Nazis, it merely ridiculed them, portraying them "harmlessly with paper helmets and wooden swords," despite the increasingly deadly fights between storm troopers and Communists. One number in particular illustrated how slapstick humor could get the better of a serious political message. Actors depicting Hitler, Strasser, Goebbels, and other Nazi bosses appeared on stage wearing porcelain chamber pots in place of helmets. When they got into one of their perennial fights over Nazi policy, they used wooden sticks to crack the potties on each others' heads. The audience would invariably roar with laughter at such infantile humor. After one performance, however, some workers protested that in reality the Nazis were not beating up each other but killing proletarians. Stung by that criticism, the troupe gave the scene a coda in future performances. After the slapstick and the inevitable peals of laughter, the actors would halt the show and ask the audience: "Is that what the Nazis really look like? Aren't they killing workers every day?" Then an actor wearing an authentic storm-trooper uniform would appear on stage, and others held up posters listing the names of workers killed by Nazis.[66] That story highlights the limits of using humor for serious political ends, as well as the Communist rank-and-file's greater perspicacity in recognizing the Nazi threat. Nevertheless, agitprop troupes continued to perform far more numbers attacking Social Democrats right up to the end of the republic.

The KPD was even less perceptive when it came to assessing the Nazis' anti-Semitism. Just as the Communists believed that a "sham battle" took place between Nazis and Social Democrats, they contended that the hostility toward Jews was also feigned: it was a capitalist ploy to divert workers away from class struggle by fomenting racial conflict. The Communist inability to acknowledge serious ideological splits within the bourgeoisie was made manifest in an agitprop skit that Georg Pijet wrote for the 1930 Reichstag elections. In grotesque defiance of political reality, one scene depicted both a "Jewish capitalist" and an "Aryan capitalist" giving money to Hitler. When some Nazis shouted "Death to the Jews!!! Germany awake!!!," even the Jewish capitalist applauded, since he (qua capitalist) believed that such racial demagoguery would divert the workers from class struggle. The Nazis in the skit tried to throw the Jewish capitalist out, but Hitler stopped them with the comment: "Good Lord, you don't have to take everything so literally!"[67] This denial of the reality of the Nazis' anti-Semitism was not isolated, but a central precept of Communist thought of the time. It appeared in other agitprop skits, and even formed the basis for Brecht's dramatic analysis of fascism, *The Roundheads and the Peakheads* (1932).

Neither the bourgeois satirists nor their Communist counterparts were able to comprehend the true nature of National Socialism. Liberal notions of rational, responsible political engagement and Communist beliefs in simplistically bipolar class struggle were equally limited in their ability to understand the Nazi menace. Satire was unable to fathom Hitler, much less stop him. When he finally came to power, he remembered his opponents. The liberals, Jews, and Communists who had constituted the bulk of people engaged in bourgeois cabaret and proletarian agitprop were destined to be victims of the new regime.

# CHAPTER EIGHT

# Cabaret under National Socialism

The National Socialist takeover in the spring of 1933 nearly destroyed the cabaret movement, for most of the entertainers had been liberal, leftist, or Jewish. Many of these fled Germany in the first days and weeks of Nazi rule. The remaining "Aryan" performers who desired to ply their trade had to make significant compromises with the new regime. Whereas Trude Hesterberg took the route of subscribing (or pretending to subscribe) to Nazi ideals, Werner Finck persisted in making sly jokes about life in the Third Reich. For that offense, his Catacombs cabaret was closed in May 1935, as was the Tingel-Tangel, another refractory stage. In the wake of that affair, the authorities called for the creation of a "positive cabaret" that would applaud the Nazis' goals and mock those of their enemies. The project, which was totally alien to the spirit of cabaret, was a failure; consequently in 1937 Goebbels banned all political themes from German stages. Thereafter cabaret degenerated into pure vaudeville, the seedbed from which it had sprung in the 1890s. With the increasing mobilization of the male population after 1939, only women remained to populate the cabaret and revue stages. The "Girls" dominated the shows until the bombardment of Berlin destroyed the remaining centers of entertainment.

## The Suppression of Critical Cabaret

Although the outside world might have viewed Berlin as the seat of Hitler's rule, the Nazis themselves regarded the metropolis with great suspicion. To be sure, they made impressive electoral inroads into the traditionally "red" city after 1930. The despair brought on by mounting unemployment led to a polarization of Berlin's electorate. In the Reichstag elections of September 14, 1930, the Communists received 27.3 percent of the Berlin vote, narrowly surpassing the Social Democrats, who won 27.2 percent. The Nazis, who had made a negligible showing in 1928, received almost 15 percent of the ballots cast in the capital. They continued to make dramatic gains as the economic crisis worsened. On November 6, 1932, in the last Reichstag elections before Hitler's chancellorship, more Berliners supported the Nazis (26 percent) than the Social Democrats (23 percent). Nevertheless, the Communists attained a considerable lead (31 percent), and the Nazis fared significantly worse in the capital than they did in the national vote (where they attracted 33 percent of the electorate). For liberal Berliners, the November elections were a catastrophe: almost 70 percent of their neighbors voted against the Weimar democracy (if one combines the votes of the Nazis, the Communists, and the German National People's Party, at 11 percent). Yet from a Nazi perspective, the results were far from ideal: some 54 percent of Berliners were still voting "red" (SPD or KPD). Thus when Hitler was appointed chancellor on January 30, 1933, he knew that he would govern from a city that was largely enemy territory.

Given the city's leftist propensities, the Nazis' purge of Berlin was especially brutal. Upon being appointed minister of the interior for Prussia, Hermann Göring put Nazi party members in charge of police departments, and he declared that the storm troopers would function as "auxiliary police." This inaugurated a reign of terror, as the SA and SS used their new authority to wreak vengeance on the leftists whom they had battled in the preceding years. Thousands of Communists, Social Democrats, and trade union officials were detained in over fifty hastily created jails and concentration camps in and around Berlin. Among the most notorious were the Columbiahaus at the Tempelhof airport, run by the SS, and the concentration camp at Oranienburg just north of the city. An early highpoint of terror came in June, when a hundred Communists and socialists were tortured to death by the SA and SS during the "Köpenick Blood Week."

While outright violence was used to intimidate the leftists, pseudo-legal means were used to cow liberals and Jews of all political persuasions. Following the Reichstag fire of February 27, which the Nazis claimed was a Communist signal for a proletarian uprising, Hindenburg promulgated an emergency degree based on article 48 of the Weimar constitution. The decree gave Hitler de facto authority to suspend freedom of speech, the press, and political assembly. Despite these powers, the Nazis still could not gain a majority of votes in the Reichstag elections of March 5, where they received 44 percent of the national vote, and 35 percent of ballots cast in the capital. Nevertheless, the new Reichstag—meeting in the Kroll Opera House, ironically the site of many avant-garde performances in the twenties—suspended the constitution and gave Hitler dictatorial powers on March 23. The two-thirds majority needed to pass this so-called Enabling Act was attainable because all KPD mandates had been invalidated, and storm troopers prevented many SPD delegates from attending the session. That law spelled the end of the Weimar Republic. By summer the Nazis had banned all other political parties, dissolved the trade unions, and forced all newspapers to toe the National Socialist line. Moreover, they began to institute their anti-Semitic policies: on April 1 they proclaimed a one-day boycott of Jewish businesses, and on April 7 they passed a law dismissing almost all Jews from the civil service.

These events could not help but have a traumatic impact on Berlin's cultural life, including cabaret. Since the Nazis moved most swiftly against Communists and Social Democrats, whom they considered their most serious enemies, members of agitprop troupes were in immediate danger. Many of them were arrested, and in November 1933 Hans Otto, a leader of the German Workers' Theater League and a supporter of the agitprop movement, was killed in the Columbiahaus. Other outspokenly leftist associates of the cabaret movement suffered as well. Erich Mühsam, a frequent performer in Berlin's pub-cabarets at the turn of the century, was killed in Oranienburg in July 1934 for having played a commanding role in the Bavarian Soviet Republic of 1919.

Nor was Nazi terror limited to the far left. Many of Berlin's liberal and "bourgeois" luminaries in literature and the arts also were very high on the Nazi hit list. Some of them had been outspoken opponents of Hitler, even if they often underestimated the threat that he posed. Goebbels disliked the cabarets in particular. In January 1930 he had gone to the Kadeko in order to see a guest appearance by Karl Valentin. Goebbels had liked the famous (and non-Jewish) comedian from Munich, but as for the rest of the show: "A totally Jewish affair. In part insufferable, in part weak, but also in part not without wit. Naturally it was all asphalt."[1] Having been the ranking Nazi in Berlin for several years, Goebbels had observed and castigated that city's "asphalt literature," a right-wing buzzword designating all cosmopolitan and critical art.

Goebbels was particularly anxious to cleanse Berlin's cultural scene, which he considered a cesspool of "decadent," "Bolshevik," and "Jewish" culture. The first of several well-choreographed attacks came on May 10, when university students throughout Germany tossed thousands of books by undesirable writers into huge bonfires. The most publicized of these conflagrations occurred in front of Berlin's university, in the presence of Goebbels. To the text of a ritual incantation denouncing decadent values and extolling nationalist virtues, the works of Marx, Freud, Remarque, Heinrich Mann, and others were consigned to the flames. Two stalwarts of Weimar cabaret were mentioned explicitly. Erich Kästner's works were burned to the cry of: "Against decadence and moral decay! For discipline and decency in the family and the state!" And while Tucholsky's books were being cremated, the students intoned: "Against impudence and arrogance, for respect and reverence toward the immortal German people's soul!"[2]

Kästner actually witnessed the book-burning, but most of the prominent cabaret writers and performers had fled Germany by then. Unlike Kästner, they were almost all Jewish: Kurt Gerron, Valeska Gert, Paul Graetz, Fritz Grünbaum, Annemarie Hase, Friedrich Hollaender, Margo Lion, Walter Mehring, Paul Morgan, Rudolf Nelson, Kurt Robitschek, Mischa Spoliansky, and many others. All of them faced hardships in exile; some succumbed to despair. Paul Nikolaus, the political conferencier of the Kadeko, already had committed suicide in Lucerne on March 30. In a last letter he wrote: "For once, no joke: I am taking my own life. Why? I could not return to Germany without taking it there. I cannot work there now, I do not want to work there now, and yet unfortunately I have fallen in love with my fatherland. I cannot live in these times." A week earlier Paul Simmel, the well-known cartoonist for the *Berliner Illustrirte Zeitung,* had committed suicide in Berlin. And two years later Kurt Tucholsky ended his life in Sweden.[3]

Those cabaret artists who remained in Germany faced great difficulties. The economic depression had forced many cabarets to fold. The establishment of Nazi rule killed off almost all the others, as leftists, liberals, and Jews were silenced. Erwin Lowinsky, Elow of the Cabaret of the Nameless, was one of the few intrepid Jews who attempted to run a cabaret under the new conditions. When his contract to be conferencier at the Wilhelmshallen am Zoo was canceled, he decided to open his own cabaret in October 1933 (owing to "an optimism that I no longer understand," he wrote in his postwar memoirs). Unlike his previous venture, which made fun of amateurs, Elow's Künstlerspiele Uhlandeck on the Kurfürstendamm was a more conventional cabaret in which he acted as conferencier, cracking jokes and introducing the various singers and entertainers. The shows received very favorable reviews in many of Berlin's papers, which often noted that Elow's humor was still "biting" *(bissig)* but strictly apolitical. One reason why he was able to stay in business for several months was the fact that he was forced to hire some members of the Nazi's Battle League for German Culture (Kampfbund für Deutsche Kultur). Unemployment among actors and entertainers was very high (over 40 percent in 1932), and Nazi sympathizers were happy to have a contract, even if it involved signing with a flourishing "Jewish" enterprise. That situation ended in April 1934, however, when Elow's venture was finally "Aryanized." It passed into the hands of Paul Schneider-Duncker, who had founded the Roland von Berlin with "the Jew" Rudolf Nelson thirty years earlier, but now was an outspoken supporter of the Nazi regime.[4]

By then the major vehicle for keeping Jews, liberals, leftists, and other undesirables out of Germany's cultural life was the Reich Culture Chamber (Reichskulturkammer). Founded in September 1933 at the urging of Goebbels, who became its president, the organization was divided into sub-chambers for literature, the visual arts, theater, music, film, the press, and radio. Anyone seeking to be active in any of these fields was required to become a member, but membership invariably was denied to "non-Aryans" and politically suspect individuals. In its first two years, much of the Culture Chamber's time was spent ascertaining the racial credentials of applicants. When Elow sought to become a member of the subchamber for literature, which would have allowed him to appear in print, he received a letter of rejection that argued: "Given the great importance of intellectual and culturally creative work for the life and the future development of the German people, doubtlessly only those personalities are qualified to undertake such activity in Germany who belong to the German people not only as citizens but also through profound bonds of race and blood. Only someone who feels tied and obligated to his people through racial commonality is allowed to exert influence upon the inner life of the nation by means of the far-reaching and momentous type of work represented by intellectual and cultural production. Because of your status as non-Aryan, you are incapable of perceiving and appreciating such an obligation."[5]

Having been shut out of the public sphere, Jewish performers were forced to restrict their activities to Jewish audiences. Eventually the only context in which they were allowed to act was in events sponsored by the Culture League of German Jews (Kulturbund deutscher Juden). Founded in Berlin in June 1933, the League's membership was restricted to Jews, and only the Jewish press was allowed to report on its activities. The only "Aryans" permitted at performances were official observers, often from the Gestapo. Most of the League's performances consisted of classical music or drama. Rosa Valetti, who had founded the Cabaret Megalomania in the early twenties, emigrated to Austria in 1933, but she was allowed to make guest appearances in the League's Berlin theater until July 1934. As of October 1935 the League even had a section for cabaret (Kleinkunst) headed by Max Ehrlich, a popular comic actor of the twenties who had appeared at the Kadeko. Ehrlich became one of the League's most active performers, as he mounted numerous cabaret evenings, musical comedies, and revues. Their purpose was pure entertainment and diversion, and his shows invariably succeeded, in the words of a reviewer for the *Jüdische Rundschau* of April 1937, in "relieving us of cares and fears for a couple of hours." That was precisely what his increasingly imperiled audience desired from the stage. In September 1938 that same paper objected to a League performance of *Ghosts*, Ibsen's grimmest drama, claiming: "we need consolation and we need release from tension." At the same time that the League's audiences sought diversion, they also would have objected to overly boisterous comedies, owing to the increasing gravity of the Jews' situation. That point was made explicit by Elow, who founded the Tourists (Touristen), a "cabaret of Jewish authors," in 1937. In his opening number he proclaimed: "The time of jokes is past. We are committed to providing you with joy and a cheerful mood. One can take even joy seriously." A far cry from his previous Cabaret of the Nameless, Elow's new, "literary" venture presented poems, songs, and skits in a lightly humorous vein.[6]

While the expulsion of Jews from public stages decimated the cabaret movement, the restrictions imposed by Nazi cultural policy crippled the remaining "Aryan" stars of popular entertainment. All non-Jews who attempted to keep cabaret alive found themselves forced to make major compromises with the times. One such case involved Trude Hesterberg, who had been closely associated with the Weimar cultural scene. After managing and singing at the Wild Stage from 1921 to 1923, she had been a frequent performer in the Haller revues, and had appeared in controversial productions such as Brecht's and Weill's *Rise and Fall of the City of Mahagonny.* Toward the end of the Weimar Republic, however, she must have experienced a political change of heart, for in January 1933—even before Hitler's appointment as chancellor—she joined the Nazi party and the Fighting League for German Culture, and she even became a member of an SS support group. That show of enthusiasm for the new regime did not, however, spare her trouble in the ensuing months. In the spring of that year she starred in a touring production of a new operetta by Oscar Straus, who had been the in-house composer of Wolzogen's Motley Theater over thirty years earlier. The show had no difficulties in Dresden, but was closed down by Nazi authorities in Stuttgart as a "decadent" and "immoral" work whose music and lyrics had been written by Jews.

Suddenly worried about her status with the authorities, Hesterberg wrote a letter to Hans Hinkel, the secretary general of the Fighting League and the recently appointed commissioner for theater in the Prussian Ministry of Science, Art and Education. Describing herself as "Berliner, German, Christian," she claimed: "as a woman and an artist I naturally have been influenced by all tendencies of the times, but I never became a politician. I have always instinctively considered my art a megaphone of the popular opinions of the day. Out of this sense of artistic duty, I became a member of the Nazi party and the Fighting League." Following this perhaps unwitting, but still rather blatant, admission of opportunism, Hesterberg conceded that the condemnation of Straus's operetta was probably justified "from a racial [*völkisch*] standpoint," and expressed the hope that her appearance in the work would not be regarded as an act of "national disloyalty."[7]

Hinkel replied cordially to Hesterberg, assuring her that she would face no difficulties because of her involvement in the Straus operetta. However, she did not seem to have learned the proper lesson in Nazi racial policy, because thereafter she joined a show touring Austria and Czechoslovakia which was put together by Kurt Robitschek, who had fled Berlin in March. Moreover, in the ensuing weeks various denunciations of Hesterberg seem to have filtered in to Hinkel's office. For example, in July a certain Charlotte Jungmann, a member of the Nazi party who described herself as having been Hesterberg's maid for many years, wrote a letter asserting that it was "doubtful" that Hesterberg was "reliable from the standpoint of the National Socialist state." Jungmann requested an audience with Hinkel, which was granted. By September, Hesterberg had clearly fallen from Hinkel's favor. He wrote to one of her friends that she had been engaged to Heinrich Mann, "who has had his citizenship revoked," and that she "was always glad to be seen in public with Herr Mann during the Marxist period." Moreover, she had performed cabaret numbers in Paris that promoted reconciliation among the nations. According to Hinkel, there was "no guarantee that she stands on the ground of the National Socialist worldview." He concluded the letter by expressing doubts about her political change of heart: "Since Frau Hesterberg, according to your own description, has a very strong personality, she could not have changed her attitude credibly in such a short period of time."[8]

Hesterberg responded to this letter, which her friend had passed on to her, with a long missive to Hinkel. She denied ever having appeared in Parisian cabarets and stressed her long-standing nationalist sentiments. She noted that during World War I she had "conducted German cultural propaganda in Switzerland and Scandinavia," and that on her recent stint in Czechoslovakia she had "expressly stood up for the German government." Moreover, "in accordance with my duty I broke my contractual obligations to Herr Robitschek and consequently suffered very considerable difficulties due to breach of contract," including numerous attacks on her in the Austrian press. Hesterberg was most perturbed about the stories linking her to Heinrich Mann. She admitted that she had had a friendly relationship with him in 1928 and that he had proposed marriage to her. Yet she had rejected that proposal, and, more important, she claimed to have rejected his politics as well: "Never in any way did I identify with the opinions of Herr Mann. In particular I always disapproved of all of Mann's Marxist and subversive ideas." As for her own attitude, she wrote that "in my capacity as artist I have always tried to stand above things and have always sought to support my fatherland." For that reason, "I stand completely on the ground of the National Socialist worldview and would like to point out that I have been a supporting member of an SS unit [*Förderndes Mitglied einer SS-Standarte*] since January, that is, before the national upheaval."[9]

By November, Hesterberg had regained enough credibility to open her own cabaret, the Muses' Swing (Musenschaukel). The program booklet of the first production struck the proper national chords. One short essay, "Into the New Era," stressed that the cabaret was not located in western Berlin, but in the Pavillon Mascotte, which had been a fashionable establishment in the older Friedrichstadt entertainment district at the turn of the century. That was a transparent way of saying that the venture was not part of Kurfürstendamm, the newer (and in many people's minds, Jewish) center of nightlife in the twenties, but harked back to prewar traditions. The program booklet's introductory essay, written by Megerle von Mühlfeld, the cabaret's literary director, stressed the venture's apolitical nature: "Far be it from us to illuminate politics from our small stage. These grave times demand a more serious treatment of such themes . . . We pursue just one goal: to coax a few cheerful hours from hard-working and productive people." The cabaret explicitly sought to provide pure diversion, but it would be distraction with a properly German basis: "we want to welcome our city-dwellers once more into a popular cabaret [*Volkskabarett*], which contains nothing foreign. Thus you will hear only numbers that are anchored in our nature and whose music is derived from folk songs. For the people's voice is genuine. It is honest and free."[10] The cabaret thus subscribed to the Nazi vision of bringing corrupt urbanites back in touch with the *völkisch* soul, by reintroducing them to "popular" culture and keeping all foreign (French, American, Jewish) influences at bay.

Such statements might have been music to the ears of Nazi authorities, but in practice they did not prove commercially viable. The Muses' Swing folded in February 1934, after its second production. It had provided an uneasy combination of folk-type songs, nostalgic looks back to prewar Germany (with numbers entitled "Kaiser Waltz" and "1905 in the Mascotte"), as well as parodies. Understandably, the latter were the most successful numbers; nevertheless, takeoffs on Hungarian operettas (in the November–December program) or grand opera (in January) hardly addressed gripping issues. By March 1934 Hesterberg's ensemble had relinquished the Pavillon Mascotte, and was presenting its more successful parodies at the Kadeko as part of the evening entertainment.[11] Soon thereafter the ensemble disbanded, and Hesterberg spent the rest of the Nazi era making guest appearances at the Kadeko and various variety stages, as well as playing character roles in numerous films.

An "Aryan" performer who encountered much greater difficulties was Werner Finck, the founder and star of the Catacombs, which had moved to a small hall on the premises of the Scala variety theater in 1932. Finck's ensemble was able to carry over into the Nazi era almost completely intact because it included very few Jews. Indeed, that was one reason for the cabaret's name, aside from the fact that it initially played in a basement. On the opening night in October 1929 Finck explained: "Two thousand years ago the catacombs were the place of refuge for the first Christians, today they are the place of refuge for the last ones." This reference to the prevalence of Jews in the entertainment business was not Finck's only joke at the expense of "non-Christians"; after all, he was the one who had quipped that if it should rain on a Nazi parade, all Jews in the vicinity would be shot. Moreover, he had begun his stage career with a number in questionable taste. At a dress rehearsal of the short-lived cabaret Impossible (Die Unmöglichen) in 1928, he had presented a parody of a play by a Yiddish theater group. This had led to "angry protests" by the "predominantly Jewish public," according to Finck's own autobiography. Such incidents, combined with the fact that he had broken away from his leftist colleagues in 1930, indicated to the Nazis that he was not part of the "Bolshevik Jewish" scene. The ensemble continued to perform uninterruptedly into the Nazi era, save for the dismissal of the non-"Aryan" members of the troupe (the actresses Inge Barsch and Dora Gerson, and Trude Kolman, the cabaret's literary adviser).[12]

What the authorities failed to realize was that Finck, though no militant leftist, occasionally aimed his barbs against the right. In 1929, for example, he performed a parody of the Wandervögel, a middle-class back-to-nature youth movement that had acquired nationalist and anti-Semitic overtones (fig. 35). Like most of Finck's "critical" numbers, its attitude was one of playful ridicule. Finck indicated that he would continue his sly attacks at the opening of a new show in March 1933. He emerged from the curtain asking "What will the Catacombs do?" and replied: "We're still here!" For the next two years Finck's troupe continued to make rather benign jokes about conditions in Germany. What is even more surprising is the fact that newspaper reviews were uniformly positive, even in flagship Nazi papers. The Völkischer Beobachter praised the program of March 1935, which soon caused the Catacombs' demise, for being "full of cheerful, witty, and sharp good humor," and approved of its "gladly conceded fool's license." To be sure, some cautionary notes appeared amid the rave reviews. The 12 Uhr Blatt, one of the most sycophantic pro-Nazi papers, wrote that "Werner Finck probably goes too far with some of his allusions." The Catholic Germania noted with cautionary sympathy: "this Finck is not harmless, but never malicious. Even when he becomes 'political'—and this time he is especially fond of being so—everyone still senses: this is a person who makes jokes not out of malicious glee, but rather

35. Werner Finck (center) parodies the Wandervogel youth movement.

because of a general cheerfulness . . . There is a type of constructive criticism. There is also constructive humor! Under its aegis stands the Catacombs—hopefully for some time longer!"[13]

That hope was not to be realized, because by then the cabaret had provoked the ire of Joseph Goebbels as well as Reinhard Heydrich, the virtual head of the Gestapo. The trouble started in December 1934, when the Gestapo ordered a check on a Nazi party member's complaint that "the measures of the Reich government are ridiculed and criticized in the Catacombs cabaret, which attracts very many Jews." After viewing the show, the agents reported that the audience was one-third Jewish, and that only one number could be considered political. Set in a dentist's office, it featured Finck as a new patient who refused to open his mouth because, as he told the dentist, "I don't know you." This reference to fear of expressing one's opinion was not sufficient reason for police intervention, but the agents recommended checking out the subsequent program when it opened.[14]

Even though the ensuing show, which opened at the end of March, received highly favorable reviews in the press, the Nazi authorities detected nothing but subversion. By that time secret observers were being sent by both Heydrich's Gestapo and Goebbels' propaganda ministry. From their reports we learn that at the very outset Finck told his audience to listen for undertones: "We're not too open, but we're open enough to just barely stay open" (Wir sind nicht zu offen, aber wir sind offen genug, um gerade noch offen zu bleiben). The ensuing presentations illustrated that point. In one number Walter Trautschold sketched drawings while Finck commented. Finck told the audience that Trautschold would draw a famous figure whose name began with "Gö..." Trautschold then began to sketch what appeared to be a military lapel, and Finck said it had to be especially wide so that it could hold numerous medals. By then the audience obviously was thinking of Göring's great girth as well as his ostentatious display of military decorations. At that point, however, Trautschold added a few more strokes to his picture, turned it upside down, and revealed a portrait of Goethe.

Other numbers were more direct. In a scene entitled "Editors, As They Should Not Be," Heinrich Giesen played a newspaper editor who copied editorials from other papers because "the same things are said in every newspaper anyway." Another skit had Finck enter a packed café. He was about to sit down at a table with a woman, but then hesitated when he noticed that she was a prostitute. At that point, however, another woman entered, asking for donations to the Winterhilfswerk, the ubiquitous Nazi-sponsored charity whose money reputedly flowed into party bosses' pockets. Finck proceeded to sit down at the prostitute's table after all. After she made a donation, Finck declined to give money by telling the collector: "No thank you, we're a couple." The moral of the story—that it was less disreputable to be associated with a prostitute than to give to the Nazis' fake charity—particularly incensed the agents. The other unusually provocative number was set in a tailor's shop, with Finck playing a customer who resisted having his body measurements taken because he imagined that was being sized for a soldier's uniform. The skit referred to Hitler's recent introduction of universal military conscription, in clear violation of the Treaty of Versailles. The audacious tone of the whole evening was summed up when Finck told his audience: "What you hear here, you cannot hear anywhere else in Berlin."[15]

A couple of the agents recommended that the entire cast, as well as the audience, which laughed and applauded appreciatively, should be arrested and sent to a concentration camp. But the higher authorities initially were more circumspect. After all, one observer conceded that Finck was "too cautious and clever to expose himself to attack with any of his comments."

Because he said nothing directly, but rather operated with puns and innuendos, it was impossible to nail down his own opinion. In a subsequent interrogation Finck even made the disingenuous claim that his cabaret supported official policy. For example, he claimed that the number in the café made fun of people who were too cheap to donate to the charity, and that the tailor skit ridiculed draft evaders. The other members of the cast employed similar ruses. One agent noted that Giesen had "very wisely" entitled his number "Editors, As They Should *Not* Be," in order to protect himself from the charge that he was characterizing the Nazi press in general.[16]

Finck and the others could claim that if their words were misinterpreted, then it was the fault of the audience. The authorities were in fact distressed that Finck could receive so much applause from some two hundred different people night after night. Some agents tried to blame this on a prevalence of Jews, but the observers could not agree on the "racial" composition of Finck's public: their estimates of its "Jewishness" ranged from 3 to 70 percent. One observer noted, with what reads now like inadvertent humor, that the audience was "60 percent Jews and intellectuals, the rest Aryans." Finck himself believed that some 20 to 25 percent of his audience was Jewish. But he also could point to the fact that many Nazis, including high-ranking ones, attended and applauded his show. Moreover, the Catacombs' manager, Erich Kuntzen, had joined the NSDAP as early as January 1932, and one of its three investors was a party member. At pains to explain why the many Nazis in the audience did not protest the program, Heydrich wrote to Goebbels that "every decent racial comrade [*Volksgenosse*] assumes with good reason that in entertainment locales in National Socialist Germany there will be no presentations that pursue ends inimical to the state. He has faith in the vigilance of the authorities." Moreover, the newspapers had published unanimously positive reviews. According to Heydrich, these factors would have overridden any suspicions that Nazi viewers of the show might have harbored, lulling them into believing that they were watching acceptable entertainment.[17]

It was not always to one's advantage to have a manager who was a member of the Nazi party. At the same time that the Catacombs was being observed, the Gestapo received a report from NSDAP member Max Elsner that horrible things were being said in the cabaret that he managed, the Tingel-Tangel. Having been abandoned by Friedrich Hollaender after the Nazi takeover, that cabaret was resurrected in February 1935 by the actor Günther Lüders as well as Trude Kolman, who had been dismissed from the Catacombs for being Jewish. The Gestapo's agents, sent at Elsner's behest, found the Tingel-Tangel as bad as Finck's venture. Playing before what Heydrich described as a "Jewish and in part also homosexual public," the Tingel-Tangel presented a series of numbers that defamed the National Socialist state. The ostensible theme of the show was the triumph of spring over winter, but the Gestapo observers feared that it was an allegorical expression of hope that the Nazi regime would be ousted. One song praised weeds that grew in a garden that was too rigidly cultivated, and seemed to imply that the Nazi state was manure *(Mist)*. The message of another song, entitled "Thoughts Are Free" (Die Gedanken sind frei), was all too apparent. Two agents claimed to have seen an actress give the fascist salute, and then very quickly touch her finger to her forehead (a common German gesture to denote lunacy). Most horrifying of all, during a card game on stage the players appeared to insult Hitler: one Gestapo observer claimed that "das As" (the ace) was pronounced "det Aas" (that beast), and "without doubt the Führer was meant by the latter comment."[18]

The authorities decided to move against both the Tingel-Tangel and the Catacombs on May 10, 1935, after Elsner reported rumors that some storm troopers, disgusted by the Tingel-Tangel's program, planned to attack it that evening. Heydrich and Goebbels agreed that three performers from each group—Finck, Giesen, and Trautschold from the Catacombs; Walter Lieck, Walter Gross, and Eckehard Arendt from the Tingel-Tangel—would be taken into "protective custody." They were held at the dreaded Columbiahaus, and were interrogated for several days (albeit in a "polite" manner, by Gestapo standards). All of the prisoners denied harboring any anti-Nazi sentiments, and they insisted that too much was read into their metaphorical statements either by the audience or by the overly suspicious police agents. The case for the Tingel-Tangel performers was not helped by the testimony of Elsner, their manager. He even asserted that they received material from the muzzled author Erich Kästner, who had befriended Herti Kirchner, an actress at the Tingel-Tangel. After several days Goebbels had Arendt released, because he was an Austrian citizen and a Nazi party member to boot; he was, however, forbidden to appear on German stages again. Goebbels further ordered that Günther Lüders be added to the group of arrested performers, and that all of them be sent to a labor camp for six weeks. They were thus transferred to the concentration camp at Esterwegen, near the Dutch border.[19]

In the end the six served only half of their sentence, since they were released on July 1 on orders of Göring. The actress Käte Dorsch, reputed to have been Göring's lover in earlier years, had appealed to him to help the entertainers. Moreover, as Prussian minister president and thus overlord of Berlin's state theaters, Göring was probably happy to countermand Goebbels, his frequent rival in matters of the stage. Whereas Goebbels had sent the six delinquent cabaretists to a camp by dictatorial fiat, Göring ordered that they be tried in court. The judges who eventually heard the case in Berlin over a year later, in October 1936, found themselves in a very uncomfortable position. They must have realized that a decision for or against the defendants would offend either Goebbels or Göring. They opted to declare the defendants innocent, owing to lack of incriminating evidence. Angering Goebbels proved to be the wrong decision, inasmuch as the judges were relegated to a provincial court thereafter. In any case, Goebbels already had managed to prolong the misery of the six performers, for he had them expelled from the Reich Culture Chamber until April 1936. Thus for nearly a year they were unable to find employment and suffered great material hardship.[20]

## From "Positive Cabaret" to Total Depoliticization

The authorities sent a warning to all entertainers by having the German press give prominent coverage to the Gestapo's closing of the cabarets. Newspapers that had praised the Catacombs six weeks earlier now changed their tune. The *12 Uhr Blatt* placed much of the blame on the audience. It contended that the cabarets had started out by serving a useful function, insofar as they had engaged in constructive criticism, but soon they fell under the destructive sway of "a clientele consisting mainly of Jews and other state-negating elements." For this reason the performers would be given the "opportunity" to reconsider their views, "while performing proper and robust work in a camp." The *Völkischer Beobachter* placed more of the blame on the entertainers themselves, whom it described as "rootless and subversive elements that sprang from the school of Jewish cabarets." More important, both papers used the occasion to define the purpose of satire in the Nazi state. The *Völkischer Beobachter* claimed to support "freedom of political satire," but said that it could be granted "only to people who possess the ethical disposition of subordinating their personal freedom to that of the state, to that of the nation." The *12 Uhr Blatt* asserted that "cabaret can be political, it should be political in a certain sense—but then in the *sense of the state,* which through its struggle has given performing artists the opportunity and encouragement to exercise their art." Thus the closing of the cabarets should serve as a "serious warning" to other stages with similar inclinations: "They can exist and continue to operate if they finally fall into the marching line of the entire German people. We all want to laugh and we like to laugh, but not about things that have become sacred to us through great conviction and struggle."[21]

Such comments pointed to a major dilemma in Nazi attitudes toward cabaret, which was discussed more or less openly in the ensuing months. The authorities in principle wanted to encourage cabaret, since, like the Communist sponsors of agitprop, they believed that a successful combination of propaganda and humor would be an effective way of feeding official values to the population at large. At the same time they realized that in practice, the cabaret movement was freighted with tendencies which they opposed. Various articles criticized the cabarets of both Wilhelmine and Weimar Germany for having undermined respect for the state and national values, and thus having contributed to disaster. The *12 Uhr Blatt* contended that "National Socialism will not repeat the mistake of prewar Germany, which could not prevent the mocking of its great supporting institutions, such as the army, the schools, and so on, and thus collapsed in the hour of danger." According to another article, the situation deteriorated even more after 1918, when censorship was abolished and almost the entire entertainment scene fell under Jewish control: "German visitors to these amusement locales were served up the strongest doses of Zionist, erotic, and perverse vulgarities! One has every right to assert: Since 1918 everything exalted and holy, belief in God, sense of family, sublime German womanhood, glowing love of people and fatherland, was sullied, throttled, and undermined. *That was a pure culture of cultural Bolshevism!*"[22]

The Nazi ideologues conceded far too much influence to cabaret and satire by blaming them for the disasters of 1918 and the "decadence" of Weimar society. Nevertheless, such arguments were necessary in order to justify the Nazis' imposition of censorship and their banishment of Jewish performers from the stage. In contrast to the supposedly negativistic cabarets of the Wilhelmine and Weimar eras, Nazi ideology supported a type of "positive cabaret" that would aid the nation "in its desire for reconstruction, for advancement, for community."[23] On the surface, the Nazi attack on purely negativistic or cynical cabarets sounded like earlier Communist or liberal strictures against the Weimar entertainers. Agitprop advocates had asserted that Communist values had to be supported at the same time that capitalism was attacked; committed liberals had argued that "bourgeois" cabarets should forgo criticizing the prorepublican parties and aim their barbs against the enemies on the left and the right. After 1933 Nazi writers likewise asked: Should cabaret attack all parties, or defend a specific standpoint? By then, however, the question was merely rhetorical, since the new political context had changed the rules of the game drastically.

The Nazi regime had totalitarian aspirations. It sought to control all aspects of everyday existence, including thought and culture. Goebbels made this clear in a speech to theater professionals as early as May 8, 1933: "A revolution does not limit itself to the confines of politics, but instead gradually conquers all areas of public life, if it is a real and genuine revolution . . . This revolution will be carried out to the extreme end. It stops at nothing . . . The revolution conquers the folk and public life, it stamps its mark on culture, the economy, politics, and private life. It would be naive to believe that art could be spared this, that it could lead a Sleeping-Beauty existence, far from life, beside or behind the times, that it could assert that art transcends parties, that art is international, that art has higher tasks than politics."[24] Goebbels' diatribe meant that sooner or later all forms of theater, including cabaret, revue, and vaudeville, would be forced to toe the Nazi line.

No previous regime had sought to use cabaret for its own ends. To the extent that it was political, cabaret had always satirized those in power. Now, however, the Nazi apparatus sought to transform it into a tool for official propaganda. That was a tricky task, which ultimately proved a failure. Not that there was a lack of volunteers for the Nazi effort. As noted in Chapter 5, the Weimar years witnessed numerous "political humorists" who entertained variety show audiences with right-wing attacks on the republican system. Their political views, combined with the high unemployment rate of performers in the early thirties, made them particularly hopeful of achieving fame and fortune under the National Socialists. Their appetite was whetted even more by the numerous vacancies caused by the emigration or dismissal of Jewish entertainers. The Reich Culture Chamber, and Goebbels in particular, received many letters from right-wing actors offering their services, either as performers or as managers of enterprises that had been abandoned by their Jewish owners. The Culture Chamber did not, indeed it could not, do anything to help such people in a material sense, since cabarets and variety shows remained private enterprises and were not funded by the state. Nevertheless, the letters betrayed many of the resentments that had been building up during the Weimar era.

In June 1933, for example, Goebbels received a letter from the wife of Wilhelm Millowitsch, an actor who served as provisional director of the Kadeko after Robitschek's flight. It may be assumed that Frau Millowitsch, rather than her husband, wrote the letter because she was a member of the NSDAP. She asked Goebbels whether the "state or the Party" could grant them a loan of 35,000 marks in order to put the cabaret on a secure financial footing. She claimed that "we intend to dedicate the house to healthy folk humor based on unconditionally German qualifications." She noted further that they planned to begin the fall season with a production of Paul Lincke's *Frau Luna,* with the composer conducting. She contended that Lincke knew her husband from earlier years, and that, "like many experts in the field, he is of the opinion that this would provide the proper tone with which to inaugurate the heavily Jewish-dominated house on

Kurfürstendamm under new 'German' management." Frau Millowitsch finally noted that she and her husband were especially "eager to grab this position" because a Jew had "cheated us out most of our capital."[25] Although Millowitsch did not receive the money, nor even remain in charge of the cabaret, the letter is significant because it provides just one of many examples of how anti-Semitic rhetoric was routinely used for self-promotion and to curry favor with the new regime.

The reference to Lincke was also noteworthy, because it anticipated the Nazis' reactionary desire to turn back the cultural clock. Having been a highly successful composer in the Wilhelmine era, Lincke saw his operettas disappear from the stage during the Weimar years, owing to the shift in popular taste toward American musical forms. After 1933, however, his works enjoyed a renaissance. This resulted in part from the fact that Lincke was one of the few non-Jewish operetta composers, along with Franz Lehar and Walter and Willi Kollo. Even the Johann Strauss family was a potential problem, because of partial Jewish ancestry; but since Hitler (along with millions of other Germans) adored their works, mention of their "racial" background was forbidden and their music continued to be performed. Lincke did not enjoy a similar popularity, but his music was promoted owing to its "healthy," prewar, and non-American style.[26]

This harking back to Wilhelmine taste could be seen in other cultural spheres as well. In the visual arts the Nazi era witnessed a resurgence of painters trained in nineteenth-century academic styles. Having been shunned and denigrated by proponents of the more modern movements in the twenties (Expressionism, New Objectivity), they gave vent to their resentments after 1933 by retaking leading positions in art institutes and museums, and by conducting an all-out assault on avant-garde art. A similar development occurred in the realm of "high" music: atonality was vilified, as the Nazis sponsored those composers who imitated late Romantic orchestrations and harmonies. The attack on Weimar culture reached a climax in 1937 and 1938, when the regime sponsored major exhibitions denigrating "degenerate art" and "degenerate music." Yet in place of the execrated works, all the Nazis could offer was artistic mediocrity.[27]

There were specific reasons why the Nazi polity could not produce "great" cabaret to serve its purposes. Aside from the fact that the best talent (a subjective concept, to be sure) was liberal, leftist, or Jewish, the official call for "positive cabaret" was self-defeating from the start. Cabaret acquires its bite from its ability to challenge prevailing values, successful fashions, and the political powers that be. It seeks to make people reexamine their preconceived notions, and it attacks figures, institutions, and symbols of authority. Even when nonpolitical, cabaret questions social mores in areas like sexuality or commercialism. Such themes are inherent in cabaret because they constitute its form of humor. Satire consists of juxtaposing stated ideals with practiced reality, and hence can be used to unmask assertions ranging from political slogans to advertisements. Parody may be employed to highlight, through exaggeration, conventions in art and everyday life that are unthinkingly taken for granted.

None of these practices served the purposes of the Nazi authorities; the last thing they wanted was critical thought. Instead, the Nazis demanded that all people conform to a "healthy folk mentality," wherein independent spirits would find no home. In May 1933 Goebbels told his audience of actors and theater directors that "individualism will be smashed" and replaced by dedication to the *Volk*.[28] The "positive cabaret" desired by the Nazis was supposed to attack people who disturbed the homogeneous mindset. Of course, those same individuals were being persecuted by the state's repressive apparatuses. Far from defending the underdog, Nazi cabaret was supposed to side with the victorious bully. That fact seriously limited the success of the Nazis' "positive" cabarets. Audiences found little humor in seeing someone already on the ground being kicked gratuitously.

One well-publicized example of a "positive cabaret" was named the Unfettered Eight (Die 8 Entfesselten)—a rather ironic appelation, given the fact that they were tied strictly to official ideology. The troupe was founded by the NS-Cultural Community (NS-Kulturgemeinde), a successor to the Fighting League for German Culture, in early 1936. They performed in Berlin during the winter months and toured the rest of the nation during the summer. In their first program they distanced themselves from the past by parodying conventions of earlier cabarets, such as the songs about prostitutes or vamps. They also made fun of various types of modern dance as well as American-style music. Other send-ups were less focused, being aimed at kitschy or mediocre aspects of popular literature, films, and advertisements. As for social commentary, the troupe satirized "the people of yesterday" (Die von Gestern), an attack on pretentious or eccentric types of individuals who did not fit the new era's homogeneous mold.[29]

"Positive cabaret" might have seemed possible in theory, but it had numerous problems in practice. Criticizing aspects of contemporary life— even those that were hindering the development of National Socialism— might be misunderstood, since any attack on the status quo could be interpreted as an assault on the Nazi state. Conversely, outright support for the regime might come across as sycophancy, and fall flat with the audience. Eventually Goebbels decided that politics had no place on the stage at all. On December 8, 1937, he issued a decree which prohibited theaters, variety shows, and cabarets from making any reference—even positive ones—to politics, the state, religion, the police, or the army. This sweeping decree was intended to spell the end of political cabaret. The following day Goebbels wrote in his diary: "This is a real deliverance for me."[30]

Goebbels rejoiced too soon, however, since the ban on contemporary references proved very difficult to enforce. His own propaganda ministry immediately weakened its impact by making exceptions. Officials debated among themselves whether the Unfettered Eight also had to follow the new guidelines. After all, the troupe had been created as "a decidedly political cabaret with indubitable National Socialist premises," whose program "has found complete approval throughout party circles." Yet it was also obvious that if an exception were made for the Unfettered Eight, then other performers would not take the decree seriously. The old difficulties would then recur: "All of our officials would be confronted with the problem of determining whether a political allusion is positive or negative, a problem that is all too easily governed by subjective perceptions."[31] In the end, the Unfettered Eight were allowed to continue with their contemporary references—and, as feared, other entertainers did not heed the decree too strictly either. An increasingly frustrated Goebbels had to reissue similar orders on May 6, 1939, and December 11, 1940, but he never succeeded in totally abolishing contemporary references from the stage.

Despite great support in the press and by Nazi cultural organizations, the Unfettered Eight disbanded in 1939, in part because of poor texts. No other performers were able to devise a more successful formula for "positive cabaret" under National Socialist rule. Most so-called cabarets contented themselves with parodies of previous cabaretic styles or current fashions. In September 1935 several members of the Catacombs and the Tingel-Tangel who had not been indicted took over the stage of the Catacombs. Calling their new venture the Dragon (Tatzelwurm), they too performed only insipid parodies. A police report to the Gestapo confirmed that "the presentations were unobjectionable from a moral, religious, and political standpoint." The venture folded by the following spring. Like Hesterberg after the failure of the Muses' Swing, many of the Dragon's performers ended up joining the Kadeko. Robitschek's former theater, now properly "Aryanized," became a holding tank for all of the entertainers whose ventures had failed or been closed after 1933. Even Werner Finck appeared there regularly, after he was permitted to perform again in April 1936.[32]

The Kadeko remained the most successful cabaret in the Nazi era, just as it had been prior to 1933 under Robitschek's direction. After the death of Hanns Schindler, who had taken it over in September 1933, it passed into the hands of Willi Schaeffers in 1938. Schaeffers had been a prominent entertainer on cabaret and revue stages in the Weimar era, and he assiduously sought to maintain good contacts with the authorities after 1938. He also tried to provide a modicum of free speech on his stage. The program booklet of October 1938 even had an article entitled "The Hot Potato, or the Political Joke," which indirectly argued for more leniency. The article contended that permission to make political jokes was a sign of national strength: "The firmer the foundations of the Reich, the less likely it is to be shaken by a political joke. That's a simple fact. The more someone finds a political joke 'unbearable' ['*untragbar*'], the less he is convinced of the sturdiness [*Tragfähigkeit*] of our Reich."[33] By suggesting that detractors of political humor were unpatriotic, the article sought to turn the tables against those who considered political jokes subversive.

Neither arguments like that nor Schaeffers' efforts to mollify the authorities could protect some of the Kadeko's performers from the wrath of Goebbels. Once again Werner Finck was one of the troublemakers. Referring to his previous problems with the authorities and his consequent need to watch his language, he would introduce himself as "the fink, slightly throttled" (Ich bin der Finck, leicht gedrosselt)—a pun on the words "drosseln" (to throttle) and "Drossel" (songbird). In a similar vein, when he bent down to pass through a low doorway on stage, he said: "Even if I stoop this much I still might bump my head against the higher-ups" (Jetzt habe ich mich schon so geduckt und wäre doch beinahe wieder oben angestossen). He would end his number by looking at his watch and saying he had better stop, because he did not want to "discuss the(se) time(s)." Other individuals who annoyed Goebbels included a trio of singers entitled the Three Rulands (Die Drei Rulands), who had started out at the Catacombs. To be sure, the three men (Helmut Buth, Manfred Dlugi, Wilhelm Meissner) were not unwilling to put their efforts into the service of Nazi causes. In the wake of the "crystal night" pogrom of November 1938, they wrote a song that accused Jews of being money-grubbing exploiters in the twenties, and of still being filthy rich even under National Socialism. The song, which was broadcast by the Leipzig radio station, made fun of the Jews' complaints about having to pay for the destruction caused by the pogrom, and joked about Jewish emigration to Holland. Despite this contribution to the worst type of anti-Semitic rhetoric at a time when the assault against Jews had moved into full gear, the Rulands also made light of certain Nazi policies, albeit in a much more genial mode. The authorities were especially annoyed by a song that joked about the restructuring of Berlin undertaken by Albert Speer in close consultation with Hitler. Dressed as architects in white smocks, the trio sarcastically claimed that Berlin had been an ugly city until recently, but now all the ditches and mounds of dirt made it look beautiful.[34]

As in 1935, the official Nazi press found this song and the rest of the

Kadeko's program amusing, but Goebbels was infuriated by the reports
his agents sent him. He wrote in his diary that on February 1, 1939, he
had "a lengthy battle over the Cabaret of Comedians. I kick Schaeffers
into shape. He whines some nonsense to me. But I stick to my standpoint.
Political jokes will be stamped out. Wiped off the map." Two days later
German newspapers reported that Finck, the Three Rulands, and the
conferencier Peter Sachse had been dismissed from the Reich Culture
Chamber, and hence banned from all German stages. The following day
Goebbels published an article entitled "Do We Still Have Humor?" (Haben
wir eigentlich noch Humor?). The title referred to a recent series of articles
in the *Berliner Tageblatt* (under the rubric "Haben wir eigentlich Humor?"), to which various comedians, including Finck, had contributed.
Goebbels attacked that newspaper, which "with skeptical, suggestive
winks of the eye, concerned itself with the question, whether today in
Germany we still have any humor." The minister's answer was unequivo-
cal: "We believe that there is no country in Europe where there is as much
joy as in Germany." This was, he contended, mainly the result of Strength
through Joy (Kraft durch Freude), the Nazi institution that organized
evenings of entertainment as well as vacations for workers and employees.[35]

Goebbels argued that he had been "broad-minded," even with respect
to political jokes, but his liberality had a limit where the "sacred" ideals
of National Socialism were called into question. He repeated the assertion
that Jewish satire aimed at officers, Junkers, and industrialists had contributed to the weakening of the Wilhelmine state and its consequent
collapse in time of crisis. The Nazis would not make the same mistake:
"Political joking-around is a remnant of liberalism. In the previous system
one could still accomplish something with it. We are too smart and too
experienced in such matters to let them continue on their course." Goebbels was aware that German émigrés and Western democracies would
protest his actions, but that did not concern him: "to hell with freedom
of opinion" (Freiheit der Meinung hin, Freiheit der Meinung her). Referring to the annexation of Austria and parts of Czechoslovakia, Goebbels
set the priorities straight: "Last year the Führer reconquered ten million
Germans for the Reich. Now that is something." Goebbels concluded that
"this nation has humor; but it follows the clear principle, learned from
the Prussian army, that the only person who has a right to mock, to
complain, or even to curse once in a while, is someone who is marching
in step."

On February 5 Goebbels could write in his diary: "My article against
political jokesters along with my decrees hit like a bombshell. Now the
intellectual cowards are quivering with fear." The attack put an end to

Finck's public apperances, but it also made him an unwitting symbol of opposition to National Socialism (an honor Finck modestly denied after the war). Critical citizens credited him with many of the anti-Nazi jokes circulating at the time, even though he had never told them on stage. Some of the lines falsely imputed to him were even reported in the foreign press, which commented acerbically on Finck's dismissal, as Goebbels had predicted.[36]

Another person who received unearned credit for oppositional jokes was Claire Waldoff. Although no supporter of the regime, she remained in Germany and appeared frequently in cabarets and variety shows. Given her contentious stage personality, and the fact that she had sung at benefit concerts for leftist charities during the Depression, it was assumed that she made sly cuts against the Nazi authorities. At some point someone devised a satire of Göring, based upon "Hermann," Waldoff's signature song:

> Links Lametta, rechts Lametta,
> Und der Bauch wird immer fetta.
> Und in Preussen ist er Meester—
> Hermann heesst er!

"Medals to the left, medals to the right / And his stomach gets fatter and fatter. / He is master in Prussia—/ Hermann's his name!" Waldoff not only did not write it; she also never sang that parody in public. However, the joke was widely known, and audiences assumed she had composed it. It certainly was in many people's minds whenever she sang the original version of "Hermann"; at least the authorities thought so, and considered banning the innocuous "Hermann" from her repertory. But no action was taken, and even direct allusions to the Göring parody went unpunished. In May 1940 a mayor of Bremen reported to the propaganda ministry that when Schneider-Duncker introduced Waldoff on stage, he referred to the "Hermann" song and said: "But it doesn't have anything to do with that" (das habe damit aber gar nichts zu tun). Despite the obvious reference to the Göring parody, the ministry responded that, "owing to the complete harmlessness of the reported remark, nothing more will be undertaken."[37]

By the outbreak of World War II Goebbels had indeed ensured the "complete harmlessness" of all entertainment. The enforced depoliticization caused cabaret to suffer a backward evolution, as it regressed to the type of noncritical vaudeville that had been so prominent in the 1890s. At the same time, variety shows themselves underwent a similar process of *Gleichschaltung* at Goebbels' instigation. Berlin's three major vaudeville halls in the 1930s were the Wintergarten, the Scala, and the Plaza. The Plaza's program booklet of October 1935 claimed that its stage would be devoted to a revival of the Berlin *Volksstück,* a type of popular theater which it claimed had been destroyed by cosmopolitan and Jewish elements: "The internationalization of eastern and northern Berlin by intellectual Kurfürstendamm politicians destroyed, along with the Berlin homeland [*Heimat Berlin*], the Berlin Volksstück as well." For the Plaza, the return to "genuine" folk theater meant a revival of Lincke's operettas, as well as the staging of new musicals about Berlin's past scripted by Hans Brennecke and composed by Willi Kollo. These works were nostalgic recollections of nineteenth-century Berlin, from the Biedermeier to the Imperial era. In 1938 the Plaza was taken over by Strength through Joy, which turned it into a pure vaudeville hall featuring acrobatic and show numbers.[38]

As for the two other major variety stages, the Wintergarten had never departed from its vaudeville format, but the Scala developed the *Revue-Varieté,* a mixture of revue and variety-show elements. The use of plot-lines and conferenciers allowed the Scala to include humorous, even critical references to conditions in Nazi Germany. In October 1938 Goebbels put an end to this by ordering the Scala, in the words of one propaganda ministry official, to "cultivate less the revue, and more of a vaudevillelike character." This implied that there would no longer be any plot-line, dramatic action, or even conferenciers, merely a simple juxtaposition of acrobatic or other numbers. By December an observer of the propaganda ministry could confirm: "In contrast to their presentations of the recent past, which promoted the revue-type variety show [*Revue-Varieté*], the Scala's program this month has been converted to a pure acrobatic-number variety show [*Nummern-Varieté*]. Thus the individual acrobatic presentations are no longer tied to a revue-type frame, but are simply strung together without any such connection." The observer confirmed that "comedians and conferenciers do not appear." Yet he also recorded the downside of the new strictures: the program was mediocre.[39]

### Only the "Girls" Remain

In order to enliven their emasculated programs, variety show directors retained two "American" aspects of Weimar entertainment: jazz and Girls. Nazi attitudes toward the mass culture of the United States were mixed. Generally, it was considered shallow and materialistic. Not only did Americans lack the profundity of German *Geist* and *Kultur,* but their racially mixed society prevented them from attaining the type of *völkisch* homogeneity that the Nazis considered a prerequisite for cultural greatness. At the same time, though, Nazi officials were aware of the appeal of American popular culture, and they sometimes succumbed to it themselves. In 1937 Goebbels' Christmas present to the Führer included not only thirty feature films, but also eighteen reels of Mickey Mouse. The propaganda minister could proudly confide to his diary: "He is very pleased with them. Is most happy with this treasure, which I hope will give him much joy and recreation."[40]

Mickey could entertain both democrats and fascists, but the same could not be said about jazz. As we have seen, American jazz and its German variants had come under severe attack by cultural conservatives in the twenties, and Hitler shared that distaste. When the musical reactionaries attained positions of authority after 1933, they sought to banish jazz, as well as swing, its updated version of the mid-thirties, from German cultural life. That proved to be difficult, however, owing to the popularity of the newer dance rhythms. Despite Nazi claims of a homogeneous folk-community, millions of Germans did not want to revert to polkas and waltzes. German jazz and swing musicians often were able to dupe officials, who knew next to nothing about the newer music, by reorchestrating tunes to give them "softer" melodic lines, or by withholding the true names of the composers (especially if these happened to be black or Jewish). Even though Goebbels banned jazz from German airwaves in October 1935, radio programmers were still able to sneak in suspicious tunes.

Predictably, some of the most refractory institutions were cabarets and variety shows, which needed to keep musically up-to-date in order to attract their domestic public as well as the foreign tourists upon whom they continued to depend. Many jazz combos that had appeared in Weimar cabarets and revues had consisted of Jewish musicians, and groups like Weintraub's Syncopators had to leave Germany in the first months of Nazi rule. Nevertheless, there were enough "Aryan" jazz enthusiasts to provide Berlin's entertainment stages with what many Nazis considered non-"Aryan" music. Otto Stenzel, the leader of the Scala band, was one of the most prominent supporters of jazz and swing. Moreover, since Berlin's great variety shows were still tied to the international vaudeville circuit, they often imported big-band groups from abroad. Thus throughout the thirties jazz enthusiasts were able to play cat-and-mouse games with the authorities, despite repeated protests by Nazi musical purists.[41]

The issue of Girls was more complicated, because it underscored an obvious contradiction, indeed hypocrisy, within Nazi ideology and cultural practice. National Socialist writers repeatedly castigated the Girl shows of the Weimar era as the epitome of Jewish decadence and perversion. In 1935 the Institute for the Study of the Jewish Question published a thick volume on Jews in Germany, which included a large section concerning revues. It began with this contention: "The sexualization of reality is an expression of the Jewish spirit. The Jew Freud traced all mental processes back to sexual stimulations." The authors went on to "prove" this point by noting that all revue directors of the twenties were Jewish, and they launched into an extended attack on the shows of Herman Haller and especially James Klein. The erotic plots and the prevalence of female nudity on those stages were recounted in great detail. Weimar cabaret and revues became one of the prime markers of "Jewish perversion" in Nazi propaganda. The flagship anti-Semitic film of 1940, *The Eternal Jew,* attacked by name the Haller, Nelson, and Klein revues, as well as cabaret performers like Curt Bois, Max Ehrlich, Kurt Gerron, Paul Morgan, and Rosa Valetti.[42]

That being the case, one might have expected that Girl shows—nude dancers as well as kicklines—would have disappeared from the stage after 1933. But that did not happen because, like jazz, Girls were popular with large segments of the public. In fact, cabaret and revue directors believed that they could not sell enough tickets without some flesh as bait. Moreover, unlike jazz, the display of nude women did not per se contradict central tenants of National Socialism. The Nazis claimed to restore the "dignity of the German wife and mother" after the "decadence" of the Weimar years, and thus placed great emphasis on icons of maternal virtue. At the same time, however, Nazi ideology promoted "healthy" physicality, which explicitly sought to overcome "Jewish" (and, by implication, Christian) notions of the sinfulness of the body.[43] This lauding of "body culture" found its most obvious expression in the Nazis' extensive encouragement of sports. It was but a short step from the celebration of fit bodies to the celebration of naked bodies, and works like Leni Riefenstahl's *Olympia* film drew parallels between nudity and physical strength. This emphasis on the Body Beautiful (and, of course, the Body Aryan) could be used as an excuse for displaying flesh on stage.

Nevertheless, the presentation of nearly naked women was problematic because many Nazi sympathizers could not tell the difference between the "perverse" and "Jewish" shows of the twenties and those on German stages after 1933. In December 1935 a Nazi women's newspaper, the *Völkische Frauenzeitung,* ran an article protesting the persistence of "Girl-Kultur" on German stages. Men too were disturbed by the phenomenon. In March 1939 a young party member wrote to the propaganda ministry to inform its agents, in case they did not know, that "insufficiently dressed or completely undressed" dancers had become commonplace on variety stages; he was especially shocked by an Adam and Eve scene at the Scala. He wondered how there could be such a reversion to the Weimar era, "which thank God is past," and he asked: "Is it not disgraceful for us Aryans, when we allow the appearance of dancers whose 'costumes' lay bare with every movement the charms of woman—a woman who as a German mother should be holy to us, as we have intoned again and again?" Three months later a storm trooper wrote to the Reich Culture Chamber to protest the appearance of three "beauty dancers" *(Schönheitstänzerin-nen),* wearing only loincloths and "armed with huge fans," at Berlin's Stella-Palast: "One feels that one has been sent back to the worst times of the Weimar era. National Socialism has not fought its battles so that today, in the seventh year of the Third Reich, German people are offered such Semitic-oriental-erotic veil-games as diversion." That same month an observer for the propaganda ministry complained about the Scala's program: "The utilization of naked women on a very large scale also seems objectionable. It is outright embarrassing to see a rebirth of the long-dead genre of 'living sculptures,' in the form of living reproductions of the paintings of classical masters." In particular, the reproduction of a Goya painting represented the "quintessence of tastelessness."[44]

In the Wilhelmine and Weimar eras, censors had struggled to define the often fine line between artistically acceptable and prurient forms of nudity. In the ensuing Nazi era, the authorities had similar trouble separating examples of "healthy" physicality from holdovers of "Jewish obscenity." This was a touchy issue, as Willi Schaeffers discovered soon after taking over the Kadeko. In October 1938 the SS newspaper *Das Schwarze Korps* had published an article that tried to make that distinction by juxtaposing "chaste" pictures of nude young women in natural settings with "lascivious" photos of stripped-down women on stage. Since one of the latter had been taken at the Kadeko, Schaeffers quipped during the next performance: "We left our nude dancer at home today, since I have no desire to appear a second time in *Das Schwarze Korps.* I don't know if you saw that—apparently not. That just proves that the paper doesn't have the circulation that its editors think it does!" Several SS men walked out at that point, and soon strongly worded letters rained down on Schaeffers from Nazi cultural authorities. He was forced to write a lengthy, groveling letter of apology, in which he contended that he was a subscriber to, indeed an avid reader of *Das Schwarze Korps.* Moreover, he claimed that he personally could not stand nude dancers, since they had no talent; he was forced to hire one, however, because "at the moment it's all the rage."[45] The incident revealed that Nazi authorities did not look kindly on public comments concerning their double standards.

Aside from "beauty dancers" and tableaux vivants, Nazi stages also featured kicklines, which were somewhat less problematic because they did not bare as much flesh as the other numbers. In fact, kicklines enjoyed patronage at the highest levels of the Nazi state. Hitler admired types of dance that required "a training that pushes to the outer limits of human capacity, to the breaking point of the human body." He was a fan of "the fantastic Tiller Girls—in the final analysis, it was because of them that everyone went to the cabarets [sic: the Tiller Girls appeared only in revues]." Goebbels was an enthusiastic viewer of Busby Berkeley musicals, and he encouraged the German film industry to make similar "revue films." He made his taste clear in a diary entry of June 1937: "Ufa is making a dance film. I prohibit it from showcasing the philosophic dance of Palucca, Wigmann, and others [soloists famous for modern dance]. Dance must be animated and display beautiful women's bodies. That has nothing to do with philosophy." With such taste at the pinnacle of the regime, it was hardly surprising that the German movie industry continued to crank out revue films right up to 1944.[46]

One could see kicklines in Berlin's variety shows as well. The Scala Girls first took the stage in 1934. The most famous Nazi-era company featured the Hiller Girls, a troupe of Tiller Girl imitators directed by Rolf Hiller. They appeared in variety shows throughout Germany, including the Wintergarten and the Scala in Berlin. Their production numbers made explicit one reason for the Nazis' enthusiasm: their militaristic overtones. That aspect of their appeal was highlighted when they marched in uniforms that evoked the days of Frederick the Great; for that number, they had been drilled by a Wehrmacht officer. When the Hiller Girls appeared at a show celebrating the fiftieth anniversary of the Wintergarten, a newspaper reported that their parade march was "surpassed only by the music corps of the SS honor guard Adolf Hitler, which played for the Winterhilfswerk on stage and reaped thunderous applause."[47]

Ironically, the Hiller Girls became problematic after the outbreak of actual war. The Scala's program in April 1940 featured them performing parade steps to the tune of Prussian military marches, as they had done so often before (fig. 36). But now that war was once again a grim reality, the number drew complaints from various officers, and the Wehrmacht High Command lodged a protest. An observer from the propaganda ministry concurred: "The questionable numbers, supposedly found objectionable in military circles, are the military 'exercises' of the Hiller Girls. I am in fact of the opinion that these exercises may well be left out. The Girls present parade steps and shoulder arms to the strains of old Prussian military marches. To be sure, their exercises are precise, but the whole is nothing more than nationalistic kitsch and a superficial matter, which we could easily do without." Now that much of the male population was mobilized, the martial spirit embodied in the Girls was superfluous and could be dismissed as kitsch. That was not, however, the opinion of the audience, since the report proceeded to note: "There were no protests or complaints from the public; on the contrary, the spectators applauded loudly." Moreover, Eduard Duisberg, the Scala's director, noted that "in Munich, Hiller presented this performance before the Führer, who liked it very much, and a year ago at the Wintergarten he presented it before

36. No longer desirable: the Hiller Girls perform Prussian military marches at the Scala variety theater.

Reich Minister Dr. Goebbels." Needless to say, now that Germany was at war, the Wehrmacht High Command had its way. Although nonmartial kicklines persisted on German stages, the Reich Theater Chamber ordered that "dance performances which take on military forms are forbidden for the duration of the war."[48]

The "beauty dances" and tableaux vivants featuring nearly naked women also became more problematic after 1939. As during World War I, many citizens were aghast that such frivolous and tasteless entertainments could be mounted at a time of national crisis. In October 1940 Goebbels was sent an anonymous letter by a person who spelled out the issues most clearly. The missive began:

> German airplanes blown to atoms over London,
> Shot-down German pilots and seamen drowning,
> German folk-comrades, women and children killed by British bombs,

> Devastated and burning houses in city and countryside and a nation
>   fighting for its life,
> That is the picture of the present in our dear German fatherland.
> And what is going on in the Reich capital Berlin?
> Here's the answer!

The letter proceeded to recount the appearance of naked women at the Metropol, the Admiralspalast, the Scala, and the Kadeko; it even included a clipping of an advertisement for the Kadeko, which featured a drawing of a female nude. The missive contended that "not even the Jewish Robitscheks and their ghetto-comrades took the liberty of showing such things during the [First] World War." The letter concluded: "One can really lose one's faith in our dear and cherished National Socialism!"[49]

Although the authorities were disturbed by such sentiments, they did not put an end to "beauty dances." In March 1940 Goebbels confided to his diary: "Should we completely ban nude dances? Only when they are unaesthetic. Decide case by case." In fact, the Girl element became even more pronounced on Berlin stages as the war progressed. This was in part a necessity, since there was very little other "talent" available for cabaret and variety shows. Most of the male performers were at the front, either as soldiers or entertainers. Men did everything they could to join the extensive program of troop entertainment *(Truppenbetreuung),* which staged diversions for the soldiers; those who failed to do so invariably were drafted into the military. Likewise, many of the best-known female singers spent long stints performing for the troops, often near the front. For a while Berlin's cabaret and variety show directors filled the gaps by hiring performers from other Axis countries, but by 1943 such imported talent was loathe to come to Berlin owing to the heavy bombardment. Because of that, one propaganda ministry official noted that theaters like the Scala "must base their program considerably more on ballet [Girl troupes] and models."[50] That was unobjectionable, since by then soldiers on home leave constituted a major portion of the entertainment public in Berlin. For them, as for fighting men on all sides of the conflict, Girls were deemed an appropriate form of distraction.

More topical forms of entertainment were very problematic. In the first year of the war, the Nazi authorities tried to use comic dialogues to bring their message to the populace. Beginning in September 1939, two comedians, Ludwig Schmitz and Jupp Hussels, appeared weekly as "Tran und Helle" in the movie shorts preceding feature films. Tran, the "stupid" character, would express ideas or engage in actions disapproved by the regime (such as hoarding goods or listening to the BBC). Helle, the "smart" one, would set him right. These numbers were very popular, and the act was occasionally performed "live" at venues like Berlin's Scala. Nevertheless, the authorities had their suspicions about the duo's popularity. The Nazis were smart enough to know that ideological conformity was not the major basis of their appeal. Audiences simply might have admired the comic talents of the two actors, regardless of the political message. But the authorities also feared that at least some viewers might have sympathized with Tran, who voiced ideas that no one dared express publicly. The issue became so murky that by the fall of 1940 the series of movie shorts had been terminated.[51]

Other entertainers who tried to deal with topical issues were equally at a loss. After 1939 cabaret and variety shows joked about wartime inconveniences, such as the rationing of food and clothing. Goebbels, however, believed that such numbers were anything but funny, and were demoralizing to boot. In order to put a halt to such comments, he issued the last of his sweeping decrees against cabarets on March 14, 1941. Not only did he repeat his injunction against references (even positive ones) to public events or personalities, but he also banned the position of conferencier, which was the usual source of contemporary quips. Thereafter all cabarets became simple variety shows, as they had no choice but to present an unconnected string of numbers to their audience.

Goebbels' pronouncement destroyed the last vestiges of the cabaret forms that had been inaugurated forty years earlier. Only variety acts featuring female dancers and models were left, and they did not survive much longer. The Kadeko was bombed in February 1943, the Scala was destroyed the following November, and the Wintergarten was flattened in June 1944. All remaining stages were closed at the end of August at Goebbels' behest, as the nation mobilized its last resources. In November 1944 an official of the propaganda ministry described the final remnants of cabaret in the capital of the Third Reich: "In Berlin there are two nighttime cabarets for soldiers passing through, which only play at night (midnight to five in the morning), and which may be visited only by soldiers in transit without any accompanying persons. This arrangement was made in order to provide a shelter for soldiers waiting for train connections, since Berlin's railway stations have been largely destroyed."[52]

# Cabaret in Concentration Camps

While the Nazis systematically muzzled cabaret in Berlin after 1933, some of the entertainers who had fled the Third Reich attempted to perform in exile. They had some, albeit limited success in cities like Zurich, Vienna, Prague, Paris, and London. But in the United States there was no demand for their style of cabaret. Kurt Robitschek's attempt to revive the Kadeko in New York ended in failure. Calling himself Ken Robey, he had better luck as a producer of American-style vaudeville shows. Valeska Gert opened the Beggar's Bar in Greenwich Village in 1938, but it had a very limited clientele. She fared somewhat better when she returned to Berlin in 1950, where she founded the Witch's Kitchen (Hexenküche). Friedrich Hollaender went to Los Angeles, but his attempt to revive the Tingel-Tangel on Santa Monica Boulevard was a total failure, despite the fact that he used English-language texts. Thereafter he made a comfortable living writing music for Hollywood films. In the 1950s and 1960s he again mounted cabaret-revues in Germany, primarily in Munich.

America was inhospitable territory for Berlin-style cabaret, but at least it provided the exiles with a safe haven for the duration of the Third Reich. The European continent was somewhat more receptive to Berlin's émigré entertainers—until the Wehrmacht started marching. In 1943 and 1944 some of the Jewish stars of the twenties mounted shows again, but this time as prisoners in the concentration camps of Westerbork and Theresienstadt. Their story concludes the history of Berlin cabaret.

The Netherlands hosted the two most successful "Berlin" cabarets in exile, those of Rudolf Nelson and Willy Rosen. Various factors allowed German entertainment to take root there. For one, Holland had long been susceptible to the cultural influence of its neighbor. Their languages were very similar, so that most Dutch audiences could understand literary nuances and wordplays in German. Moreover, since the number of German artists and writers greatly outnumbered those in the Netherlands, the Dutch could not help but be swamped by Germany's cultural products. In fact, the Dutch were well acquainted with Berlin cabaret since its beginnings. Wolzogen took his Motley Theater to Amsterdam in 1902, and other touring troupes followed. Holland was especially attractive to German performers in the early twenties, since they could earn hard currency there at a time when the German mark was rendered worthless by inflation. By the end of the decade many of Berlin's stars also became known to Dutch audiences through the medium of film.[1]

Another, very different factor that allowed German cabaret to establish itself in the Netherlands after 1933 was the local tradition of granting asylum. In the early months of the Nazi regime hundreds of Jews, liberals, and leftists crossed the border seeking a temporary or more permanent haven. The Dutch Social Democrats as well as the Dutch Jewish community, which numbered over a hundred thousand, organized relief efforts for the exiles. That was another reason why Berlin's Jewish cabaretists believed they would be welcomed in the Netherlands.

In reality German émigré entertainers faced considerable difficulties, as a result of economic and political circumstances. The depression hit Holland particularly hard, and up to 1936 unemployment continued to rise. As the steady stream of refugees strained resources, and native citizens worried that the incoming Germans might compete for scarce jobs, asylum regulations were tightened. In the realm of popular arts, Dutch entertainers feared the competition of the German performers, and their professional organization (Nederlandse Artiesten Organisatie) regularly mounted protests in the press and with the government against the foreigners. Their opposition forced Willy Rosen's troupe to terminate its stay in Holland in the summer of 1933; it did not return until 1937. Political factors further impeded overly critical cabarets. Dutch politics was dominated by conservative and strongly antileftist Protestant and Catholic parties; many of them actually welcomed Hitler's coming to power, inasmuch as they regarded him as a bulwark against "Bolshevism." Antifascist cabaret thus did not find much sympathy among large sectors of the public. Moreover, the Dutch government did not want to alienate its powerful neighbor, and it threatened to ban performances and even expel troupes that criticized foreign regimes, including that of Hitler.[2]

These factors plagued Ping-Pong, the earliest exile cabaret in Holland. It opened in Amsterdam in May 1933, and included various performers from Berlin, many of whom had appeared in the Catacombs. Ping-Pong's most prominent members were the chanteuse Dora Gerson, the dancers Chaja Goldstein and Julia Marcus, and Kurt Egon Wolff as conferencier; the singer and composer Curt Bry joined the troupe in August. Their numbers included texts by Brecht, Hollaender, Kästner, and Tucholsky, and Marcus often performed dances with an antimilitarist bent. Several conservative newspapers attacked this politicization of entertainment, by foreigners to boot, and soon the troupe had to blunt its critical edge. By the end of the year Ping-Pong had trouble extending its work permit, so it moved to Switzerland. It returned the following fall, but was allowed to perform only if it agreed to hire Dutch entertainers as part of its program. Since these new additions proved to be mediocre, and since most of Ping-Pong's stars (Gerson, Goldstein, and Marcus) had started solo careers, the cabaret soon disbanded.[3]

Another troupe that faced problems was Erika Mann's Peppermill (Pfef-fermühle). Founded in Munich in January 1933, that cabaret had to leave Germany in March, and it reconstituted itself in Zurich the following October. The Peppermill was the most political of all the exile cabarets. Although it did not explicitly name Germany or its leaders, its songs and skits consisted of parables that clearly dealt with conditions under Hitler. This led to protests by the German ambassador, and eventually attacks by Swiss Nazis. Fearing for law and order, the canton of Zurich banned its appearance in 1935. The Peppermill then toured other Swiss cantons, and also performed in Czechoslovakia, Belgium, Luxemburg, and the Nether-lands. Although it appeared in Holland in 1934 and 1935 without much difficulty, in October 1936 it provoked strong protests by Dutch National Socialists, as well as by local entertainers fearful of the competition. The government accordingly withdrew its license to perform, amid a storm of protest in many newspapers and even the parliament. The troupe moved on to New York in January 1937, where it presented its songs and skits in English. After several weeks it disbanded for good, due to lack of interest on the part of the American public.[4]

Rudolf Nelson was able to avoid these problems insofar as politics was concerned. He had always been a cautious and astute manager, and after 1933 he fully depoliticized his cabaret. His first stops in exile were Austria and Switzerland, where the Basel National Zeitung noted in November: "The Nelson revue hardly desires to inspire serious thoughts, it wants simply to entertain." Another Swiss newspaper reported that Nelson "clings to neutral ground," and remained "unconcerned with politics and the economic crisis." The same apolitical tone prevailed when Nelson brought his troupe to Amsterdam in April 1934 at the instigation of Louis Davids, one of the founders of Dutch cabaret at the turn of the century. Since Erika Mann's troupe was touring Holland at the time of Nelson's arrival, the Catholic De Tijd could compare the two: "The Peppermill in the Centraal-theater is more thoughtful and literary, while the Nelson revue in the Leidscheplein-theater is more superficial, charming, more entertain-ing." The Social Democratic Het Volk noted that Nelson offered "good amusement art; it does not aspire to be more." Two years later the Alge-meen Handelsblad reported that Nelson's "idea is that there can be no place for politics on his stage, he exclusively wants diversion to be offered to the visitor who has come there to forget for a moment the sword of Damocles that perhaps has been hanging over his head for the entire day." Ironically, in November 1936 Nelson's revue included a song that pleaded: "Oh please, do not be silent, / is not a war in sight?" (Ach, bitte, schweige nicht, / ist nicht ein Krieg in Sicht?).[5] Yet such comments were rare on Nelson's stage, as he generally kept silent on contemporary events. It seemed that he too ignored the sword of Damocles over his own head.

Nelson was able to maintain his troupe in the Netherlands up to the German occupation not just because he avoided political statements, but also because he provided varied and high-quality entertainment. He changed his program every two weeks, and mounted over a hundred different revues during his stay in Amsterdam. He regularly performed his old hits from the twenties, and even the Wilhelmine era, but he continually composed new music as well. The texts were usually scripted by his son Herbert; they consisted of sometimes sentimental, sometimes ironic love songs, as well as parodies of film, advertisements, and other cultural and commercial fashions of the day. Much of Nelson's success resulted from the talent of his entertainers. Dora Paulsen was his star chanteuse, and Kurt Lilien his principal comic actor. He also brought other prominent émigré entertainers into his troupe as they decided to leave Germany or (after the Anschluss) Austria. For example, the famous Viennese conferencier Karl Farkas appeared in Nelson's revues in 1938, before he moved on to New York. Although Dutch entertainers occasionally protested that these shows lured away some of their own audience, the government did not intervene because they were genuinely popular with broad sectors of the well-off public. Moreover, no Dutch stage offered the same type or quality of entertainment, so the issue of competition was moot.[6]

A similar venture was Willy Rosen's Prominents (Theater der Prominenten). As its name suggested, it featured well-known actresses, and especially actors. Many of them, such as Otto Wallburg and Siegfried Arno, were known to the Dutch audience from Weimar films. Rosen himself had been a star at the Kadeko. He was one of the few people who both scripted and composed his songs, and performed them while playing a piano. He proudly introduced his numbers with the phrase: "Text and music by me!" (Text und Musik von mir!). Having been evicted from Holland in the summer of 1933 because of protests by Dutch performers, Rosen toured non-Nazi Europe with his troupe. He also maintained ties to Berlin, since he regularly composed music for Max Ehrlich's shows for the Cultural League of German Jews. The Prominents did not return to the Netherlands until 1937, when they performed at the summer resort town of Scheveningen. That became their home for the next three summers; the rest of the year they performed in Amsterdam, Rotterdam, and Belgium. Rosen mounted several new programs each year, which featured love songs and numerous comic skits. Like Nelson, he assiduously avoided politics. The program book for the 1940 season in Scheveningen proclaimed: "When you want to forget your worries, then come to us, the theater without politics. (Without politics! For three years we have stuck to that strictly and we want to stay with it.)"[7]

Scheveningen's 1940 summer season had barely begun when politics intruded violently. On May 10 German forces invaded the Netherlands, and the country was conquered in a matter of days. The entertainers who had fled Germany after 1933 were now once again in Nazi hands, under much more frightening conditions. Nevertheless, the occupiers were able to allay outright panic among Holland's Jews by introducing anti-Semitic policies in incremental stages. The delays resulted in part from the Nazis' realization that their attacks on Jews were highly unpopular with the Gentile population. In February 1941 a near-general strike occurred in Amsterdam and surrounding communities to protest the rounding up of Jews, and the Nazis had to use force to terminate the work stoppage. Within this atmosphere of public solidarity, Rosen's Prominents were permitted to perform in Amsterdam from December 1940 to January 1942. Nelson too continued to mount revues in that city. In November 1941 his troupe was reconstituted as the Jewish Cabaret Ensemble (Joodsch-Klein-kunst-Ensemble). It appeared in the Hollandsche Schouwburg, which was renamed the Joodsche Schouwburg. As in Berlin, only Jews were allowed to attend the performances.

Nelson's revues acquired a new theme song, with words by his son Herbert, that tried to hold out hope for his exclusively Jewish public. The lyrics claimed that "the great waltzes" and "the old songs" not only inspired a melancholic nostalgia, but revived a feeling of youth that gave strength to carry on. The refrain then proclaimed:

> Life keeps on going, it never stands still.
> Life keeps on going, we must follow its will.
> Music, our escort, lends wings to our stride.
> Life keeps on going, we have hope at our side.

> Das Leben geht weiter, es bleibt niemals stehn.
> Das Leben geht weiter, wir müssen mit ihm gehn.
> Musik als Begleiter beflügelt den Schritt.
> Das Leben geht weiter, voll Hoffnung gehn wir mit.[8]

Such hopes were soon dispelled. Nelson and Rosen gave a final revue together in May 1942. The next month the Nazis began a massive roundup of Dutch Jews. Now that the extermination camps in Poland were fully operational, the occupiers could begin instituting their plan of making Holland "Jew-free" *(judenrein)*. With the assistance of Dora Paulsen, his star chanteuse, Nelson and his family were able to go underground and survive the war. Herbert Nelson even managed to organize weekly matinees of oppositional cabaret while in hiding, and his father eventually mounted a revue again in Berlin in 1949. Rosen was not so fortunate. Kurt Robitschek, who was trying with little success to revive the Kadeko in New York, had arranged a benefit performance to raise money for Rosen's trans-Atlantic passage, and Rosen had been granted a visa for Cuba and was in the process of procuring one for the United States. America's entry into the war in December 1941, however, blocked his ability to escape.[9] He thus shared the fate of more than a hundred thousand Jews in Holland. Over the course of several months, the Jews of Amsterdam were assembled at the Joodsche Schouwburg, where Nelson's Jewish Cabaret had performed. Their first stop thereafter was the "transit camp" at Westerbork.

Ironically, Westerbork had been inaugurated by the Dutch government in 1939 as a holding camp for Jewish refugees from Germany. By 1938 the Netherlands had practically halted all immigration from the Nazi state, but the atrocities of the "crystal night" pogrom in November of that year led to public demands to admit a new wave of asylum seekers. The authorities did not, however, want to make conditions too comfortable for the refugees, in the hope that they would eventually move on to other countries. Thus a holding camp was established at Westerbork, in the desolate moors in the northeast part of the nation. Several hundred German Jews lived there until July 1942, when the camp was taken over by the SS. Thereafter its population burgeoned to several thousand at any one time, as it became a way station for Dutch Jews being transported to Auschwitz, Sobibor, Bergen-Belsen, and Theresienstadt.[10]

Westerbork holds a troubled place in the history of cabaret because six revues were staged there between July 1943 and June 1944. The numbers were written and composed by Rosen and Erich Ziegler, a musician who had been a long-time member of the Prominents. The stars of the show were Max Ehrlich and Camilla Spira, an operetta singer who had gained fame in Charell's production of *The White Horse Inn* in 1930. She later appeared in many of Ehrlich's shows for the Cultural League of German Jews. Spira left Berlin for Holland in the wake of the "crystal night" pogrom, and Ehrlich followed in May 1939. They performed with Rosen's and Nelson's troupes until their deportation to Westerbork. The large casts of the camp's revues included Johnny and Jones, a popular Dutch musical duo, but most of the entertainers were German Jews.

Philip Mechanicus, a Dutch journalist whose diary chronicled life in

37. Max Ehrlich (right) performs a scene set in a barrack room of the Westerbork camp.

Westerbork, noted: "The revue was a mixture of antiquated sketches and
mild ridicule of the conditions and circumstances prevailing at the camp.
Not a single sharp word, not a single harsh word, but a little gentle irony
in the passing, avoiding the main issues. A compromise." That characterization is borne out by the extant documentation on the shows: typed
program booklets, photographs, even film clips. The second revue, entitled
*Humor and Melody (Humor und Melodie),* which opened on September
4, 1943, was a mixture of mild satire about camp conditions and pure
diversion. It began with a "roll call" *(Appell)* of the cast members on stage,
in imitation of the outdoor roll calls of camp inmates. Other numbers
dealing with Westerbork were set in the crowded barracks (fig. 37) and
the infirmary. Yet many scenes were nostalgic looks back at the past: there
was a waltz number set in the 1880s and a "postcoach idyll" from the
even earlier Biedermeier era. Other scenes were more modern, such as one
that parodied a jazz band. The show even concluded with a "Girl" number,
inasmuch as a skit set in a classroom allowed six "schoolgirls" to parade in
very short skirts (fig. 38). Similarly, the subsequent revue, entitled "Bravo!
Da capo!", included a scene called "The Westerbork-Girls Dance!" (Die
Westerbork-Girls tanzen!). The shows were invariably well-rehearsed, and

props and costumes were often elaborate. Mechanicus could rightly note that "Westerbork has the best cabaret in Holland."[11]

One might well wonder how it was possible to mount such elaborate shows in the context of a concentration camp. Obviously, it would not have been possible without the encouragement and active support of the camp's SS commandant, Konrad Gemmeker. This rather bland career bureaucrat, who worked his way up office ladders in the Düsseldorf police force and then the SS, was put in charge of Westerbork in October 1942, after three other SS camp commandants had been dismissed in rapid succession for incompetence. Among Westerbork's inmates Gemmeker was a subject of much speculation and confusion. He regularly would give token signs of "largesse" toward the interned Jews, such as encouraging the cabaret, for which he even allotted large sums for props and costumes. Of course, he too was a beneficiary of the shows, since he was an enthusiast of popular music. On September 5, 1943, Mechanicus noted in his diary: "The Commandant was enjoying himself like a schoolboy—blessed are the poor in spirit." Etty Hillesum, another inmate who chronicled the camp's life, wrote in a letter two weeks earlier: "On one occasion he came three times in succession to see the same performance and roared with laughter at the same old jokes each time." Even Ferdinand Aus der Fünten, one of the most feared Nazis in Holland, who was in charge of the overall

38. Schoolgirl scene in *Humor and Melody*.

deportation program for Dutch Jews, made regular trips from Amsterdam to attend the Westerbork shows.[12]

Although the performances were immensely popular with the inmates of Westerbork—they were invariably sold out, and tickets were often hard to acquire—they also were highly controversial. Many prisoners saw them as part of a larger strategy of manipulation that ensured the proper functioning of Westerbork—and Westerbork's main function was to fill the weekly quota of "transport material," the official term for deportees to the Polish camps. Gemmeker was able to remain Westerbork's commandant until the end of the war because he, unlike his predecessors, never failed to meet the quotas and simultaneously to keep order in the camp. His main ploy was a policy of divide-and-conquer, which pitted German Jews against Dutch Jews. Gemmeker favored Westerbork's "long-term residents," those German Jews who had been settled there before the Nazi invasion. He granted them preferential treatment in areas such as housing, inasmuch as they could live in small cottages instead of the huge, cramped barracks. More important, Gemmeker appointed some of them to run the camp on a day-to-day basis.

The most important function of Westerbork's German Jewish administrators was to select the names of their fellow inmates who would be sent on the weekly transports, which numbered anywhere from a thousand to three thousand souls. This reflected a widespread tactic: throughout their empire, the Nazis tried to turn Jews against each other, by making some of them responsible for the selection of "transport material." Holland was not spared this cynical ploy. The Jewish Council for the Netherlands, formed at the Nazis' behest and based in Amsterdam, selected the citizens who were to be sent to Westerbork. Within that camp, the German Jews selected "transport material" for deportation to Poland.

Few if any of the inmates knew what awaited them at Auschwitz or Sobibor. They were told that they were being sent to "labor camps." Even astute and informed observers like Hillesum and Mechanicus had no inkling of the gas chambers, the fearsome death that awaited most Jews within hours of their arrival at the extermination camps. Nevertheless, all inmates knew that deportation to the east was something to be avoided at all costs. They imagined the Polish camps as places where poor housing, meager food, and intense physical labor resulted in high mortality rates. Since conditions at Westerbork were relatively tolerable, and above all survivable, it was obviously desirable to prolong one's stay there as long as possible. This gave tremendous power—power over life and death—to those German Jews who drew up the transport lists. In the process, they protected their friends, generally favoring German over Dutch Jews. Mechanicus, who devoted many agonized pages of his diary to the issue, believed that the German Jews were wreaking revenge for the presumed lack of support from Dutch Jews prior to 1940. The Dutch Jews, in turn, became increasingly hostile toward their German coreligionists as the favoritism in drawing up the transport lists became obvious. Mechanicus even feared that if the war were to end and Westerbork be liberated, the German inmates would be massacred by the Dutch prisoners.[13]

Various aspects of the Westerbork revues revealed these tensions. For one, the shows reflected Gemmeker's preference for German over Dutch Jews. Even though the star performers were not "long-term residents," since they did not arrive in Westerbork until 1943, they were granted the privilege of living in private cottages. Gemmeker would even socialize with some of them, by inviting them to his house and talking with them late into the night. But by far the greatest favor bestowed upon them was exemption from deportation. Becoming a member of the cast was thus a life-or-death matter. Since the revues were performed almost exclusively by German Jews, the performances caused resentment among the Dutch Jews. As early as July 27, 1943, rumors about irregularities and favoritism in the casting reached such a level that Gemmeker became peeved, and he issued a proclamation threatening to cancel the shows completely if the bad-mouthing did not stop. The complainers became more circumspect, and the shows continued.

Three months later the greatest reward of all was granted to Camilla Spira, the star of the first two revues: she was pronounced "Aryan." This was made possible by the false testimony of her (Gentile) mother, who claimed that Camilla was not the offspring of her legal (Jewish) father. That white lie, combined with a hefty bribe from a friend in Amsterdam, allowed Spira, her Jewish husband, and their two children to be released from Westerbork. She gave a farewell performance at the premiere of the third revue. On October 18 Mechanicus noted laconically in his diary: "Camilla Spira, the star of the revue, has departed for Amsterdam, Aryanized. A great loss for the revue." Mechanicus envied Spira's good fortune, but he could not be too critical, for several weeks later he himself tried unsuccessfully to prove that he had an "Aryan" background. He noted in his diary: "There is no disgrace about passing oneself off as an Aryan, although it is not pleasant to accept a gift from the hands of the oppressor. The main thing is to get out of his clutches."[14]

At the same time that the Westerbork revues fueled the tensions between German and Dutch Jews, they also played into Gemmeker's hands by acting as a diversionary and quieting force within a camp whose ultimate goal was the destruction of Dutch Jewry. This was the heart of the problem, and it provoked numerous debates among Westerbork's inmates concerning the propriety of attending the shows. Many prisoners boycotted the revues because they considered them tasteless at best, and sacrilegeous at worst. After all, the wood for the stage at Westerbork had been taken from the demolished synagogue of a nearby town. Israel Taubes, a survivor of the camp, noted bitterly after the war: "On the wooden boards from the old synagogue of Assen, which were used for the construction of the stage, the choicest young girls, specially chosen by experts, will swing their legs to the rhythm of jazz music." Even more shocking to many was the fact that the shows were performed in what was normally the registration hall, where newly arrived inmates were processed, and where one had to go to apply for exemption from deportation. In the words of Mechanicus, it was "the same hall where the transport people are brought, where men sigh and women and children weep and every week the walls resound to the entreaties of those who want to escape the awful calamity of being sent to Poland."[15]

Etty Hillesum did not attend the premiere of the first revue, but her letter of July 9, 1943, revealed great distress:

> It is a complete madhouse here; we shall have to feel ashamed of it for three hundred years . . . In the middle of this game with human lives, an order suddenly comes from the commandant: the *Dienstleiters* [Jewish section leaders in the camp] must present themselves that evening at the first night of a cabaret which is being put on here. They stared open-mouthed, but they had to go home and dress in their best clothes. And then in the evening they sit in the registration hall, where Max Ehrlich, Chaya Goldstein, Willy Rosen, and others give a performance. In the first row, the commandant with his guests . . . The rest of the hall full. People laughed until they cried—oh yes, cried. On days when the [newly arriving inmates] from Amsterdam pour into the camp, we put up a kind of wooden barrier in the big reception hall to hold them back if the crush becomes too great. During the cabaret this same barrier served as a piece of decor on the stage; Max Ehrlich leaned over it to sing his little songs. I wasn't there myself, but Kormann just told me about it, adding, "This whole business is slowly driving me to the edge of despair."

Mechanicus too was loathe to attend the "unsavoury cabaret shows," but he felt compelled to go in his capacity as chronicler of Westerbork for posterity. He vented his own feelings on October 17, 1943, after the opening of the third show, which featured the "Westerbork Girls": "Attended the premiere of the new revue yesterday evening. Absolutely packed out. Old numbers that had been refurbished, well acted. A great part of the programme consisted of dancing by revue girls with bare legs. The *Obersturmführer* [Gemmeker] present with Aus der Fünten. Went home with a feeling of disgust."[16]

Israel Taubes reported that there was often a total lack of understanding between "the majority" who attended the shows and those who refused to go: "There were earnest and intelligent people who maintained that those doomed to die were not likely to be helped by a boycott, and some might get a little comfort, if only for a few hours. Others, disagreeing, thought that going to the shows was an offence to Jewish self-respect." Mechanicus too pondered both sides of the issue, which he called "a psychological mystery. Light music beside an open grave." He recognized that the inmates, especially the younger ones, craved distractions from their situation. Even before the revues commenced, he noted in his diary: "People's nerves are at a breaking point. It is a relief, even at Westerbork, to escape from the nervous strain for a moment and break the tension."[17]

The shows provided such relief, and to the extent that they made life more bearable, they were a welcome attraction to the inmates. Moreover, it seems that the revues sometimes tried to achieve concrete, practical goals. Certain scenes probably attempted to be conduits between the inmates and the camp's commandant, by appealing for good treatment. For example, one number in the second revue had Camilla Spira proclaiming the joys of receiving packages from relatives or friends outside the camp. The importance of the text was highlighted by being spelled out on stage (fig. 39). Since such shipments, which flowed quite freely into Westerbork at that time, were invaluable supplements to the meager food and clothing rations provided by the camp authorities, the number might have been an indirect means of "thanking" Gemmeker for the "privilege" of receiving packages, as well as an appeal not to infringe on that benefit.

Occasionally the performers even expressed a note of defiance. In a photo album presented to Gemmeker by the entertainers, the picture of the package scene bore the commentary: "Spira is slowly becoming Aryan." That caption suggested that the official "Aryanization" of a half-Jewish person revealed the sham nature of the Nazis' racial "science." Whereas that comment was reserved for the eyes of the commandant, other defiant notes were heard by a larger public. A recurring theme of the second revue was the line: "When you sit up to your neck in shit, you're not supposed to chirp!" (Wenn man bis zum Hals im Dreck sitzt, hat man nicht zu zwitschern!). Ehrlich's reply was: "In spite of that, I'm chirping!" (Ich zwitschere trotzdem!).[18] By whistling in the face of adversity, Ehrlich implied that one should resist being destroyed emotionally and psychologically by the demeaning conditions of the camp.

Many inmates believed that the shows provided not only temporary diversion but also gave them the mental strength to carry on. This faith was shared in other, much harsher camps than Westerbork, such as Dachau and Buchenwald. There the maintenance of self-respect and the will to live was often considered a prerequisite for survival; those least likely to survive, it was believed, were the *Muselmänner* (Moslems), the camp jargon for people who had given up all hope. The will to live found its clearest expression in unofficial camp anthems. Two of the most famous were

DER TEXT IST BEINAH LITERARISCH
DIE SPIRA WIRD SCHON LANGSAM ARISCH...

39. Camilla Spira and the dance ensemble of the Westerbork revue celebrate the arrival of gift parcels. The two-line ditty below refers ironically to the sudden "Aryanization"—and hence liberation—of the half-Jewish star.

composed by writers associated with cabaret. The "Buchenwald Song" was scripted by Fritz Löhner, best known as Beda, who had written numerous cabaret skits and hit songs, as well as the libretti for some of Franz Lehar's operettas. Like many of Vienna's entertainers, he was arrested after the annexation of Austria. Transferred to Buchenwald, he wrote a song that was paradigmatic of so many camp anthems. While it evoked the grim conditions, it held up the hope that the day of freedom would surely come. In the meantime:

> Comrade, don't lose courage, keep in step, bear the pain,
> For we all have the will to live in our veins
> And faith, yes faith in our hearts!

> Halte Schritt, Kamarad, und verlier nicht den Mut,
> Denn wir tragen den Willen zum Leben im Blut
> Und im Herzen, im Herzen den Glauben![19]

A similar song was composed in Dachau, where other prominent Austrian entertainers were detained. They included the Viennese comedian Paul Morgan, who had been a cofounder of the Kadeko in 1924, as well as the Austrian conferencier Fritz Grünbaum, who had appeared regularly on Berlin's cabaret stages since the days of Nelson's Chat noir. Morgan and Grünbaum performed numerous impromptu shows at Dachau, sometimes with, sometimes without, the knowledge or acquiescence of the guards. Also at Dachau was the young, highly talented Viennese cabaretist Jura Soyfer, who performed the most hard-hitting numbers in the camp and also scripted the "Dachau Song." Like Beda's verses, it evoked the brutal conditions—the barbed wire, the armed guards, the cynicism of the promise "Arbeit macht frei"—and it too ended with a vision of eventual freedom. Its formula for survival was grimmer than Beda's, since it called upon the inmates to become "steel and stone." Yet it also urged them to cling to their humanity: "Remain a human being, comrade, / Be a man, comrade" (Bleib ein Mensch, Kamerad, / Sei ein Mann, Kamerad).[20]

Such songs were extremely popular among inmates, who sang them often and considered them a crutch for survival. Karl Röder, who outlived Dachau, recalled: "In an incarceration without forseeable end, whose sole purpose is the mental and physical destruction of thousands of human beings, the flight into unconsciousness becomes the greatest danger . . . By means of the manifold performances the world outside could be brought alive and with it the strength to resist . . . Seen in this light, the performances were a valuable component of inner resistance, and it is no exaggeration to say that with their help many people's lives were saved." Be that as it may, the songs did not alter the fate of most inmates. Morgan and Soyfer were transferred to Buchenwald, where they died in December 1938 and February 1939 respectively. Löhner was transported from Buchenwald to Auschwitz, where he succumbed to overwork in December 1942. Grünbaum died in Dachau in January 1941, shortly after performing on New Year's Eve in an extremely sick and weak condition.[21]

It cannot be denied that in Westerbork as well, the revues provided some short-term psychological benefits to many inmates. Yet there too the shows did nothing to change the fate of the detainees. Even lesser appeals went unheeded: the "privilege" of receiving packages was curtailed drastically in the fall of 1943. Above all, the transports kept rolling eastward every Tuesday morning. Insofar as the revues were a palliative, they might even have served the interests of the Nazi commandant, as Mechanicus noted with dismay: "Man wants to mourn with those who have been struck down by fate, but he feels compelled to live with the living. Is the *Obersturmführer* such a good psychologist that he knows this law of life and has put it into effect here? Or is he merely a brutal egoist who lets the Jews amuse themselves for his own amusement and gives them something at the same time? You cannot see the workings of his heart." Mechanicus' worst suspicion was that it was part of a deliberately sadistic ploy: "The henchmen of the *Führer* play a cat and mouse game with the Jews—they chase them from one corner to the other and take pleasure in their fear and gradual exhaustion. The henchman at Westerbork mocks and derides them by laying on a cabaret with light and airy music as a change from the macabre Tuesday morning transports. And the Jews are not ashamed to go to the cabarets."[22]

This dilemma was real, but Mechanicus never lost sight of the fact that it was the Nazi system which forced Jewish prisoners to make such inhuman choices. It need hardly be said that the inmates of Westerbork had no say over their ultimate fate. They could make only minor choices, such as that regarding cabaret: To play or not to play? To attend or not to attend? In favor of cabaret, one could say that at the very least it offered distraction; at best, it might have provided some amounts of courage, strength, and fortitude. Against it, a minority of inmates could and did hurl charges of bad taste, indeed blasphemy: there was no room for light entertainment while weekly transports to an unknown but doubtlessly terrible fate were taking place. But beyond the question of juxtaposition, there was that of linkage. Some inmates could not suppress the thought that the shows were somehow complicit in the Nazi "cat and mouse game." As we have seen in other, much less threatening contexts, cabaret's venting of frustration could serve the interests of the powers that be. The reduction of outright anger made Westerbork function more smoothly, which meant, ultimately, that the transports left with little commotion. But did that tenuous linkage make the cabarets complicit? The boxcars would have left under any conditions, with their full quotas of "transport material." Etty Hillesum overheard a fellow inmate say: "Once upon a time we had a commandant who used to kick people off to Poland. This one sees them off with a smile."[23] The worst charge one could level against the Westerbork cabaret was that it was one facet of that smirk.

If the Westerbork entertainers believed they could save at least their own lives by mounting the shows, most of them were tragically deceived. The last Westerbork revue, which opened in June 1944, was dominated quite literally by gallows humor. *Totally Crazy! A Grotesque Cabaret Show (Total verrückt! Groteske Kabarettschau)* included numbers such as "The Guillotine" (according to the program, "not for people with weak nerves!!"), and even an operatic parody of Gothic horror plays entitled "Ludmilla, or Corpses on a Conveyor Belt" (Ludmilla, oder Leichen am laufenden Band). On August 3, Gemmeker suspended all cabaret and other types of performance; a month later he announced that Westerbork was being closed. While some trains left for Auschwitz, the stalwarts of the revues—Rosen, Ehrlich, and Ziegler—had the "honor" of being sent to Theresienstadt. That was merely a diversion. After only two weeks there, Ehrlich and Rosen were sent on to Auschwitz, where they were gassed on September 29. Only Ziegler survived the camps.[24]

The inmates of Westerbork had long harbored illusions about Theresienstadt. It was considered a "favorable" camp, much like Westerbork. Mechanicus noted that when the issue of transports arose, discussions centered around "Theresienstadt, Theresienstadt, Theresienstadt, Auschwitz, Auschwitz, Auschwitz." Being sent to the former was considered a sign of "clemency." Even the means of transport to the two camps were different: those to Auschwitz were the notorious boxcars, those to Theresienstadt were often third-class passenger trains. After the departure of one of the latter in January 1944, Mechanicus mused: "The word 'Theresienstadt' has had a magnetic effect on people's minds, like Wengenrode or the Isle of Wight or Capri. Fantastic tales were going the rounds. It was said that life there was so good that the residents were not imprisoned behind barbed wire, but could move freely through the little old fortress town and live in small houses . . . So the train departed with men and women who took their leave of Holland and their friends with rather heavy hearts, but consoled themselves with the thought that they were going to a place remote from the scourge of war, the cruelty of the concentration camp and the callousness of the slave-driver who is master in Poland. A pleasure train and a little bit of sightseeing." Mechanicus was, however, skeptical. He guessed correctly: "Hitler wants to exterminate the Jews . . . He exterminates them in separate classes, just as a firm of undertakers buries its dead clients according to different categories." A friend of Mechanicus expressed the matter most succinctly: "Theresienstadt is the cat's whiskers, but the cat stinks."[25]

Theresienstadt (Terezín in Czech) was indeed a giant deception. Originally an Austrian garrison town founded in the late eighteenth century, it had less than four thousand Czech inhabitants in 1939. They were moved out in October 1941, and the city was declared a "ghetto" exclusively for Jews. It became a holding pen with up to 53,000 inmates at a time. They consisted not only of Jews from Bohemia and Moravia, and later Holland and Denmark, but also "distinguished" Jews from German-speaking territories. These included decorated veterans of World War I, as well as noted scholars, writers, artists, and musicians. The Nazis had special reasons for creating a supposedly "model" ghetto at the time that the mass extermination of Jews was entering its most intense phase. In the face of mounting reports of atrocities, the Germans could invite outside commissions, such as those of the International Red Cross, to Theresienstadt in order to counter reports of bad treatment, let alone mass murder, in the camps. In particular, the Nazis could demonstrate that various well-known Jewish personalities, whose disappearance caused concern abroad, were alive and well.

With respect to the Jewish victims, the myth of Theresienstadt likewise served Nazi interests. We have seen that many of Westerbork's inmates were happy to join the transports to Theresienstadt. Throughout Central Europe many Jews willingly signed over their life savings in exchange for a promise of good care in clean, well-furnished, and private rooms; at times the Nazis even touted the locale as a retirement spa—"Theresienbad." Even more insidiously, the myth of Theresienstadt could be used to drive wedges within Jewish communities. Those individuals who acquiesced to Nazi policies without complaint could be "rewarded" with transport there, while those who made trouble were guaranteed a trip to Auschwitz, Sobibor, or Treblinka. Of course, the true nature of the reward became brutally clear upon arrival at Terezín. Compared to Westerbork, the dormitory barracks were more crowded; medical treatment was much more primitive; physical labor was harder and lasted longer; and the food supply was significantly worse, since most inmates of Theresienstadt rarely received the packages that made such a difference in the Dutch camp. These conditions produced a high mortality rate: of the 141,000 Jews sent to Theresienstadt, 33,000 died there of overwork, malnourishment, and disease. Another 88,000 were shipped on to extermination camps, primarily Auschwitz. Like Westerbork, Theresienstadt was essentially a deceptive way station along the path to the "final solution."[26]

Despite the harsh conditions, the inmates of Theresienstadt managed to develop an incredibly rich and active cultural life. Recitals and readings began informally in early 1942, even though they were forbidden by the camp authorities. By the end of that year, however, the official policy was reversed, and cultural life was actively encouraged. Throughout 1943 and up to October 1944, when massive transports to Auschwitz decimated the camp's population, Theresienstadt witnessed numerous events of every conceivable type: lectures, poetry readings, recitals, chamber music, symphony concerts, oratorios, even several operas. Cabaret too proliferated, owing to the versatility it had demonstrated throughout its history: it did not require elaborate sets and costumes or extensive scripts, but could be pieced together quickly from diverse sources. Moreover, it could be performed in every conceivable venue. Theresienstadt's numerous cabarets appeared not only in the (very few) performance halls, but also in barracks, attics, courtyards, and infirmary wards. Of the Czech-language cabarets, the most popular was headed by Karel Svenk, who scripted the most critical numbers presented in the camp. The majority of cabarets performed in German. Several different ensembles were formed by professional entertainers, most of whom hailed from Vienna (Egon Thorn, Hans Hofer, Bobby John, Ernst Morgan, Walter Steiner, Walter Lindenbaum). One notable group was headed by Leo Strauss; despite the second "s," he was the son of Oscar Straus, who had been the in-house composer of Wolzogen's Motley Theater forty years earlier. Carl Meinhard, one of the "Bad Boys" of the Imperial era, was likewise interned in Theresienstadt, but he took little part in the ghetto's stage life.[27]

January 1944 saw the arrival of Kurt Gerron, one of Berlin's greatest stars of the twenties. He had appeared in every major cabaret and revue of the time: the Wild Stage, Megalomania, the Kadeko, the revues of Hollaender and Nelson. He had played the role of Tiger Brown at the premiere of *The Threepenny Opera* and the vaudeville director in the film *The Blue Angel*. After Hitler's takeover he moved to Amsterdam, where he directed several successful films, until protests by Dutch filmmakers, who disliked the competition, put an end to his involvement. He subsequently appeared in Nelson's and Rosen's revues. Following the Nazi invasion, Marlene Dietrich tried to bring him to the United States, but he loathed the thought of emigrating once again, so he turned down the offer. He also rejected the opportunity to go into hiding in Holland, as Nelson had done. As a decorated veteran of World War I, Gerron trusted the certificate given him by the Germans that supposedly exempted him from deportation. Like all other Nazi promises, it was soon broken. In September 1943 he was sent to Westerbork, where he appeared in the third revue. At the beginning of 1944 he was transported to Theresienstadt.

Whereas Gemmeker often went to the Westerbork revues, Karl Rahm, the German commandant of the Terezín ghetto, rarely attended any of its inmates' performances. Nevertheless, he had seen Gerron on screen and was pleased to have such a famous actor in his camp; he even arranged to have Gerron give a special performance for the SS. Having been shown supposed good-will at the top, Gerron proceeded to mount the most lavish of the Theresienstadt cabarets. Known as the Carousel (Karussell), it performed over fifty times, most frequently during June and July 1944 (fig. 40). Gerron could draw upon the best talent in the camp. The music was usually arranged, and often composed and played, by Martin Roman. This German musician, another who had arrived in Terezín via Westerbork, was also the leader of The Ghetto Swingers, the Theresienstadt jazz band. Sets for the cabaret were designed by František Zelenka, who had been a prominent stage designer for the Czech National Theater in Prague. For his texts Gerron drew on the talents of Leo Strauss and another writer, Manfred Greiffenhagen.[28]

As in Westerbork, the Theresienstadt cabarets led to serious questions of propriety and complicity. The performers could not be accused of

40. Kurt Gerron as director of the Carousel cabaret in Theresienstadt, portrayed by his fellow inmate, the artist Fritta (Fritz Taussig) in 1944.

entertaining Nazi officers, since attendance by the SS was very exceptional; otherwise, all of the other qualms resurfaced. Performers had a vested interest in their activities, which raised them to the ranks of so-called "prominents." This usually guaranteed private sleeping quarters, better food rations, and above all protection from transports. The fact that thousands were constantly being shipped "to the east" again made many inmates question the propriety of light entertainment. H. G. Adler, a survivor who wrote the most extensive account of Theresienstadt, was thoroughly disgusted by the "unhealthy to-do" and the "dissipated thoughtlessness" of the cabarets; he contended that "human dignity was eroded from the inside out, without the victims noticing it." Zdenek Lederer, another survivor and chronicler of the camp, contended that the entertainments served Nazi purposes in two ways: by distracting the inmates, and by putting on a facade of leniency for outside inspectors. Lederer argued that "the Germans were not inspired by generosity when granting cultural freedom to their victims. They only cared for the success of their propaganda stunt and the smooth progress of deportations: cultural freedom would lull the prisoners into a false sense of security and would also provide a harmless outlet for any will to resistance." Another survivor, Jacob Jacobson, took issue with such sentiments, claiming that "it would be unjust to blame the people for using those institutions and, by using them, helping the Nazis indirectly to carry out this manoeuvre of camouflage and deceit." He claimed that distraction was a psychological necessity for most inmates, a welcome "counterbalance" to "horror and despair": "Just because the danger of deportation was menacing everyone at every moment, the people in the Ghetto had to live as if this danger did not really exist, as if a life of freedom and human dignity was waiting round the corner."[29]

The surviving texts from Gerron's cabaret allow us to examine the ways in which the shows attempted to cope with the inmates' psychological needs. Although the Carousel presented much old material—for example, Gerron often sang tunes from *The Threepenny Opera*—a number of new songs addressed conditions in Theresienstadt. Leo Strauss wrote most of these lyrics, including the theme song for the cabaret. Likewise entitled "Carousel," it described life as a "strange voyage, / a journey without a destination" (Das ist eine seltsame Reise, / Das ist eine Fahrt ohne Ziel); only when the turning stopped could you see where you stood. In this confusing world, there was one great need: "Illusion, oh please, please, illusion" (Illusion, ach bitte, bitte, Illusion). This appeal for illusion, for suppressing the present, characterized many of the Carousel's numbers. Several of them harked back to friendships and romances in the past, and promised that friends and lovers would find each other in the future. The first half of the "Theresienstadt Viennese Song" (Theresienstädter Wiener Lied) described how the singer and his "sweetie" *(Schatzerl)* used to rendezvous at the Prater, Vienna's amusement park. In the second half, he sang that he was now in Theresienstadt, while she was "somewhere in the east"; yet the refrain contended that every night he still met her in the Prater in his dreams, and it held out the hope that they would be reunited there some day. Such numbers, which swept the audience out of the present into an idyllic past and a hopeful future, were evidently very popular. One inmate, Frieda Rosenthal, even wrote Leo Strauss a poem thanking him for his songs, since "thanks to the dear cabaret" (Dank dem lieben Cabaret), she could forget temporarily about hunger and the travails of the day. In particular, numbers that spoke of "once upon a time" (Es war einmal) and "it will be once again" (Es wird einmal wieder sein) stilled the "longing" in her heart.[30]

Not all of the cabaret's numbers contributed to illusion, however; some of them cautioned against it. That was the case with "From the Strauss Family" (Aus der Familie der Sträusse). The number essentially described the confusion generated by the numerous, often unrelated composers of that name (Josef; Johann father and son; Richard; and Leo's father Oscar). But punning on the word *Strauss* (ostrich), the song contended that of all the Strausses, the most respected one in Theresienstadt was the ostrich, because it could stick its head in the sand. In general, the Carousel shows treated illusions ambivalently. On the one hand, Leo Strauss recognized that visions of hope were necessary for survival, or at least for maintaining sanity. On the other hand, he realized that certain delusions could be deadly, especially since Theresienstadt itself was a city built upon deception. Perhaps the most popular Strauss text was "As If" (Als ob), which described Terezín as an as-if city with as-if occupations, as-if celebrities, as-if food, and as-if beds. Significantly, a note of self-criticism entered the last stanza, which suggested that visions of a better future might also be as-if hopes:

> Oppressive fate we carry
> As if it were quite light,
> And speak of better futures,
> As if they were in sight.

> Man trägt das schwere Schicksal,
> Als ob es nicht so schwer,
> Und spricht von schönrer Zukunft,
> Als obs schon morgen wär.[31]

Strauss spoke of disillusionment because that was the first, overwhelmingly shocking experience of all new arrivals in Terezín. Almost all survivors' accounts describe the horror of the people who came expecting to find a pleasant town, only to be treated like animals. Upon reaching Terezín, they had to drag their baggage for over a mile until they reached what inmates called the "sluice" *(Schleuse)*, where all of their belongings promptly were confiscated. Not yet fully disillusioned, many people would request special accommodations: double rooms, for example, or balconies with southern exposure. The final, irreversible blow came when they were herded into the crowded barracks, with their three-tiered wooden bunk beds. Many inmates, finally realizing the massiveness of the deception, went into shock or deep depression—a condition that made them prime candidates for the next transport to Auschwitz. Strauss addressed this phenomenon in one of his most bitterly humorous songs. It took the form of a dialogue between a newly arrived lady and a long-term inmate of the camp. The fashionable woman's conceptions of what food, lodging, and clothes she expected were fundamentally, if wittily, destroyed in the course of the conversation.[32] What is interesting about the song is that it made fun of the new arrival, and thus spoke to an audience that was presumed to consist of long-term residents. In addition to giving this public a sense of superiority vis-à-vis the newcomers, it suggested that their ability to survive was a product of their adaptability, their realism, and even their sense of humor.

Once again, it is hard to speak of "humor" in the context of a concentration camp, but the Carousel's songs implied that wit was one component of survival. Many numbers tried to laugh off the annoyances of the inmates' lives, such as the seemingly endless standing in line for meager food rations. Strauss even wrote a song on that subject which parodied "Here Comes the Music," one of his father's hits at Wolzogen's Motley Theater forty years earlier. Liliencron's text had described the passing of a military band; now Strauss's "Here Comes the Grub" (Die Menage kommt) recounted the hierarchic order in which people were allowed to line up for their servings.[33] Whereas such songs attempted to come to terms with facts of camp life that could not be changed, other, more serious numbers tried to correct modes of behavior whereby the inmates hurt each other and themselves. One of the most important of such themes was the prejudice rampant among the Czech, Austrian, and German Jews incarcerated in Terezín. As in Westerbork, the German Jews were perceived to have a superior attitude, and so were resented by the Austrian and Czech Jews; yet the German and Austrian Jews together looked down upon the eastern European prisoners.

Several cabaret numbers combated anti-Semitic prejudices among the Jewish inmates themselves. Many had come from thoroughly assimilated families, and were even baptized. Some of these people not only did not consider themselves Jewish but also despised Jews in general, or east European Jews in particular. In Strauss's dialogue between the new arrival at Terezín and the long-term inmate, the former's first complaint was that she was suddenly surrounded by "Polish Semites." As conferencier, Strauss would tell the following joke: "A gentleman who lives in the same room with me said to me today: 'I'm really suffering from a great injustice. Never in my life have I socialized with Jews—and now I'm forced to live in a room with so many Jews.' I replied to him: 'And I suffer from an even greater injustice. In my whole life I have socialized only with Jews—and now I'm forced to live in a room full of anti-Semites.'" While Strauss indirectly appealed for tolerance by underscoring the absurdity of anti-Semitism among Jewish prisoners, Manfred Greiffenhagen, the other major lyricist at the Carousel, wrote a song that pleaded overtly for solidarity among the interned Jews, be they Czech, German, Austrian, Dutch, or Danish citizens.[34]

The Carousel thus made serious attempts to alleviate the situation of the prisoners in Terezín. At the very least it offered them distraction, at best it sought to improve their behavior toward each other. Nevertheless, as in Westerbork, that did not alter the ultimate fate of the inmates, nor did it obviate the fact that the cabaret was part of an elaborate Nazi charade. Indeed, the performances took place most frequently in June 1944, at the height of the notorious "beautification project" *(Verschönerungsaktion)*. In anticipation of a visit by the International Red Cross on June 23, Theresienstadt's population was mobilized to clean up the town. Facades were repainted, gardens planted, and fictitious shops, schools, playgrounds, and even a bank were concocted. Performances, including those of the Carousel, were spruced up. Worst of all, over seven thousand elderly prisoners were shipped off to Auschwitz, in order to give the city a less crowded look. When the Red Cross observers arrived, they were taken on a carefully choreographed eight-hour tour of the ghetto, which gave them the impression of a peaceful, happy, and culturally thriving community. They did not observe the cabaret, but saw instead a few minutes of Hans Krása's *Brundibar,* a children's opera that was the inmates' favorite production.[35]

The Nazi officials were so thrilled by the success of their ruse that they planned one final deceit: they decided to use the cleaned-up camp as the backdrop for a propaganda film which would show for all time how well they treated the Jews. The film was cynically entitled *The Führer Presents a City to the Jews (Der Führer schenkt den Juden eine Stadt)*. It was to be Gerron's last work, and his most terrible concession to the Nazis. As a famous actor and film director, he was the most obvious candidate for the project. Since refusal to comply would have meant certain death, he felt compelled to undertake it. He worked out a detailed scenario, and the shooting took place on twelve days between August 16 and September 11. The film showed clean barracks, well-equipped workshops, a well-supplied hospital, and several activities that were unthinkable to the prisoners in reality, such as tilling private garden plots or swimming in the nearby river. Naturally, the cultural life of the camp was highlighted: there were clips from *Brundibar,* a symphony concert, and a performance of Verdi's *Requiem*. Since Gerron was the film's director, his cabaret naturally appeared as well. That segment too underscored the film's duplicity. The Carousel always performed within the ghetto, since the prisoners were forbidden to venture beyond the moats of the former garrison. Nevertheless, the film's cabaret sequence was shot in an open field well beyond the town, to give the impression that the inhabitants were free to roam the countryside.

Alice Randt, a survivor of Terezín, witnessed the filming of the cabaret segment on August 19. She and hundreds of the other prisoners were told to put on summer clothes, which had been given to them as part of the "beautification project," and to assemble for a performance of the Carousel, at which ice cream would be served. Most of the inmates were loathe to participate in the filming, since they had been mortified and infuriated by the Red Cross visit. However, they had no choice but to comply; and a chance to walk in the countryside, taste ice cream, and see the stars of the Carousel (tickets for which were hard to come by) certainly sweetened the pain. Under heavy guard the "audience" was marched to an outlying meadow. What awaited them was disappointment. There was no ice cream, and they heard only short snippets of songs, repeated several times for outtakes; Gerron sang "Mack the Knife" and the "Cannon-Song" from *The Threepenny Opera,* among other things. The crowd was supposed to provide images of "happy spectators." The shooting was delayed because there were too many blond-haired people in the audience. Since Gerron had been ordered to show only "Jewish-looking" individuals in the film, he had to await a delivery of more dark-haired prisoners.

The whole situation—including the fact that they were surrounded by armed SS guards, just out of camera range—put the spectators into anything but a jovial mood, and Gerron had to work hard to get them to laugh. Randt remembered:

> "Whoever looks into the camera, makes faces or speaks into the camera, will be arrested immediately." Bathed in sweat, Gerron urged us, implored us, begged for discipline, for us to follow orders absolutely. He cracked jokes and made despairing efforts. "Please, no incidents, don't provoke any use of force!" He begged us urgently: "Do what I show you, when I laugh, laugh with me!" And he began a contagious, irresistable laugh, during which he wobbled his fat belly, so that we really had to laugh, even though the situation for him and for us was anything but laughable. *Laugh, Pagliacco!* Thus he stood before us, pale, sweaty, laughing loudly, with a wobbling belly. And thus they filmed peals of laughter from three thousand cheerful country dwellers enjoying their glorious summer variety show!

She recalled further that they all returned "furious" and "full of shame."[36]

The soundtrack was not added to the film until March 1945, and it was shown to a Red Cross commission on April 6. By then the fictitious scenes could do little to whitewash the Nazis' crimes, as irrefutable proof of German atrocities were being uncovered daily by the advancing Allied armies. In the fall of 1944, however, clips of Gerron's film already had appeared in the weekly newsreels shown in German cinemas. Images of "Jewish-looking" people sitting in the Terezín café were juxtaposed with shots of fighting German soldiers, and the voice-over proclaimed: "While the Jews in Theresienstadt dance and consume coffee and cake, our soldiers bear all the burdens of a terrible war, its dangers and deprivations, in order to defend the homeland." Since German cities were being systematically leveled by bombs at that time, the German spectators could not but have felt resentment at the privileged and protected residents of the idyllic Theresienstadt.[37]

In reality, by the time the clips were shown on German screens, the population of Terezín had been decimated. Having duped the Red Cross commission and shot the film, the Nazis had no further use for their "model ghetto." September and October 1944 were the most terrible months in the history of the camp, as almost twenty thousand prisoners were transported to Auschwitz. Among them were Kurt Gerron and Leo Strauss, who died in the gas chambers. Manfred Greiffenhagen was sent on to Dachau, where he perished in January 1945.

Cabaret usually tried to end the evening on an upbeat note. In part, that was commercially astute: it sent the audience home in a "feel-good" mood. It would be possible to give this book a "happy end" as well. After all, Friedrich Hollaender and Rudolf Nelson not only survived the war, they even mounted cabaret shows and revues in the Federal Republic. Werner Finck and Erich Kästner, who had remained in the Nazi state, also contributed to West Germany's postwar cabaret scene. The more leftist entertainers and veterans of the agitprop movement gravitated toward the German Democratic Republic, which developed a distinctive cabaret culture of its own.

But those later developments cannot blind us to the fact that an entire era of Berlin cabaret had come to a tragic end by 1945. *Kabarett* in the Federal Republic and the GDR was quite unlike that of the previous eras: it was less showy, and much more focused on political themes. By contrast, the Wilhelmine and Weimar tradition of cabaret was an unstable but vital combination of satire and parody dealing with love, fashion, art, and—at times—politics. This mixture constantly shifted in response to Germany's volatile political, cultural, and economic climate. The genre was strained to the limit in the concentration camps, and it was there that Berlin cabaret died. It perished not because it could not cope with the inhuman conditions; it managed to retain a blend of art and entertainment, of humor and seriousness, even in those impossible circumstances. Berlin cabaret died because the Nazis murdered so many of the human beings who sustained it—women and men, writers and composers, actors and musicians, professionals and amateurs, entertainers and audience.

# Notes · Index

# Notes

## 1. Cabaret as Metropolitan Montage

1. Friedrich Hollaender, "Cabaret," *Weltbühne*, February 2, 1932, 169.
2. A complete listing of works on the history of modern Berlin would, of course, have thousands of entries. For a comprehensive, up-to-date, and eminently readable history of Berlin, see Wolfgang Ribbe, ed., *Geschichte Berlins*, 2 vols. (Munich: 1987); the work includes an extensive bibliography. Werner Hegemann's *Das steinerne Berlin: Geschichte der grössten Mietskasernenstadt der Welt* (Lugano: 1930) remains a classic account of city planning and real-estate speculation in Berlin. For a general work in English dealing with the Wilhelmine era, see Gerhard Masur, *Imperial Berlin* (New York: 1970). For a short introduction to the city's history, see Peter Jelavich, "Berlin's Path to Modernity," in *Art in Berlin, 1815–1989* (Atlanta: High Museum of Art, 1989), 13–40. The information in the ensuing paragraphs is taken from that essay.
3. Anon. [Walter Rathenau], "Die schönste Stadt der Welt," *Die Zukunft* 26 (1899): 39.
4. Karl Scheffler, *Berlin: Ein Stadtschicksal* (Berlin: 1910), 267; and Arthur Eloesser, "Gedanken in einem Grillroom" (1912), in *Die Strasse meiner Jugend: Berliner Skizzen* (Berlin: 1987), 78–80.
5. Leo Colze, *Berliner Warenhäuser* (Leipzig: 1908), 9; Franz Hessel, *Ein Flaneur in Berlin* (1929; reprinted Berlin: 1984), 32–33; Eloesser, "Unter den Linden" (1911), in *Strasse meiner Jugend*, 53; and Walter Benjamin, *Berliner Chronik* (Frankfurt am Main: 1970), 79. See also Julius Posener, *Berlin auf dem Wege zu einer neuen Architektur: Das Zeitalter Wilhelms II* (Munich: 1979), 453–474.
6. Karl Scheffler, *Die Architektur der Grossstadt* (Berlin: 1913), 3; Hans Simmel, "Auszüge aus den Lebenserinnerungen," in *Ästhetik und Soziologie um die Jahrhundertwende: Georg Simmel*, ed. Hannes Böhringer and Karlfried Gründer (Frankfurt am Main: 1976), 265; Georg Simmel, "Die Grossstädte und das Geistesleben," in *Jahrbuch der Gehe-Stiftung zu Dresden* 9 (1903): 188, 193, 195.
7. Georg Simmel, "Berliner Gewerbe-Ausstellung," *Die Zeit* (Vienna), July 25, 1896, 59, 60.

8. Georg Simmel, *The Philosophy of Money,* trans. Tom Bottomore and David Frisby (Boston: 1978), 474, 484.

9. Charles Baudelaire, "Le Spleen de Paris," in *Oeuvres,* ed. Y.-G. le Dantec (Dijon: 1944), 1: 405–406.

10. Richard Hamann, *Der Impressionismus in Leben und Kunst* (Cologne: 1907), 201. For an account and critique of this work, see Rudolf Zeitler, "Richard Hamanns Buch 'Der Impressionismus in Leben in Kunst,' 1907: Noten zur Ideengeschichte," in *Ideengeschichte und Kunstwissenschaft: Philosophie und bildende Kunst im Kaiserreich,* ed. Ekkehard Mai et al. (Berlin: 1983), 293–311.

11. For discussions of the importance of collage and montage in various arts, see the essays in Denis Bablet, ed., *Collage et montage au théâtre et dans les autres arts durant les années vingt* (Lausanne: 1978); and Katherine Hoffman, ed., *Collage: Critical Views* (Ann Arbor: 1989).

12. Ludwig Rubiner, "Variété und Kultur," *Das Leben: Illustrierte Wochenschrift* 1 (1906): 889.

13. Definition of Tingeltangel according to the Strafsenat des Kammergerichts, September 22, 1904; reported by Glasenapp, Polizeipräsidium Berlin, to Landgericht Magdeburg, letter of May 23, 1914; in Brandenburgisches Landeshauptarchiv, Pr. Br. Rep. 30 Berlin C, Pol. Präs. Tit. 74 (hereafter cited as BLHA), Th 1499, f. 303. For a general history of variety shows, see Ernst Günther, *Geschichte des Varietés* (Berlin: 1978), and Wolfgang Jansen, *Das Varieté* (Berlin: 1990). For Imperial Berlin, see the contemporary survey of Eberhard Buchner, *Variété und Tingeltangel in Berlin* (Berlin: 1905); as well as Ingrid Heinrich-Jost, *Auf ins Metropol: Specialitäten- und Unterhaltungstheater im ausgehenden 19. Jahrhundert* (Berlin: 1984). It should be noted that at the turn of the century, the German word for variety show was usually spelled "Variété." Now, however, "Varieté" is the accepted spelling.

14. For more information on the Wintergarten, see the commemorative booklet *Festschrift 50 Jahre Wintergarten, 1888–1938* (Berlin: 1938). On the first film projection, see Gisela Winkler, "Die Bilder lernten das Laufen—im Varieté," in *Kassette: Ein Almanach für Bühne, Podium und Manege,* 5 (1981): 197–204.

15. Günther, *Geschichte des Varietés,* pp. 125–126, 138; Gerhard Wahnrau, *Berlin—Stadt der Theater* (Berlin: 1957), 460–462; anon., "Ueberbrettl und Variété," *Modernes Brettl,* January 15, 1902, 49; and Conrad Alberti, "Die Chansonnière," *Münchener Salonblatt,* June 2, 1901, 363. For a detailed account of how one Munich theater that opened as a home for modern drama was rapidly converted into a vaudeville hall, see Peter Jelavich, *Munich and Theatrical Modernism: Politics, Playwriting, and Performance, 1890–1914* (Cambridge, Mass: 1985), 115.

16. Artur Moeller-Bruck, *Das Varieté* (Berlin: 1902), 22; Victor Ottmann, cited in Heinrich-Jost, *Auf ins Metropol,* 64; and Alberti, "Die Chansonnière," 363. Moeller-Bruck later called himself Moeller van den Bruck and became an important spokesman for *völkisch* renewal, best known for his book *Das*

*Dritte Reich* (Hamburg: 1923); see Fritz Stern, *The Politics of Cultural Despair: A Study in the Rise of Germanic Ideology* (Berkeley: 1961).

17. Wolzogen in the *Vossische Zeitung*, October 31, 1900; and Otto Julius Bierbaum, ed., *Deutsche Chansons (Brettl-Lieder)*, third edition (Berlin: 1901), xi–xii.

18. Oskar Panizza, "Der Klassizismus und das Eindringen des Variété," *Gesellschaft* 12/10 (October 1896): 1253, 1256, 1267. For further information on Panizza, see Jelavich, *Munich and Theatrical Modernism*, 54–74; and Michael Bauer, *Oskar Panizza: Ein literarisches Porträt* (Munich: 1984).

19. Hugo Haan, "Oper und Brettl," *Signale für die musikalische Welt*, March 13, 1901, 322; and Richard Batka, "Bunte Bühne," *Kunstwart*, 14/18 (2. Juniheft 1901): 211, and 15/9 (1. Februarheft 1902): 407.

20. For analyses of the Parisian cabarets of the 1880s and 1890s, see the discussions in Charles Rearick, *Pleasures of the Belle Epoque: Entertainment and Festivity in Turn–of–the–Century France* (New Haven: 1985), 53–79; and Jerrold Seigel, *Bohemian Paris: Culture, Politics, and the Boundaries of Bourgeois Life, 1830–1930* (New York: 1986), 215–241. For a short, well-illustrated survey of several establishments, see Mariel Oberthur, *Cafés and Cabarets of Montmartre* (Salt Lake City: 1984).

21. Moeller-Bruck, *Variété*, 36; and Otto Julius Bierbaum, *Stilpe: Ein Roman aus der Froschperspektive* (1897; reprinted Munich: 1963), 171–173.

22. Bierbaum, *Deutsche Chansons*, ix–x.

23. Buchner, *Variété*, 94; Bierbaum, *Deutsche Chansons*, xv; and Moeller-Bruck, *Variété*, 21.

24. Friedrich Nietzsche, "Von alten und neuen Tafeln," section 23, in *Also sprach Zarathustra; Menschliches, Allzumenschliches*, part 1, section 213; *Die fröhliche Wissenschaft*, sections 107, 382. For a survey of the diverse uses to which Nietzsche was put in Wilhelmine Germany, see Peter Pütz, *Friedrich Nietzsche* (Stuttgart: 1967), 61–88; and R. Hinton Thomas, *Nietzsche in German Politics and Society, 1890–1918* (La Salle, Ill.: 1983).

25. Bierbaum, *Stilpe*, 171; Ernst von Wolzogen, *Wie ich mich ums Leben brachte: Erinnerungen und Erfahrungen* (Braunschweig: 1922), 197; Nietzsche, *Menschliches, Allzumenschliches*, vol. 1, section 290; *Die fröhliche Wissenschaft*, sections 280, 329.

26. Nietzsche, "Schopenhauer als Erzieher," section 6, in *Unzeitgemässe Betrachtungen;* "Wo ich Einwände mache," in *Nietzsche contra Wagner*.

27. *Goethes Gespräche mit Eckermann*, entry of December 4, 1823.

28. For a history and analysis of Berlin humor, see Gustav Sichelschmidt, *Die Berliner und ihr Witz: Versuch einer Analyse* (Berlin: 1978). For the Berlin dialect, see the various editions of Hans Meyer, *Der Richtige Berliner in Wörtern und Redensarten*, which first appeared in 1878 and continues to be updated; see also Walter Benjamin, "Wat hier jelacht wird, det lache ick" (1929), in *Schriften* (Frankfurt am Main: 1972), 4: 537–542. During the *Vormärz*, Glassbrenner's works were particularly important: see Ingrid Heinrich-Jost, *Literarische Publizistik Adolf Glassbrenners (1810–1876): Die List*

*beim Schreiben der Wahrheit* (Munich: 1980); Heinrich-Jost, *Adolf Glassbrenner* (Berlin: 1981); and Mary Lee Townsend, "The Politics of Humor: Adolph Glassbrenner and the Rediscovery of the Prussian Vormärz (1815–48)," *Central European History* 20 (1987): 29–57.

29. Ernst Dronke, *Berlin* (1846; reprinted Darmstadt: 1987), 17; and "Berlin," in *Meyers Konversations-Lexikon: Eine Encyklopädie des allgemeinen Wissens* (Leipzig: 1874), 3: 12–13.

30. Hamann, *Impressionismus*, 204, 205.

31. Walter Benjamin, *Versuche über Brecht* (Frankfurt am Main: 1966), 113.

32. Sigmund Freud, *Jokes and their Relation to the Unconscious*, trans. James Strachey (New York: 1963), 101, 179.

33. See Gary Stark, "The Censorship of Literary Naturalism, 1885–1895: Prussia and Saxony," *Central European History* 18 (1985): 341–342; and Peter Jelavich, "Authorial Games: Confronting Censorship and the Market," in Karin MacHardy and Gisela Brude-Firmau, eds., *Fact and Fiction: German History and Literature, 1848–1924* (Tübingen: 1990), 70–72.

## 2. Between Elitism and Entertainment: Wolzogen's Motley Theater

1. Ernst von Wolzogen, *Wie ich mich ums Leben brachte*, 6–8. For general histories of cabaret, which include accounts of Wolzogen's Motley Theater, see Heinz Greul, *Bretter, die die Zeit bedeuten: Die Kulturgeschichte des Kabaretts* (Munich: 1971); Rainer Otto and Walter Rösler, *Kabarettgeschichte: Abriss des deutschsprachigen Kabaretts* (Berlin: 1977); Walter Rösler, *Das Chanson im deutschen Kabarett 1901–1933* (Berlin: 1980); Helga Bemmann, *Berliner Musenkinder-Memoiren: Eine heitere Chronik von 1900–1930* (Berlin: 1981); Klaus Budzinski, *Pfeffer ins Getriebe: Ein Streifzug durch 100 Jahre Kabarett* (Munich: 1982); Volker Kühn, *Das Kabarett der frühen Jahre* (Berlin: 1984); Ingrid Heinrich-Jost, *Hungrige Pegasusse: Anfänge des deutschsprachigen Kabaretts in Berlin* (Berlin: n.d.); and Harold B. Segel, *Turn-of-the-Century Cabaret* (New York: 1987). The most comprehensive history of cabaret in English is Lisa Appignanesi, *The Cabaret* (New York: 1976). Two very useful handbooks are the cabaret encyclopedia of Klaus Budzinski, *Das Kabarett* (Düsseldorf: 1985), and the massive compendium of cabaret and popular music gramophone recordings by Berthold Leimbach, *Tondokumente der Kleinkunst und ihre Interpreten, 1898–1945* (Göttingen: 1991). That work is printed privately; for copies, send inquiries to the author (Berthold Leimbach, Nikolausberger Weg 84, W-3400 Göttingen, Germany).

2. Wolzogen to Polizei Präsident Berlin, letter of June 9, 1900, in BLHA, Th 793.

3. Ibid.; and see Wolzogen, *Wie ich mich*, 53–54, 136.

4. Wolzogen, "Das Ueberbrettl," *Vossische Zeitung*, December 16, 1900.

5. "Vom 'Ueberbrettl zum rasenden Jüngling,'" *Vossische Zeitung*, October 31, 1900.

6. "Festvorstellung im Opernhause," *Berliner Tageblatt*, January 19, 1901; and Wolzogen, *Wie ich mich*, 208.

7. *Vossische Zeitung,* October 31 and December 16, 1900. The poem is reprinted in Kühn, *Das Kabarett der frühen Jahre,* 32–33.

8. Oscar Straus/Peter Schlemihl [Ludwig Thoma], "Zur Dichtkunst abkommandirt," sheet music (Berlin: 1901). See the criticisms in *Die Zeit,* January 26, 1901, 56; *Deutsche Zeitung,* January 20, 1901; and *Berliner Tageblatt,* January 19, 1901. See also Ludwig Thoma to Albert Langen, letter of February 12, 1901, in Thoma, *Ein Leben in Briefen (1875–1921),* ed. Anton Keller (Munich: 1963), 71.

9. Otto Julius Bierbaum, "Der lustige Ehemann," in *Deutsche Chansons,* 4–5. For a musical analysis of the piece, see Rösler, *Das Chanson im deutschen Kabarett,* 80–81. See the reviews in *Bühne und Welt* 3 (1900–01): 465; and *Das litterarische Echo,* March 1901, 713.

10. Review in *Deutsche Zeitung,* January 20, 1901.

11. "Das Laufmädel" and "Madame Adèle" in Wolzogen, *Verse zu meinem Leben,* third edition (Berlin: 1907), 134–138; review in *Berliner Lokal-Anzeiger,* January 19, 1901.

12. See Christian Morgenstern, "Das Mittagsmahl," *Die Zeit,* September 8, 1900, 158–160; Detlev von Liliencron, "König Ragnar Lodbrok," in *Gesammelte Werke* (Berlin: 1911), 2: 11–13. On pantomime, see Oscar Geller, "Die Pantomime," *Das moderne Brettl,* January 15, 1902, 51–53.

13. Audience reaction to the various works was noted in *Berliner Tageblatt* and *Berliner Lokal-Anzeiger,* both of January 19, 1901; *Deutsche Zeitung,* January 20, 1901; and *Bühne und Welt,* 3 (1900–01): 465.

14. *Deutsche Zeitung,* January 20, 1901; *Berliner Tageblatt* and *Berliner Lokal-Anzeiger,* January 19, 1901; and Bierbaum, *Deutsche Chansons,* x.

15. *Berliner Börsen Courier,* January 19, 1901; Wolzogen, *Wie ich mich,* 196–197; *Berliner Lokal-Anzeiger,* January 19, 1901.

16. Report of February 9, 1901, in BLHA, Th 793; *Berliner Börsen-Courier,* January 19, 1901; and Julius Elias, "Cabaret—Brettl—Petit théâtre," *Die Nation,* 19/11 (1901): 173. For successful challenges to the censor, see Gary Stark, "The Censorship of Literary Naturalism, 1885–1895: Prussia and Saxony," *Central European History* 18 (1985): 326–343.

17. *Norddeutsche Allgemeine Zeitung,* March 10, 1901; *Berliner Lokal-Anzeiger,* January 19, 1901; Richard Batka, "Bunte Bühne," *Kunstwart* (2. Juniheft 1901), 210; and *Vorwärts,* June 9, 1901.

18. *Frankfurter Zeitung,* May 11, 1901; Oscar Straus/Theodor Etzel, "Bettelbubenlied," sheet music (Berlin: 1901); and Ferdinand Gregori, "Das Ueberbrettl," *Volkserzieher,* 1901, 183.

19. Report of February 9, 1901, in BLHA, Th 793; and *Norddeutsche Allgemeine Zeitung,* March 10, 1901.

20. Arthur Seidl, "Biedermeier in Decadence? Zur Psychologie des 'Überbrettls,'" *Gesellschaft,* 17/2 (1901): 143; Walter Gensel, "Berliner Brettlseuche," ibid., 17/4: 217; Ernst Heilborn, "Das Ueberbrettl," *Die Zeit,* January 26, 1901, 56; and Johannes Gaulke, "Die Ueberbrettl-Seuche," *Magasin für Litteratur,* October 12, 1901, 978.

21. Maximilian Harden, "Tingeltangel," *Zukunft,* March 9, 1901, 396. Bourgeois satisfaction at being entertained by nobles was also noted by Johannes Gaulke, "Zur Renaissance des Tingeltangels," *Magasin für Litteratur,* March 30, 1901, 307.

22. Joc., "Sonntagsplauderei," *Vorwärts,* June 9, 1901; H. Ströbel, "Das Ueber-brettl," *Neue Zeit,* 20/1 (1901–02), 175; and Johannes Gaulke, "Die Ueber-brettl-Seuche," *Magasin für Litteratur,* October 12, 1901, 977.

23. Bogumil Zepler/Fritz Engel, "Der Marschallstab," sheet music (Berlin: 1901).

24. On the tour, see note of Bausenwein, June 10, 1901, in BLHA, Th 793; and Heinrich Hart, "Ein Abend im Bunten Theater, 7. Juli 1901," in *Ausgewählte Aufsätze. Reisebilder. Vom Theater* (Berlin: 1907), 243.

25. *Kleines Journal,* July 26, 1901; *Norddeutsche Allgemeine Zeitung,* July 31, 1901; and *Das Moderne Brettl,* November 15, 1901, 23; December 15, 1901, 45; January 15, 1902, 61; and July 1902, 159.

26. *Bühne und Brettl,* November 10, 1901; and *Das Moderne Brettl,* November 15, 1901, 24.

27. *Münchener Post,* August 30, 1901; *Berliner Lokal-Anzeiger,* September 1, 1901; and *Illustriertes Salonblatt,* 3 (1901): 604. See also the reports in *Theater Kourier,* September 7, 1901, and *Münchener Post,* September 14 and 22, 1901.

28. Walter Gensel, "Berliner Brettlseuche," *Gesellschaft,* 17/4 (1901), 219; Alfred Kerr, "Fluch der bösen Tat: Liliencrons Auftreten (27. September 1901)," in *Das neue Drama* (Berlin: 1917), 337; and Detlev von Liliencron, *Ausgewählte Briefe* (Berlin: 1910), 2: 210 (letter of December 15, 1901).

29. *Das litterarische Echo,* October 1901, 73; also in numerous newspapers throughout Germany around September 18.

30. See in general *August Endell: Der Architekt des Photoateliers Elvira 1871–1925* (Munich: Museum Villa Stuck, 1977); *Hermann Obrist: Wegbereiter der Moderne* (Munich: Museum Villa Stuck, 1968); and Peg Weiss, *Kandinsky in Munich: The Formative Jugendstil Years* (Princeton: 1979), 28–40.

31. August Endell, *Um die Schönheit: Eine Paraphrase über die Münchener Kunst-ausstellung 1896* (Munich: 1896), 13; and Endell, *Die Schönheit der grossen Stadt* (Stuttgart: 1908), 13, 23.

32. August Endell, "Das Wolzogen-Theater in Berlin," *Berliner Architekturwelt* 4 (1902): 384.

33. Fritz Stahl, "Buntes Theater: Das Haus," *Berliner Tageblatt,* November 29, 1901; and Karl Scheffler, "August Endell G.m.b.H.", *Lotse,* March 8, 1902, 702, 705.

34. "Wolzogens Beichte: Ein Interview," *Berliner Tageblatt,* November 27, 1901; *Kleines Journal* and *Berliner Lokal-Anzeiger,* both of November 29, 1901.

35. Letters of October 20, November 16, and December 5, 1901 in Thoma, *Briefe,* 92, 96, 105. Compare Wolzogen's announcement in *Berliner Tageblatt,* November 12, 1901, with Thoma's correction, ibid., November 28. See also the account in Thoma, "Erinnerungen" (1919), in *Gesammelte Werke* (Munich: 1968), 1: 195–196.

36. "Wolzogens Beichte," *Berliner Tageblatt,* November 27, 1901; "Buntes Thea-ter: Die Eröffnungsvorstellung," *Berliner Tageblatt,* November 29, 1901. See

also Ludwig Thoma, "Die Protestversammlung," in Karl von Levetzow, ed., *Buntes Theater: Ernst von Wolzogen's offizielles Repertoire* (Berlin: 1902), 1: 20–31.

37. *Das moderne Brettl,* April 1902, 108; *Kleines Journal,* April 15, 1902; and *Neue Preussische Zeitung,* April 15, 1902. See examples of Schattenbänkel in Levetzow, *Buntes Theater,* 2: 77–82.

38. *Berliner Tageblatt,* January 8, 1901; *Kleines Journal,* November 29, 1901. On the Eleven Executioners, see Jelavich, *Munich and Theatrical Modernism,* 167–185.

39. The increase of one-act plays was noted in the *Kleines Journal* and the *Neue Preussische Zeitung,* both of April 15, 1902. On the causes of burnout at the Eleven Executioners, see Jelavich, *Munich and Theatrical Modernism,* 182–183.

40. Wolzogen, "Das Überbrettl: Nachwort," in *Ansichten und Aussichten: Ein Erntebuch* (Berlin: 1908), 238–239; and Hanns Heinz Ewers, *Das Cabaret* (Berlin: 1904), 40–42.

41. *Kleines Journal, Tägliche Rundschau* and *Berliner Börsen Zeitung,* February 14, 1902; and *Berliner Tageblatt,* April 13, 1902.

42. Wedekind, letter of August 5, 1902, in *Gesammelte Briefe,* 2: 91. On Adolf Philipp, see *Berliner Börsen Zeitung,* June 24, 1903; and the special issue of *Bühne und Brettl,* vol. 6, no. 5.

43. *Berliner Kurier,* May 22, 1902; and Wolzogen, *Wie ich mich,* 229–243.

44. Compare Wolzogen, "Das Ueberbrettl," *Vossische Zeitung,* December 16, 1900, with *Das literarische Echo,* January 1901, 547, where an ellipsis replaced the sentence quoted; and Wolzogen, "Das Überbrettl: Nachwort," 234, 235, 241.

45. Wolzogen, *Wie ich mich,* 198–199, 101–103.

46. Ewers, *Das Cabaret,* 33–34.

### 3. From Artistic Parody to Theatrical Renewal: Reinhardt's Sound and Smoke

1. On the origins of the Volksbühne movement in Berlin, see Heinrich Braulich, *Die Volksbühne: Theater und Politik in der deutschen Volksbühnenbewegung* (Berlin: 1976), 31–65.

2. Chlodwig zu Hohenlohe-Schillingsfürst, *Denkwürdigkeiten* (Stuttgart: 1907), 2: 507; and Oskar Blumenthal, *Verbotene Stücke* (Berlin: 1900), 16.

3. Reinhardt to Berthold Held, fall 1894; and "Über ein Theater, wie es mir vorschwebt" (1901), in Max Reinhardt, *Ich bin nichts als ein Theatermann: Briefe, Reden, Aufsätze, Interviews, Gespräche, Auszüge aus Regiebüchern,* ed. Hugo Fetting (Berlin: 1989), 37, 64.

4. Citation from Gottfried Reinhardt, *Der Liebhaber: Erinnerungen seines Sohnes Gottfried Reinhardt an Max Reinhardt* (Munich: 1973), 180.

5. *Berliner Tageblatt,* January 24, 1901.

6. "L'Intérieur," in Max Reinhardt, *Schall und Rauch* (Berlin: 1901), 207–214. See also the description of the "Zehn Gerechten" in *Theater Kourier,* March 23, 1901.

7. The first three versions are published in Reinhardt, *Schall und Rauch*, 27–125.

8. Reinhardt to Berthold Held, letter of March 9, 1895, in Reinhardt, *Ich bin nichts*, 61.

9. Kayssler to Morgenstern, letters of January 27 and undated (ca. March 1901), in Christian Morgenstern, *Ein Leben in Briefen* (Wiesbaden: 1952), 117, 123.

10. See "Diarrhoesteia" and "Das Regiekollegium," in Reinhardt, *Schall und Rauch*, 127–206.

11. On the theatrical projects of the Darmstadt Artists' Colony, see Jutta Boehe, "Theater und Jugendstil—Feste des Lebens und der Kunst," and "Darmstädter Spiele 1901: Das Theater der Darmstädter Künstlerkolonie," both in Gerhard Bott, ed., *Von Morris zum Bauhaus* (Hanau: 1977), 145–181. Behrens presented his ideas in *Feste des Lebens und der Kunst: Eine Betrachtung des Theaters als höchstes Kultursymbol* (Leipzig: 1900), and "Die Lebensmesse von Richard Dehmel," *Die Rheinlande*, January 1901, 28–40. For the ideas of Fuchs, see Jelavich, *Munich and Theatrical Modernism*, 187–208.

12. See "Carleas und Elisande" in Reinhardt, *Schall und Rauch*, 112–113.

13. *Freisinnige Zeitung*, October 11, 1901, and *Kunstwart* (2. Aprilheft 1902), 85. See also the descriptions in *Vossische Zeitung*, *Tägliche Rundschau*, and *Berliner Börsen-Courier*, all of October 10, 1901, and *National Zeitung*, *Deutsche Zeitung*, and *Norddeutsche Allgemeine Zeitung*, all of October 11, 1901.

14. "Des 43. Überbrettlmenschen Höllenfahrt" is reprinted in Peter Sprengel, ed., *Schall und Rauch: Erlaubtes und Verbotenes* (Berlin: 1991), 71–97; see also the description in *Vossische Zeitung*, October 10, 1901.

15. Literary satire at Wolzogen's Überbrettl was criticized in *Die Zeit*, January 26, 1901, 56. Others reviews cited from *Neue Preussische Zeitung*, *Das Kleine Journal*, and *Berliner Börsen-Zeitung*, all of October 10, 1901; and *Berliner Morgenpost* and *Norddeutsche Allgemeine Zeitung*, October 11, 1901.

16. For reviews of the opening night of the Bad Boys, see *Berliner Tageblatt*, November 17, 1901; *Welt am Montag*, November 18, 1901; and *Deutsche Zeitung* and *Das deutsche Blatt*, November 20, 1901.

17. Parts of the Ibsen parody are quoted in Rudolf Bernauer, *Das Theater meines Lebens: Erinnerungen* (Berlin: 1955), 132–135. Meinhard and Bernauer characterized their public and their repertory in letters to the police dated December 26, 1903, September 29, 1904, and November 8, 1904, in BLHA, Th 1490.

18. *Freisinnige Zeitung*, October 11, 1901; *Vossische Zeitung*, November 16, 1901.

19. Reinhardt to Bertold Held, undated letter, fall 1894, in Reinhardt, *Ich bin nichts*, 48. For the debate on Hauptmann's play, see Hans Schwab-Felisch, ed., *Hauptmann: Die Weber: Dichtung und Wirklichkeit* (Frankfurt an Main: 1963). The reasons for canceling the Kaiser's loge are described in Alfred Dreifuss, *Deutsches Theater Berlin* (Berlin: 1987), 117–120.

20. Friedrich Kayssler, "Die Weber. Soziales Drama. Auf Wunsch Sr. Durchlaucht von Serenissimus für eine Sondervorstellung bearbeitet von Freiherrn von Kindermann," reprinted in Sprengel, *Schall und Rauch*, 54. See also the de-

scriptions of the skit in *Berliner Tageblatt, Tägliche Rundschau,* and *Das Kleine Journal,* all of May 23, 1901.

21. Ernst Johann, ed., *Reden des Kaisers: Ansprachen, Predigten und Trinksprüche Wilhlems II* (Munich: 1966), 102. For the Kaiser's conflicts with modern art more generally, see Peter Paret, *The Berlin Secession: Modernism and its Enemies in Imperial Germany* (Cambridge, Mass: 1980).

22. Heinrich Mann, *Professor Unrat* (orig. 1905), chapter 6.

23. Oberländer to Police Praesidium, letter of November 13, 1901, in BLHA, Th 804. The reappearance of Serenissimus was described in *Vossische Zeitung,* November 16, 1901; the text of his comments is reprinted in Sprengel, *Schall und Rauch,* 148–152.

24. Police notes of November 31 and December 1, 1901, in BLHA, Th 804; and Police Praesidium to Ministry of the Interior, letter of December 2, 1901, in BLHA, Th 804.

25. The letter to the Empress is quoted in Leonard Fiedler, *Max Reinhardt in Selbstzeugnissen und Bilddokumenten* (Reinbek: 1975), 35. Police Praesidium to Schall und Rauch, letter of December 3, 1901, and memorandums of December 17, 1901 to January 9, 1902, in BLHA, Th 804.

26. Possart to Ministry of the Interior, letter of January 4, 1902, in BLHA, Th 804. For the "Caligula" affair, see Ludwig Quidde, *Caligula: Schriften über Militarismus und Pazifismus,* ed. Hans-Ulrich Wehler (Frankfurt am Main: 1977).

27. *Deutsche Zeitung,* January 24, 1902; Possart to Ministry of the Interior, letter of January 4, 1902.

28. *Tägliche Rundschau,* February 10, 1902; *Vorwärts,* November 17, 1901.

29. *Berliner Courier,* November 16, 1901.

30. Police report of March 21, 1902, in BLHA, Th 804; "Karle" and "Diarrhoesteia," in Reinhardt, *Schall und Rauch,* 79, 129.

31. The invitation list to *Salome* accompanies Oberländer to Glasenapp, letter of October 23, 1902, in BLHA, Th 804. A police observer of a New Year's Eve party sponsored by the Bad Boys reported that "three-quarters" of the audience consisted of "people of Jewish faith"; see report of January 1, 1903, in BLHA, Th 1490.

32. For the protests in the Weimar era, see Chapter 7. For a nuanced account of Jewish caricatures in liberal journals during the Wilhelmine age, see Henry Wassermann, "Jews in Jugendstil: Simplicissimus, 1896–1914," Leo Baeck Institute, *Year Book* 31 (1986): 71–104. Examples of benign Jewish jokes told during the Wilhelmine era may be found in Alexander Moszkowski's *Die Unsterbliche Kiste: Die 333 besten Witze der Weltliteratur* (Berlin: 1907).

33. Morgenstern, *Ein Leben in Briefen,* 120; and Oberländer to Police Praesidium, letter of April 15, 1902, in BLHA, Th 804.

34. Reinhardt, "Über ein Theater, wie es mir vorschwebt" (1901), in *Ich bin nichts,* 74–75.

35. Ibid., 75; "Zweite Kindheit in Wien," 26.

36. Kayssler's letter is quoted in Julius Bab, *Das Theater der Gegenwart* (Leipzig:

1928), 121. The revolutionary theatricality of *Earth Spirit* is discussed in Jelavich, *Munich and Theatrical Modernism,* 105–115.

37. Hugo von Hofmannsthal, "Eine Monographie: 'Friedrich Mitterwurzer' von Eugen Guglia" (1895), in *Reden und Aufsätze* (Frankfurt am Main: 1979), 1: 480–481.

38. Hofmannsthal, "Elektra," in *Dramen* (Frankfurt am Main: 1979), 2: 233.

39. Bernauer, *Theater meines Lebens,* 109; Max Halbe, *Jahrhundertwende: Erinnerungen an eine Epoche* (1935; reprinted Munich: 1976), 339; Schlaikjer paraphrased in *Tägliche Rundschau,* October 17, 1901.

## 4. Cosmopolitan Diversions, Metropolitan Identities

1. Karl Storck, "Vom Überbrettl," *Monatsblätter für deutsche Literatur,* October 1901, 19.

2. Paul Block, "Zum hungrigen Pegasus," *Berliner Tageblatt,* October 28, 1901. See also the accounts in Ewers, *Das Cabaret,* 48–51; and *Das moderne Brettl,* January 15, 1902, 57. For Mühsam's appearances in Berlin cabarets, see his article "Die zehnte Muse," in *Vossische Zeitung,* December 28, 1927. For other aspects of his literary career, see Jelavich, *Munich and Theatrical Modernism,* 268–283.

3. "Berliner 'Cabarets,'" in *Das Moderne Brettl,* January 15, 1902, 57; and Block, "Zum hungrigen Pegasus."

4. *Berliner Lokal-Anzeiger,* February 18, 1902; Benjamin, *Berliner Chronik,* 48; Block, "Zum hungrigen Pegasus."

5. *Freisinnige Zeitung,* November 6, 1901; and Mühsam, "Die zehnte Muse."

6. For a character report on Tilke, see the police report of May 9, 1902 in BLHA, Th 1490.

7. *Freisinnige Zeitung,* November 6, 1901; and police report of December 19, 1902, BLHA, Th 1493. See also the descriptions in Ewers, *Das Cabaret,* 51–54; and *Das moderne Brettl,* May 1902, 121–123.

8. Ewers, *Das Cabaret,* 54–61; *Berliner Courier,* November 12, 1903; and Kurt Tucholsky, "Berliner Mutterlaut" (1922), in *Gesammelte Werke* (Reinbek: 1975), 3: 288.

9. Police reports of December 27 and 31, 1901, in BLHA, Th 1491; and *Vorwärts,* November 28, 1901. The political poem in question was published in *Welt am Montag,* December 9, 1901. For other examples of Hyan's verse, see "Preussische Kunst" and "Der bestohlene Kommerzienrat," in *Das moderne Brettl,* May 1902, 124.

10. Police reports of August 24 and November 13, 1902, and December 23, 1903, in BLHA, Th 1491.

11. Police reports of August 24 1902, and December 5 and 11, 1903, in BLHA, Th 1491.

12. Police report of December 11, 1901, in BLHA, Th 1491; *Berliner Börsen-Courier,* October 9, 1902; and Glasenapp to Minister des Innern, report of May 15, 1902, in BLHA, Th 804, f. 289r–290. The counterproductive nature of the censors' actions in the previous decade is the subject of Gary Stark,

"The Censorship of Literary Naturalism, 1885–1895: Prussia and Saxony," *Central European History* 18 (1985): 326–343.

13. Ewers, *Das Cabaret*, 67.

14. "Fort mit den Schmarotzerpflanzen!" in *Internationale Artisten-Zeitung*, June 14, 1903. See also the earlier article in another vaudeville trade publication: "Die Cabarets," in *Der Artist*, February 9, 1902.

15. "Kabaretts," in *Deutsche Warte*, November 13, 1904; and Erich Mühsam, "Das Kabarett," in *Fackel*, March 23, 1906, 19.

16. Inquiry of the Gewerbe-Kommisariat, July 29, 1903, in BLHA, Th 1499; *Berliner Tageblatt* and *Berliner Zeitung*, both of October 24, 1904; Possart to Minister des Innern, March 23, 1905, in BLHA, Th 1499, f. 41; *Neue Gast-wirths-Zeitung*, April 16, 1905; and *Vossische Zeitung*, April 27 and 29, 1905.

17. Franz Hoeniger, "Das Recht der Kabaretts," in *Berliner Tageblatt*, December 9, 1905. That is the second part of an article that began on December 2.

18. Bethmann Hollweg to Polizei-Präsident, letter of July 5, 1905, BLHA, Th 1499, f. 108; order of Polizei-Präsident Börries, May 5, 1906, ibid., ff. 126–127.

19. "Polizei und Kabaretts," in *Berliner Tageblatt*, November 26, 1910; and "Vom Berliner Nachtvergnügen," in *Frankfurter Nachrichten*, December 2, 1910.

20. Egon Jameson, *Am Flügel: Rudolf Nelson* (Berlin: 1967), 58. This work consists of Nelson's reminiscences, recorded during the 1950s.

21. Rudolf Nelson/O. A. Alberts, "Rechts ein Puppchen, links ein Puppchen!" sheet music (Berlin: 1904).

22. Kurt Tucholsky, "Berliner Cabarets" (1913), in *Gesammelte Werke*, 1: 87–88.

23. Rudolf Nelson/Willy Hagen, "Jacques Manasse," sheet music (Berlin: 1912).

24. Nelson to Glasenapp, letter of October 14, 1910, in BLHA, Th 1499, ff. 170–171.

25. Police report of October 25, 1912, in BLHA, Th 2693, f. 18r; and Rudolf Nelson/Willy Wolff, "Das Ladenmädel," sheet music (Berlin: 1904). For the events in Donaueschingen, see Jameson, *Am Flügel: Rudolf Nelson*, 89–91; *Vossische Zeitung*, November 9, 1908; and *Berliner Tageblatt*, *Berliner Mor-gen-Zeitung*, and *Vorwärts* of November 10, 1908.

26. For an example of how those events were reported in Berlin, see "Allerhöchster Trost" and "Wovon man spricht," in *Der Roland von Berlin: Eine Wochen-schrift für das Berliner Leben*, November 12 and 17, 1908. That journal was unrelated to the cabaret of the same name.

27. Walter Rathenau, "Die schönste Stadt der Welt," in *Zukunft*, January 7, 1899, 38.

28. Claire Waldoff, *Weeste noch...! Aus meinen Erinnerungen* (Düsseldorf: 1953), 25–26. For details on her life, see that autobiography, as well as Helga Bem-mann, *Wer schmeisst denn da mit Lehm? Eine Claire-Waldoff-Biographie* (Berlin: 1982).

29. Luc Gersal, *Spree-Athen: Berliner Skizzen von einem Böotier* (Leipzig: 1892), 85; Trust, "Passagetheater," in *Sturm*, December 1911, 720; and Tucholsky, "Berliner Cabarets" and "Cabaret," in *Gesammelte Werke*, 1: 88, 125.

30. "Hermann heesst er!" (lyrics and music by Ludwig Mendelssohn), in Helga

Bemmann, ed., *Die Lieder der Claire Waldoff* (Berlin: 1983), 23. Waldoff made recordings of this song in the 1920s, and they are reissued frequently to this day. For a description of her performance of this song, see Tucholsky, "Cabaret," 124–125. He noted her ability to get around the censor in "Berliner Cabarets," 89.

31. Waldoff, *Weeste noch ...!*, 48; and Tucholsky, "Berolina ... Claire Waldoff," in *Die Weltbühne*, August 27, 1929.

32. *Vossische Zeitung*, October 10, 1901. For the history of operetta in Berlin, see two works by Otto Schneidereit: *Berlin wie es weint und lacht: Spaziergänge durch Berlins Operettengeschichte* (Berlin: 1976); and *Paul Lincke und die Entstehung der Berliner Operette* (Berlin: 1974). For a survey of musical theater in Berlin at the end of the nineteenth century, see Ingrid Heinrich-Jost, *Auf ins Metropol: Specialitäten- und Unterhaltungstheater im ausgehenden 19. Jahrhundert* (Berlin: 1984).

33. The origins and history of the Metropoltheater are recounted in Walter Freund, "Aus der Frühzeit des Berliner Metropoltheaters," in *Kleine Schriften der Gesellschaft für Theatergeschichte*, no. 19 (Berlin: 1962), 45–66.

34. For the complete script, see Julius Freund, *"Neuestes!! Allerneuestes!!!"* (Berlin: 1904).

35. *Vossische Zeitung* and *Berliner Tageblatt*, both of January 7, 1903.

36. For relations with the police, see Walter Freund, "Aus der Frühzeit des Berliner Metropoltheaters," 62–63.

37. For the fate of "Annemarie," see ibid., 54–56.

38. Arthur Eloesser, "Gedanken in einem Grillroom" (1912), in *Die Strasse meiner Jugend: Berliner Skizzen* (Berlin: 1987), 78.

39. Ibid., 77–79.

40. Georg Simmel, "Fashion" (1904), in *Georg Simmel: On Individuality and Social Forms*, ed. Donald Levine (Chicago: 1971), 298–299.

41. Dora Duncker, "Das Metropoltheater und die Berliner Revue," in *Bühne und Welt*, 10/1 (1907–08): 49–50.

42. The description of the silken legs comes from a "contemporary account" quoted, but not identified, in Scheidereit, *Berlin wie es weint und lacht*, 122. The actual condition of seamstresses in Berlin is described in Robyn Dasey, "Women's Work and the Family: Women Garment Workers in Berlin and Hamburg Before the First World War," in Richard Evans and W. R. Lee, eds., *The German Family: Essays on the Social History of the Family in Nineteenth- and Twentieth-Century Germany* (London: 1981), 221–255.

43. On prostitution at the Metropol, see Schneidereit, *Berlin wie es weint und lacht*, 128–129.

44. Julius Freund, *Chauffeur—in's Metropol!* (Berlin: 1912), act 2, numbers 8 and 9.

## 5. Political Satire in the Early Weimar Republic

1. Max Herrmann-Neisse, "Mein Weihnachtswunsch fürs Kabarett," in *Neue Schaubühne* 3 (1921): 169.

2. "Der Wintergarten im Kriege," in *Berliner Börsen-Courier,* November 4, 1914; and reprint of article from the *Königsberger Anzeiger,* in *Organ der Variétéwelt,* November 20, 1915.

3. *Berliner Börsen-Courier,* December 9, 1914.

4. Fritz Friedmann-Frederich, "25 Jahre Metropol-Theater," in *Jahrbuch der Berliner Bühnen 1925/26.*

5. Otto Reutter, *Berlin im Krieg,* act 1, 26 (1917; typescript in Landesarchiv Berlin); Reutter, *1914,* act 3, 15–18 (1914; typescript in Landesarchiv Berlin).

6. Walter Kollo et al., *Extrablätter: Heitere Bilder aus ernster Zeit* (Munich: 1914), 15.

7. "Ein Sieg der Willenskraft. Die Füsse als Ersatz der Hände," in *Weltspiegel,* May 30, 1915.

8. Police reports of February 9 and 12, and April 19, 1915, in BLHA, Th 2693, ff. 116, 121, 129.

9. Police reports of January 14, February 5, 9, 12, and April 19, 1915, in BLHA, Th 2693, ff. 107–108, 116–117, 121–122, 132, 135.

10. Police reports of January 14, April 19, and April (undated) 1915, in BLHA, Th 2693, ff. 107–108, 133, and 127.

11. For the Jewish woman's protests, see the anonymous letter of January 15, and police report of January 29, 1915, in BLHA, Th 1514, ff. 1–3.

12. Article reprinted in the *Neue Preussische Zeitung,* September 6, 1916.

13. Police reports of September 9 and 27, 1916, in BLHA, Th 2693, ff. 182, 191r.

14. Letters to the police of September 19, 12, and 23, 1916, in BLHA, Th 2693, ff. 196/204, 194, and 185.

15. See the reports in *Vossische Zeitung* and *Berliner Börsen-Courier,* March 30, 1921, and *Berliner Morgenpost,* March 31, 1921.

16. Max Herrmann-Neisse, "Mein Weihnachtswunsch fürs Kabarett," in *Die neue Schaubühne,* December 1921, 171; and review in *Kritiker,* 4 (1922): 7.

17. Dr. Allos, " 'Gemachte' Kabarett-Literatur," in *Das Kabarett Jahrbuch 1921,* 24; and Kurt Tucholsky, "Vom Radauhumoristen" (1922), in *Werke,* 3: 171–172.

18. Fritz Grünbaum, "Kabarett und Politik," in *Das Kabarett Jahrbuch 1922,* 34; Max Herrmann-Neisse, in *Kritiker,* 4 (1922): 7; and Kurt Tucholsky, "Schlager" (1924), in *Gedichte,* ed. Mary Gerold-Tucholsky (Reinbek: 1983), 419–420.

19. Ernst Troeltsch, *Spectator-Briefe: Aufsätze über die deutsche Revolution und die Weltpolitik 1918–1922* (Tübingen: 1924), 15.

20. Otto Reutter, *Geh'n Sie bloss nicht nach Berlin,* act 2, 20–21 (1917; typescript in Landesarchiv Berlin).

21. On Serenissimus, see *Berliner Tageblatt* and *Berliner Börsen-Zeitung,* December 9, 1919. Wangenheim's songs "He! Halloh!" and "Abschied von der Bohème" are reprinted in Friedrich Hollaender, *Schall und Rauch: Lieder und Chansons des gleichnamigen Berliner Kabaretts aus der Zeit nach dem 1. Weltkrieg* (Mainz: 1983), 22–27.

22. There is considerable secondary literature on Tucholsky. On his politics, particularly useful essays may be found in Irmgard Ackermann, ed., *Kurt Tuchol-*

*sky: Sieben Beiträge zu Werk und Wirkung* (Munich: 1981). His political milieu is analyzed in Istvan Deak, *Weimar Germany's Left-Wing Intellectuals: A Political History of the Weltbühne and its Circle* (Berkeley: 1968). His relations to cabaret are the subject of Alan Lareau, "Kurt Tucholsky and German Cabaret: A Documentation," in *Michigan German Studies* 13 (1987): 58–83; and Helga Bemmann, *In mein' Verein bin ich hineingetreten: Kurt Tucholsky als Chanson- und Liederdichter* (Berlin: 1989). Many of Tucholsky's cabaret songs are reprinted, with piano accompaniment, in Mary Gerold-Tucholsky and Hans Georg Heepe, eds., *Das Kurt Tucholsky Chanson Buch: Texte und Noten* (Reinbek: 1983).

23. "Wenn der alte Motor wieder tackt," in Hollaender, *Schall und Rauch*, 10–13.
24. Max Herrmann-Neisse, "Berliner Kabaretts," in *Neue Schaubühne*, March 1922, 73; "Das ist der Herzschlag," in Hollaender, *Schall und Rauch*, 62–65. That song is criticized in Rösler, *Das Chanson im deutschen Kabarett*, 230.
25. Letter of October 21, 1919, in Kurt Tucholsky, *Unser geliebtes Leben: Briefe an Mary* (Reinbek: 1982), 275; *BZ am Mittag, Vorwärts,* and *Freiheit* of December 9, 1919. For Tucholsky's account of his pseudonyms, see Tucholsky, *Mit 5 PS* (Berlin: 1927), 11–15.
26. Tucholsky, "Was darf die Satire?" and "Wir Negativen," in *Werke,* 2: 42–44, 52–57.
27. Ignaz Wrobel, "Politik im Cabaret," *Schall und Rauch,* June 1920, 1; Tucholsky, "Politische Satire" and "Politische Couplets," in *Werke,* 2: 171–172, 93–94.
28. Tucholsky, "Politische Couplets;" letter to Hans Erich Blaich, March 6, 1920, in Tucholsky, *Ausgewählte Briefe, 1913–1935* (Reinbek: 1962), 76. Joachim Ringelnatz, another important performer with Sound and Smoke, also noted that political allusions could lead to protests from the audience: see the letter of September 1920 in Joachim Ringelnatz, *Reisebriefe an M.* (Berlin: 1964), 21–22. For his cabaret performances, see Helga Bemmann, *Daddeldu, ahoi! Leben und Werk des Dichters, Malers und Artisten Joachim Ringelnatz* (Berlin: 1980), 105–156.
29. Kurt Tucholsky, "Auf dem Nachttisch," in *Gesammelte Werke,* 7: 102; and "Immer um die Litfasssäule rum," in Hollaender, *Schall und Rauch,* 32–35. Texts and music of the other songs mentioned are reprinted in that volume.
30. Report on the new management in *Berliner Börsen-Courier,* March 2, 1921; Max Herrmann-Neisse in *Kritiker* 4 (1922): 25, and *Neue Schaubühne,* March 1922, 70.
31. For texts of these songs, and Ebinger's commentary, see Blandine Ebinger, *"Blandine ..."* (Zurich: 1985), 71–77.
32. "Die Rote Melodie," in *Tucholsky Chanson Buch,* 263–267.
33. Rudolf Nelson/Willi Prager, "Berlin, ich kenne dich nicht wieder!," sheet music (Berlin: 1919); police report of October 20, 1920, BLHA, Th 2693, f. 227. For a passing comment on the bad location of Sound and Smoke, see *Kritiker* 3 (1921), 1. Maiheft, 16.
34. Police report of October 25, 1920, BLHA, Th 2693, ff. 237–238. For reviews

of the premiere, see *Berliner Börsen-Zeitung* and *Berliner Tageblatt* of October 15, 1920, as well as the *BZ am Mittag* of October 16.

35. Rudolf Nelson/Theobald Tiger, "Unterm Stadtbahnbogen," sheet music (Berlin: 1920).

36. Fritz Walter, review of Hollaender's *Jetzt kommt jeder dran,* in *Berliner Börsen-Courier,* August 12, 1928.

37. "Nelsontheater," in *Tagebuch* 3 (1922): 1552; Rudolf Nelson/Theobald Tiger, "Raffke," sheet music (Berlin: 1922); *Vossische Zeitung,* October 13, 1922; *Berliner Börsen-Zeitung,* October 11, 1922.

38. "Mir ist heut so nach Tamerlan," in *Tucholsky Chanson Buch,* 218–224.

39. "Kleine Geschichte des deutschen Kabaretts" (1924), in Max Herrmann-Neisse, *Kabarett: Schriften zum Kabarett und zur bildenden Kunst* (Frankfurt am Main: 1988), 57–58; letter of September 1, 1922, in Tucholsky, *Ausgewählte Briefe,* 95; cf. letter of March 1923, ibid., 457–458; "Requiem" (1923), in Tucholsky, *Werke,* 3: 332.

40. Walter Mehring, *Einfach klassisch! Eine Orestie mit glücklichem Ausgang* (Berlin: 1919), 5, 6, 8, 21.

41. Mehring, *Einfach klassisch!,* 19–20.

42. Georg Grosz and Wieland Herzfelde, "Die Kunst ist in Gefahr: Ein Orientierungsversuch" (1925), in Wieland Herzfelde, *Zur Sache* (Berlin: 1976), 118; Raoul Hausmann, "Pamphlet gegen die Weimarische Lebensauffassung" (1919), reprinted in Karl Riha, ed., *Dada Berlin: Texte, Manifeste, Aktionen* (Stuttgart: 1977), 50. For Herzfelde's experiences in captivity, see "Schutzhaft: Erlebnisse vom 7. bis 20. März bei den Berliner Ordnungstruppen" (1919), in *Zur Sache,* 31–50. For discussions of Dada politics, see J. C. Middleton, "'Bolshevism in Art': Dada and Politics," *Texas Studies in Literature and Language* 4 (1962–63): 408–430; and Richard Sheppard, "Dada and Politics," *Journal of European Studies* 9 (1979): 39–74.

43. Baader quoted in Walter Mehring, *Berlin Dada: Eine Chronik* (Zurich: 1959), 53; Herzfelde, "George Grosz, John Heartfield, Erwin Piscator, Dada und die Folgen oder Die Macht der Freundschaft," in *Zur Sache,* 447–448; *Vorwärts,* December 9, 1919.

44. Wangenheim, "Abschied von der Boheme," 24–25; *Rote Fahne,* July 25, 1920.

45. For Mehring's life, see the biography and critical analysis by Frank Hellberg, *Walter Mehring: Schriftsteller zwischen Kabarett und Avantgarde* (Bonn: 1983).

46. "Das kesse Lied," in Walter Mehring, *Das Politische Cabaret: Chansons Songs Couplets* (Dresden: 1920), 40–42.

47. "Achtung Gleisdreieck!" in Walter Mehring, *Das Ketzerbrevier: Ein Kabarettprogramm* (Munich: 1921), 19–20.

48. "Couplet en Voltige der Contorsionistin Ellen T," in Mehring, *Das Politische Cabaret,* 88–91.

49. "Heimat Berlin," in Mehring, *Ketzerbrevier,* 28–30; *Berliner Tageblatt,* October 2, 1920; *Berliner Börsen-Zeitung,* October 3, 1920; Kurt Tucholsky, "Auf dem Nachttisch" (1929), in *Werke,* 7: 102. At the time of the first performance,

"Heimat Berlin" was known (like the trio as a whole) as "Berliner Tempo"; the published version specified the title as "Heimat Berlin."

50. Friedrich Hollaender, "Das neue Chanson," *Schall und Rauch*, 2/2 (October 1920), 16; Tucholsky, "Das neue Lied" (1920), in *Werke*, 2: 447, 449.

51. "Berlin simultan," in Mehring, *Das Politische Cabaret*, 44–46.

52. See the autobiography, Trude Hesterberg, *Was ich noch sagen wollte ...* (Berlin: 1971), for accounts of Bendow (93–96), Lion (115–117), Kästner (98), and Brecht (106–109). For an example of Bendow's comments as the "Tattooed Lady," see Wilhelm Bendow and Marcellus Schiffer, *Der kleine Bendow ist vom Himmel gefallen* (Berlin: 1925), 80–85.

53. "Das Börsenlied," in Walter Mehring, *Wedding-Montmerte* (Berlin: 1922), 22–25; Herrmann-Neisse in *Kritiker* 4 (1922), 1. Märzheft, 10; "Dressur" and "Der Rattenfänger von Hameln," in Walter Mehring, *Europäische Nächte* (Berlin: 1924), 10–13, 42–46.

54. Karl Wilczynski in *Berliner Börsen-Zeitung*, October 24, 1920; Alfred Richard Meyer in *National-Zeitung*, October 3, 1920; and Herrmann-Neisse in *Neue Schaubühne*, March 1922, 68.

55. Herrmann-Neisse in *Kritiker* 6 (1924), September–October, 17; and *Berliner Tageblatt*, October 10, 1925.

## 6. The Weimar Revue

1. Harry de Rheidt [Alfred Seweloh], "Von Celly de Rheidt und ihren Schönheits-tänzen," in program booklet, December 1919, BLHA, Th 1505, f. 13.

2. Felix Langer, "Nackttanz," *Berliner Tageblatt*, March 29, 1920; police reports of December 15, 1919, and August 24, 1920, in BLHA, Th 1505, ff. 14, 115. On advertisements for the ensemble, see also Stefan Grossmann, "Celly de Rheidt," *Tagebuch* 1 (1920): 590.

3. Max Herrmann-Neisse, "Berliner Kabarett," *Neue Schaubühne*, March 1922, 69; Grossmann, "Celly," 591–592.

4. Grossmann, "Celly," 591–592; Seweloh's comment reported by Prof. Dr. Brunner, March 31, 1920, in BLHA, Th 1505, f. 42.

5. Nelson to police, August 21, 1921, in BLHA, Th 1505, f. 181; and summary of judgment, Schöffengericht Berlin-Schöneberg, November 5, 1921, BLHA Th 3316. On the hesitation to take the Sewelohs to court, see Generalstaats-anwalt, Ermittlungsverfahren, August 24, 1920, in BLHA, Th 1505, f. 115.

6. "Schönheitsabende in Berlin," *Volkswart*, May 1920; report of March 16, 1922, in BLHA, Th 1508, f. 3.

7. For Hoppe's assertions, see *Berliner Tageblatt*, January 18, 1922; the trial was described in detail in that paper from January 10 to 22.

8. For the director's comments, see *Berliner Tageblatt*, January 15 and 18, 1922; and the judges' ruling on the case, March 17, 1922, in BLHA, Th 1506, f. 12r.

9. BLHA, Th 1506, ff. 9, 10r.

10. BLHA, Th 1506, ff. 14r-15.

11. On the confiscation of postcards, see Ludwig Leiss, *Kunst im Konflikt: Kunst*

*und Künstler im Widerstreit mit der Obrigkeit* (Berlin: 1971), 247–267; Gary Stark, "Pornography, Society, and the Law in Imperial Germany," *Central European History* 14 (1981): 224–225; and Jelavich, *Munich and Theatrical Modernism*, 82–83.

12. BLHA, Th 1506, f. 14r.

13. BLHA, Th 1506, f. 17.

14. Restrictions on Celly's troupe noted in letter of February 8, 1922, in BLHA, Th 1507, ff. 27–28; Hermann-Neisse in *Kritiker,* April 1922, 7; Lola Bach Ballet reported on February 13, 1922, in BLHA, Th 1507, f. 31; and Seweloh conflict reported in *BZ am Mittag*, September 9, 1923, and *Berliner Zeitung,* October 15, 1923.

15. For Severing's statement, see *Deutsche Bühne* 15 (1923): 28–29.

16. Polizei-Präsident Berlin to Polizeipräsidium Dresden, November 4, 1924, in BLHA, Th 1504, f. 102.

17. Report of August 9, 1926, in BLHA, Th 1504, f. 168; report of May 16, 1921, in Th 1507, f. 1. For examples of Herrmann-Neisse's views on Anita Berber, see *Kritiker,* July–August 1924, 14, and May 1925, 57. For a biography of Berber, see Lothar Fischer, *Tanz zwischen Rausch und Tod: Anita Berber, 1918–1928 in Berlin* (Berlin: 1984).

18. Mehring, *Ketzerbrevier,* 95.

19. For a general history of the Weimar revues, see the informative and well-illustrated volume by Wolfgang Jansen, *Glanzrevuen der Zwanziger Jahre* (Berlin: 1987). A shorter comparative account is provided by Franz-Peter Kothes, *Die theatralische Revue in Berlin und Wien 1900–1938:. Typen, Inhalte, Funktionen* (Wilhelmshaven: 1977). A general history of "Girls" in revue and film, with emphasis on the American and English dimension, may be found in Reinhard Klooss and Thomas Reuter, *Körperbilder: Menschenornamente in Revuetheater und Revuefilm* (Frankfurt am Main: 1980).

20. "Wenn der alte Motor wieder tackt," in Hollaender, *Schall und Rauch,* 10–13.

21. Walter Kollo/Herman Haller, Rideamus, Willi Wolff, "Linden-Marsch," in *Drunter und Drüber: Textbuch der Gesänge* (Berlin: 1923), 8–9.

22. "Rekord der Revue: Neun Berliner Theater wollen Revue spielen!" in *Berliner Tageblatt,* July 7, 1926; Ernst Bloch, "Berlin, Funktionen im Hohlraum," 212, and "Revueform in der Philosophie" (1928), 368–369, both reprinted in Bloch, *Erbschaft dieser Zeit* (Frankfurt am Main: 1962); Siegfried Kracauer, "Kult der Zerstreuung" (1926), in *Das Ornament der Masse: Essays* (Frankfurt am Main: 1977), 314–315.

23. Maximilian Sladek, "Unsere Schau," in program book, *An Alle ...! Die grosse Schau im Grossen Schauspielhaus,* reproduced in Jansen, *Glanzrevuen,* 146; and Jacobs' review of *An Alle* in *Vossische Zeitung,* October 23, 1924.

24. Frank Warschauer, "Berliner Revuen," *Weltbühne* 20 (1924): 920–921.

25. Theodor Lücke, "Gedanken der Revue," in *Scene* 16 (1926): 114. American popular music in Weimar Germany is discussed in Michael Kater, "The Jazz Experience in Weimar Germany," *German History* 6 (1988): 145–158; and two essays in Sabine Schutte, ed., *Ich will aber gerade vom Leben singen: Über populäre Musik vom ausgehenden 19. Jahrhundert bis zum Ende der Weimarer*

*Republik* (Reinbek: 1987): Fred Ritzel, "'Hätte der Kaiser Jazz getanzt ...':
US-Tanzmusik in Deutschland vor und nach dem Ersten Weltkrieg," 265–293,
and Ulrich Kurth, "'Ich pfeif' auf Tugend und Moral': Zum Foxtrott in den
zwanziger Jahren," 365–384.

26. Hans Pfitzner, "Die neue Ästhetik der musikalischen Impotenz," in *Gesam-melte Schriften* (Augsburg: 1926), 2: 115–116; Hans Siemsen, "Jazz-Band,"
*Weltbühne* 17 (1921): 288.

27. *Berliner Tageblatt,* January 4, 1926; and Oskar Bie in *Berliner Börsen-Courier,*
May 26, 1925, and January 4, 1926. For examples of Dadaist use of black
imagery, see Walter Mehring, "If the man in the moon were a coon," in
*Europäische Nächte,* 73–76; and George Grosz, "Gesang an die Welt," in
Wieland Herzfelde and Hans Marquardt, eds., *Pass auf! Hier kommt Grosz:
Bilder, Rhythmen und Gesänge, 1915–1918* (Leipzig: 1981), 16–18, as well as
other verses in that volume. For discussions of the image of blacks in Germany,
see the essays in Reinhold Grimm and Jost Hermand, eds., *Blacks and German
Culture* (Madison: 1986).

28. Hildenbrandt in *Berliner Tageblatt,* May 26, 1925; Harry Graf Kessler, *Tage-bücher 1918–1937* (Frankfurt am Main: 1961), 458.

29. Josephine Baker, *Memoiren* (Munich: 1928), 110–111.

30. Iwan Goll, "Die Neger erobern Europa," *Die literarische Welt,* January 15,
1926, 3. On Douglas, see *Berliner Börsen-Courier,* January 4, 1926.

31. For examples of wartime hostility to French colonial troops, see the covers of
*Berliner Illustrirte Zeitung,* April 8 and July 22, 1917. On "die schwarze
Schmach," see Keith Nelson, "'The Black Horror on the Rhine': Race as a
Factor in Post–World War I Diplomacy," *Journal of Modern History* 42
(1970): 606–627; Sally Marks, "Black Watch on the Rhine: Propaganda,
Prejudice and Prurience," *European Studies Review* 13 (1983): 297–334; and
Gisela Lebzelter, "Die 'Schwarze Schmach': Vorurteile—Propaganda—My-thos," *Geschichte und Gesellschaft* 11 (1985): 37–58.

32. On the Lola Bach ballet, see police report of 23 February 1922, in BLHA, Th
1507, f. 47; on Erna Offeney's troupe, see *Freiheit, Morgenpost,* and *Deutsche
Allgemeine Zeitung,* all of March 7, 1922.

33. On the origin of the Tiller Girls, see Derek and Julia Parker, *The Natural
History of the Chorus Girl* (Indianapolis: 1975), 102–106; and "Tiller und
Tillergirls," Wintergarten program book, January 1930, 10–14.

34. Ihering in *Berliner Börsen-Courier,* August 28, 1924.

35. For an indirect attack on Klein's revues by a spokesman for Charell, see Stefan
Grossmann, "Inszenierung der Nacktheit," in *Für Dich! Revue-Magazin
Charellrevue 1925–1926.*

36. Fritz Giese, *Girlkultur: Vergleiche zwischen amerikanischem und europä-ischem Rhythmus und Lebensgefühl* (Munich: 1925), 122; Theodor Lücke,
"Gedanken der Revue," 114; Adam Kuckhoff, "Grösse und Niedergang der
Revue," *Die Volksbühne,* April 1928, 4; Siegfried Kracauer, "Das Ornament
der Masse" (1927), in *Das Ornament der Masse,* 52; Joseph Roth, "Die Girls,"
*Tagebuch* 11 (1930): 549.

37. Alfred Polgar, "Girls" (1926), in *Auswahl: Prosa aus vier Jahrzenten* (Reinbek:

1968), 187; Hildenbrandt, review of *Für Dich*, in *Berliner Tageblatt*, September 2, 1925.

38. Paul Morgan, "Kleine Tragödie," *Querschnitt* 8 (1928): 655.
39. See Giese, *Girlkultur*, passim; and compare with the accounts of Weimar Germany's white-collar women in Ute Frevert, *Women in German History: From Bourgeois Emancipation to Sexual Liberation* (New York: 1989), 176–185; and Atina Grossmann, "*Girlkultur* or Thoroughly Rationalized Female: A New Woman in Weimar Germany?" in Judith Friedlander et al., eds., *Women in Culture and Politics: A Century of Change* (Bloomington: 1986), 62–80. The Girl image in the workplace, the media, and on stage is discussed in Günter Berghaus, "*Girlkultur*—Feminism, Americanism, and Popular Entertainment in Weimar Germany," *Journal of Design History* 1 (1988): 193–219.
40. For examples of questionable interviews, see Berghaus, "*Girlkultur*," 203–204. It is interesting to note that the myth of the Tiller Girls' marriages to rich men was parodied in a program book of the Haller revue; see E. Breitner, "Das Tiller-Girl und die Liebe," in program book, *Wann und Wo* (1927), 26.
41. Polgar, "Girls," 186; Walter Benjamin and Bernhard Reich, "Revue oder Theater," *Querschnitt* 5 (1925): 1043; Oscar Bie in *Berliner Börsen-Courier*, September 3, 1927; Kracauer, "Das Ornament der Masse," 52.
42. Siegfried Kracauer, "Girls und Krise," *Frankfurter Zeitung*, May 26, 1931. The machine imagery appeared in *Vossische Zeitung*, August 19, 1926; Giese, *Girlkultur*, 15, 111; and *Vossische Zeitung*, March 19, 1927.
43. For representative essays on "Americanism," see the selections in Anton Kaes, ed., *Weimarer Republik: Manifeste und Dokumente zur deutschen Literatur 1918–1933* (Stuttgart: 1983), 265–286. The impact of Taylorism and Fordism on European thought in the interwar period is the subject of Charles Maier, "Between Taylorism and Technocracy: European ideologies and the vision of industrial productivity in the 1920s," *Journal of Contemporary History* 5/2 (1970): 27–61. See also Thomas Hughes, *American Genesis: A Century of Invention and Technological Enthusiasm, 1870–1970* (New York: 1989), 284–294.
44. Polgar, "Girls," 186–187; Paul Lindau, "Von der Amerikanisierung Europas," *Westermanns Monatshefte*, January 1927, 566–567.
45. Kracauer, "Das Ornament der Masse," 53, 54; Erich Kästner, "Chor der Girls," in *Lärm im Spiegel* (Leipzig: 1929), 84. The line makes a pun on the words *Bein* (leg) and *Einerlei* (uniformity, monotony).
46. *Hannah Höch, 1889–1978* (Berlin: Berlinische Galerie, 1989), 215. For designs for the antirevue, see 174–175.
47. Hildenbrandt, "Tanzabend Valeska Gert," *Berliner Tageblatt*, October 27, 1927; review in *Kritiker*, November 1926, 169; Herrmann-Neisse, "Endlich eine Revueparodie," *Kritiker*, April 1926, 61; review in *Die literarische Welt*, March 5, 1926, 3. See also Valeska Gert, *Mein Weg* (Leipzig: 1930); Fred Hildenbrandt, *Die Tänzerin Valeska Gert* (Stuttgart: 1928); and Frank-Manuel Peter, *Valeska Gert: Tänzerin, Schauspielerin, Kabarettistin* (Berlin: 1985). Gert appeared in many important films of the Weimar era; she was the pro-

curess Frau Greifer in Pabst's *Joyless Street* (1925) and Mrs. Peachum in his version of *The Threepenny Opera* (1931). Late in her life she appeared in Fellini's *Juliet of the Spirits* (1965).

## 7. Political Cabaret at the End of the Republic

1. On *Die Welt ohne Schleier,* see *Berliner Lokal-Anzeiger* and *Berliner Börsen-Courier,* October 10, 1923. Work was praised in *Der Herr der Welt,* 1921; *Europa spricht davon,* 1922; and *Streng verboten!,* 1927: see *Berliner Tageblatt,* October 5, 1921, and September 19, 1922; and *Vossische Zeitung,* March 17, 1927.
2. Walter von Hollander, "Erziehung durch Revue," *Die Premiere,* March 1925, 11; Ihering in *Berliner Börsen-Courier,* August 19, 1926; Monty Jacobs in *Vossische Zeitung,* August 20, 1925; "Dann ist es wieder richtig," in Walter Kollo/Herman Haller, Rideamus, Willi Wolff, *Achtung! Welle 505! Textbuch der Gesänge* (Berlin: 1925), 15. Berlin's radio station transmitted on the 505 wavelength.
3. Jacobs in *Vossische Zeitung,* October 23, 1924, and September 2, 1926. See also Friedrich Hollaender, "Raus mit den Männern!" sheet music (Berlin: 1926).
4. Jacobs in *Vossische Zeitung,* September 2, 1926; *Berliner Tageblatt* and *Berliner Lokal-Anzeiger,* both of September 8, 1923; "Linden-Marsch," in Kollo et al., *Drunter und Drüber: Textbuch der Gesänge,* 9.
5. *Berliner Tageblatt,* October 1, 1924; Oscar Bie, "Musik und Tanz in der Revue," program for *Achtung! Welle 505!,* Haller-Revue 1925–26, 32.
6. *Vossische Zeitung,* September 13, 1926.
7. Max Herrmann-Neisse, "Endlich eine Revueparodie," in *Kritiker,* April 1926, 60–61. See also the reviews in *Berliner Börsen-Courier* and *Vossische Zeitung,* February 20, 1926. Hollaender's life is recounted in his not always credible autobiography, *Von Kopf bis Fuss: Mein Leben mit Text und Musik* (Munich: 1965); see also Volker Kühn, *Spötterdämmerung: Vom langen Sterben des grossen kleinen Friedrich Hollaender* (Frankfurt am Main: 1988).
8. Ihering in *Berliner Börsen-Courier,* April 8, 1927.
9. For the text, see Mischa Spoliansky/Kurt Robitschek and Marcellus Schiffer, *Rufen Sie Herrn Plim!* (Berlin: 1932).
10. Herrmann-Neisse, "Kabarett," *Kritiker,* March 1925, 44. Both songs are printed in Mischa Spoliansky/Marcellus Schiffer, *Es liegt in der Luft: 5 Haupt-Schlager* (Berlin: 1928), 2–3, 8–9.
11. "Ich weiss, das ist nicht so," in Spoliansky/Schiffer, *Es liegt in der Luft,* 10–11; Hollaender, "Vielleicht, kann sein, vielleicht auch nicht!" in *Querschnitt* 7 (1927): 140–142.
12. *Berliner Tageblatt,* May 16, 1928.
13. *Berliner Tageblatt,* July 22, 1927.
14. Ibid.; Lutz Weltmann in *Weltbühne,* 23/2 (1927): 154; Arthur Eloesser, "Revue," ibid., 24/1 (1928): 28.
15. Friedrich Hollaender, "Der Potsdamer Edelfasan, oder Die letzte Haarnadel,"

and "Die Trommlerin: Eine Schiessbudenfigur," lyrics reprinted in Volker Kühn, ed., *Hoppla, wir beben: Kabarett einer gewissen Republik 1918–1933* (Weinheim: 1988), 194–195, 297–298. The comments of Kraus appear in *Fackel*, 31, nos. 827–833, February 1930, 89.

16. Ad from *BZ am Mittag*, June 1, 1926. For accounts of the venture, see Heinz Pol, "Die Namenlosen: Bajazzi des Podiums," *Vossische Zeitung*, July 27, 1926; Bernhard von Brentano, "Kabarett der Namenlosen," in *Wo in Europa ist Berlin?*, 153–158; and the articles in the following note. The "Sammlung Elow" of the Akademie der Künste in West Berlin has a large collection of clippings on the venture. In the 1980s American television had a similar "attraction"—"The Gong Show."

17. Manfred Georg, "Trauerspiel der Eitelkeit: Menschenzoo im Kabarett," *Neues Wiener Journal*, February 27, 1927; Bernhard Zebrowski, "Berliner Talent-Arena," *Welt am Montag*, March 28, 1927; Erich Kästner, "Kabarett der Namenlosen," *Magdeburger General-Anzeiger*, April 7, 1929; and Kästner, *Fabian: Die Geschichte eines Moralisten* (1931), chapter 7.

18. For examples of Herrmann-Neisse's positive reviews, see *Kritiker*, March 1925, 44–45, and May 1925, 57–58; and *Berliner Tageblatt*, September 14, 1926, and October 20, 1927.

19. For a description of the Mendelsohn theater, see *Berliner Tageblatt*, September 21, 1928.

20. Kurt Robitschek, "Schrei nach Hilfe," *Frechheit*, April 1926, 2; Robitschek, "5 Jahre Kabarett der Komiker," ibid., December 1929, 6.

21. Robitschek, "5 Jahre Kabarett der Komiker," 5; and Robitschek, "Zeitungs-parodie," *Frechheit*, September 1929, 3–6. Paul Morgan made a recording of the newspaper parody in 1930.

22. Paul Morgan, "Wie wir uns die Kritiken gedacht haben," *Frechheit*, January 1926, 11–12.

23. Kurt Robitschek and Paul Morgan, eds., *Die einsame Träne: Das Buch der guten Witze* (Berlin: 1924), 7; and accounts of protests in *Berliner Börsen-Courier*, *Berliner Tageblatt*, and *Vossische Zeitung*, April 23, 1926. For other examples of the Central Association's protests, see Donald Niewyk, *The Jews in Weimar Germany* (Baton Rouge: 1980), 89.

24. *Tägliche Rundschau*, April 24, 1926; Harry Kessler, *Tagebücher*, 646–647. For the anti-Remarque demonstrations, see Martin Broszat, *Hitler and the Collapse of Weimar Germany* (Leamington Spa: 1987), 32–36; and Bärbel Schrader and Jürgen Schebera, *The "Golden" Twenties: Art and Literature in the Weimar Republic* (New Haven: 1988), 216–222.

25. Joseph Goebbels, "Rund um die Gedächtniskirche (23. Januar 1928)," in *Der Angriff: Aufsätze aus der Kampfzeit*, third edition (Munich: 1936), 338–340. On the events of September 1931, see Annemarie Lange, *Berlin in der Weimarer Republik* (Berlin: 1987), 1015–1017; and Karl-Heinz Metzger and Ulrich Dunker, *Der Kurfürstendamm: Leben und Mythos des Boulevards in 100 Jahren deutscher Geschichte* (Berlin: 1986), 155–156.

26. Robitschek, "Randbemerkungen zum Jahre 1930," *Frechheit*, January 1931, 1–2; "Die Preise fallen!," ibid., March 1931, 2; "Das siebente Jahr," ibid.,

June 1931, 1. For an example of Kracauer's criticism, see *Frankfurter Zeitung,* August 6, 1930; Robitschek's self-defense against another critic appears in *Frechheit,* April 1931, 1. The public discussion is described in *Berlin am Morgen,* September 16, 1930; the political evening in Robitschek, "Geschriebene Conferencen," *Frechheit,* December 1930, 2. The Charlott-Casino's announcement is reported in *Berliner Tageblatt,* February 15, 1930.

27. *Berliner Börsen-Zeitung,* April 12, 1930. On the Wasps, see Wolfgang Schütte, *"Mit Stacheln und Sticheln ...": Beiträge zur Geschichte der Berliner Brettl-Truppe "Die Wespen" (1929–1933)* (Leipzig: 1987).

28. For the text and music to the "Stempellied," see Bemmann, *Berliner Musenkinder-Memoiren,* 208–211. For Busch's appearances at the Catacombs, see Ludwig Hoffmann and Karl Siebig, *Ernst Busch: Eine Biographie in Texten, Bildern und Dokumenten* (Berlin: 1987), 78–93.

29. *Berlin am Morgen,* March 27, 1931; *Berliner Tageblatt,* September 25, 1931. On the Charlott-Casino, see ibid., February 15, 1930; on the division in the Catacombs, see ibid., December 19, 1930, and *Berlin am Morgen,* December 20, 1930.

30. Kästner, *Lärm im Spiegel,* 51. The most complete recent biography, which includes a discussion of his relations to cabaret, is Helga Bemmann, *Humor auf Taille: Erich Kästner, Leben und Werk* (Berlin: 1983). For a more general discussion of "Gebrauchslyrik," see J. J. White, "The Cult of 'Functional Poetry' during the Weimar Period," in Alan Bance, ed., *Weimar Germany: Writers and Politics* (Edinburgh: 1982), 91–109.

31. Kästner, "Ganz besonders feine Damen" and "Eine Mutter zieht Bilanz" in *Lärm im Spiegel,* 10–12, 14–15; "Ankündigung einer Chansonette" and "Und wo bleibt das Positive, Herr Kästner?" in *Ein Mann gibt Auskunft* (1931; reprinted Munich: Knaur, n.d.), 47–48, 94–95.

32. *Berliner Börsen-Zeitung,* August 9, 1929; *Berliner Tageblatt,* August 7, 1929.

33. Friedrich Hollaender, "Der Spuk persönlich" and "An allem sind die Juden schuld!" in *Spuk in der Villa Stern,* piano-vocal selection (Berlin: 1931), 4–7.

34. "Münchhausen," in Hollaender, *Spuk,* 2–3.

35. Kurt Robitschek, "Sieg des Theaters über die Weltgeschichte," *Frechheit,* July 1931, 1.

36. Nazi citation from Gordon Craig, *Germany, 1866–1945* (New York: 1978), 550; Finck cited in *Berliner Tageblatt,* December 6, 1931.

37. *Berliner Tageblatt,* September 19, 1931; Walter Benjamin, "Linke Melancholie," in *Gesammelte Schriften* (Frankfurt am Main: 1972), 3: 280–281.

38. *Die Rote Fahne,* 14 June 1925; italics in the original. On the Dadaists' turn toward the KPD, see Wieland Herzfelde, "George Grosz, John Heartfield, Erwin Piscator, Dada und die Folgen, oder Die Macht der Freundschaft," in *Zur Sache,* 430–467.

39. Erich Weinert, "Politische Satire, Politisches Kabarett," *Kulturwille* 3/8 (1926): 151, 152; Mehring cited in Urs Bader, "Walter Mehring: Eine Biographie des Jahrhunderts," *Basler Zeitung,* April 25, 1981.

40. Erwin Piscator, *Das politische Theater* (Berlin: 1929), 60–61.

41. On the *Revue Roter Rummel*, see Ludwig Hoffmann and Daniel Hoffmann-Ostwald, eds., *Deutsches Arbeitertheater* (Berlin: 1977), 1: 154–166.

42. Nuko, "Unsere Agitproptruppen" (1927), and Robert Leibbrand, *Deutschlands junge Garde* (1959), quoted in Hoffmann and Hoffmann-Ostwald, *Deutsches Arbeitertheater,* 1: 343, 184.

43. Police report in Geheimes Staatsarchiv Preussischer Kulturbesitz [hereafter cited as GStA PK], I. HA, Rep. 219, Nr. 155, ff. 13–14; and "Bericht des Bezirks Berlin-Brandenburg über die Jugendtag-Kampagne," in *Der junge Bolschevik,* 6/2: 10–11.

44. Police report cited in Hoffmann and Hoffmann-Ostwald, *Deutsches Arbeitertheater,* 2: 306.

45. "Des deutschen Spiessers Wunderwelt" reprinted ibid., 1:374–387; the program of the Rotes Sprachrohr can be found in GStA PK, I. HA, Rep. 219, Nr. 69, f. 136; and the "Niggersong" in *Rote Raketen: Textbuch der Berliner Spieltruppe des Roten Frontkämpfer Bundes* (1928), 20–22, in GStA PK, I. HA, Rep. 219, Nr. 68.

46. *Wintersonnwende 1928. Material zur Ausgestaltung von Winter-Sonnwend-veranstaltungen,* ed. ZK der KJVD, Abteilung Agitprop, in GStA PK, I. HA, Rep. 219, Nr. 178, f. 119; and police report of December 20, 1929, in Rep. 219, Nr. 179, f. 390.

47. Tucholsky's song appears in *Wintersonnwende 1928,* f. 122; "Heiliger Antonius, schütze uns ... gegen Gotteslästerung," *Rote Fahne,* April 18, 1930.

48. See police report of April 6, 1927, in GStA PK, I. HA, Rep. 219, Nr. 177, f. 79; and *Rote Fahne,* March 28, 1927.

49. Police reports in GStA PK, I. HA, Rep. 219, Nr. 155, f. 65; and Rep. 219, Nr. 69, f. 89. "Schlaflied" in *Rote Raketen: Textbuch,* 26; "Gigolo-Song" in *Schlager der Roten Raketen,* in Rep. 219, Nr. 68, f. 25.

50. *Das rote Sprachrohr,* June 1929, 10–11.

51. "Bericht des westeuropäischen Büros des IATB über die Lage des Arbeiter Theaters in den kapitalistischen Ländern," in GStA PK, I. HA, Rep. 219, Nr. 73, f. 143.

52. Police report of November 20, 1926, in GStA PK, I. HA, Rep. 219, Nr. 155, f. 345.

53. Police report of April 2, 1931, in GStA PK, I. HA, Rep. 219, Nr. 69, f. 5; *Rote Fahne,* April 29, 1931.

54. Police reports of July 5, 1930 and March 30, 1931, in GStA PK, I. HA, Rep. 219, Nr. 69, ff. 179r, 213; and *Reichsbote,* March 3, 1931.

55. Report of November 5, 1930, in GStA PK, I. HA, Rep. 219, Nr. 69, ff. 184–185.

56. "Bericht des westeuropäischen Büros des IATB," f. 145; flyer in GStA PK, I. HA, Rep. 219, Nr. 69, ff. 56–57.

57. "Unsere Sommer-Agitation" in GStA PK, I. HA, Rep. 219, Nr. 138, f. 102; and Bertolt Brecht, *Kuhle Wampe: Protokoll des Films und Materialien,* ed. Wolfgang Gersch and Werner Hecht (Frankfurt am Main: 1969), 67–76. The film also includes an open-air performance of the Red Megaphone troupe.

58. Freud, *Jokes and their Relation to the Unconscious*, 102.

59. Reports of September 11 and December 2, 1928, in GStA PK, I. HA, Rep. 219, Nr. 69, ff. 75r, 91–93.

60. Hoffmann and Hoffmann-Ostwald, *Deutsches Arbeitertheater*, 1: 341, 310. Italics in original.

61. Ibid., 1: 299; and 2: 70, 283, 132.

62. Ibid., 1: 195, 300.

63. "Bericht des westeuropäischen Büros des IATB," f. 154; and "Resolution" of the Reichstruppenkonferenz des ATDB, April 5, 1931, in GStA PK, I. HA, Rep. 219, Nr. 73, f. 40.

64. Ibid.; "Einführungskurse. Schult euch für den Befreiungskampf des Jungproletariats. Für neue Mitglieder," in GStA PK, I. HA, Rep. 219, Nr. 138, f. 192; and talk by Walter Däumig at agitprop conference in Hamburg, September 16, 1932, as leaked to the police, in Rep. 219, Nr. 69, f. 284.

65. Scene from Roter Rummel in GStA PK, I. HA, Rep. 219, Nr. 68, f. 253.

66. Helmut Damerius, *Über zehn Meere zum Mittelpunkt der Welt: Erinnerungen an die "Kolonne links"* (Berlin: 1977), 148–158. For the struggles between Nazis and Communists, see Eve Rosenhaft, *Beating the Fascists? The German Communists and Political Violence, 1929–1933* (Cambridge: 1983); and Conan Fischer, *The German Communists and the Rise of Nazism* (London: 1991).

67. Georg Pijet, "Wenn die Firma verkrachte ...," *Das rote Sprachrohr*, August–September 1930, 17–18.

## 8. Cabaret under National Socialism

1. Elke Fröhlich, ed., *Die Tagebücher von Joseph Goebbels: Sämtliche Fragmente* [hereafter cited as *Goebbels-Tagebücher*] (Munich: 1987), 1: 490 (entry of January 26, 1930).

2. The incantations are cited in Friedemann Berger et al., eds., *In jenen Tagen: Schriftsteller zwischen Reichstagsbrand und Bücherverbrennung: Eine Dokumentation* (Leipzig: 1983), 285–286.

3. For obituaries of Simmel and Nikolaus, see the *Berliner Tageblatt*, March 23 and 31, 1933. Nikolaus' letter is quoted in Volker Kühn, ed., *Deutschlands erwachen: Kabarett unterm Hakenkreuz 1933–1945* (Weinheim: 1989), 335.

4. Elow recounts his experiences in 1933 and 1934 in his memoirs, "Von der Jägerstrasse zum Kurfürstendamm," reprinted in Frauke Deissner-Jenssen, ed., *Die zehnte Muse: Kabarettisten erzählen* (Berlin: 1986), 266–269. A typescript with excerpts from numerous positive reviews between October 1933 and April 1934 is located in the "Sammlung Elow" of the Akademie der Künste, West Berlin.

5. Präsident der Reichsschriftumskammer, letter of February 19, 1935, in "Sammlung Elow." For the organization of the Reich Chamber of Culture, and especially the subchamber for theater, see Jutta Wardetzsky, *Theaterpolitik im faschistischen Deutschland: Studien und Dokumente* (Berlin: 1983), 25–42; Boguslaw Drewniak, *Das Theater im NS-Staat: Szenarium deutscher Zeit-*

geschichte 1933–1945 (Düsseldorf: 1983), 13–22; Volker Dahm, "Anfänge und Ideologie der Reichskulturkammer," *Vierteljahreshefte für Zeitgeschichte* 34 (1986): 53–84; and Alan Steinweis, "The Professional, Social, and Economic Dimensions of Nazi Cultural Policy: The Case of the Reich Theater Chamber," *German Studies Review* 13 (1990): 441–459.

6. *Jüdische Rundschau*, quoted in Volker Dahm, "Kulturelles und geistiges Leben," in Wolfgang Benz, ed., *Die Juden in Deutschland, 1933–1945: Leben unter nationalsozialistischer Herrschaft* (Munich: 1988), 174, 187. Elow's opening number is reprinted in Kühn, *Deutschlands Erwachen*, 174–176. On the theaters of the Culture League of German Jews, see Dahm, 125–194; and Herbert Freeden, *Jüdisches Theater in Nazideutschland* (Tübingen: 1964).

7. Hesterberg to Hinkel, letter of May 14, 1933, in Berlin Document Center, Reichskulturkammer (hereafter cited as BDC/RKK), Hesterberg file. The text of Oscar Straus's *Eine Frau, die weiss, was sie will*, by Alfred Grünwald, later was attacked explicitly in one of the Nazis' major anti-Semitic books: see Institut zum Studium der Judenfrage, *Die Juden in Deutschland* (1935; reprinted Munich: 1939), 334–335.

8. Charlotte Jungmann to Hinkel, July 16, 1933; and Hinkel to Else Ehser, September 30, 1933, in BDC/RKK, Hesterberg file.

9. Hesterberg to Hinkel, October 7, 1933, BDC/RKK, Hesterberg file.

10. Program booklet for "Die Musenschaukel," dated December 2, 1933, in Akademie der Künste, West Berlin, Theatersammlung.

11. For the appearance of the Hesterberg ensemble at the Kadeko, see *Berliner Herold*, March 11, 1934.

12. For the opening nights of the Impossible cabaret and the Catacombs, see Werner Finck, *Alter Narr, was nun? Die Geschichte meiner Zeit* (Munich: 1972), 37–38, 53. The dismissal of the Jews is mentioned in the letter of the Catacombs' lawyer, Eberhard Nitschke, to the Geheimes Staatspolizeiamt, May 12, 1935, reprinted in Helmut Heiber, *Die Katakombe wird geschlossen* (Munich: 1966), 46. That volume reprints much of the Gestapo documentation, located in the Bundesarchiv Koblenz, concerning the closing of the Catacombs and the Tingel-Tangel.

13. *Berliner Tageblatt*, March 14, 1933; *Völkischer Beobachter*, March 29, 1935; *12 Uhr Blatt*, April 2, 1935; and *Germania*, March 30, 1935.

14. See the documents in Heiber, *Katakombe*, 14.

15. For Gestapo and propaganda ministry reports on these and other numbers, see Heiber, *Katakombe*, 16–30. For Finck's recreation of the tailor scene, which differs somewhat from the police reports, see Finck, *Alter Narr, was nun?*, 66–67.

16. See the reports reprinted in Heiber, *Katakombe*, 17, 20, and the transcript of Finck's interrogation, 40–44.

17. See Staatspolizei report in Heiber, *Katakombe*, 15–16; Finck's interrogation, 41; and Heydrich's report to Goebbels, 50.

18. See the reports reprinted in Heiber, *Katakombe*, 19–21, 30–32. The texts of three of the offending numbers are reprinted in Kühn, *Deutschlands Erwachen*, 83–91.

19. Elsner's accusations of Kästner's complicity appear in Heiber, *Katakombe*, 58, and Bundesarchiv Koblenz, R 58 (Reichssicherheitshauptamt), number 739, f. 137.

20. For the difficulties caused by expulsion from the Reichskulturkammer, see Walter Gross's plaintive letter begging for readmission, dated August 28, 1935, in BDC/RKK, Walter Gross file.

21. *12 Uhr Blatt*, May 11, 1935, separate articles on pages 2 and 8, italics in original; *Völkischer Beobachter*, May 12, 1935.

22. *12 Uhr Blatt*, May 11, 1935, 2; Max Wolf, "Nationalsozialistische Kleinkunst!" in *Die deutsche Artistik*, September 29, 1935, italics in original.

23. Helmuth Jahn, "Das positive Kabarett," in *Die deutsche Artistik*, September 29, 1935.

24. Joseph Goebbels, "Erobert die Seele der Nation: Rede über 'Die Aufgaben des deutschen Theaters,'" in *"Goebbels spricht": Reden aus Kampf und Sieg* (Oldenburg: 1933), 67, 74.

25. "Pg. Frau W. Millowitsch" to Goebbels, letter of June 9, 1933, in BLHA, Th 2644, f. 8.

26. For Lincke's revival during the Nazi era, see Otto Schneidereit, *Paul Lincke und die Entstehung der Berliner Operette* (Berlin: 1974), 124–132; Drewniak, *Das Theater im NS-Staat*, 338; and Ingrid Grünberg, "'Wer sich die Welt mit einem Donnerschlag erobern will ...': Zur Situation und Funktion der deutschsprachigen Operette in den Jahren 1933 bis 1945," in Hanns-Werner Heister and Hans-Günter Klein, eds., *Musik und Musikpolitik im faschistischen Deutschland* (Frankfurt am Main: 1984), 229.

27. For the visual arts in Nazi Germany, see Berthold Hinz, *Art in the Third Reich* (New York: 1979); and Stephanie Barron, ed., *"Degenerate Art": The Fate of the Avant-Garde in Nazi Germany* (Los Angeles: 1991). For the attack on modern music in the Nazi era, see Albrecht Dümling and Peter Girth, eds., *Entartete Musik: Eine kommentierte Rekonstruktion* (Düsseldorf: 1988).

28. Goebbels, "Erobert die Seele," 74.

29. A booklet for the first program of the Unfettered Eight, dated August 7, 1936, is located in the Akademie der Künste, West Berlin, Theatersammlung. The troupe is described in Günter Meerstein, "Das Kabarett im Dienste der Politik" (dissertation, Leipzig University, 1938), 65. Despite the title, that work is of little interest, given its brevity and the overly general nature of its argumentation.

30. *Goebbels-Tagebücher*, 3: 361 (entry of December 9, 1937).

31. Letter to Goebbels, December 9, 1937, in Bundesarchiv, Abteilungen Potsdam, Reichsministerium für Volksaufklärung und Propaganda (hereafter cited as BArchP/RMVP), number 472, f. 27.

32. On the Dragon, see Polizeipräsident Berlin to Gestapo, October 16, 1935, in Bundesarchiv Koblenz, R 58, number 739, f. 194; and reviews in *BZ am Mittag* and the *Berliner Börsen-Zeitung*, September 7, 1935, and *Querschnitt* 15 (1935): 585–586. Finck's appearance at the Kadeko was noted in the *Berliner Börsen-Zeitung*, April 7, 1936.

33. C. H. Petersen, "Das heisse Eisen oder der politische Witz," in *Eulenspiegel*, October 1938, 26–28.

34. Werner Finck, *Alter Narr, was nun?*, 113; Drei Rulands, "Neubau Berlins" and "Ham Se nicht den kleinen Cohn gesehn?" reprinted in Kühn, *Deutschlands erwachen*, 166–169, 220–223.

35. *Goebbels-Tagebücher*, 3: 567 (entry of February 3, 1939, reporting events of two days prior); and Goebbels, "Haben wir eigentlich noch Humor?" *Völkischer Beobachter*, February 4, 1939. The issue was picked up in other newspapers, e.g. "Humor—staatsgefährlich?" *Das Schwarze Korps*, February 16, 1939.

36. *Goebbels-Tagebücher*, 3: 568 (entry of February 5, 1939). For foreign reports of Finck's jokes in the wake of his dismissal from the Reich Culture Chamber, see *Daily Express* and *Chicago Daily Tribune*, February 4, 1939; and *Daily Mail*, February 6, 1939.

37. Waldoff denied having written the "Hermann" parody in her autobiography, *Weeste noch*, 91. For the correspondence between Bremen's mayor and the propaganda ministry, see the letters of April 25 and May 7, 1940, in BArchP/RMVP, number 472, ff. 246–247. Göring had somewhat more tolerance for jokes than Goebbels; it will be recalled that he intervened to release the Catacombs actors from a concentration camp, even though they had made a visual joke about Göring/Goethe. Göring probably considered such jokes, as well as the "Hermann" verses, a sign of what he believed to be his enormous popularity.

38. "Das neue Berliner Volksstück," in "Berlin, wie es weint, Berlin, wie es lacht," program of Plaza, October 1935.

39. Regierungsrat Kleinschmidt to Minister Gutterer and Staatsrat Hinkel, October 27, 1938, in BArchP/RMVP, number 474, f. 92; and report of Kleinschmidt, December 5, 1938, ibid., f. 94. For the Scala in the Nazi years, see Karl Pütz and Wolfgang Jansen, eds., *... und abends in die Scala* (Berlin: 1991).

40. *Goebbels-Tagebücher*, 3: 378 (entry of December 22, 1937).

41. For a detailed discussion of jazz during the Nazi era, see Michael Kater, "Forbidden Fruit? Jazz in the Third Reich," *American Historical Review* 94 (1989): 11–43; as well as Kater's fascinating and comprehensive study, *Different Drummers: Jazz in the Culture of Nazi Germany* (Oxford: 1992). See also the essays in Bernd Polster, ed., *"Swing Heil": Jazz im Nationalsozialismus* (Berlin: 1989).

42. Institut zum Studium der Judenfrage, *Die Juden in Deutschland*, 329–347; see similar arguments in Hans Diebow, *Der ewige Jude: 265 Bilddokumente* (Munich: 1937), 55–61.

43. For an example of a Nazi attack on prudery with regard to the body, see "Anstössig?" in *Das Schwarze Korps*, April 16, 1936. This article, illustrated by paintings and photos of nudes, called for a healthy physicality among both men and women.

44. "Noch immer Girl-Kultur in Deutschland?" *Völkische Frauenzeitung*, December 1, 1935; W. Hanke to propaganda ministry, March 31, 1939, in

BArchP/RMVP, number 472, f. 186; Harmut Reichenbach to Reichskulturkammer, June 26, 1939, ibid., f. 206; and report of Kleinschmidt, June 5, 1939, in ibid., number 474, f. 102.

45. Schaeffers' quip is quoted in Hans Hinkel to Benno von Arent, October 27, 1937; and Schaeffers to Hinkel, November 4, 1938, both in BDC/RKK, Willi Schaeffers file. The pictures and accompanying articles ("Für echte und edle Nacktheit" and "Wenn zwei dasselbe tun ...") appeared in *Das Schwarze Korps,* October 20, 1938.

46. Henry Picker, *Hitlers Tischgespräche im Führerhauptquartier, 1941–1942,* second edition (Stuttgart: 1965), 209; and *Goebbels-Tagebücher,* 3: 187 (entry of June 27, 1937). For kicklines in Nazi films, see Helga Belach, ed., *Wir tanzen um die Welt: Deutsche Revuefilme 1933–1945* (Munich: 1979).

47. Unidentified newspaper clipping reproduced in Maria Milde, *Berlin Glienicker Brücke: Babelsberger Notizen* (Berlin: 1978), 20. Milde was a member of the Hiller Girls. Training by a Wehrmacht officer is reported in Robert Wilschke, *Im Lichte des Scheinwerfers: Erinnerungen und Erzählungen eines Varieté- und Zirkusagenten* (Berlin: 1941), 350.

48. Report of Scherler, May 8, 1940, BArchP/RMVP, number 474, f. 127; Duisberg to the propaganda ministry, June 14, 1940, ibid., ff. 135–136; "Rundschreiben" of the president of the Reich Theater Chamber, July 2, 1940, ibid., number 472, f. 260.

49. Anonymous letter to the propaganda minister, October 25, 1940, in BArchP/RMVP, number 472, f. 306.

50. *Goebbels-Tagebücher,* 4: 83 (entry of March 22, 1940); and theater division of the propaganda ministry, letter of September 10, 1943, in BArchP/RMVP, number 474, f. 166. For examples of entertainers at the front, see Kater, *Different Drummers,* 117–118, 185–188.

51. For information on Tran und Helle, as well as an example of their act, see Kühn, *Deutschlands Erwachen,* 226–227, 354–355.

52. Letter of Dr. Schloesser, November 9, 1944, in BArchP/RMVP, number 473, f. 79.

## Epilogue: Cabaret in Concentration Camps

1. For Dutch interest in German cabaret before 1933, see Jacques Klöters, "Denk vandaag niet aan morgen: Cabaret en revue in Duitsland en Nederland," in Kathinka Dittrich et al., eds., *Berlijn-Amsterdam: Wisselwerkingen* (Amsterdam: 1982), 168–177. The remainder of the article (177–185) surveys German cabaret in Holland from 1933 to 1944. For general studies of the German exile experience in Holland, see Kathinka Dittrich and Hans Würzner, eds., *Die Niederlande und das deutsche Exil, 1933–1940* (Königstein: 1982); and Klaus Hermsdorf et al., *Exil in den Niederlanden und in Spanien* (Frankfurt am Main: 1981).

2. On the initial Dutch response to the Nazi regime, see Harry Pappe, "Die Niederlande und die Niederländer," in Dittrich and Würzner, *Die Niederlande,* 18.

3. See Jacques Klöters, "Momente so, Momente so: Dora Gerson und das erste Emigranten-Kabarett 'Ping-Pong'," in Dittrich and Würzner, *Die Niederlande,* 174–185.

4. See Hermsdorf, *Exil in den Niederlanden,* 74–76; and Klöters, "Denk vandaag niet aan morgen," 180–181.

5. *National Zeitung,* November 19, 1933; *Zürichsee Zeitung,* December 5, 1933; *De Tijd,* May 3, 1934; *Algemeen Handelsblad,* September 11, 1936; song quoted in ibid., November 19, 1936.

6. For an account of Nelson's revues in Amsterdam, see Klöters, "Denk vandaag niet aan morgen," 178–180.

7. "4 Jaar Theater der Prominenten," in program booklet, Theater der Prominenten, Lutine Palace, Scheveningen, Seizoen 1940, copy in Nederlands Theater Instituut. For an account of the Prominents, see Klöters, "Denk vandaag niet aan morgen," 181–182.

8. Herbert Nelson, "Das Leben geht weiter," reprinted in Kühn, *Deutschlands Erwachen,* 206.

9. Rosen's attempts to reach the United States are recounted by his widow, Elsbeth Rosen, "Mein Mann Willy Rosen," in Will Meisel, *Willy Rosen: "Text und Musik von mir"* (Berlin: 1967), 6.

10. For accounts of Westerbork, see J. Presser, *The Destruction of the Dutch Jews,* trans. Arnold Pomerans (New York: 1969), 406–464; and Jacob Boas, *Boulevard des Misères: The Story of the Transit Camp Westerbork* (Hamden, Conn.: 1985). The most direct and complete accounts are diaries and letters by two inmates who eventually perished in Auschwitz: Philip Mechanicus, *Year of Fear: A Jewish Prisoner Waits for Auschwitz,* trans. Irene Gibbons (New York: 1968); and Etty Hillesum, *An Interrupted Life: The Diaries of Etty Hillesum, 1941–1943,* trans. Arnold Pomerans (New York: 1983), and *Letters from Westerbork,* trans. Arnold Pomerans (New York: 1986). See also the account by Israel Taubes, "The Persecution of Jews in Holland, 1940–1944: Westerbork and Bergen-Belsen," typescript, Jewish Survivors Report, Documents of Nazi Guilt, no. 2 (London: Jewish Central Information Office, 1945). For further reflections on the Holocaust in the Netherlands, see Louis de Jong, *The Netherlands and Nazi Germany* (Cambridge, Mass: 1990), 1–25.

11. Mechanicus, *Year of Fear,* 146, 89. Typed program booklets for five of the six revues are located at the Rijksinstituut voor Oorlogsdocumentatie, Amsterdam. The photographs, from an album documenting "Humor und Melodie" that was presented to Gemmeker, are housed in Yad Vashem, Jerusalem.

12. Mechanicus, *Year of Fear,* 147; Hillesum, *Letters,* 136.

13. For Mechanicus' discussion of the hostilities between Dutch and German Jews, and his plans to assuage them, see *Year of Fear,* 30–33, 101, 104, 113, 120–124, 147, 151, 175, 183, 191, 218–219, 239, 246.

14. Mechanicus, *Year of Fear,* 176, 202. For Gemmeker's socializing with the entertainers and other favors, see ibid., 99; and Hillesum, *Letters,* 133, 136.

15. Taubes, "Persecution of the Jews in Holland," 26; Mechanicus, *Year of Fear,* 46.

16. Hillesum, *Letters,* 89; Mechanicus, *Year of Fear,* 103, 176.

17. Taubes, "Persecution of the Jews in Holland," 27; Mechanicus, *Year of Fear,* 147, 22.

18. Ehrlich's line is quoted at the beginning of the photo album of "Humor und Melodie" presented to Gemmeker; Mechanicus also refers to it, ibid., 147.

19. Beda, "Buchenwald-Lied," in Kühn, *Deutschlands Erwachen,* 309. For an early account of performances at Dachau and Buchenwald by a former inmate, see Curt Daniel, "'The Freest Theatre in the Reich': In the German Concentration Camps," *Theatre Arts* 25 (1941): 801–807. The origins of the first camp anthem, composed at Börgermoor ("Wir sind die Moorsoldaten"), are recounted in Wolfgang Langhoff, *Die Moorsoldaten* (1935; reprinted Halle: 1986), 165–186.

20. Jura Soyfer, "Dachau Lied," in Kühn, *Deutschlands Erwachen,* 316–317.

21. Röder is quoted in Walter Rösler, ed., *Gehn ma halt a bisserl unter: Kabarett in Wien von den Anfängen bis heute* (Berlin: 1991), 273. Grünbaum's last days are described by a fellow inmate in Karl Schnog, "Das Ende eines Spassmachers," in Helga Bemmann, ed., *Mitgelacht—dabeigewesen: Erinnerungen aus acht Jahrzehnten Kabarett* (Berlin: 1984), 285–289.

22. Mechanicus, *Year of Fear,* 159, 100.

23. Hillesum, *Letters from Westerbork,* 136.

24. The murders of Ehrlich and Rosen are mentioned in Max Mannheimer, "Theresienstadt, and From Thersienstadt to Auschwitz," typescript, Jewish Survivors Report, Documents of Nazi Guilt, no. 3 (London: Jewish Central Information Office, 1945), 8–9.

25. Mechanicus, *Year of Fear,* 152, 154, 230, 230–231, 228.

26. The two most complete accounts of Thesienstadt were written by survivors: Zdenek Lederer, *Ghetto Theresienstadt* (1953; reprinted New York: 1983); and H. G. Adler, *Theresienstadt 1941–1945: Das Antlitz einer Zwangsgemeinschaft* (Tübingen: 1955), as well as Adler's volume of primary sources, *Die verheimlichte Wahrheit: Theresienstädter Dokumente* (Tübingen: 1958). For important recent studies, see Ruth Bondy, *"Elder of the Jews": Jakob Edelstein of Theresienstadt* (New York: 1989); and Ruth Schwertfeger, *Women of Theresienstadt: Voices from a Concentration Camp* (Oxford: 1989).

27. Cabaret in Theresienstadt is described in Eva Somorova, "Kabarett im Konzentrationslager Terezín (Theresienstadt), 1941–1945," in *Kassette 5* (1981): 161–169; and Joza Karas, *Music in Terezín, 1941–1945* (New York: 1985), 143–156. Karas describes the other musical activities in Terezín, as does Milan Kuna, *Hudba na hranici života: O činnosti a utrpení hudebníků z českých zemí v nacistických koncentračních táborech a věznicích* (Prague: 1990), 167–257, 328–345; unfortunately, Kuna does not mention cabaret. The visual arts are described in Gerald Green, *The Artists of Terezín* (New York: 1969); and in Johanna Branson, ed., *Seeing through "paradise": artists and the Terezín concentration camp* (Boston: 1991). Some of the thousands of children's drawings, and dozens of children's poems that survived their young creators are reproduced in *I never saw another butterfly: Children's Drawings and Poems from Terezín Concentration Camp, 1942–1944* (New York: 1962).

28. Martin Roman, who survived the camps, mentioned the special performance

for the SS in an interview cited in Karas, *Music in Terezín,* 147. The total number of performances by the Carousel is unknown; however, an accounting of performances in Theresienstadt made in the summer of 1944 (Yad Vashem, document 064/415) indicates performances almost every other day from June 13 to July 2, and notes that the troupe had appeared forty-five times by July 20. For Roman's "Ghetto Swingers," see Karas, *Music in Terezín,* 151–152; and Kater, *Different Drummers,* 177–179.

29. Adler, *Theresienstadt,* 579, 589, 588; Lederer, *Ghetto Theresienstadt,* 126; Jacob Jacobson, "Terezín: The Daily Life, 1943–1945," typescript, Jewish Survivors Report, Documents of Nazi Guilt, no. 6 (London: Jewish Central Information Office, 1946), 12.

30. Typescripts of the surviving Theresienstadt lyrics are housed at Yad Vashem. Almost all of them have been reprinted in Ulrike Migdal, ed., *Und die Musik spielt dazu: Chansons und Satiren aus dem KZ Therezienstadt* (Munich: 1986). For Leo Strauss, "Karussell" and "Theresienstädter Wiener Lied," see 59–61, 65–67; and Frieda Rosenthal, "Dank dem lieben Cabaret," 70–71.

31. Leo Strauss, "Aus der Familie der Sträusse" and "Als ob," in Migdal, *Und die Musik,* 67–70, 106–108.

32. Leo Strauss, "Theresienstädter Fragen," in Migdal, *Und die Musik,* 71–74.

33. Leo Strauss, "Die Menage kommt," in Migdal, *Und die Musik,* 87.

34. Strauss, "Theresienstädter Fragen," 72; "Aus den Theresienstaedter Conférencen von Leo Strauss," typescript in the archives of Památník Terezín, Herrmann collection, no. 4092/1; and Manfred Greiffenhagen, "Die Ochsen," in Migdal, *Und die Musik,* 105–106.

35. On the "beautification project," see Adler, *Theresienstadt,* 162–175.

36. Alice Randt, "Die Schleuse: Drei Jahre Theresienstadt" (typescript, given to Yad Vashem in 1951), 94–96. For more on the film, see Adler, *Theresienstadt,* 178–191, and the documentation reprinted in Adler, *Die verheimlichte Wahrheit,* 324–351. The documents indicate that 1800 prisoners were marched to the meadow. No copy of the completed film survives; however, about a half-hour of out-takes are housed in Yad Vashem. The cabaret scenes are not among them.

37. The use of the clips in the "Wochenschau" is mentioned in Adler, *Die verheimlichte Wahrheit,* 325.

# Index

Adler, H. G., 276
Aeschylus, 130; parodied, 141–143
Agitprop, 214–227, 230; criticism of mass culture, 214–216; criticism of Christianity, 216–217, 220; attacks on SPD, 217–221, 225; censored, 219–222; criticism of Nazis, 225–227
Alberti, Conrad, 22, 23
Alberts, O. A., 96
Allos, Dr., 127
Anti, 204
Anti-Semitism: in Berlin, 13, 124, 125, 202–203, 209; of Wolzogen, 60–61; Sound and Smoke accused of, 79–80; satirized or criticized, 141, 149–150, 188, 200–201, 207–208, 226–227, 269, 279; Weimar cabarets accused of, 201–202; and Nazi cabaret, 243–244, 247, 251–252. *See also* Jews; Terezín; Westerbork
Arent, Benno von, 173
Arno, Siegfried, 261
Arnold, Victor, 73–74, 77
Artists' Café (Künstlercafé, Küka), 204, 206
Aus der Fünten, Ferdinand, 265, 268

Baader, Johannes, 145
Bad Boys (Böse Buben), 71–72
Baker, Josephine, 170, 171–173
Baudelaire, Charles, 18–19
Bausenwein, Victor, 51, 52
Beaurepaire, Gustav, 74
Behrens, Peter, 69
Bendow, Wilhelm, 150
Benjamin, Walter, 16, 33, 87, 180, 209
Berber, Anita, 164
Berlin: history, 10–14; as metropolis, 12,

16–17, 35, 93, 94, 106, 112–114, 169; wit, 30–33, 102–103, 137–138; depicted on stage, 105, 106, 109, 138, 166–167, 169, 190, 250
Bernauer, Rudolf, 71–72, 83, 120
Bethmann Hollweg, Theobald von, 94; portrayed on stage, 123
Bie, Oscar, 180, 190
Bierbaum, Otto Julius, 24, 27–28, 40, 41
Bismarck, Otto von, 11–12; portrayed on stage, 107–108, 123
Blacks: on Weimar stages, 169–175; depicted in agitprop, 216, 223
Bloch, Ernst, 167
*Blue Angel*, 1, 21, 75, 191, 275
Böcklin, Arnold, 69
Bois, Curt, 252
Bradsky, Bozena, 41, 42, 43, 51, 59
Brahm, Otto, 62–63, 68
Brecht, Bertolt, 1, 2, 33, 150, 222, 227, 259
Bruant, Aristide, 26–27, 89, 136
Brüning, Heinrich, 219; attacked by agitprop, 221
Bry, Curt, 259
Buchenwald, 269–270
Busch, Ernst, 204, 205

Cabaret: defined, 1–2; in Paris, 26–27, 45–46, 85–86, 136; as "safety valve," 34, 40, 78, 100, 134–135, 209, 223–224, 272
Cabaret of Comedians (Kabarett der Komiker, Kadeko), 192, 198–201, 203, 235, 246–248, 253, 257, 261
Cabaret of the Nameless (Kabarett der Namenlosen), 197–198
Cabaret-revues, 190–196

Calderon, Philip, 161
Carousel (Karussell), 275, 276, 277–280
Catacombs (Katakombe), 204–205, 209, 235–241, 259
Celly de Rheidt Ballet, 136, 155–164; trial, 159–164
Censorship: in Imperial Germany, 34–35, 40, 46, 76–77, 88, 103, 123; public as censor, 34, 49, 135, 195, 298n28; in Weimar era, 154–155; of nude dancing, 157–164; of agitprop, 219–222; in Nazi era, 230–232, 237–242, 247–250
Charell, Erik, 165, 166, 168, 169, 176, 186, 188, 189
Chat noir (Berlin), 99, 103, 119, 122
Chat noir (Paris), 26, 85
Chocolate Kiddies, 170, 171, 172
Communist Party of Germany (KPD), 145–146, 209–227, 228–229, 230; theory of "social fascism," 218–219, 225. *See also* Agitprop; Red Revues

Dachau, 269, 271
Dada, 19, 143–146, 147, 170, 183, 209
Damerius, Helmut, 226
D'Annunzio, Gabriele: parodied, 44, 45
Davids, Louis, 260
Dehmel, Richard, 47, 52, 69
Department stores, 13, 14–16, 48, 114, 202; depicted on stage, 106, 116–117, 192
Destrée, Olga, 43, 44, 51
Dietrich, Marlene, 1, 167, 193, 275
Dolorosa, 86, 90
Douglas, Louis, 170, 172, 173–174

Ebert, Friedrich, 129; satirized, 131, 138–139, 149
Ebinger, Blandine, 137, 190, 196, 206
Ehrlich, Max, 232, 252, 261, 263, 268, 269, 273
Eisler, Hanns, 204
Eleven Executioners (Elf Scharfrichter), 57–58
Ellington, Duke, 170
Eloesser, Arthur, 14, 15, 112–113, 195
Elow. *See* Lowinsky, Erwin
Endell, August, 53–55
Engel, Fritz, 189, 194, 195
Ewers, Hanns Heinz, 50–51, 58, 61, 91

Farkas, Karl, 261
Finck, Werner, 204, 205, 209, 235–241, 246, 247, 248, 249, 282
Ford, Henry, 181, 182
Frederick the Great, 11; portrayed on stage, 123, 127; Frederician guards portrayed on stage, 186, 189, 254–255
Freud, Sigmund, 33, 223, 230, 251
Freund, Julius, 106, 108, 109
Frey, Hermann, 102
Frick, Wilhelm, 175
Fuchs, Georg, 69

Geller, Oscar, 44
Gemmeker, Konrad, 265, 266, 267, 268, 269, 271–272
Gerron, Kurt, 1, 151, 202, 231, 252, 275, 276, 277, 280–282
Gerson, Dora, 236, 259, 260
Gert, Valeska, 184–185, 190, 231, 258
Giampietro, Joseph, 111
Giese, Fritz, 177, 179
Giesen, Heinrich, 238, 239, 240
Gilbert, Jean, 120
Gilbert, Robert (David Weber), 205
"Girls": in Weimar era, 175–186, 189–190; mechanistic overtones, 180–183; militaristic overtones, 181, 183, 186, 189–190, 254–255; in agitprop, 217; in Nazi era, 251–257; in Westerbork revues, 264, 268. *See also* Tiller Girls
Glasenapp, Kurt von, 91, 109
Goebbels, Joseph, 202–203, 230, 231–232, 237–248 passim, 251, 254–257 passim; satirized or criticized, 221, 226
Goethe, Johann Wolfgang von, 31
Goldstein, Chaja, 259, 260, 268
Goll, Iwan, 172
Göring, Hermann, 229, 241, 311n37; satirized, 238, 249
Graetz, Paul, 32, 131, 141, 146, 148, 152, 166
Greiffenhagen, Manfred, 275, 279, 282
Grosz, George, 142, 143, 144, 145, 146, 170, 210
Grünbaum, Fritz, 127, 138, 231, 271
Grzesinski, Albert, 220; attacked by agitprop, 221

Habsburg, Leopold Ferdinand von, 126
Haller, Herman, 165, 166, 175, 176, 186, 188, 189, 190
Hamann, Richard, 19, 32
Harden, Maximilian, 48–49
Hart, Heinrich, 50
Hase, Annemarie, 195, 206, 231
Hauptmann, Gerhart, 63; parodied, 73–75, 107
Hausmann, Raoul, 144, 145
Heartfield, John, 142, 143, 144, 145, 146, 210
Herrmann-Neisse, Max, 118, 126, 127, 133, 136, 140, 152, 153, 162, 164, 185, 190, 192, 198
Herzfelde, Wieland, 144, 145, 146
Hessel, Franz, 15
Hesterberg, Trude, 150–151, 153, 196, 206, 233–235
Heydrich, Reinhard, 237, 238, 239, 240
Hildenbrandt, Fred, 171, 184
Hiller Girls, 254–255
Hillesum, Etty, 265, 266, 268, 272
Hinkel, Hans, 233, 234
Hitler, Adolf, 250–251, 253–254; satirized or criticized, 198, 199, 200, 207–209, 221, 226, 240
Höch, Hannah, 183
Hofmannsthal, Hugo von, 82–83
Hohenlohe-Schillingsfürst, Chlodwig zu, 63
Hollaender, Friedrich, 1, 7, 10, 136–137, 143, 148, 189, 190, 191, 192, 194, 195, 196, 207, 208, 209, 221, 231, 258, 259, 282
Hollaender, Viktor, 105–106, 108
Huelsenbeck, Richard, 144, 145
Hungry Pegasus (Zum hungrigen Pegasus), 86–88
Hussels, Jupp, 256–257
Hyan, Hans, 86, 89–90

Ibsen, Henrik, 63, 232; parodied, 72
Ihering, Herbert, 176, 188, 192
Isherwood, Christopher, 1

Jacobs, Monty, 168, 188, 189
Jacobson, Jacob, 277
Jagow, Traugott von, 110
Jazz, 169–170, 250, 251
Jews: satirized, 79–80, 96–97, 236; Central Association of German Citizens of Jewish Faith, 201–202; banned from performing by Nazis, 231–232; Culture League of German Jews, 232–233, 261. *See also* Anti-Semitism; Terezín; Westerbork

Kästner, Erich, 150, 183, 197–198, 203, 205–206, 209, 230, 231, 240, 259, 282
Kayssler, Friedrich, 64, 65, 66, 67, 68, 80, 82
Kerr, Alfred, 40, 52
Kessler, Harry, 171, 202
Klein, James, 165, 166–167, 176, 186, 188, 252
Kollo, Walter, 102, 120, 121, 166, 244
Kollo, Willi, 244, 250
Kolman, Trude, 236, 239
Koppel, Robert, 41, 42, 51
Kracauer, Siegfried, 167, 177–178, 180, 183, 185–186
Kraus, Karl, 196

Larifari, 204
Lauff, Josef, 40; parodied, 40, 72
Lederer, Zdenek, 276
Levetzow, Karl von, 51
Lilien, Kurt, 261
Liliencron, Detlev von, 44, 47, 51, 52, 279
Lincke, Paul, 105, 108, 111, 169, 243, 244, 250
Lion, Margo, 191, 193, 231
Löhner, Fritz (Beda), 270, 271
Lola Bach Ballet, 162, 174
Lowinsky, Erwin (Elow), 197–198, 231, 232, 233
Ludendorff, Erich, 126; satirized or criticized, 137, 201
Lüders, Günther, 239, 240

Maeterlinck, Maurice, 64, 67, 83; parodied, 65, 67, 72, 107
Mann, Erika, 260
Mann, Heinrich, 75–76, 230, 234
Marcus, Julia, 259, 260
Mechanicus, Philip, 263–269 passim, 271–272, 273
Megalomania (Cabaret Grössenwahn), 136–137, 149, 150

Mehring, Walter, 143, 146–153, 165, 170, 199, 205, 209, 231

Meinhard, Carl, 71–72, 275

Mendelsohn, Erich, 198, 199

Metropol-Theater, 105–117, 120, 166, 188; and fashion, 113–115

Minnelli, Liza, 1

Mirliton, 26

Moeller van den Bruck, Artur, 23, 25, 28

Morgan, Paul, 178, 198, 200–201, 231, 252, 271

Morgenstern, Christian, 44, 45, 64

Motley Stage Boards (Buntes Brettl), 51, 52, 59, 91

Motley Theater (Buntes Theater), 39–61, 85, 258; opening night, 39–45; criticized, 45–50; new theater, 53–59; demise, 59

Mühsam, Erich, 86, 88, 93, 230

National Socialism: opposition to "Negro art," 175; satirized or criticized, 198, 199, 200–201, 207–209, 225–227, 236–238, 239–240, 260, 269; in Berlin, 202–203, 228–229; attacks on critical cabaret, 230–242, 247–248, 257; notion of "positive cabaret," 241–243, 244–245. See also Goebbels, Joseph; Hitler, Adolf

Nelson, Herbert, 261, 262, 263

Nelson, Rudolf, 7, 95–100, 103, 108, 120, 122–125, 137, 138, 139, 140, 157, 158, 165–166, 169, 190, 231, 252, 258, 260–261, 262, 263, 282

Nietzsche, Friedrich, 28–30, 38, 56, 64

Nikolaus, Paul, 199–200, 203, 231

Noske, Gustav, 129; satirized or criticized, 131, 132, 133, 146, 211

Nude dancing, 155–165; in Weimar revues, 176, 177, 178–179; in Nazi era, 252–253, 255–256. See also Celly de Rheidt Ballet; Lola Bach Ballet

Oberländer, Hans, 68, 76, 77, 79, 81

Offeney, Erna, 136, 174

Operetta, 105, 119–121, 186, 235, 244, 250

Otto, Hans, 230

Panizza, Oskar, 24–25

Paulsen, Dora, 261

Peppermill (Pfeffermühle), 260

Pfitzner, Hans, 170

Pijet, Georg, 224, 226–227

Ping-Pong, 259–260

Piscator, Erwin, 211–212; parodied, 194

Plaza, 249, 250

Polgar, Alfred, 178, 180, 181

Prager, Willy, 123, 193, 194

Prostitution: theaters as venues for, 115–116, 156

Pub-cabarets (Kneipenbrettl), 85–95

Rahm, Karl, 275

Randt, Alice, 280–281

Rathenau, Walter, 11, 100

Red Revues (Red Revels), 212–214, 218. See also Agitprop

Reicher, Emanuel, 79

Reinhardt, Max: early years, 62–64; founding of Sound and Smoke, 64–68; turn to drama, 80–84; parodied, 109, 138, 141; and postwar Sound and Smoke, 130

Remarque, Erich Maria, 196, 202, 230

Reutter, Otto, 102, 120

Revues: defined, 3; Metropol revues, 104–117; in Weimar era, 165–169, 187–190. See also Cabaret-revues; Charell, Erik; Haller, Herman; Klein, James; Metropol-Theater; Red Revues; Tiller Girls

Riefenstahl, Leni, 252

Rigardo, Marietta de, 89

Ringelnatz, Joachim, 298n28

Robitschek, Kurt, 192, 198, 199–200, 201, 202, 203, 208, 231, 234, 258, 263

Röder, Karl, 271

Roland von Berlin, 95–96, 102, 103

Roman, Martin, 275

Rosen, Willy, 198, 258, 259, 261–262, 263, 268, 273

Roth, Joseph, 178

Salis, Rodolphe, 26, 27, 85

Scala, 185, 186, 249, 250, 252, 253, 254–255, 256

Schaeffers, Willi, 139, 246–247, 248, 253

Scheffler, Karl, 14, 16, 54–55

Schiffer, Marcellus, 7, 150, 190, 191, 192

Schiller, Friedrich: parodied, 65–67, 79

Schmitz, Ludwig, 256–257

Schneider-Duncker, Paul, 95, 96, 97, 102, 231, 249
Schnitzler, Arthur, 44
Schoenberg, Arnold, 58
Schultz, Richard, 105, 106, 108
Schulz, Georg David, 86, 88–89
Serenissimus, 72–79, 106, 130, 140
Seventh Heaven (Zum siebenten Himmel), 88–89
Severing, Carl, 163; attacked by agitprop, 221
Seweloh, Cäcilie (Celly de Rheidt). *See* Celly de Rheidt Ballet
Sexuality: as theme in cabarets and revues, 5, 34, 43, 47, 49, 86, 90, 96–98, 99, 103, 115–116, 136, 137, 139, 140, 146, 193, 200. *See also* "Girls"; Nude dancing
Siemsen, Hans, 170
Silver Punchbowl (Silberne Punschterrine), 89–91
Simmel, Georg, 16–18, 113–114, 117
Simmel, Paul, 181, 182, 231
Social Democratic Party (SPD), 13, 128–129, 218, 219, 228, 229, 230; satirized, 57, 107, 129–130, 131, 133, 138–139; criticized by agitprop, 217–221, 225. *See also* Ebert, Friedrich; Noske, Gustav
Sound and Smoke (Schall und Rauch): opening night, 64–68; in new theater, 68–71; Serenissimus scenes, 72–79, 130; portrayal of Jews, 79–80; turn to drama, 80–83; postwar, 130–131, 132, 141, 146
Soyfer, Jura, 271
Speer, Albert: satirized, 247
Spira, Camilla, 263, 267, 269, 270
Spoliansky, Mischa, 150, 190, 192, 198, 231
Stenzel, Otto, 251
Stöcker, Adolf, 13, 80
Strasser, Otto, 225; satirized, 226
Straus, Oscar, 41, 47, 51, 59, 233, 275
Strauss, Leo, 275, 277, 278, 279, 282
Stresemann, Gustav: satirized or criticized, 194–195, 211, 218
Svenk, Karel, 274

Taubes, Israel, 268
Taussig, Fritz (Fritta), 276

Taylor, Charles, 181
Terezín (Theresienstadt), 273–282
Thoma, Ludwig, 41, 56, 89
Three Rulands (Die Drei Rulands), 247, 248
Tilke, Max, 86, 87, 88
Tiller, John, 175, 181
Tiller Girls, 165, 175–186, 190; parodied, 183–184, 185, 190; admired by Hitler, 253
Tingeltangel: defined, 1, 21. *See also* Variety shows
Tingel-Tangel: under Hollaender, 183, 207–208; in Nazi era, 239–240
Trautschold, Walter, 238, 240
Tucholsky, Kurt, 4, 89, 96, 103, 127, 131–141, 148–149, 152, 153, 165, 166, 199, 203, 205, 209, 217, 230, 231, 259

Überbrettl, 29, 39, 45, 60, 85. *See also* Motley Theater
Unfettered Eight (Die 8 Entfesselten), 245, 246
Unthan, Carl Hermann, 121

Valentin, Karl, 230
Valetti, Rosa, 1, 136–137, 149, 150, 198, 204, 232, 252
Vallentin, Maxim, 213
Van Elben, Grit and Ina, 183–184
Variety shows (vaudeville, Variété), 20–28; licensing of, 91–92. *See also* Plaza; Scala; Wintergarten

Waldersee, Alfred von: parodied, 49–50
Waldoff, Claire, 32, 100–104, 120, 123, 188, 189, 249
Wallburg, Otto, 261
Wangenheim, Gustav von, 130, 145, 209
Wedekind, Frank, 57, 59, 81, 82; parodied, 72, 107, 109
Weill, Kurt, 1, 2
Weinert, Erich, 199, 210–211, 219
Weintraub's Syncopators, 1, 191, 251
Westerbork, 263–269, 271–273
Wild Stage (Wilde Bühne), 150, 153
Wilde, Oscar: *Salome*, 79, 81, 82
Wilhelm II: aesthetic opinions, 73, 75; satirized or criticized, 75, 77, 108,

Wilhelm II (cont.)
    110–111, 141, 194, 195–196; host to
    Nelson, 99–100
Wilson, Woodrow: satirized, 141, 142, 189
Wintergarten, 21–22, 43, 119, 183, 186,
    249, 250, 254
Wohlbrück, Olga, 43
Wolff, Kurt Egon, 259
Wolzogen, Ernst von, 23–24, 29, 36–61,
    85, 258; elitism of, 38–39, 46; political

views, 40; anti-Semitic views, 60–61;
    parodied, 107
Wooding, Sam, 170


Zelenka, František, 275
Zickel, Martin, 59, 64, 65, 66, 67
Ziegler, Erich, 263, 273
Zille, Heinrich, 12
Zörgiebel, Karl, 218

SMCL

3 5151 00225 8127